THE COAST SALISH
AND THEIR NEIGHBORS

From the map Native Languages of the Northwest Coast. Cartography and graphics by Cameron Suttles. Published in 1985 by Western Imprints, The Press of the Oregon Historical Society, Portland, Oregon. Reproduced with permission of Western Imprints.

COAST SALISH

ESSAYS

Wayne Suttles

WAYNE SUTTLES

Talonbooks
Vancouver

University of Washington Press
Seattle and London

1987

Published with the assistance of the Canada Council

Talonbooks
104 - 3100 Prodction Way
Burnaby, British Columbia
Canada V5A 4R4

Compiled and edited with the assistance of Dr. Ralph Maud.

Typeset in Times by Pièce de Résistance Ltée., and printed and bound in Canada by Hignell Printing Ltd.

Fourth Printing: January 2000

Canadian Cataloguing in Publication Data
    Suttles, Wayne P., 1918-
    Coast Salish Essays

    Bibliography: p.
    ISBN 0-88922-212-6 (pbk.)

    I. Salish Indians 2. Indians of North America — Northwest, Pacific.
3. Coast Salish Indians. I. Maud, Ralph, 1928- II. Title.
E99.S2S88   1986   970.004'97   C86-091521-2

Contents

Part III: Adaptation and Survival Through the European Invasion

Part IV: Inferences About Prehistory

List of Illustrations

Foreword

The sixteen essays in this collection span three decades in which a great deal has been learned about Northwest Coast cultures, and the number of practitioners in the allied disciplines of anthropology, archaeology, and linguistics has multiplied several times. And throughout this period, as these essays testify, Wayne Suttles has been influential in shaping the direction of Northwest Coast studies. His work has stood as a model for students and colleagues alike, and it has held true to its own course. It occupies a secure place in the forefront of the study of this culture area.

Until the midpoint of this century North American anthropology was overwhelmingly concerned with reconstructive ethnography. First Boas and his students, and then his students' students, sought to salvage from the memories of older Indians the data necessary to build descriptive accounts of cultures already gone or quickly slipping away. As one of those pedagogical "grandchildren" of Boas, Wayne Suttles stepped easily into the field of Northwest Coast research. In his doctoral dissertation he provided a full and most welcome account of the economic organization of Straits Salish. From that time his main interest and effort has remained focussed upon Coast Salish culture, and this collection of essays constitutes a book on that subject.

But it is not at all such a book as his mentors would have made. While Suttles did collect texts in Indian languages and enquire persistently about old-time hunting equipment and ritual practices, his was never the kind of ethnography that attempted to describe model systems fixed in timeless place. There has always been a sense of history in his work. Informants, identified in time and place are there, so that the reader may draw from them an informed grasp of culture change. This is but part of a larger theme which has integrated his work and ties these essays together: it is a concern with cultural adaptation and evolution. Where earlier Northwest Coast scholars were content to describe culture areas and societies from the long distant past, and to give the occasional nod to "migration" or "diffusion" in explanation of change, Suttles has set us on the path towards a more satisfactory and powerful understanding of how Northwest Coast cultures came to be what they are.

While a concern with evolution and adaptation set Suttles' work apart, in another aspect he has followed more strongly than other contemporaries the lead of Boas. This is in attention to linguistics. Throughout the time spanned by these essays Suttles has laboured, as time and circumstance allowed, on collection of Halkomelem texts and completion of a grammar of that language. These foundations have informed his research on spirit dancing, kinship, ritual, and art. They have enabled occasional penetrating glimpses of underlying cultural patterns—patterns that integrate experience and ideas, patterns that make the fundamental distinction between humans and non-humans, and give distinctive emphases to Coast Salish culture. In Suttles' work a richness of understanding emerges from painstaking collection and consideration of the facts.

This careful approach has earned respect from colleagues and collaborators alike. I know that Suttles' unflagging persistence with pen and notebook has wearied more than one informant. But the weariness was that which comes from fatigue, not from impatience with repetition, or frustration while instructing a fumbling tongue. He has a deserved reputation among Salish people as a scholar and an authority on Salish culture. And he has shared with them, as generously as he has with academic colleagues, his files and notes. These have contributed to community genealogical charts, to lists of place names, to village histories, and to courtroom evidence on land claims.

Although this collection of essays centres on the Coast Salish and for that fact will be an essential book of readings for all students of that culture group, it will find equal use in courses which take the whole Northwest Coast culture area as their subject. For too long the available overviews of that area have been outdated. Far from offering an understanding of the place of potlatching in modern Indian life, or even describing such activities, they have at times denied their continued existence. They have not attempted to tell us how the incredible linguistic and cultural diversity of the area arose, nor how these small scale societies responded to incorporation in modern North American society.

Answers to such questions do not jump at you from Suttles' writing. But you will find them there among the facts he gives. This is a source book that gives answers and shows how to find answers, and that will be its enduring value.

Michael Kew
Vancouver, B.C.
January 1987

Introduction

This is a collection of articles written over a period of three decades. The earliest dates back to 1950, when I was a student at the University of Washington; six date from the years 1951-1963, during which I taught at the University of British Columbia; three date from 1963-1966, while I was at the University of Nevada in Reno; and six were written during the 1970s and early 1980s at Portland State University. They are concerned with the Central Coast Salish of southwestern British Columbia and northwestern Washington, the wider Coast Salish region, the whole Northwest Coast of North America, or, in one instance, the Interior Salish of the Plateau. Putting these articles together into a book has allowed me to express some second (or third) thoughts about some of the things I have written and some of the issues they deal with. I have done so in square brackets added to each article. I have corrected a few typographic errors and transcriptions of native terms, but otherwise the articles appear as originally published. The original maps have been omitted and new ones added as endpapers.

Rather than presenting these papers in chronological order, I have arranged them topically in four groups, keeping a chronological order within each group. Part I, Models of Historic Social Systems, consists of four attempts to describe the social systems of the Central Coast Salish and other Native peoples of the Northwest Coast at the time of the European invasion in the late 18th and early 19th century. Part II, Knowledge, Belief, and Art in Historic Culture, consists of three essays on these topics, dealing mainly with the Central Coast Salish. In Part III, Adaptation and Survival Through the European Invasion, two articles deal with the Coast Salish in general and two deal more specifically with the Central Coast Salish. Part IV, Inferences About Prehistory, consists of articles dealing with attempts to reconstruct history from ethnological, archeological, and linguistic evidence, again ranging in scope from the narrower to the broader area.

If there is any unity to these pieces apart from their common subject, it may come from three concerns that I sense were present in different strengths when I wrote them. First, I was concerned with ethnographic description, initially with the goal of presenting the insider's view of the culture but soon hoping to combine this goal with that of presenting the culture in its larger setting, allowing us to see things as the participants do but also to step back and see how the whole thing works. Second, I was concerned with the reconstruction of culture history, prehistoric and historic, initially perhaps satisfied with evidence of one culture's influence on another, but soon looking for something beyond cultural determinism. And third, I became increasingly concerned with what I saw as a stereotyping of "the Coast Salish" as culturally homogeneous and a pale reflection of the "real Northwest Coast" to the north.

The first two of these concerns were no doubt both the product of and a reaction to my anthropological upbringing in the Boasian environment of the University of Washington department in the late 1930s, when I was an undergraduate, and in the middle and late 1940s, when I was a graduate student. (During the intervening period I was translating Japanese for the U.S. Navy.) Of my earliest teachers, Erna Gunther, Melville Jacobs, and Viola Garfield had been students of Franz Boas, while Verne Ray had studied with one of Boas's more historicist students, Leslie Spier. From all four I got a strong dose of Northwestern North American ethnography, something on ethnographic field methods, and the Boasian ideal of seeing the culture from the inside. In classes with Jacobs I learned to hear, produce, and write the sounds of the Native languages of the region and came to feel that linguistic work ought to accompany ethnographic work. Ray in particular taught a Boasian historical reconstruction in which the causes of culture change are to be found within culture.

My non-Boasian interests, especially the interest in the relationship of people to their environment that drew me toward what became ecological anthropology, had other sources. First was surely the experience of growing up on the Northwest Coast with cousins and friends who pursued its natural history. Other contributing experiences, when I was a graduate student, were reading in evolutionary biology, hearing what Viola Garfield and Melville Jacobs were saying about Northwest Coast economics, reading Julian Steward (whom I never got to see), taking courses with Fred Hulse and with Paul Kirchhoff and a seminar with K.A. Wittfogel, listening to Bill Elmendorf on the Twana, and perhaps as much as anything the experience of doing field work.

I began field work during the summer of 1946, six months after returning from the navy and three months before starting graduate work. My parents were living at Friday Harbor in the San Juan Islands, and my wife and I were staying there. Arden King of the Anthropology Department at the University of Washington was conducting a dig on San Juan Island, and students were scheduled to do a site survey of the islands. I had talked with Erna Gunther about returning to the University in the fall. She suggested that I begin ethnographic work immediately with the objective of discovering what Native peoples had occupied the San Juan Islands and what they did there that would have left evidence for the archeologists to discover.

That assignment was congenial from the start and became a powerful determinant in my career. Since the San Juan Islands were no longer occupied by any group of Indians, I had to visit the Swinomish and Lummi reservations on the Washington mainland and the Saanich and Songhees reserves on Vancouver Island to find people reported to have visited the islands in earlier times. This immediately led me into the old yearly round and the earlier and persisting network of kin ties that extended throughout the region. I collected place names, genealogies, and information about who went where and did what. Thinking of archeological sites, I tried to locate activities as precisely as I could in time and space. Inevitably, and happily, I was drawn into the study of the region and away from the dead end that a "community study" might have been. During five years of graduate work I spent about three months of each year in the field, which meant visiting Indian friends on both the Washington and B.C. sides of the border, eliciting more on aboriginal subsistence activities and technology, attending the winter dances, and finally developing the ethnography that became my Ph.D. dissertation (Suttles 1951a). Work with historical materials resulted in a ethnohistorical study of the Lummi (Suttles 1954).

As a graduate student I worked with the Coast Salish people whose territories lay about Haro and Rosario Straits, the two main channels that connect the Strait of Juan de Fuca with Georgia Strait. These were the speakers of a language I came to call "Straits." I worked, of course, in English. I could record Native names and technical terms fairly accurately, and in the beginning I astonished my Indian friends by being able to pronounce the words fairly accurately. But at the time there was nothing of much use on any of the Coast Salish languages—no grammars, dictionaries, or compilations of handy phrases, and I did not spend much time trying to record texts or do grammatical analysis myself.

While teaching at the University of British Columbia, I began work with speakers of Halkomelem, the next language to the north, doing ethnographic work at Katzie (Suttles 1955) and at Musqueam, and finally, in the late 1950s, finding the opportunity to begin linguistic work on Halkomelem. This work has occupied me from time to time over the years since. It has been a source of great satisfaction to learn how the language works (though I cannot yet claim to be fluent in it), to collect texts in the language, and to pursue the Boasian goal of exploring the culture through it. Meanwhile I have also been fortunate enough to have had some contact with speakers of other Salish languages, with Kwakiutl people, and with Native people from elsewhere on the coast.

I am grateful to my early teachers of anthropology, already mentioned, and to my Native teachers, whose names appear in some of the essays that follow. I must also thank Harry Hawthorn, who invited me to the University of British Columbia and made much of my work there possible, A.P. Vayda, who asked the right questions and inspired me to do things I would not otherwise have done, and dozens of students whose contributions to my classes have made teaching about the Northwest Coast the pleasure it has been. I must thank my friend Ralph Maud for urging me to put this collection together, my son Cameron for the maps that appear as end-papers, and finally my wife, Shirley, for a lifetime of encouragement and advice.

Wayne Suttles
Portland, Oregon
January 1987

Part I

Models of Historic Social Systems

1. Private Knowledge, Morality, and Social Classes among the Coast Salish[1]*

An exchange of views in a recent issue of the *American Anthropologist* shows that social stratification on the Northwest Coast is still a live issue. The principal question is whether Northwest Coast society had, apart from slaves, distinct social classes of nobles and commoners or merely a single class of freemen within which there were only ranked individuals. The recent exchange began with Ray's suggestion that Boas neglected the culture of the lower class among the Northwest Coast tribes. Lowie countered that if Drucker's analysis is right, there were only ranked individuals and no social classes, and hence no lower class to neglect. Ray then returned with quotations from several ethnographers who reported social classes and has promised us an analysis of the whole body of published Northwest Coast ethnography, which will demonstrate the existence of a lower class. Since this exchange, Codere has presented an analysis of some of Boas's Kwakiutl material, which seems to support Drucker's and Lowie's position—that there was no distinguishable lower class

[1]An abridged version of this paper was read at the 55th Meeting of the American Anthropological Association held at Santa Monica, December 1956.

*[Originally published in the *American Anthropologist* 60:497-507 (1958). Reproduced by permission of the American Anthropological Association; not for further reproduction. Reprinted in *Indians of the North Pacific Coast*, edited by Tom McFeat (Toronto: McClelland and Stewart 1966), reprinted with the Postscript in *The Human Experience* edited by David H. Spain (Homewood, Illinois: The Dorsey Press 1975), pp.262-73. My views have not changed since writing the Postscript.]

among the Kwakiutl (Ray 1955; Lowie 1956; Ray 1956; Codere 1957).

One of the bases of disagreement may be simply a difference in terms or in emphasis on different factors in a definition of "class."[2] But another basis for disagreement may lie in real differences among the various Northwest Coast societies.

In this paper I will deal with a small segment of the Northwest Coast—the area of the Coast Salish of Northern Puget Sound, the Strait of Juan de Fuca, and Southern Georgia Strait.[3] My purposes are: (1) to call attention to evidence for the existence of a distinct, though probably relatively small, lower class; (2) to postulate a relationship between class and certain Coast Salish beliefs about morality; and (3) to suggest the possibility that the Coast Salish theory of morality and the absence of any very developed system of ranked individual positions may have allowed for a sharper definition of social classes among the Coast Salish than among the supposedly more rank-obsessed Kwakiutl.

When we enquire among the Coast Salish about social classes we are likely to encounter a paradox. We find among our informants a strong feeling that social classes did indeed exist in the past. Informant after informant will tell us that there were high-class people and low-class people. Yet if we ask for an identification of the descendants of former low-class people, our informants are likely to say they do not know or refuse to talk about the matter. Later, after we establish good relations with an informant, he will probably tell us that while he is of high-class descent, certain other families are of low-class descent. When we go to members of these other families, we may be told that our new informants' families are of high-class origin but certain other families, including that of our first informant, are really of low-class descent.

This is what happened to me on the Lummi Reservation. Two persons, each associated with one of the two leading lineages, told a story accounting for a low-class origin for the other lineage. One story was an account of a known ancestor of the lineage in question; the other story was really a local adaptation of a widespread folktale. Both stories, however, demonstrated the prior residence of the narrator's lineage, the former slave or serf-like status of the

---

[2]For the purposes of this paper, I can best follow Codere in accepting Goldschmidt's minimal definition of a social class as "a segment of the community, the members of which show a common social position in a hierarchical ranking" and his characterization of the true class-organized society as "one in which the hierarchy of prestige and status is divisible into groups each with its own social, economic, attitudinal and cultural characteristics, and each having differential degrees of power in community decisions." "Such groups," he writes, "would be socially separate and their members would readily identify" (Goldschmidt 1950:491-2; Codere 1957:473).

[3]I have done fieldwork in this area at various times since 1946. This work has been supported successively by the University of Washington, a Wenner-Gren Pre-doctoral Fellowship, and the University of British Columbia.

other lineage at some other place, and the generosity of the teller's lineage in allowing the other to settle at Lummi. Both informants agreed, as did others, in ascribing a still lower status to the family of a pair of slaves who had been freed in the 1860s.

This situation, which could undoubtedly be encountered in many Coast Salish communities, suggests that except for the former slaves, social class was more a myth than a reality. Perhaps the accusation of lower-class ancestry is merely part of the gossip that all families enjoy relating about all others and which enables each to make claims of superior status, none of which has any more validity than another.

But there is other evidence for the reality of social classes in the past. The best evidence comes from descriptions of village structure and intervillage relations. We encounter again and again descriptions of villages in which there was a division of residence between upper-class and lower-class people. In some villages, households of lower-class people were at one end or on one side of the village. In other villages, the lower-class people were somewhat separate and often in an exposed position where an enemy might strike first. Then we are also told of villages set quite apart but in a serf-like status as vassals of high-class villages or villages with high-class inhabitants.

Barnett (1955:19, 30) reports that the Saanich village at Brentwood Bay and the Sechelt village had an upper-class section in the center and lower-class sections at the ends. I was told that the old Semiahmoo village on Tongue Spit consisted of two rows of houses, one facing outward and the other facing inward; the outer row was occupied by upper-class people and the inner row by lower-class people. Gunther (1927:183-4, 261) reports lower-class settlements on exposed spits among the Klallam,* and Barnett (1955:23) reports the same thing at Nanoose and possibly Chemainus. I was told that the principal Skagit village at Snakelum Point consisted of a great stockade enclosing a long house divided into three segments, each with its own named group of high-class people; outside the stockade were "camps" of low-class people who served as "scouts" and were not allowed inside the stockade. Haeberlin and Gunther (1930:15, 58) report a separate lower-class village, also unprotected, for the Snohomish. I was told of lower-class villages at Warm Beach on Port Susan, possibly vassal to the Stillaguamish or the Snohomish; at Greenbank on Whidbey Island, possibly vassal to the Skagit; and on Dugualla Bay, Whidbey Island, vassal to the Swinomish. According to an informant, the Dugualla people had to bring fuel to the Swinomish during the coldest part of the winter. Boas (1894:455), Hill-Tout (1902:407-8) and Jenness (1955:86) report that the Coquitlam on the Lower Fraser were vassals of the

---

*[Klallam has been the usual anthropological spelling, but I would now write Clallam as in Clallam County. I would also now write Songhees, as the name is spelled locally, rather than Songish, as I did here.]

Kwantlen. And while Barnett reports that the Nanoose had a divided village, Jenness's and some of my own informants regarded the Nanoose as wholly lower class. They were the group with which the Coquitlam could marry, said one. One informant told of a tradition of open conflict between the lower- and upper-class segments of a village at Oak Harbor on Whidbey Island, and something similar was hinted at for a Songish village.

This is only a rough outline of the data on residence. There is no question in my mind about the existence of a lower class in this area. Its existence is also indicated by some data on marriages and inherited privileges, and it is reflected in the native terms used.

A person of high status was called si⁊ɛ́m.* This term is often translated as "chief," but it is clear that the whole institution of chieftainship as it now exists developed after European contact. Si⁊ɛ́m meant and still means simply "Sir" or "Madam" in address and "gentleman" or "lady" in reference. One could speak of the si⁊ɛ́m of a house, if it had one clearly recognized leader, perhaps the man who had organized the building; but not all houses had such leaders. One could also say the si⁊ɛ́m of the village, but the title did not imply a political office. If there were a si⁊ɛ́m, he was probably the wealthiest man, the leader in the potlatch. Leadership in other matters was apt to be in the hands of others, depending upon their special abilities. The plural, si·⁊ɛ́m, is usually translated "high-class people."

People who are not "high class" are referred to by terms which are translated as "poor people," "nothing people," or "low-class people." According to one old man, the most polite term is səsəláyčən, the diminutive plural of "younger sibling." The term used in the Lkungeneng (Straits) and Halkomelem languages for the people of the vassal village is stɛ́šəm: their status is clearly distinguished from that of sk̓ʷə́yəs, "slave." Slaves were private property, captured or purchased; vassals were simply in a low status as a group destined to serve other villages.

Thus it appears that Coast Salish society was in fact stratified. In addition to slaves, there were at least an upper class and a lower class. The proportions of upper- to lower-class people in each community probably varied, just as the spatial relationship between the two groups varied. But in the area as a whole, the vassal tribes were relatively few and the villages said to have lower-class sections were in the minority. It is difficult to get information on the subject but I believe the evidence strongly suggests that, taken as a whole, the upper class considerably outnumbered the lower class.

I suggest that the structure of Native society was not that of a pyramid. There was no apex of nobles, medium-sized middle class, and broad base of commoners. Instead, Native society had more the shape of an inverted pear. The greater number of people belonged to an upper or respectable class,

---

*[The phonetic symbols used for writing Native words are explained in the Appendix.]

from which leaders of various sorts emerged on various occasions. Mobility within this group was fairly free. A smaller number of people belonged to a lower class, upon which the upper class imposed its will and which it treated with contempt. Movement from this lower class into the upper class was probably difficult. A still smaller group of slaves lived with their masters, who were always of the upper class.

The principle of ranking individuals or groups in a numbered series seems to have been poorly developed among these tribes; it finds its most significant expression among the Nootka and Kwakiutl in seating and receiving order at potlatching. Among these Coast Salish tribes, there were two kinds of gatherings at which gifts were given: the sƛ̓ésʼən (from ƛ̓ésʼən, to invite), an intra-household or intravillage gathering at which one person as host shared an unexpected surplus of food; and the sƛ̓énəq (from ƛ̓énəq, to potlatch), an intervillage gathering at which the household or village as host gave away wealth. The second of these was the potlatch proper. The reason for giving away wealth at a potlatch was to pay guests from other communities to witness a change in the status of some member of the potlatcher's family. Such changes were life crises marked by the use of inherited privileges, or merely transfer of privileges themselves, as in the bestowal of an ancestral name. While such changes might be marked by intragroup gatherings, the larger gathering was preferable. And while one man might lead in organizing the potlatch, it was more typically an occasion when the several leaders (siʔ·ə́m̓) of a household or village pooled their life crises, name-givings, and so forth, for a joint endeavor vis-à-vis other households and/or villages. At such an occasion, each of the hosts might have his own list of guests to whom he owed gifts from previous potlatches. Whenever gifts are given to individuals there must of course be an order of giving, but it is my strong impression that there was no permanent receiving order among these Coast Salish tribes; each host had an ad hoc order based on his own debts and his own evaluations of persons.[4]

If we ask what gave a man high status, we are apt to find different persons emphasizing different attributes, but generally we hear first that a man must be of good birth and must be wealthy. Being of good family, of high birth, and so forth, is sometimes put negatively as "having no black marks against one"—that is, having no taint of slave ancestry, low-class ancestry, or disgraceful conduct in the family. High-class people are those who had good

---

[4]W.W. Elmendorf has indicated (personal communication) that there is evidence for a series of ranked individuals among the Twana and the Klallam, but that they constituted only a small part of the society. My position here is not that this principle is totally absent from the area but that it is relatively unimportant, and that such series, if they existed at all among some groups, were quite unstable. Among the tribes I have worked with I have not heard any accounts of conflict over position within a series; I would expect to hear such stories if the principle were of any great importance.

family trees, with a stock of good hereditary names and a few other hereditary rights.

Wealth was of course important. A man had to have wealth to give away when taking or bestowing an hereditary name or exercising some other hereditary right. But wealth was itself only the product of and the proof of possession of more important things. In some cases, wealth came from the possession of hereditary rights, as in the case of a Songish or Lummi reef-net owner; but even then, the man not only owned the right to use a net at a certain place but also usually possessed the special practical and ritual knowledge necessary for its successful operation. This knowledge was acquired from other persons, usually older kinsmen. Other kinds of ritual knowledge were a source of wealth to persons who functioned as ritualists at life crises.

But many of the activities that led to the accumulation of wealth were due, in Coast Salish theory, to the possession of spirit power. The shaman, the warrior, the gambler, the hunter, the carpenter, all persons likely to accumulate wealth, were successful in doing so, it was thought, because they had guardian spirits which made them a shaman or a warrior or a gambler. In theory, spirits could be obtained by anyone—anyone, that is, who had the courage and endurance to fast and bathe and seek a spirit vision. Of course, some families knew better than others how to train their children for spirit questing, and the location of the best places for encountering certain spirits. But poor-boy-meets-spirit-and-makes-good stories are numerous and some of them are told of actual people, so we may assume that a man without inherited fishing sites and without ritual knowledge could also become wealthy and attain high status. Over a period of several generations there was probably a good deal of social mobility. The leaders were at various times fishermen, hunters, warriors, doctors, gamblers, ritualists—men who owed their material wealth to the possession of various types of incorporeal property.

One other possession theoretically necessary to upper-class status was a sort of private or guarded knowledge; in the Straits (Lkungeneng) language this was called *snǝp*, usually translated "advice." Advice consisted of genealogies and family traditions revealing family greatness, gossip about other families demonstrating how inferior they are, instruction in practical matters such as how to quest for the right kind of guardian spirit, secret signals for indicating that someone is of lower-class descent, and a good deal of solid moral training.

If we ask what accounts for the status of a low-classed person, we will probably be told that low-classed people are those who don't have anything and don't know anything. One informant, who often returned to this subject, said repeatedly that low-class people were people who had "lost their history," who "had no advice" (*ʔǝwǝnǝ snə́ps*). High-class people preserved the knowledge of their own heritage and valued it, and possessed a knowledge of good conduct. Low-class people were those who, through their own or their forebears' misfortune or foolishness, had lost their links with the past and their knowledge of good conduct.

The moral training contained in "advice" included such warnings as "don't lie," "don't steal," "be polite to your elders," and so on. Such injunctions are presented as knowledge restricted to us few truly high-class families. It is hard for an outsider to believe that it was not generally known that one should not lie, steal, or throw rocks at his grandmother, but this was the Coast Salish fiction.

It is important to note that morality among the Coast Salish had little if any relationship to supernaturalism. Its sanctions were social, not supernatural. Children were not told that the supernatural would punish them if they misbehaved. And since there was no organized government, they could not be told that a policeman would come for them. What they were told was that if they misbehaved, they would be called "low-class." In a society that stressed private property as the Coast Salish did, it must have been very effective to present moral training as private property, in the context of secret knowledge on the gaining of wealth and the maintenance of status.

Thus the theory that knowledge of good behavior was restricted to the upper class made a contribution to social control and was therefore of some value to society. The visible existence of a genuine lower class (even though small) served to remind one of the necessity of leading a moral life, but the myth of a lower class was more important than the reality. For this reason, many Coast Salish will let you understand that there are many low-class people lurking about, but you rarely find one yourself.

How could low-class groups have come into existence in Coast Salish society? At one time, most villages consisted each of a single lineage which regarded itself as descended from an ancestor left on the site by the Transformer, or dropped from the sky. Each prided itself on the antiquity and continuity of its traditional ties with its country—the village site, fishing sites, and other productive places—and hereditary rights to names and other privileges. Kinship was reckoned bilaterally but residence was patrilocal, so membership in such a lineage was usually through the male line. (With these qualifications, Boas's early use of the term "gentes" for Coast Salish villages was probably quite proper.) According to one native tradition, certain vassal villages were simply lineages whose ancestors had been assigned this status by the Transformer. According to another native explanation, the vassal villages were descendants of slaves who no longer had individual masters; and according to yet another, they were the descendants of originally high-class people who had been forced by famine to sell themselves into slavery.

I see several possible factors in the formation of lower-class groups:

(1) *Private ownership of resources.* While the lineage (or village) identified itself with its country, exploitation of the most productive fishing and other sites was often in the hands of certain individuals who were able to use whatever surplus might be produced. Persons unrelated to the owners

9

would thereby suffer some poverty. Yet some activities were unrestricted, and the development of skill—in hunting, for example—interpreted as due to the possession of spirit power might bring wealth to anyone.

(2) *Primogeniture and other limitations in inheritance.* Primogeniture was often the practice and is implied by the kinship terms, which differentiate senior and junior lines of descent. Use of the term "little younger siblings" for lower-class people suggests that historically they may be the descendants of propertyless junior lines. But of course it may also be a way of extending a fictitious kinship to them when something is to be gained by doing so. However, primogeniture was not always the practice; it seems that rights such as great names often went to the child judged to be potentially the most successful. In the case of guarded knowledge such as the genealogies and family traditions contained in "advice," the child with the best memory might be the one who could later use the knowledge and assume or bestow the ancestral names. But again, a name was perhaps valued principally in relation to what was given away at the time it was assumed, so that a person with wealth might take any known ancestral name and make it great.

(3) *Slavery.* Slave status was hereditary. If household slaves became too numerous they might be turned out to form a separate settlement, which might then become the nucleus of a group formed by the accretion of illegitimates, orphans, tramps, and those reduced by chance to beggary.

The taint of slave ancestry was most undesirable. A person captured and made a slave could be cleansed by a *čx̌ʷtén*, "cleansing rite." Such ceremonies form an important class of inherited privileges. But while the paraphernalia and ritual knowledge required were restricted by primogeniture or other means to certain members of a lineage, the rite might be performed by the owner for any member of the lineage. Thus the only persons who could not be "cleansed" were those without close ties to families which had cleansing rites. Even after a cleansing rite had been performed, gossip about the taint of slavery was important in any rivalry and made possible implicit and private rankings not usually made explicit by seating and receiving. The mere existence of a pattern of warfare and enslavement of captives led to the social evaluation of freemen.

(4) *The social function of the myth of "advice."* Private property, the prevention of its dispersal through restrictions on inheritance, and the existence of slavery as a status into which freemen may fall, all these must have contributed to the differentiation of freemen into higher and lower. Still, there were mitigating factors with each. I believe that these causes are not quite sufficient to explain the existence of the strong feelings among the Coast Salish society—the inverted pear with the large upper class and the small lower class. I suggest that the additional factor needed is ideological; it is the myth that morality is the private property of the upper class.

This myth made it necessary (or at least useful) for the lower class to exist as evidence for its truth, but the myth probably also acted as a check on the growth of the lower class. If the lower class grew too large, its existence would no longer be compatible with the myth; a large lower class would be seen by the upper class as a threat to society, and the attitude of the upper class would become intolerable to the lower class. The two segments of such a community could only split, or fight it out. According to traditions, both interclass fighting and the splitting of communities did occur. As to the latter, Snyder (1954) has described how the rather complex tribal relations in the Lower Skagit area are the result of a process by which a community would segregate into an upper and lower class and then split to form two separate communities, each of which again became stratified. Later marriages might link the more successful families of the new community with the old community. Snyder offers no explanation as to why the division was into two parts, except to suggest an underlying duality in Coast Salish culture. I believe the hypothesis presented here supports the suggestions and clarifies the process.

Let me summarize briefly. Coast Salish society consists of three classes (Fig. 1): a large upper class of good people, a smaller lower class of worthless people, and a still smaller class of slaves. Within the upper class there were certainly differences in status, due mainly to differences in wealth. Wealth came to some persons because of their hereditary rights, to others because of spirit powers (and practical skills) acquired through their own efforts. Mobility upward within this larger class was quite possible. Moreover, there were neither clear divisions within the upper class, nor a series of ranked individuals. There was, however, a fairly clear line dividing the upper class from the lower class, especially when they were spatially separated. Movement upward from the lower group was evidently much more difficult; if a group became large enough, greater separation and the formation of a new community was probably the usual way out.

I suggest, then, that when Coast Salish informants speak of social mobility and tell folktales and historic accounts of poor boys who became successful, they are thinking of poor (but good) families within the upper class, which included the bulk of the population. When they speak of "low-class people" they are thinking of the smaller worthless class. And when they hint that other families who claim high status are really low, they are thinking of possible links with the worthless people. Perhaps all families had such links, but as long as a family produced an occasional great man it was secure. At any rate, the Coast Salish myth about "advice" may have made gossip a necessity.*

Kwakiutl society seems to have been organized along somewhat different lines. There is no indication that there were separate settlements of lower-class people. Within each group, many—and perhaps most—individuals held

---

*[On the importance of gossip, I ought to have cited Colson 1953:188-90.]

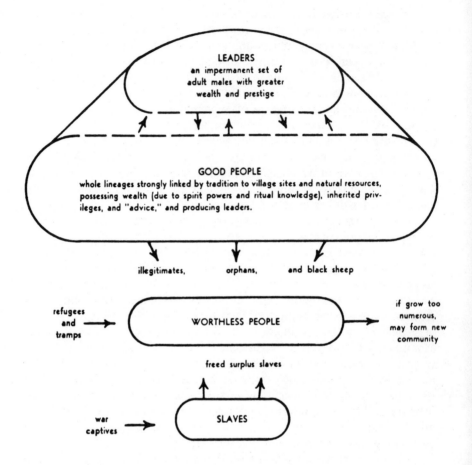

Fig. 1. Stratification in a Coast Salish Community according to the present hypothesis.

positions that were ranked in a numerical series made explicit by seating and receiving order at potlatches. Local groups were also ranked by number in a series. This ranking had two consequences. One was that everyone stood at a different place and all differences were small; if Drucker is right (and I believe he may be right for the Kwakiutl), ranking prevented any tendency toward segregation into distinct classes. The second consequence is that ranking within a series brings into being a social unit with discernible limits, whether it is a small local group or a confederacy of tribes.

In contrast, the Coast Salish of the area that I am discussing had only a poorly-developed system of ranking in numbered series for individuals, and none for local groups. Membership in a local group was not as clear a matter as among the Kwakiutl, and there were no social units larger than the local group. Thus, in one respect, Coast Salish society was more fluid than Kwakiutl society. But on the other hand, because Coast Salish society did not stress the ranking of individuals in series, it may have been easier for distinct social classes to develop.

Moreover, Kwakiutl culture does not seem to show the same emphasis on private knowledge in relation to social status as does Coast Salish culture. Among the Kwakiutl, feeling about social status seems to have been strongest at the potlatch when the relative standing of individuals was made explicit by their seating and receiving order. Among the Salish, feeling was posssibly strongest when a grandparent was telling a grandchild how he should conduct himself.

I present this as one interpretation of the data at hand, in order to point out where generalizations about the Northwest Coast as a whole may be wrong. Principles of organization may be different in its different segments. We need not assume that because the Kwakiutl show the highest development of "paranoid" behavior at potlatches, they have the strongest development of social classes. I have suggested factors in Coast Salish organization which could have led to a greater development of social classes among them. I might also point to two other factors: the Coast Salish area under discussion had more varied and probably richer natural resources than did that of the Kwakiutl, and it supported a larger population (Kroeber 1939:135); if resources and population are necessary to stratification, then the area might have supported a more stratified society.

Finally, I would urge that the relationship between the existence of a small class of worthless people and their society's ethical system, a relationship presented here more as hypothesis than as demonstrated fact, be studied in other primitive societies.

POSTSCRIPT, 1974

This paper was written in 1956. Since then I have continued to work with

Coast Salish materials and I think I now see the Coast Salish more clearly than I did then, especially in the contexts of ecology and areal ethnography. (My more recent papers listed in the Bibliography are attempts at developing this understanding.) While I see no reason to change the model of social stratification presented in this paper, I would now change some of the terms I used eighteen years ago. Perhaps the term ''Coast Salish'' itself is misleading, since the people I was concerned with are not all of the Coast Salish but only one segment of a Coast Salish continuum that extends on to the north and to the south and southwest and exhibits cultural differences, especially between the extremes. This segment lies about at the center of the continuum and so I should have said ''Central Coast Salish.'' The term ''lineages'' now seems inappropriate, since that term generally refers to the discrete descent groups found with unilineal descent, whereas the (Central) Coast Salish cognatic descent groups are non-discrete (i.e., overlapping) extended families or ''stem kindreds.'' ''Patrilocal'' now seems misleading if not plain wrong, since it may imply a clearly formulated rule that a couple should live with the husband's family, whereas the (Central) Coast Salish asserted that a couple was free to live with either family. In practice perhaps two-thirds (the data have not been properly pulled together) of all couples did live with the husband's family, but those who lived with the wife's family did not suffer any loss of status because of it; there was nothing like the deplorable condition of being ''half-married'' that was endured by the northwest California men who lived with their wives' families. The Central Coast Salish could and did change residence according to kin and marital ties and this freedom may have been one of the ways they accommodated to local fluctuations in the abundance of resources. I would now avoid ''community,'' since it often implies a social unit with a high degree of cohesiveness, in-group feeling, internal social control, and so forth, and the Central Coast Salish village may not have been such a unit. ''Village'' or simply ''settlement'' would be more appropriate, since these terms are more neutral in what they imply about social cohesion, and so on. I would now strike the word ''primitive'' from the last sentence of the paper, because of the implications of the word itself and because I should not have suggested any restriction in comparisons. In fact, my ''inverted pear'' image of the Central Coast Salish village could have been inspired by West's (1945) diamond-shaped representation of ''Plainville, U.S.A.'' and/or Kroeber's (1948:269-72) discussion of Plainville and other U.S. ''communities,'' though I do not remember it. Finally, the term ''social classes'' is one I would still use, though perhaps only because I am not yet convinced that it is inappropriate. For a somewhat different view of Coast Salish social stratification see Elmendorf (1971).

2. Affinal Ties, Subsistence, and Prestige among the Coast Salish[1]*

The nature of Northwest Coast social stratification and the nature of the institution most intimately related to it, the potlatch, are problems of widely recognized importance. Yet attempts at solving these problems have not been wholly satisfactory. Generalizations about social stratification have been betrayed by failure to give sufficient weight to all of the differences in social structure that existed among the various Northwest Coast tribes. Explanations of the potlatch have been only partial ones, finding its function in the expression of the individual's drive for high status or in the fulfillment of society's need for solidarity. Relating these functions to man's other requirements for survival

---

[1]This paper was presented in somewhat shorter form at the 12th Annual Northwest Anthropological Conference held at Portland State College in April 1959. The field research upon which it is based has been done at various times over the last twelve years and has been supported successively by the University of Washington, a Wenner-Gren Pre-doctoral Fellowship, the University of British Columbia, and the Leon and Thea Koerner Foundation. The interpretation presented here has evolved from one presented in my Ph.D. dissertation (1951), modified by late work on the Lower Fraser, and further developed and broadened by collaboration with Dr. A.P. Vayda and discussion with our students at the University of British Columbia. [One of the sources of inspiration for this article must have been Vayda's interpretation of Pomo trade feasts presented in our joint seminar (see Vayda 1966).]

*[Originally published in the *American Anthropologist* 62:296-305 (1960). Reproduced by permission of the American Anthropological Association; not for further reproduction. Reprinted as Bobbs-Merrill Reprint Series in the Social Sciences No. A-219 (1962) and in *Issues in Cultural Anthropology: Selected Readings* edited by David W. McCurdy and James P. Spradley (Boston and Toronto: Little, Brown 1979), pp. 244-51.]

has often been inhibited by an assumption that the satisfaction of alimentary needs through the food quest and the satisfaction of psychological needs through the manipulation of wealth form two separate systems, the "subsistence economy" and the "prestige economy." Or if a relationship between the two is hypothesized, the hypothesis usually makes the "prestige economy" dependent upon the "subsistence economy"; it is assumed that a rich habitat provides an abundance of food which in turn supports the prestige economy which in turn maintains social stratification. I believe, however, that it is more reasonable to assume that, for a population to have survived in a given environment for any length of time, its subsistence activities and prestige-gaining activities are likely to form a single integrated system by which that population has adapted to its environment. I will try to show how this may be true of one group of Northwest Coast tribes, the Coast Salish of Southern Georgia Strait and the Strait of Juan de Fuca,[2] and in particular I will try to show that in the socio-economic system of these tribes a role of crucial importance was played by the ties established through intercommunity marriage.

Native social organization in this area was characterized by a seeming looseness. Kinship was reckoned bilaterally. Residence was usually, but not always, patrilocal. The nuclear families of brothers, cousins, and brothers-in-law

---

[2]There is no general term for the tribes of this area. They are all speakers of two closely related Coast Salish languages, Halkomelem and Straits (Lkungeneng). Dialects of Halkomelem are spoken by the Stalo tribes, including the Chilliwack, Katzie, Kwantlen, Musqueam, and others on the Lower Fraser, and by the Nanaimo, Chemainus, and Cowichan of Vancouver Island. Straits dialects are spoken by the Semiahmoo, Lummi, and Samish on the mainland south of the Fraser and by the Saanich, Songish, and Sooke on Vancouver Island. The Klallam, on the south shore of the Strait of Juan de Fuca and at Becher Bay on Vancouver Island, speak a more divergent dialect of Straits. There are few significant cultural differences among these tribes. That they have some kind of social unity is suggested by the fact that the system of kin terms described here is identical in Straits, Halkomelem, and Nooksack, but different in structure to the north and to the south. The system of affinal exchange described here, however, seems to have extended somewhat beyond this area, but my data are not sufficient to permit me to draw any neat boundaries.

My data are mainly from work done with informants of the Straits tribes and of the Katzie and Musqueam. The personal recollections of the oldest of these people did not take them back earlier than the 1870s and 80s, though traditional genealogies and bits of history allow for some inferences about conditions during the first half of the 19th century. The present paper is thus an interpretation based on an ethnographic reconstruction.

Portions of this area have been covered in the published ethnographic works of Boas, Hill-Tout, Jenness, Gunther, Stern, Barnett, and Duff. I have used these as guides for enquiry, but the material this paper is based on is almost wholly my own field notes.

Native terms have been transcribed in the system of phonetic symbols used in the more recent publications on this area. Unless otherwise indicated, Native terms are given in the Musqueam dialect of Halkomelem. Dr. W.W. Elmendorf and I are preparing a comparative study of Halkomelem dialects to be presented elsewhere. [See Elmendorf and Suttles 1960.]

formed extended families (*xʷnəċéləwəm*), occupying great cedar-plank houses and claiming rights to certain local resources and to certain inherited privileges. One or more such extended families formed a village or community. The community was linked through ties of marriage and kinship with other communities and these with still others to form a social network with no very clear boundaries. Groups of villages like the Lummi and Cowichan were linked by common dialect and traditions as "tribes" but in recent generations these village groupings were certainly not separate "societies."

Within most communities there seem to have been three distinct social classes—a majority identified as "high class," a somewhat smaller group identified as "low class," and a still smaller group of slaves. The slaves lived in the households of the upper class; the lower class often occupied separate houses in its own section of the community or in a location sufficiently separate so that it might be regarded as a lower class community subservient to an upper class group. In Native theory the lower class consisted of people who "had lost their history," that is, people who had no claim to the most productive resources of the area and no claim to recognized inherited privileges, and who furthermore "had no advice," that is, they had no private knowledge and no moral training.[3]

For the upper class the most proper and usual sort of marriage was one arranged between families of similar social standing in different communities. The arrangements usually included preliminary negotiations by members of the prospective groom's family, a vigil kept by the young man at the girl's house, and an exchange of property between the two families. This exchange was the wedding itself. It was held in the bride's house. The groom's family brought wealth for the bride's family; the bride's family gave wealth, perhaps nearly an equal amount, to the groom's family; and the bride's father also gave, if possible, an inherited privilege or privileges, such as a name or the right to use a rattle or mask, to the couple for their child or children. After the wedding the couple usually went to live with the groom's family. The two families could continue to exchange property as long as the marriage endured. And the marriage might be made to endure longer than the life of one party to it, for if one or the other died the family of the deceased might provide another spouse for the survivor.

The kinship terms seem to indicate something of the nature of these relationships. The terms for blood kin form a system in some respects like the English, bilateral with lineal and collateral kin distinguished in parents' and children's generations, the most important difference being that the sibling

---

[3]I have discussed this in greater detail in "Private Knowledge, Morality, and Social Classes among the Coast Salish" (1958). [No. 1 in this volume]

17

terms distinguish older and younger siblings and are extended to cousins to distinguish senior and junior lines of descent.*

But the affinal terms form an entirely different system. For the relationships indicated by the English terms "father-in-law," "mother-in-law," "son-in-law," "daughter-in-law," "brother-in-law," "sister-in-law," there are four Native terms: *sk̓ʷíɬəw* (spouse's parent, wife's brother), *scəwtéɬ* (child's spouse, man's sister's husband), *smétəxʷtən* (man's sister-in-law, woman's brother-in-law), *šxʷʔéləx* (woman's sister-in-law). Thus the affinal terms, quite unlike the consanguineal terms, may lump persons of different generations and distinguish by sex of speaker. The English affinal terms form a structure that mirrors that formed by the consanguineal terms; the Native affinal terms form an entirely different sort of structure. The key to this structure seems to be that it shows the "direction of the marriage," that is, the direction of the movement of women as wives, and it shows the possibility of secondary affinal marriage. A man calls by the term *sk̓ʷíɬəw* his wife's father and brother, that is, the men from whom he received her, and he is called *scəwtéɬ* by them. And, conversely, he uses the term *scəwtéɬ* for his sister's husband and daughter's husband, that is, the men who have received women from him, and they will of course call him *sk̓ʷíɬəw*. Siblings-in-law of the opposite sex, that is, men and women who might marry through the operation of the levirate or sororate, call each other *smétəxʷtən*. Sisters-in-law call each other *šxʷʔéləx*, which means literally "one who functions as sister."† If a spouse dies, his or her relatives are all called by a single term *céyʔɛ* by the widow or widower. To marry one's *céyʔ·ɛ* is called *céyʔɛm*. If this is done the former terms are again used.

The most important remaining affinal kinship term is *sk̓ʷálwəs*, child's spouse's parent. Since there is no usual English term for *sk̓ʷálwəs*, I propose to use a term of my own, "co-parent-in-law."‡ This relationship is one of the most important in the whole social system. Co-parents-in-law are people linked by the marriage of their children. These are the people who exchange wealth at the wedding and who may continue to make exchanges as long as the marriage lasts. After the death of one party to the marriage they become *ćɬx̌é·m* ("those who weep together") until the marriage is reconstituted.

According to informants from several tribes in the area, a man could at any time take food to a co-parent-in-law and expect to receive wealth in return.

---

*[For a further discussion of the consanguineal terms see No. 13 in this volume.]

†[Correction: *ʔéləx* is "sibling of the opposite sex," i.e., a male's sister or a female's brother; the compound prefix *šxʷ-* gives the sense "locus of" or "possessor of"; and so *šxʷʔéləx* seems to be "one who has (my) sibling of the opposite sex."]

‡[The term "co-parent-in-law" rose out of my unconscious, I suppose, but I must admit with some embarrassment that I clearly did not invent it. Kroeber (1960) used it as the English for the Yurok term. The Halkomelem term applies not only to the child's spouse's parent but to any consanguine's spouse's consanguine.]

18

To make such a trip was called *ʔíst* (literally "to paddle") or *ɬəwɛ́n* in Straits, *ʔə́xəl* or *kʷəlwəsɛ́·n* in Halkomelem. The person taking food invited members of his community to help him take it; these people were called *šq̓áʔwəɬ*. The person or family receiving the food then invited members of their own community to share the food in a feast (*sx̌éxən*, from *x̌éxən*, "to invite"). At this time they hired a speaker (*šq̓ʷiʔqʷél'*) to "pay the paddles"and to "thank" the co-parent-in-law. To "pay the paddles" (*q̓éʔwəlwɛʔs*, from *q̓éʔwət*, "to pay for services," and *-əlwɛʔs*, "paddle") meant to pay each of the *šq̓áʔwəɬ* who had helped bring the food, and also to make payments for the canoes themselves, the paddles, and even the bailers. The Swinomish, Lummi, and Katzie seem to have spoken of "paying" the co-parent-in-law for the food, using the verb (in Halkomelem) *nə́wnəc*, "to pay for something bought." A Lummi informant stated that on Vancouver Island people did not pay their co-parents-in-law. My Musqueam informants likewise stated that they and the Cowichan did not pay for the food. But then they explained that you had to "thank" (*čí·t*) your co-parents-in-law. The Vancouver Island people still do this—at Cowichan "you ought to thank them with between ten and twenty dollars." The difference then is only in the terms used. Everywhere one can take food and expect to receive wealth.

This sort of exchange is not confined to co-parents-in-law; it may take place between father-in-law and son-in-law or between brothers-in-law, or between cousins in different communities as well. But informants usually speak of the exchange first in relation to co-parents-in-law, probably because this is the relationship of the two families who have established the tie through marrying their children to one another and who begin the series of exchanges. Exchanges between other relatives are, I believe, simply the continuation of exchanges begun by co-parents-in-law.

Several informants indicated that the exchanges of food and wealth between affinals could become competitive. The amount of wealth extracted from an in-law could be increased by increasing the amount of food taken and by increasing the number of fellow villagers invited to help take it. But if the amount of wealth required were very great, the recipient of the food might "pay for it with a song," that is to say, he might sing an inherited song (*səyə́-wənəm* or *shəẏwiʔnaqʷ*) or (perhaps only among the Klallam) a spirit song bestowed by a wealth spirit (*yúɬməx*). If the recipient of the food had such a song which he might sing at this time as additional payment, the bringer of the food might then feel obliged to thank him for this performance with a gift of wealth, or treat him in the same fashion when the situation was reversed.

Two things must be made clear. First, this sort of exchange between affinals is not simply a repayment of the bride price or a balancing out of the exchanges that took place at the wedding. Historically it may be derived from this, or in individual cases it may begin with this, but families seem to have continued and developed the series of exchanges long after the original connection was established. Second, this sort of exchange is not to be confused with the potlatch. The potlatch (sx̣ʼə́nəq) is an occasion when the host or hosts invite members of other communities to the host community to receive gifts of wealth to validate changes of status and exercise inherited privileges. The sponsor may be an individual, but it seems that more often a number of persons in the host community pooled their occasions for the validation of claims to high (or at least new) status and invited guests at the same time so that the community as a whole served as host.

As I said earlier, I believe the exchange between affinals that I have just described plays an important part in the Native socio-economic system. First, it is an important link in the relationship between food, wealth, and high status, a relationship that has not been very thoroughly explored for any Northwest Coast society.

Among the Coast Saiish of the area I am describing, food and high status are directly related. High status comes from sharing food. The variety of Native subsistence techniques and property rights, together with individual differences in skill (generally interpreted in Native ideology as resulting from differences in supernatural support), made for considerable differences in productivity. And, of course, the man who produced more than others was honored. A man was expected to share food with his close relatives and housemates. Certain types of food, such as sea mammals, were usually shared at feasts (sx̣ʼéxən) at which someone from each family was served and given a portion called mə́qaʔθ to take home. And, as I have indicated, a man used food brought by his co-parents-in-law for a feast for his own people, so that having productive affinals meant being a food provider yourself—as long as you could thank your affinals properly for their gifts.

People also shared food with neighbors and relatives from other communities by sharing access to their techniques and/or resources. One conjugal family working alone had the instruments for equal access to most types of resources within the territory of its community. But some of the most productive techniques required the cooperation of several persons. Moreover, access to some of the most productive sites was restricted by property rights. Not all, but the best camas beds, fern beds, wapato ponds, and clam beds were owned by extended families with control exercised by individuals. Most duck-net sites were so owned; deer-net sites were not but the investment of material and labor in the nets was such that only a few hunters had them, and the same was probably true of seal nets. Weirs and traps for salmon seem usually to have been built by a whole community, perhaps under the direction of the head of an extended family, but with no distinction in access. However, the houses standing at the weir sites, which were necessary for smoking the catch, were owned by individuals or extended families. Some other types of fishing were more restricted by property rights. The sturgeon traps of the

Musqueam belonged to extended families. The reef-net locations of the Straits tribes, (Lummi, Saanich, Songish) were owned by individuals. But in one way or another access was shared, both within the community and among communities. The director of a Musqueam sturgeon trap might give permission to members of other extended families to help take fish from it for a share. The owner of a Straits reef-net location might "hire" a crew from members of other extended families or even other communities. Some Cowichans fished in the summer on reef nets belonging to Saanich and some of the Saanich, who had no important stream in their territory, went to the Cowichan River for the fall runs of fish caught at weirs. The Katzie were hosts to people from up and down the Fraser when it was time to take wapato from their ponds or pick berries on their bogs.

High status also comes from directing food production. Perhaps every kind of joint enterprise had a director in the owner of the gear or the "owner" of the site. The actual degree of control given to an individual probably varied with the complexity of the process and the responsibility required of him. The Straits reef net was a complex device that had to be carefully made and skillfully operated; the reef-net location was always said to be "owned" by one man or at most two brothers, who evidently had considerable authority over it. On the other hand, the Musqueam sturgeon trap was simply a kind of tidal pound from which fish could be easily drawn out at low tide; members of the extended family that had built the trap were its "owners" and were free to come and take fish at any time without consulting the director—it being expected they would share the fish; while the only responsibility of the director was to see that the trap was repaired once a year and to give permission to nonmembers to participate in the taking of the fish. But even the Katzie wapato ponds and berry bogs had an "owner" who gave permission to outsiders to collect there. Thus, for some subsistence techniques there may be technical reasons for control by a director while for others there are not. But with such widespread sharing of access to resources, there are surely social reasons why there may be an "owner" even when technical reasons are minimal, simply in order to show outsiders that *somebody's* permission had to be asked.

The potlatch very likely played an important part within this system of sharing access to resources. By potlatching, a group established its status vis-à-vis other groups, in effect saying "we are an extended family (or a village of several extended families) with title to such-and-such a territory having such-and-such resources." And when a leading member assumed a name that harked back to the beginning of the world when the ancestors of the group first appeared on the spot, this not only demonstrated the validity of the group's title but perhaps also announced in effect "this is the man in charge of our resources." But could not any sort of spectacle serve the same ends? It seems to me that these functions are not sufficient to explain that feature which is most typical of the potlatch—the lavish giving of wealth.

The relationship between wealth and high status is quite clear. As in other Northwest Coast societies, by giving wealth at a potlatch a man validates a claim to noble descent and inherited privilege and thus converts wealth into high status. It may be argued then that the relationship of wealth and high status only parallels that of food and high status, but the argument is convincing only if food and wealth are unrelated.

Food and wealth are indeed separate categories of goods in Native culture. "Wealth" (ʔə́wkʷ) consisted of blankets, shell ornaments, fine baskets, hide shirts, bows and arrows, canoes, slaves—items of varying utility but all relatively imperishable. Blankets were the most important such item, especially since they could be ripped apart and the wool rewoven time after time. Food was not classed as "wealth." Nor was it treated as wealth. There is some evidence that food was seen as a gift from the supernatural; xéʔxɛ sʔíłəŋ, "holy food," a Semiahmoo informant called it. It should be given freely, he felt, and could not be refused. Food was evidently not freely exchanged with wealth. A person in need of food might ask to buy some from another household in his community, offering wealth for it, but food was not generally offered for sale.

Food and wealth were *indirectly* related in one important way. A man who could produce more food could release some of the members of his household from food-producing activities and let them produce wealth, and he could attract more food-producing and wealth-producing persons to his household as wives for himself (polygyny being permitted) and for his sons, brothers, and nephews, and as sons-in-law (residence with wife's family being permitted). Thus food could be indirectly converted into wealth. But of course a larger household means more mouths to feed at all times and conditions of production must have set limits to the size of a household.

And finally, as described above, food could be taken to affinal relatives and wealth received in return. This then appears to have been the most important mechanism for *directly* converting food into wealth. The relationship of food, wealth, and high status is complete. They all form a single system.

Thus the first thing I want to point out about the food-for-wealth exchange between affinals is its importance within the total system of food, wealth, and high status. The second is that through it the total system is an adaptive one.

The environmental setting of native culture was characterized by four significant features: 1) *variety of types of food*, including sprouts, roots, berries, shellfish, fishes, waterfowl, land and sea mammals; 2) *local variation* in the occurrence of these types, due to irregular shore lines, broken topography, differences between fresh and salt water, local differences in temperature and precipitation; 3) *seasonal variation*, especially in vegetable foods and in anadromous fishes; 4) *fluctuation from year to year*, in part due to the regular cycles of the different populations of fish, in part to less predictable changes, as in weather.

The first three of these four environmental features are no doubt closely related to the clearly patterned yearly round of subsistence activities. In the spring the different families occupying the sections of a big house left the community, perhaps separately, to spend a good part of the year moving from place to place accumulating stores of food. But this food quest was not at all a random movement. People knew quite well where and when they were likely to find what food and so they generally exploited a certain place at a certain time for a certain thing. Their choice was determined largely by the first three of the environmental features just mentioned, together with technological and social factors factors suggested earlier. But the fourth of the environmental features, fluctuation from year to year, must have demanded versatility and adaptability. While these environmental features were characteristic even of the small territory identified with each community, they were of course of greater significance for the whole area under consideration. The rather pronounced differences in resources among communities, plus year-to-year fluctuation in quantities, must have put a premium on intercommunity cooperation.

The sharing of access to resources was a form of intercommunity cooperation that must have made for greater efficiency in the exploitation of the environment. But this form of cooperation was probably one that required some planning, as when a Saanich reef-net captain hired Cowichan net pullers or when a Musqueam family decided to visit their Katzie relatives at wapato harvesting time, and worked out best for predictable differences in resources. But the availability of food was clearly not always predictable; there were temporary unforeseen shortages and surpluses. Under all of these conditions any mechanism by which members of one community could "bank" a temporary surplus of some particular item of diet with members of another community would be advantageous. The exchange between affinals was such a mechanism. If one community had a sudden oversupply of, say, herring, its members could take canoeloads to their various co-parents-in-law, receive mountain-goat wool blankets in exchange, with which they might later "thank" their co-parents-in-law for gifts of camas bulbs or dried sturgeon. Wealth then was good credit for food received. Wealth was a part of this adaptive system.

Looking now at that most famous institution, the potlatch, I find that *within this total socio-economic system*, its most important function is to be found neither in the expression of the individual's drive for high status nor in the fulfillment of the society's need for solidarity, neither in competition nor in cooperation, but simply in the redistribution of wealth.* Wealth has been accumulated by various means—producing it within one's own household,

---

*[I would stick by this statement, with the emphasis given. There may also be other systems—psychological, ideational, etc.—in which the potlatch had different functions.]

23

receiving it for services, receiving it as gifts validating the status of donors at previous potlatches, and receiving it in thanks for food taken to one's in-laws in other communities. Since wealth is indirectly or directly obtainable through food, then inequalities in food production will be translated into in-equalities in wealth. If one community over a period of several years were to produce more food than its neighbors, it might come to have a greater part of the society's wealth. Under such circumstances the less productive communities might become unable to give wealth back in exchange for further gifts of food from the more productive one. If amassing wealth were an end in itself the process of sharing surplus food might thus break down. But wealth, in the Native view, is only a means to high status achieved through the giving of it. And so the community that has converted its surplus food into wealth and now has a surplus of wealth gets rid of its wealth by giving it away at a potlatch. And this, though the participants need not be conscious of it, by "restoring the purchasing power"* of the other communities, enables the whole process to continue. The potlatchers have converted their surplus wealth into high status. High status in turn enables the potlatchers to establish wider ties, make better marriages with more distant villages, and thus extend the process farther.

This interpretation of the potlatch among this particular group of tribes suggests that it serves as a regulating mechanism within the total socio-economic system. The drive to attain high status emerges from this interpretation as a prerequisite to the sorts of behavior that keep the system operating. Satisfying this drive is a "function" of the potlatch only in a secondary or instrumental sense (i.e. it serves an end that is only a means to another end); by satisfying the individual potlatcher's and the community's drive to attain high status, the potlatch provides the rewards necessary to keep others striving to rise. The drive for high status is itself a part of the total system. Since it is necessary to the system, we may assume that values stimulating and support-ing it have developed at the expense of values inhibiting it. Some of the values stimulating and supporting the drive to attain high status are seen in Native ethical theory, which insists that knowledge of good behavior is the monop-oly of the "good" families and that the lower class are "without advice" (i.e. without properly enculturated values), and some are seen in Native super-naturalism, which insists that success in any practical activity is achieved with supernatural support and thus gives the seeker for supernatural power† both the confidence and the incentive to succeed in the practical. These values are given to the individual early in life and are reaffirmed until the end. They

---

*[A phrase suggested by a student whose name I do not know.]

†[I would now avoid the term "supernatural" as implying a distinction that may not have existed for the Coast Salish. See No. 6 in this volume.]

provide a constant stimulation to the drive for high status, which finds its greatest satisfaction in the potlatch.

But the drive to attain high status is clearly not the explanation of the potlatch. Nor is the production of surplus. Nor the cooperation achieved by the potlatching community. The potlatch is a part of a larger socio-economic system that enables the whole social network, consisting of a number of communities, to maintain a high level of food production and to equalize its food consumption both within and among communities. The system is thus adaptive in an environment characterized by the features indicated before—spatial and temporal variation and fluctuation in the availability of resources. Values, drives, surpluses, competition, and cooperation—all of these may be as much effects as causes. The whole has probably developed through a process of variation and selection, within the limitations of environment and cultural means, that can be best described by the term "cultural evolution."

The foregoing is an interpretation of the culture of one Northwest Coast society as an adaptive system. The data on which it is based are not always as clear as I would like but I offer it with the strong feeling that, seen in this fashion, more of Native culture makes better sense than it does otherwise. I do not offer it as an interpretation of the whole Northwest Coast culture area except in a general way. In its details it may not even apply to the Coast Salish north of the Squamish and south of the Skagit. And certainly the other subareas within the Northwest Coast differ greatly in several features of social organization and they very likely differ in features of ecological setting as well. The relationship between these two sets of variables remains to be worked out.*

---

*[Vayda (1961a) suggested that a similar interpretation might be given to the potlatch of other Northwest Coast peoples, and Piddocke (1965) offered a somewhat similar one for the Kwakiutl. Drucker and Heizer (1967) criticized our approach, but see reviews of their work by Suttles (1968b) and by Hawthorn (1968). Since then there has been a literature on the potlatch too extensive to comment on here.]

3. Variation in Habitat and Culture on the Northwest Coast*

"In the early days," writes Ruth Underhill (1944:9), "the richest people in North America were Indians of the Northwest coast."

Not rich in gold and silver! Even had they been able to dig those metals from the rocks where the White man finds them now, the Indians would have thought of them only as another ornament, like bear claws and abalone shell. To them, wealth was something a man could eat, wear or use to shelter him from the weather. And it was something he could give to his friends for these purposes. In this sense, the Northwest had everything. There were fish in the streams; game in the forests; berries and roots in open places. There were trees large enough to build a banquet hall, yet splitting like matchwood. There was a climate so moist plants grew as if in the tropics, yet so mild that few clothes were necessary.

People who lived in such a climate did not need to plant. They had more berries and roots than they could use, simply by going to places where Nature had spread them. Most of them did not even hunt, unless they felt like a change of diet. Every year, they

---

*[Originally published in the *Akten des 34. Internationalen Amerikanistenkongresses, Wien, 1960*, (Vienna: Verlag Ferdinand Berger), pp. 522-37 (1962); reprinted in *Man in Adaptation: The Cultural Present*, edited by Yehudi A. Cohen (Chicago: Aldine 1968), pp. 93-106.]

26

had only to wait until the salmon came swarming up the streams, "so thick," say the old settlers, "that you could walk across on their backs." In three or four months, a family could get food enough to last a year. The rest of the time they could give to art, to war, to ceremonies and feasting. And so they did.

In the chapter on economics in their text, *An Introduction to Cultural Anthropology* (2nd ed., 1959), Ralph L. Beals and Harry Hoijer present a brief sketch of "wealth and status among the Haidas." They begin with a few lines on the habitat, reading in part:

> The region in which the Haidas live is mild and equable in climate throughout the year . . . Both land and marine fauna are exceptionally rich . . . Coastal waters and rivers teem with fish . . . *The potential food supply is consistent and dependable*, for though it is less in winter, there is no season when food is really difficult to obtain (1959:433).

After discussing technology and kinship they continue:

> The household is the producing unit and usually can find among its members all or most of the skills and labor it requires. Property is accumulated, not only by hunting, fishing, collecting, and manufacturing, but also by an elaborate technique of lending at 100 per cent interest and by trade and warfare with neighboring tribes on the mainland. Each household, *despite the ease of making a living in this rich environment*, works very hard to accumulate as large a surplus as possible, especially in storable foods, oils, furs, blankets, slaves, and shields made of native copper. The accumulations so made are not for trade, however. Indeed, *since there is little division of labor as between Haida households, such internal trade is not required; each household can amply supply its own wants.*
>
> Instead the surplus accumulated by a household is consumed in lavish feasts and elaborate entertainments called potlatches (1959:434).

Then after describing the potlatch and its relation to social status, they conclude with the following statement:

> It is clear, then, that the potlatch provides an enormous incentive to hard work and the accumulation of property among the Haidas, *even though such accumulations are not really necessary*

to survival and have no outlet in trade. The patterns of the pot-latch and its associated economic activities find their own logic in the total framework of Haida culture (1959:435). [all emphasis mine—W.S.]

In a recent essay on Boas's work on the Kwakiutl, Helen Codere (1959:72) writes:

The comparative view of Kwakiutl culture in relation to other Northwest Coast cultures seems to be based almost entirely upon studies of symbolic cultural materials, particularly those of mythology . . . probably because the Northwest Coast was an eco-logical and cultural area which shared fundamental technological and socio-economic features. Boas even considered that "the material culture of the fishing tribes of the coast of northeastern Asia, of northwest America, and of the Arctic coast of America . . . (were) . . . so much alike that the assumption of an old unity of this culture seems justifiable" (1940:338). It would follow that his work in clarifying cultural relationships within the Northwest Coast area, and the relationships of that area to the Old World, would necessarily deal largely with symbolic materials, *since the most significant variation would be found at the nonmaterial pole.* [emphasis mine—W.S.]

It is very difficult to generalize about ethnological writing on the North-west Coast, especially since there have been wide differences of opinion on certain issues. However, the statements that I have just given, taken from a semi-popular ethnographic work, from an introductory text in anthropol-ogy, and from an essay by a specialist in the area on the foremost student of the area, seem to imply a set of propositions that are contained in much, though by no means all, that has been written on the Northwest Coast. These propositions are:

1) The Northwest Coast is ecologically a single area within which the natural environment is a constant, providing everywhere abundant and dependable sources of food.

2) This habitat permits the production of surpluses, which in turn permit the development of social stratification, art, and ceremony, and the manipu-lation of prestige goods culminating in the potlatch.

3) This "prestige economy" has little relation to the problems of subsistence but is largely an expression of cultural values.

4) Cultural differences within the Northwest Coast culture area are there-fore due to the growth of differences in cultural values, to differences in cultural origins through migration or diffusion, or to combinations of these causes.

28

These propositions and the total argument that they make have perhaps never been set forth quite as explicitly as this, and perhaps not all writers who seem to have held any of them implicitly would accept them in this form. However, I do not think it is unfair to set them forth as possible implications of the writing I have quoted. I believe they should be set forth explicitly because I believe they should be as explicitly questioned.

I have already questioned the first three of these propositions as applied to one portion of the Northwest Coast in an interpretation of the culture of the Coast Salish of Southern Georgia Strait and the Strait of Juan de Fuca, which recently appeared in the *American Anthropologist.** In this interpretation several important features of Native social organization and ceremonialism appear as parts of a total socio-economic system that enabled the Native population to maintain a fairly high level of production and to reduce inequalities in consumption in a habitat characterized by a variety of types of natural resources, local diversity and seasonal variation in their occurrence, and year to year fluctuation in their abundance. In this portion of the Northwest Coast, the habitat was not a constant but a variable, and several aspects of Native culture, including the potlatch, seem to have been adapted to its variability.

In the present paper I would like to present further evidence for qualitative and quantitative variation in natural resources on the Northwest Coast and to discuss some possible implications of my interpretation of the Coast Salish material for other areas on the Coast. This paper is to be then a sort of "view of the Northwest Coast as seen from the Coast Salish." And I should add that, while my discussion of the Coast Salish is based on a number of years of first-hand experience and what I believe to be fairly good evidence, my discussion of other portions of the Coast will be largely speculation. I say this merely to give fair warning, however, rather than to apologize, for I believe that speculation is quite proper in a symposium of this sort. Let me now first outline the Coast Salish cultural system as I see it and then discuss in more detail the features of habitat under which the system seems to be adaptive.

The term "Coast Salish" usually designates a large group of tribes occupying most of the area around Georgia Strait, the Strait of Juan de Fuca, Puget Sound, and extending to the Pacific between the Olympic Peninsula and Willapa Bay. Linguistically speaking, the Bella Coola and the Tillamook could also be called "Coast Salish," though they are culturally more distinct. Even among the contiguous group of tribes, however, cultural differences are great enough that generalizations about "the Coast Salish" are probably dangerous. I must make it clear therefore that here I am concerned with only one segment of the Coast Salish area, that occupied by the speakers of only two of the ten or more Coast Salish languages.

---

*[Suttles 1960a. No. 2 in this volume.]

I am concerned here with the tribes that speak two closely related Salish languages, Lkungeneng (which I prefer to call "Straits") and Halkomelem. The speakers of Straits are the Sooke, Songish, and Saanich on Vancouver Island and the Samish, Lummi, and Semiahmoo on the opposite mainland; the speakers of Halkomelem are the Cowichan, Chemainus, and Nanaimo on the Island and, on the mainland, the Musqueam, Kwantlen, Katzie, Chilliwack, and others along the Lower Fraser River. The Lower Fraser tribes have also been called "Stalo," and Wilson Duff (1952) has called those from Chilliwack to the canyon "Upper Stalo." Although these "tribes" so-called were not united in any sort of confederacy of the Wakashan type or by any system of clans and phratries as in the north, they were by no means separate "societies," but rather loosely bound groups of communities within a social and cultural continuum that extended northward and southward somewhat beyond the area of the two languages. Biologically the Straits and Halkomelem tribes were surely a part of a single population and culturally of a single people. Unfortunately there is no way of designating these people other than with the cumbersome linguistic designation, so for convenience I will often say simply "Coast Salish" hoping that the proper qualifications will be understood.

The aboriginal culture of this Coast Salish people may be seen as having these three components:

A. A primitive technology requiring complete dependence on hunting, fishing, and gathering—but providing sound houses and watercraft, a variety of weapons, nets, traps, and containers, and preserving techniques of drying and smoking.

B. An ideology and enculturation process providing the individual with the incentive to strive for prestige through the display of supernatural power and the giving of property, the two being symbolically the same.

C. A socio-economic system containing the following—

1. Communities composed of one or more kin groups firmly identified with their locality by tradition.

2. Membership in kin group through bilateral descent, with alternate or even multiple membership possible, making the individual potentially mobile.

3. Preference for local exogamy, establishing a network of affinal ties among communities.

4. Preference for patrilocal residence, having the result that, within the community, most adult males are native and most adult females outsiders— though bilateral affiliation always makes for some exceptions.

5. Leadership within the group partly through seniority and partly through ability, kin-group headmen having control (sometimes nominal, sometimes real) over especially productive resources within the territory of the kin group. (Davenport's "stem kindred" may be a useful concept here. See Davenport 1959:564.)

6. Sharing of access to resources among communities through affinal and

blood kin ties—possibly leading to some change in residence.

7. Exchange of food for "wealth" (i.e., durable goods) between affinal relatives in different communities.

8. Redistribution of wealth through the potlatch.

The system of exchange and potlatching seems to have worked in this fashion. A kin or local group with a temporary surplus of any item of food, say the result of the run of some fish or the ripening of some berry, might take this surplus to an affinally related group in another locality and receive wealth in blankets or other imperishable items in return. Later the recipient in the first exchange might make a return visit with its own extra food and get back wealth for it. Any group that produced more food than its various affinally related neighbors would of course in time come to have more wealth. But any tendency for wealth to accumulate in a few places was controlled by the practice of potlatching, whereby the wealthy group converted its wealth into high status at the same time giving the other groups the means of continuing the whole process. Given the limitations of Native technology, and operating under the stimulus of Native ideology, this whole process was surely useful in the face of variation and fluctuation in natural resources.

Let us now look more closely at the natural resources of the territory of the Coast Salish people whose culture I have just outlined. The Straits- and Halkomelem-speaking tribes occupied the southeastern shore of Vancouver Island from Sherringham Point, west of Sooke, to Qualicum, north of Nanaimo; the Gulf and San Juan Islands; the mainland from Deception Pass northward to Burrard Inlet; and the Lower Fraser Valley up as far as Yale at the lower end of the canyon. This territory thus includes portions of two large bodies of salt water, Georgia Strait and the Strait of Juan de Fuca, and the numerous channels connecting them; it includes the lower course and delta of a large river, several smaller rivers, and bodies of fresh water; and it includes marshes, low hills and valleys, and is fringed on both the island and mainland by snow-covered mountains.

Something of the variety of climate and of flora may be seen first of all from the fact that this territory lies mainly within two separate biotic areas and borders upon two more. The biologists Munro and Cowan (1947:11-42; also Cowan and Guiguet 1956:17-29) have distinguished in British Columbia thirteen terrestrial and two marine biotic areas. Nearly all of the territory of the Straits-speaking tribes and the territory of the Halkomelem-speaking tribes on Vancouver Island lie within the "Gulf Islands Biotic Area," while the territory of the Halkomelem-speaking tribes of the mainland and a small part of that of the Straits-speaking tribes of the mainland lie within the "Puget Sound Lowlands Biotic Area." Straits territory is almost exactly coterminous with the Gulf Island Biotic Area in the south, but this biotic area extends northward beyond Halkomelem territory on Vancouver Island. Mainland Halkomelem territory is nearly coterminous with the Puget Sound Lowlands

Biotic Area in the north, but this biotic area, as the name implies, extends far to the south beyond the territory of the tribes I am concerned with here. To the north of our territory on the mainland and again to the west on Vancouver Island is the "Coast Forest Biotic Area" except at higher altitudes where it gives way to the "Southern Alplands Biotic Area." There is then a partial but not a complete correspondence of biotic area and linguistic area. There are, however, other more precise correspondences of cultural and linguistic boundaries and ecological boundaries that I will point out later.

The Gulf Islands Biotic Area is described as "moderate"in temperature and "mediterranean" in climate. Since it lies with the rain shadow of the Olympic Mountains and Island Range, it receives considerably less rainfall than the ocean coast of Vancouver Island to the west and appreciably less than the mainland shore to the east. Large areas are naturally half-open with Garry oak and madrona as the characteristic trees, with fewer of the usual conifers of the coast, and with "an abundance of spring flowering bulbous and herbaceous plants." In the Puget Sound Lowlands Biotic Area precipitation is greater—the average rainfall at New Westminster on the Fraser is 59.6 inches, as compared with 37.7 at Nanaimo and 26.7 at Victoria on the Island— and the range of temperatures somewhat greater, but winters are still mild and summers cool. The native flora was characteristically Douglas fir, western red cedar, western hemlock, Sitka spruce, and a few other conifers, but also included broad-leafed maple, red alder, flowering dogwood, vine maple, western birch, willows, and other small deciduous trees.

It should be mentioned here that the Douglas fir, which is the most common tree in the Puget Sound Lowlands and the most common conifer in the Gulf Islands Biotic Area, is not a climax type. To maintain a cover of Douglas fir the country must have periodic forest fires. If there were no fires the fir would presumably be gradually replaced by cedar, spruce, and hemlock, which are the climax trees and the characteristic cover of the areas of greater precipitation. Thus it is assumed that forest fires have periodically burned here and there throughout our area since remote prehistoric times, bringing a succession of types of cover from grasses and herbs, brush and deciduous trees to, again, Douglas fir, and thereby providing even greater variability in natural resources.

As I indicated earlier, this environment was characterized by a variety of types of natural resources, local diversity and seasonal variation in their occurrence, and year to year fluctuation in their abundance. Let us briefly consider each of these characteristics.

1) Variety of types. Vegetable foods included the sprouts of several plants, the bulbs and roots of a dozen or so species, and the berries and fruits of about twenty species. Shellfish included ten different mollusks, two sea urchins, and a crab. More than twenty species of fishes were eaten; these included all five species of Pacific salmon, steelhead trout, halibut, herring, sucker,

chub, and sturgeon, the last attaining a weight of 1800 pounds. Two or three species of upland birds were eaten, and more than forty species of waterfowl and shore birds, ranging in size from little sandpipers to twenty-pound swans. Useful land mammals included elk, deer, mountain goat, black bear, and several smaller fur-bearers, and sea mammals the seal, porpoise, and sea lion. Among these the bull elk may weigh up to 800 pounds and the bull sea lion more than a ton.*

2) Local diversity. The occurrence and abundance of these plants and animals varied greatly from place to place depending on such general factors as precipitation, altitude, and salinity of water and on many other more particular factors as well. Camas and several other edible bulbs were found almost exclusively in the drier Gulf Islands Biotic Area, while wapato grew only in ponds and sloughs along the Lower Fraser. Some of the berries also grew in quantity only on the bogs of the Fraser Delta. Blackberries, on the other hand, grow best on hillsides after forest fires.

All the shellfish are saltwater species except one, which was evidently not eaten much. But the very broken shoreline presents at one place a gravel beach, at another a spit of fine sand, and at a third a jagged face of rock. Each of these has its own types of shellfish and attracts different sorts of fishes and waterfowl. Some fishes are strictly salt-water species, but these may require different sorts of bottom. The halibut is found on banks of more than thirty fathoms; the lingcod and rockfish may be seen in shallow water off rocky shores; flounders prefer sandy bays near river mouths. Herring spawn in beds of eel grass. A few fishes, like the sucker and chub, live exclusively in fresh water. Still other fishes, and this group includes most of the really important species, are anadromous, spending part of their lives in fresh water and part in the sea. Some of these could be taken in both salt and fresh water, others only in fresh water. Sturgeon were taken in the Fraser and in the shallow bays along the mainland but rarely along Vancouver Island. Eulachon were not obtainable on the salt water but only at their spawning grounds of a few miles along the Fraser.

The habits of the five species of salmon especially limited the places where they could be taken. Two species, springs and cohoes, feed in the Straits and so can be taken in the salt water by trolling. The three other species do not feed after entering the Strait of Juan de Fuca and so cannot be taken in this way. The sockeye salmon move in fairly compact schools by the same routes each year on their way to the mouth of the Fraser and can be taken with the reef net at a limited number of locations along these routes. Sockeyes run only in the Fraser in this area; pinks and springs run largely in the Fraser.

---

*[My sources were: on forest succession, Hansen 1947; on fishes, Clemens and Wilby 1946, Rounsefell and Kelez 1938; on birds, Jewett 1953; and on mammals, Cowan and Guiguet 1956.]

In the Fraser fish could be taken only with nets. Cohoes and chums, however, run in nearly all of the smaller streams on Vancouver Island as well as the mainland, and could be taken at weirs in traps or with gaffs or harpoons.

The habitats of waterfowl also limit their availability in space. Diving ducks live on deeper water and many species live mainly on the salt water, but dabbling ducks must feed in shallow water or on land and so live along marshy shores or on lakes and streams. The mainland supported many more marsh-feeding ducks than the island.

Deer, elk, and black bear lived on both the mainland and the island. Deer were more plentiful in naturally half-open country as on the smaller islands and in areas recently burned, where feed was more abundant. Elk were most plentiful in flat country, bears probably near salmon streams. But mountain goats lived only on the mainland at higher altitudes. Porpoises and sea lions were found only in the salt water, but seals followed the salmon up the Fraser and had their hauling-out places and even breeding grounds in fresh water on Pitt and Harrison Lakes. They might be harpooned nearly anywhere, but at these places they could also be taken in greater numbers with nets and clubs.

3) Seasonal variation in abundance. Most of the vegetable foods could be harvested only in season—green sprouts in the early spring, camas bulbs in May when the blue flowers showed where they could be dug, berries of the different species from early summer to fall. Herring, smelt, eulachon, and most of the salmons could be taken only during spawning season, which might be of short duration. Some waterfowl, seals, and bears adjust their movements as well to those of the fish. Many of the waterfowl too are migratory. Some pass through this area on their way from the south to the northern interior, stopping only in spring and fall. Others winter here on the flats extending from the Fraser Delta to the mouth of the Skagit. At least nine species have been reported, even in recent winters, in flocks of thousands and even tens of thousands. Sea lions are also migratory, and were taken in this area by only a few communities in the Gulf Islands.

Besides seasonal differences in availability or abundance there were also, for some species, seasonal differences in desirability. Clams, it is said, could be dug more easily and were best at the time of the lowest tides in summer; at any rate this is the time of year when butter-clams and horse-clams were dug for preserving for winter. Weather for drying may have been an important determinant of the season. With deer, bucks are fattest and best in spring while does are best in fall. The flesh of the bear is least desirable in spring when they eat skunk cabbage, better in summer when they eat berries, and best in fall when they have fattened on salmon. The different species of salmon and even different races of the same species do not preserve equally well; weather and fat content may be the determinants.

4) Fluctuation from year to year. The various species and races of salmon also varied greatly in quantity from year to year. The most spectacular regular

fluctuations were in sockeye and pink runs. The pink salmon matures regularly in its second year and in this area the several populations are in the same cycle so that they all spawn every other year. It can be predicted then that pinks will arrive in great numbers in odd-numbered years and in even-numbered years not at all. Sockeye generally mature in their fourth year and as with pinks the various populations in the Fraser are mainly in the same cycle, with the result that every fourth year there is a run of sockeye several times larger than in any of the other three years. This four-year cycle in sockeye runs in the Fraser was recorded as far back as 1823 and presumably occurred in pre-contact times.*

Besides these regular and predictable fluctuations, there are other less predictable fluctuations in number of salmon, caused probably by various factors such as precipitation, temperature, etc., during spawning season, changes in streambeds resulting from landslides, etc. Such factors may be especially influential on smaller streams—certainly estimates of fish runs in the smaller streams of southeastern Vancouver Island for recent years show a good deal of what appears to be random fluctuation. It should also be added that other animals whose lives are related to the salmon must fluctuate in numbers accordingly.

Another source of variability from year to year is the occasional burning that must have occurred. Blackberrries and some other plants of economic importance to the Coast Salish grow best two or three years after a forest fire, and as the trees grow up again gradually lose out. Deer also find better fodder in the few years following a burn and are probably fluctuated in abundance in any single area depending upon the recency of fires. There is some reason for believing, incidentally, that the Coast Salish occasionally set fire to the woods in order to maintain the post-burn biota.†

I pointed out earlier the partial correspondence of linguistic boundaries and the boundaries of biotic areas and mentioned that there were other correspondences of linguistic, cultural, and ecological features. The most striking of these are in the relationship between the Straits language and the migration route of the sockeye salmon. The territories of the various Straits-speaking tribes lie across the channels the sockeye take on their way to the mouth of the Fraser, and there the Straits tribes caught the sockeye in their reef nets. The International Pacific Salmon Fisheries Commission has recently compiled a map (Verhoeven and Davidoff, Fig. 6) showing the routes taken by the sockeye. The reef-net locations of the Straits tribes, which I have mapped, fall very neatly along these routes. The reef net was used by the Straits tribes only; it was their most important fishing device; and it seems to have been

---

*[Jackson 1953.]

†[Norton (1979) reports evidence that prairies in Western Washington were maintained for millennia by the human use of fire.]

used wherever it was possible to take sockeye with it. The close correspondence of language, fishing method, and fish strongly suggests that we have here an ecological niche nicely filled by human beings culturally distinguishable from all others. This may surely be called "adaptation."

For the Halkomelem tribes there is no such precise correlation, but this group of tribes too has more in common than would appear at first glance. I identified earlier the Cowichan, Chemainus, and Nanaimo as living on Vancouver Island and the Musqueam, Kwantlen, etc. as living on the mainland on the Fraser. This identification refers to their winter residence, the sites of their largest permanent houses. But except for some of the Cowichan, who have a fair-sized salmon stream in the island, the Halkomelem-speaking people of Vancouver Island came across Georgia Strait each summer for the run of fish on the Fraser. Thus the Halkomelem tribes are essentially the people of the lower valley and the delta of the Fraser as the Straits tribes are the people of the channels leading to the Fraser.*

All of these data on the natural resources of the Straits and Halkomelem tribes should make it clear that I do not mean that this area was not well provided with useful plants and animals. It certainly was. What I do want to emphasize is that all things were not available everywhere at all times so that they could simply be had for the taking. On the contrary, everything useful was available more at one place than at another, and more in one season than in another, and often more in one year than in another. One may object that nobody has ever really said that this was not so, that Underhill, for example, shortly after her description of the richness of the habitat quoted earlier, describes how different foods were found at different places. But this is merely to introduce a discussion of the yearly round. So it is with much of the writing on the Northwest Coast; if spatial and temporal variation in resources gets any consideration, it is in relation to technology and seasonal movements. The extent of these variations and their implications for social organization however, are rarely considered. It is my position that the social organization and ceremonialism of the Coast Salish of the area I have studied is intelligible only in the light of these variations.

What about the rest of the Northwest Coast? Let us look first at the habitat to the northwest of the Coast Salish and then consider how the native cultures may be related to it.

The differences between the habitats of the Nootka, Kwakiutl, Bella Coola, and Tsimshian and even the Salish of Northern Georgia Strait may not be as great as the differences between the habitat of the Coast Salish that I have just described and the rest. The biologists have assigned all of Vancouver Island west of Sooke and north of Comox and all of the mainland north of Burrard Inlet to a "Coast Forest Biotic Area." This biotic area is characterized

---

*[For a development of this see Mitchell 1971.]

36

by a much greater precipitation and consequent differences in forest cover. The difference in precipitation between the Gulf Islands and Coast Forest Biotic Area is striking, to say the least—Victoria receives 26 inches of rainfall, while Jordan River, a few miles to the west, receives 133 inches. The biologists assign the habitat of the Haida to a separate "Queen Charlotte Islands Biotic Area," which has a climate similar to that of the Coast Forest Biotic Area, but because of its isolation has a more restricted fauna.

In spite of the assignment of a large portion of the coast to a single biotic area, however, there may still be less conspicuous differences between the territories of the different Native peoples. The area within which the Douglas fir is the most abundant tree extends north of the Gulf Island and Puget Sound Lowlands Biotic Areas to the northern end of Georgia Strait to include just about the same area occupied by the Salish before the recent expansion of the southernmost group of Kwakiutl. To the west and north Douglas fir is replaced by the climax trees, cedar, spruce, and hemlock. This apparent correlation of Douglas fir and Salish speech should be given further attention.*

Moreover, trees of the same species may differ in their useful qualities from one area to another. All cedar trees do not "split like matchwood." The Indian carvers working on the campus of the University of British Columbia have found some southern cedars unusable for reproducing Haida totem poles and prefer cedars from the Queen Charlotte Islands. The possibility that some regional differences in art style are related to regional differences in materials available should not be overlooked.

However, such possibilities notwithstanding, it must be granted that, more broadly speaking, the whole Northwest Coast is unquestionably a single ecological region. The principal differences between the habitat of the Coast Salish that I have described and that of the Nootka, Kwakiutl, Tsimshian, or Haida seem to be quantitative not qualitative. The habitats of each of these peoples, like that of the Coast Salish, are characterized by a variety of natural resources and by spatial and temporal differences in their abundance. But it seems to me that as we go northward along the coast we find less variety in types of resources, greater local and seasonal variation, and possibly less year-to-year fluctuation.

As soon as we leave the Gulf Islands and Puget Sound Lowlands Biotic Areas we find fewer species of edible bulbs and roots and less extensive areas where they can grow. The Kwakiutl, it is true, tended beds of cinquefoil and clover, but these could not have provided much as compared with Salish camas or wapato. Edible berries to the north may also be less plentiful. This is difficult to estimate, but we may consider that blackberries, which grow best after burns, would have less chance outside the Douglas fir area, and that in some

---

*[I believe that Wilson Duff first suggested this to me.]

37

parts of the Coast Forest Biotic Area the forest is so dense that there is no undergrowth at all, while in other parts salal and salmonberries grow profusely. Also, when we leave the Douglas fir area we find far fewer deer, perhaps less land game generally. In the Queen Charlotte Islands there were no deer at all in pre-White times.*

Shellfish are certainly plentiful to the north, but the more rugged shoreline may mean fewer good beds per mile of coast than in the south, where there are more sand and gravel beaches. Waterfowl are very likely less abundant. There is nothing resembling the great expanse of flats offered to migrating and wintering waterfowl by the Fraser and Skagit deltas. Many of the winter residents in the Salish area fly inland as they migrate northward so that the northern coast is somewhat off the Pacific flyway. A few species, however, may be more numerous in the north, as for example the Western Canada goose in the Queen Charlottes. Sea mammals are certainly as numerous off the west coast of Vancouver Island and farther north, some species undoubtedly more numerous. At the present time 70 percent of the sea lion population of British Columbia, which numbers 11,000 to 12,000, is concentrated each summer in two rookeries, one in Kwakiutl and one in Haida territory (Pike 1958). In the past there may have been more rookeries but the concentration was probably as great. Whales have no doubt always been more numerous in the ·ocean than in the more sheltered waters of Salish territory.

For some idea as to differences in fisheries resources of the different tribal areas we can consult some of the publications of the international, national, and local fisheries authorities. The Department of Fisheries of Canada issues each year a volume of *British Columbia Catch Statistics* in which the commercial salmon catch is given by species in each of 38 statistical areas within the province. These areas can be matched roughly with Native tribal areas. The figures are for recent years and are for fish taken on modern gear, but they ought to give some hint as to what was available in pre-White times. It is evident from these figures that large numbers of fish are to be had in all areas. Also there seems to be random fluctuation in catches for all species in all areas, though less perhaps for springs than for the other species. But one difference between the Salish areas and the others is very obvious—the cycles in sockeye and pink salmon that are so pronounced in the Salish area are not perceptible farther north. Thus in area 18, which includes the Saanich Inlet, Cowichan Bay, and a bit of Georgia Strait, the catch in hundred-pound units in the years 1951-58 for sockeye amounted to 154, 212, 396, 60,532, 37, 70, 10, 6,412; and for the same years for pinks 2,944, 2, 547, 52, 155,

---

*[Cowan (1945:111) estimated a deer population of about one per square mile in the coast forest near Jordan River (in Wakashan territory) and about 20 per square mile in a logged-over area in the Gulf Islands. There was a species of caribou in a limited area in the Queen Charlotte Islands.]

.5, 239, 7. In area 12, which includes most of the territory of the Kwakiutl proper, for these years the catch of sockeye amounted to 15,462, 16,321, 24,672, 6,707, 8,170, 7,379, 22,894, 124,627; and for the same years for pinks 76,250, 103,924, 187,709, 15,651, 143,630, 31,971, 160,347, 52,193. The enormous quanitity of sockeye taken in the Kwakiutl area in 1958—12,462,700 lb.—may be compared with the much smaller figure in the Cowichan area for 1958 as compared with 1954, the previous cycle year— some 600,000 lb. in '58 as compared with 6,000,000 in '54. This was the result of a quite unpredictable occurrence—in 1958 most of the Fraser run of sockeye entered Georgia Strait through Johnstone Strait instead of the Strait of Juan de Fuca. For the Skeena and Nass areas the figures vary, but with nothing like this latitude. The reasons for the absence of regularity in the figures for sockeye and pinks farther north are probably two: first, sockeye are not on any cycle because they do not spawn as regularly in their fourth year as those of the Fraser, and second, the pinks for several populations are not in step with one another and so for the area appear regular. Fluctuation may also be seen in recent figures for herring spawning (Outram 1956, 1957, 1958). I repeat, these are recent catches with modern equipment, but surely we can infer from them something of the variability of resources for the Native peoples at an earlier time.

For other salt-water fishing, fluctuation in numbers of fish was perhaps not as significant a factor in productivity as the weather. Small-craft warnings are out often enough on Georgia Strait to suggest that under aboriginal conditions the Salish could not have fished for halibut as often as they liked, regardless of how the halibut were biting. This kind of limitation must have been even more severe on Queen Charlotte Sound or on the open ocean. Drucker mentions bad weather as a cause of famine among the Nootka. The passage is worth quoting in full for the implications it has for the thesis of this paper:

> While the food resources were rich, now and then periods of scarcity occurred. Ethnographers have stressed nature's prodigality to the peoples of the Northwest Coast to the point that one is surprised by the thought they should ever have suffered want. But occasionally a poor dog salmon or herring run, followed by an unusually stormy winter or spring, as the case might be, that prevented people from going out to fish for cod and halibut, quickly brought privation. Those were the times when people walked the beaches looking for codfish heads, spurned by seals and sea lions, and storm-killed herring and pilchard. They collected and ate the tiny mussels of the inner coves and bays, and similar small mussels disdained in normal times. The spring of the year was perhaps more often a lean season than winter. Father Brabant reports two successive springs at Hesquiat when the pickings were lean and

children cried with hunger, until the weather abated long enough for the fishermen to go out. Family traditions of local groups who say they anciently lived the year around "outside," that is, on the outer beaches and islands, speak of hunger and even starvation that led them to make alliances with or make war on groups who had territories along the inner channels and owned salmon streams. Yet in general the periods of scarcity seem not to have been very frequent, and were periods of unpleasantly short rations but seldom real starvation. The specter of hunger was not constantly menacing, as it was to groups in the interior of the mainland. Most of the time food was available, and frequently it was so abundant that with the most extravagant feasting they could not use it all up (Drucker 1951:36-37; see also Rostlund 1952:23).

The data I have been presenting are fragmentary but sufficient, I believe, to suggest that, as compared with the Coast Salish, the more northern tribes rely on fewer kinds of plants and animals and get them at fewer places and for shorter times during the year, but in greater concentration, and with consequent greater chance for failure. At any rate, I would like to use this as a working hypothesis in looking at the relationship of culture to environment.

Now let us turn to the cultures of the peoples to the northwest of the Coast Salish. Probably there is general agreement that these fall into two major types: Wakashan, which includes the Nootka and the Kwakiutl proper; and Northern, which includes the Tsimshian, Haida, and Tlingit. For the purposes of this paper I will ignore the transitional Bella Bella and Haisla and the Bella Coola.

Both the Wakashan and Northern cultures, it seems to me, have technological and ideological facets rather similar to what I have indicated for the Coast Salish; they have roughly the same technological limitations and the same individual motivations—though such detail as adz types and fish nets and concepts of the supernatural may vary. But in what I have described as the third facet of culture— the socio-economic system, there are some more important differences.

Looking first at the Wakashan peoples, we find that as among the Coast Salish there are communities composed of one or more kin groups in which membership is through bilateral descent, with alternative membership and individual mobility possible but patrilocal residence preferable. The differences seem to be essentially in the addition of two features: 1) leadership is more rigidly determined by descent, that is, by hereditary "ownership" of productive resources, all of which are "owned," and leaders are fewer and more clearly defined; and 2) individuals and groups are ranked in an implicit numerical order, the principle of "seriation."*

---

*[The term "seriation" appears in Drucker 1951:220; I believe this was my source for it.]

40

The first of these features may be related directly to the ecological differences just suggested. The fewer types and greater concentration of resources that I have postulated for both the Wakashan and Northern areas might increase the importance of the "owner" as a redistributor of resources within the local group and a representative of the local group in relation to other groups. This increase in importance of the role of the "owner" may be accompanied by an increased emphasis on differences in status throughout society.

The second new feature, "seriation," does not of course automatically follow the first, but may be encouraged by it. Once introduced within the group, it has the effect of more clearly defining membership; that is to say, the series has to exist for the individual to have a position in; in contast, among the Coast Salish the lack of any series means that the individual is less easily identified with a local group. And once introduced among local groups, seriation becomes the principle by which tribes and confederacies are formed. Among the Wakashans, the ranking of local groups in series replaces the Salish principle of establishing a network of affinal ties among local groups of relatively equal status. Thus among the Wakashan local exogamy is not as important as among the Salish, and in fact there was some slight tendency towards endogamy. The potlatch among the Wakashan peoples is the means by which individuals and local groups establish and maintain rank within the series. Among the Salish the potlatch does not have this function.

Other points of similarity must also be mentioned. While seriation may make for more clearly determined groups among the Wakashan, bilateral descent, alternative membership, and individual mobility—perhaps especially for the lower ranks—all prevent the local groups from becoming rigid. This fluidity may operate advantageously for the whole population under conditions of gradually changing productivity.

Also, though local exogamy may not be as important, affinal ties are still used among the Wakashan peoples in the process of accumulating property for the potlatch. It may be that there is an underlying Northwest Coast principle here: that a man's affinals are his allies against his importunate blood kin. Perhaps a man can save better by giving to his affinals, who are honor-bound to return the gifts when he needs them for potlatching, than by keeping his food and wealth at home only to have it used up by his own blood kin, whom he is honor-bound to support.

I do not as yet fully understand the potlatch outside the Coast Salish area. The Wakashan potlatch seems to differ from the Coast Salish in that it occurred more frequently but was of shorter duration, and the Wakashan potlatch may have had a greater importance in the redistribution of food. Generally there seems to have been a freer exchange of food and wealth among the Wakashan than among the Salish. Still I suspect that there too the potlatch may have served as a regulating mechanism within the total system, as among the Coast Salish. My colleague Dr. A.P. Vayda and several of our students

41

have given some attention to this problem, as he is reporting elsewhere.*

Moving on to the Northern peoples, we find even greater differences in the socio-economic system. Among the Tsimshian, Haida, and Tlingit, the social units have become even more stable. Membership is determined by the principle of matrilineal descent, making alternative affiliation and individual mobility less possible. At the same time, matrilineal descent with exogamy and cross-cousin marriage unites pairs of social units within a system that embraces the whole population. Such pairs of social units provide services for one another and potlatch with each other. Such units stand in an *affinal* relationship to one another.

In bilateral societies such as the Coast Salish and Wakashan, affinal ties in one generation lead to consanguineal ties in the next. If the incest prohibition is observed, marriage between two families in one generation reduces the number of potential mates in the next generation. To maintain affinal bonds between two communities for several generations requires that each community be composed of several family lines alternating with each other in their marriages. Among the Coast Salish each community usually contained enough people distantly enough related to each other so that they could maintain among them affinal ties with several neighboring communities without incestuous marriages. Since each community contained several "owners" of productive resources, there was no special advantage in marrying one rather than another among the good families of a neighboring community. On the contrary, the diversity of resources and variations in productivity gave some advantage to diversity of marriage ties. But if to the north we have less diversity and greater concentration of resources and greater control over them in the hands of fewer people, then marrying into the best family is best, and best families will hope to continue to marry best families.

Now unilateral descent is a means of legitimizing kin marriage. By defining our cross-cousins as non-kin, we can marry them without breaking the incest taboo. I suggest then that matrilineal descent in the culture of the Northern tribes may be seen as a sort of crystallization of two features already suggested for the areas to the south: 1) the preference for continued marriage between groups already enjoying a reciprocal relationship, and 2) the necessity of keeping consanguineal and affinal kin separate in order to continue that relationship.

The network of affinal ties among the Coast Salish, seriation among the Kwakiutl, and matrilineal descent among the Northern tribes may all have the effect of uniting different local groups in such a way that—assuming that the potlatching system operates elsewhere somewhat as it seems to among the Coast Salish—they can accommodate to variation and fluctuation in natural resources.

---

*[Vayda 1961a, Piddocke 1965.]

One further possible mode of accommodation should be mentioned. In the southern areas, if there were long-term shifts in productivity in the territories of different groups, people would probably have adjusted to them by a process of gradual individual movement from the less productive to the more productive territory through individual ties of kinship and marriage. In the north, on the other hand, individual mobility was probably far less usual, but group movements evidently did occur. In fact, one of the most striking differences between southern and northern mythology is in the origins of the local groups; in the south most groups tell how they were either created or dropped from Heaven on the spot they now occupy, while in the north most groups tell how they migrated from somewhere else. Shifts in population probably occurred in both areas, but unilateral descent may encourage group rather that individual movements.*

I have tried to show how the environment of the Northwest Coast cultures is neither uniformly rich and dependable within any tribal area nor precisely the same from area to area. I have tried to show how some of the important features of the Coast Salish culture may be adaptive under the conditions of Coast Salish environment. And I have suggested how some of the differences in culture along the coast may be related to differences in the environment. As I said in the beginning, this is a sort of "view of the Northwest Coast as seen from the Coast Salish" and when I leave the Salish area I enter the area of speculation. To make what I have said more than speculation, we would need much more work on the ecology of the Northwest Coast, on the relations of local groups to resources, and on the system of exchange of food and wealth among groups.

I believe this sort of approach would not only make each of the cultures of the Northwest Coast more intelligible but would also lead us to reconsider some of the existing hypotheses regarding their history. If it can be shown, for example, that matrilineal descent and its accompanying features are formalizations of tendencies present elsewhere on the coast and that these tendencies are themselves adaptive, then finding an extra-areal origin for the matrilineal principle becomes less urgent. We may then also question Boas's suggestion that the Kwakiutl social organization developed as a compromise between a patrilineal south and a matrilineal north (a position Murdock has already rejected on other grounds). We may not see the Northwest Coast as simply a series of centers of diffusion with matrilineal descent emanating from the north and self-aggrandizement emanating from the Kwakiutl. Nor may we see the greater individualism of the Coast Salish as simply the result of the survival of Plateau values. Seen in a framework that includes ecology,

---

*[Adams (1973) finds evidence for a flow of people among Gitksan matrilineages and argues that the potlatch was a mechanism for legitimizing the redistribution of people in Northwest Coast societies.]

the questions of migration, diffusion, and the persistence of values assume their proper places as parts of the larger whole—the study of culture change as an evolutionary process.

I am tempted to return to Kroeber's (1923) view (which has recently received some archeological support from Borden) that the development of culture on the Northwest Coast proceeded from a river-mouth, to an inland salt-water, to a maritime adaptation, with the center of development shifting from the Lower Fraser, to the Wakashan area, to the North. I am tempted to suggest that culture on the Northwest Coast has not only developed along the general course that Kroeber has charted, but that the more specific environmental features to which it has adapted have been the decrease in variety, increase in concentration, and continued spatial and temporal variation in abundance of resources that I believe we may find upon following that course up the coast. Abandoning now all caution, I would like to suggest further that a network of affinal ties, seriation, and matrilineal descent are each crucial features of the three stages in the evolution of culture on the Northwest Coast.*

---

*[For a critique of my position here see Adams 1981:366-7. For other views on the relationship between variation in habitat and culture see Floyd 1968, Schalk 1977, Richardson 1982, and Riches 1979.]

4. Coping with Abundance: Subsistence on the Northwest Coast*

Although the aboriginal peoples of the Northwest coast of North America were not hunters so much as fishermen, they seem especially worth including in a survey of Man the Hunter for two reasons: First, their rich, maritime, temperate-zone habitat is a type in which few food-gathering peoples survived until historic times, partly because this very type of habitat elsewhere saw the growth of more advanced forms of subsistence.[1] Second, the Northwest Coast peoples seem to have attained the highest known levels of cultural complexity achieved on a food-gathering base and among the highest known levels of population density. The Northwest Coast refutes many seemingly easy generalizations about people without horticulture or herds. Here were people with permanent houses in villages of more than a thousand; social stratification, including a hereditary caste of slaves and ranked nobility; specialization in several kinds of hunting and fishing, crafts, and curing; social units larger than villages; elaborate ceremonies; and one of the world's great art styles. The area appears to have been matched in population density, among food-gathering areas, by only two or three areas adjacent to it—California and parts of the Arctic and Plateau culture areas (Kroeber 1939; but it would

---

*[From *Man the Hunter*, edited by Richard B. Lee and Irven DeVore (New York: Aldine 1968), pp. 56-68.]

[1]The Ainu, described by Watanabe in Lee and DeVore 1968:ch. 7, are perhaps the food-gathering people in the most similar habitat, but northwestern North America is climatically more like northwestern Europe than like northeastern Asia.

be good to have comparable data for the Ainu and the Lower Amur peoples). These features of Northwest Coast culture and demography are generally thought to have been made possible, or even inevitably produced, by the richness of the habitat of the area and the efficiency of the subsistence techniques of its peoples. Perhaps, then, the study of Northwest Coast subsistence can offer some guidance in estimating the possibilities of cultural development under comparable conditions in prehistoric times.

In a short paper I cannot hope to do justice to the variety and complexity of Northwest coast culture and its historic relations (for a general survey, see Drucker 1955a, 1965),[2] nor to go into the problem of aboriginal population sizes and densities except to comment that Mooney's and Kroeber's figures (Kroeber 1939:131ff.) have generally been revised upwards (Baumhoff 1963:157-61; Duff 1964:38-46; Taylor 1963). I shall simply take the cultural complexity and population density as proven, and discuss our knowledge of subsistence and its relationship to them. But as you will see, I do not consider the relationship a simple one, and so I must range through several sorts of phenomena. In general, my thesis is that while the habitat was undeniably rich, abundance did not exist the year round but only here and there and now and then, and that such temporary abundances—though they may well be a necessary condition for population density and cultural development of the sort seen on the Northwest Coast—are not sufficient to create them. Equally necessary conditions were the presence of good though limited food-getting techniques, food-storing techniques, a social system providing the organization for subsistence activities and permitting exchanges, and a value system that provided the motivation for getting food, storing food, and participating fully in the social system. I shall deal with each of these conditions in succession.

Habitat

The Northwest Coast was an area where one could find, on a single occasion, quite literally tons of food. Salmon ran into the smaller streams by the thousands and into larger streams by the tens and hundreds of thousands. Waterfowl came to the marshes by the tens and hundreds of thousands. A single sturgeon can weigh nearly a ton, a bull sea lion more than a ton, a whale up to thirty tons. But this aspect of the Northwest Coast habitat is only too well known. It has been so emphasized that the implications of the phrase used above, "on a single occasion," have been ignored and the habitat has been presented as a constant source of plenty. But as I have said elsewhere (Suttles 1960a; 1962), it was not constant. It did not provide an ever-reliable

---

[2]A complete bibliography of the area may be found in Murdock 1960a.

abundance of natural resources simply there for the taking. Abundance there consisted only of certain things at certain places at certain times and always with some possibility of failure. Describing the Central Coast Salish[3] habitat, I wrote:

> The environmental setting of Native culture was characterized by four significant features: 1) *variety of types of food*, including sprouts, roots, berries, shellfish, fishes, waterfowl, land and sea mammals; 2) *local variation* in the occurrence of these types, due to irregular shorelines, broken topography, differences between fresh and salt water, local differences in temperature and precipitation; 3) *seasonal variation*, especially in vegetable foods and in anadromous fishes; 4) *fluctuations from year to year*, in part due to the regular cycles of the different populations of fish, in part to less predictable changes, as in weather (1960a:302; see also Suttles 1962:527-29).

In their subsistence activities, the Central Coast Salish had to cope with these variable features of the habitat. It seems likely that farther north on the coast there were fewer types of resources but greater concentrations, and thus possibly greater dangers in failure, through human error or natural calamity, of resources to appear at the right place at the right time (1962:530-33). Farther south I would expect the opposite to hold. But these subareal differences have yet to be worked out.

One cause of unexpected hardship was purely climatic. Because of the Japan Current and prevailingly westerly winds from the ocean, the weather is usually mild and damp. Summers are cool and during many winters the temperature only now and again drops below the freezing point. In the Central Coast Salish area, winters without frost are not unknown. But occasionally masses of extremely cold continental air break out through the coast mountains to bring periods of as much as ten days of near-zero (Fahrenheit) weather to the outer coast. In British Columbia such severe outbreaks have been recorded at twelve- to eighteen-year intervals (Young 1954:xli-xlii).

From a number of places along the coast we have indications that there were times when food was scarce. For groups dependent upon the open ocean, the cause was usually a stretch of bad weather; for groups on rivers, it was

---

[3]The Coast Salish groups with whom I have worked on and off for a number of years are the speakers of the Halkomelem and Straits languages, whose territory includes the lower Fraser valley, the southern end of Georgia Strait, and the northern shores of the Strait of Juan de Fuca. Since they are roughly at the center of the total Coast Salish area, I call them the Central Coast Salish.

tardiness or failure in a fish run. In both situations it was of course also a matter of human failure to have accumulated enough food for the emergency.

For the Haida of the Queen Charlotte islands we have a statement by an early observer, Poole, quoted by Niblack, who writes:

> Some of these berries are collected and dried for winter's use, forming, with dried fish, the principal winter's supply. Poole (1863) says of the Haida, that they often, through feasting or improvidence, eat up all the dried berries before spring, and "were it not for a few bulbs which they dig out of the soil in the early spring-time, while awaiting the halibut season, numbers of Indians really would starve to death" (1890:276-77).

For the Tsimshian of the Nass and Skeena rivers we have Boas's statement, derived from his analysis of Tsimshian mythology, that "sometimes when the olachen were late in coming, there would be a famine on Nass River" (Boas 1916:399). In his comparison of Tsimshian data with Kwakiutl data in *Kwakiutl Culture as Reflected in Mythology*, Boas writes:

> The difficulties of obtaining an adequate food supply must have been much more serious among the Tsimshian than among the Kwakiutl, for starvation and the rescue of the tribe by the deeds of a great hunter or by supernatural help are an ever-recurring theme which, among the Kwakiutl, is rather rare. One story of this type is clearly a Tsimshian story retold . . . . Starvation stories of the Kwakiutl occur particularly among the tribes living at the heads of the inlets of the mainland, not among those who dwell near the open sea, where seals, sealions, salmon and halibut are plentiful (Boas 1935:171; see other references in Piddocke 1965:247).

For the Nootka, who occupy the west coast of Vancouver Island in less sheltered waters than the Kwakiutl, we have Drucker's statement that a poor dog salmon or herring run followed by weather bad enough to prevent people from going out for cod or halibut "quickly brought privation" when people sought foods they ordinarily disdained. He cites Father Brabant's report of "two successive springs at Hesquiat when pickings were lean and children cried out with hunger, until the weather abated enough for the fishermen to go out." He also cites family traditions of the hardships of winters on the outer coast before alliances had been made with groups with salmon streams (Drucker 1951:36-37).

Swan says of the Makah at Cape Flattery:

The ease with which these Indians can obtain their subsistence from the ocean makes them improvident in laying in supplies for winter use, except for halibut; for, on any day in the year the weather will permit, they can procure, in a few hours, provisions enough to last them for several days (1870:30).

Yet he later (p.76) describes a period in April of 1864 when the weather did not permit going out fishing or whaling and how the Ozette were concerned enough about this to accuse an old man of sorcery and threaten to kill him if he didn't stop his incantations and make fair weather. The Quileute, Swan was told, had killed an alleged sorcerer for bringing bad weather during the halibut season only a few summers earlier.

Discussing relations between the upper and lower classes among the Chinook of the mouth of the Columbia River, Ray (1938:56) says that his principal informant "declared that the upper class could infringe as much as it pleased upon the lower classes and added that famine was unknown to the former since the food of the latter was appropriated in such a circumstance." Ray adds that the informant's specific examples were acts of the chiefs. In the context of Ray's other statements, it appears that the Chinook village chief received, or seized, tribute and redistributed food to his people, favoring the upper class. My point in citing this is simply to indicate that shortages were conceivable.

Finally, we have Gould's (1966) recent re-analysis of the wealth quest among the Tolowa, an Athapaskan-speaking people on the Oregon-California border. This is the group described by DuBois (1936) as having distinctly separate "subsistence" and "prestige" economies in the paper that first introduced these terms into the study of primitive economies. According to DuBois, subsistence was not a problem; scarcity existed only in "treasures" (dentalia shells, obsidian blades, and woodpecker scalps); food circulated freely in a "subsistence economy." But Gould has found no separate "subsistence economy" in that there is no evidence for specialization in subsistence or the exchange of foods. There do appear, however, to have been differences in the productivity of households due in part to differences in the number of women available to process foods in season. It is true that "treasure" items were not constantly used to buy food, nor ideally nor publicly so used, but they were commonly used to buy food during periods of shortage. In fact, storing food to sell to others was recognized as an important method of acquiring wealth; hence, the interest the Tolowa show in acquiring women, the processors of food. Wealth is converted into prestige by its use in ceremonial displays and in payment of bride price, which establishes the social status of children to the marriage (Gould 1966:70, 77, 86). Thus recognition of the existence of periods of shortage and of problems in subsistence has made possible a reinterpretation of the data that give them a greater coherence than in the earlier analysis.[4] There is really only one Tolowa economy; in it food is converted into wealth and wealth is converted into prestige. Occasional shortages in food provided the occasions for converting wealth into food. Hungry people wanted food; greedy people wanted wealth. Why did the greedy want wealth? Because wealth brought prestige. But it seems likely that it was because indirectly prestige-seeking enabled hungry people to obtain food. Or, if this seems to imply conscious purposiveness, we may say it is because populations that have unconsciously stumbled on ways of feeding hungry members survive better than those who let them starve.

I have dwelt at length on the existence of times of scarcity on the Northwest Coast precisely because recognizing their existence may be essential to our understanding of the complexities of Northwest Coast culture. Some years ago Bartholomew and Birdsell pointed out that it is a firmly established ecological generalization, known as "Liebig's law of the minimum," that the size of a population is determined not by the mean condition but by the extremes. "A semi-arid area may have many fruitful years in succession, but a single drought year occurring once in a human generation may restrict the population to an otherwise inexplicably low density" (Bartholomew and Birdsell 1953:487-88; see also comment by Sherwood L. Washburn and June Helm, Chapter 9a, in Lee and DeVore 1968). Perhaps, also, a single, once-a-generation failure of a major fish run or prolonged period of severe weather may explain an otherwise inexplicable practice such as the Northwest Coast search for prestige.*

What we need to know for the whole coast is not merely what resources were present and when and where they were found under ordinary conditions, but also the *minimal* occurrences in space, time, and quantity. This means we should pay special attention to what foods are, or were, available in winter, even though winter was culturally defined by most peoples of the area as the ceremonial season during which people lived on stored food. As we have seen from the quotations given, stored food was not always available. It also appears that there were differences between inland river environments, sheltered saltwater bays, and the open ocean shores. There were probably also differences from south to north. None of these has been worked out in detail, but I am confident, that, with the growing body of biological and climatological data on the area, we shall one day be able to state fairly accurately what the resource base of each people's territory was.

---

[4]The fact of shortages in the Tolowa area was not just recently discovered. Driver, in his element list for northwestern California, under "Slaves," shows that "Starving person gives self for keep"was affirmed by his Tolowa informant, one of his two Karók informants, and both Yurok, while "Girls traded for food in time of famine" was affirmed by the Tolowa and both Yurok (Driver 1939:357). But Gould (1966) has indicated the relevance of the exchange of girls for food to residence rules, see the last section of this paper.

*[See postscript.]

Of course it is necessary to distinguish between what foods *could* have been hunted, fished, and gathered, and those foods actually obtained in practice. The difference between potential and actual is in part a function of the efficiency of food-getting methods.

Food-Getting Methods

The state of our knowledge in this respect, too, is certainly not as good as we would want it. We do not have and probably shall never have any figures on the quantities of food actually collected and consumed per capita, on the ratio of meat, fish, and vegetable food in the diet,[5] on the number of man-hours spent in the food quest, and on percent of the population supported in leisure or other non-subsistence activities. Moreover, for much of the area we do not even have the facts in the form of good ethnographic accounts of just how food was obtained. This is not to say there are no good works at all. Boas's material on Kwakiutl subsistence activities, mainly in the form of Native texts with translations (Boas 1909:461-516; 1921:pt. 1), gives the Native view of a number of food-getting and food-storing techniques and a great many recipes. In these texts we see what was important to the informant, but do not always find the answers to questions the ethnographer would ask. For some, however, we can make inferences about the quantities of food taken and consumed. Among the ethnographies of the area, Drucker's (1951) on the Nootka (see also Drucker 1965:chap.7, for a dramatic account of Nootka whaling) and Elmendorf's (1960) on the Twana (a Coast Salish group) are outstanding. The only specialized monograph is Kroeber and Barrett (1960) on fishing in northwestern California. But for much of the area between the Klamath and the Columbia and north of the Kwakiutl, we have only very sketchy accounts.

---

[5]While going through Central Coast Salish material for the symposium, I guessed that in the diet of adults, vegetable foods would have amounted to less than 10 percent of volume but might have been higher for children, who probably foraged for such things as cattail roots and thimble berries that adults would be less likely to bother with. I assume that in the diet of all, even small amounts of certain vegetable foods may have been very important to health. I was surprised then to note, in Murdock's *Ethnographic Atlas*, estimates of 20 percent dependence on gathering for the Nootka and 30 percent for the Kwakiutl (See also Lee, chap. 4, in Lee and DeVore 1968). As Lee notes, the *Atlas* defines "gathering" as the "gathering of wild plants and small land fauna," while "shellfishing" is included with "fishing" as is sea-mammal hunting. Since small land fauna were almost wholly ignored on the Northwest Coast, the figures must refer to vegetable foods alone.

I am willing to admit that my guess of 10 percent dependence on vegetable foods for the Central Coast Salish may be too low, but the Kwakiutl figure given in the *Atlas* is surely too high. The *Atlas* gives estimates for twenty Northwest Coast "societies." In the extreme south, the Yurok and the Tolowa proportions of gathering/hunting/fishing are

51

The reason for the deficiency in figures on subsistence is not hard to find. The purely aboriginal way of life had been greatly altered in most parts of the Northwest coast by the end of the last century and quantitative data are, as Kroeber pointed out (1939:3), not ordinarily recoverable by the method of ethnographic reconstruction we must use in western North America. The reasons for the scant attention often paid to subsistence techniques are also easy to find. Some of the techniques had disappeared by the beginning of this century or had survived in forms altered by the introduction of European goods. But, also, the very complexity of social forms and richness of art and ceremony that draw attention to the area are likely to draw attention away from mere subsistence. Thus when McIlwraith (1948) had the opportunity

---

40/10/50 percent and 40/20/40 percent respectively. This is an area where acorns were used and naturally the proportion for gathering is greater. From here northward the most common figure for gathering is 20 percent; only the Puyallup and Kwakiutl have 30 percent, while the Coos, Quileute, Twana, and Klallam have 10 percent. The Puyallup are a Coast Salish group living inland from Puget Sound who quite likely did depend more on roots and bulbs than did their salt-water neighbors, though with the complex exchange systems of the area we cannot be sure. But there seems no reason at all to give the Kwakiutl a higher figure than the Nootka, Bella Coola, and Coast Salish of northern Georgia Strait, all of them adjacent to Kwakiutl and all given 20 percent. It is true that George Hunt recorded 44 recipes for preparing vegetable foods and instructions for preserving some fifteen of them (Boas 1921, pt. 1). But the texts indicate that some of these foods were quite restricted in where they grew and the small quantities served to feast a village. Some too were described as emergency foods and evidently dangerous if eaten in quantity. Most of the roots were in fact so small that it is hard to imagine gathering large amounts of them. Altogether it does not seem to me that the Kwakiutl would have been very different from the Nootka, of whom Drucker writes:

> There was a tremendous emphasis on fats—oils and greases—in the dietary pattern. Probably the fats made up for the virtual lack of starch and sugar forms of carbohydrates. Prior to the introduction of potatoes, flour, and pilot bread in historic times, starch foods were limited to the very occasional meals of clover and fern roots, and the few other roots. It is obviously impossible to judge at this late date, but one receives the impression from informants that if the average person ate a dozen or two meals of roots in the course of the year, it was a lot. Berries provided the only sugar prior to the introduction of molasses, and were highly prized. But the berry season was rather short, except for that of salal berries, and the few baskets of them women picked seem to have adorned rather than materially augmented the diet. Instead of these things, one hears constantly of fats and oils (1951:62-63).

To me this statement hardly implies the 20 percent gathering given the Nootka by the *Atlas*. On the other hand, some of the Coast Salish groups probably did have more vegetable food in their diet than the Nootka and Kwakiutl, yet two of them (Klallam and Twana) were assigned only 10 percent—my original guess for those I am calling the "Central"groups, which include the Lummi, who are given 20 percent by the *Atlas*. I

52

to play a part himself in the Bella Coola winter ceremonies, he did so and the results form a good part of his two-volume work on that people. I find this quite understandable, but still wish we had more on Bella Coola salmon fishing than the pluses and minuses in Drucker's (1950) element list. Another reason for the neglect of subsistence probably lies in the assumption that the habitat was so rich that subsistence simply was not a problem. Finally, an understanding of just how any given subsistence technique works requires moving outside of culture and seeing the technique as part of an ecosystem; this is not easily done if one is unfamiliar with the natural history of the area and has only a few summer months to spend in it.

But the situation is by no means hopeless. In spite of the fact that year by year the purely aboriginal way of life recedes into the past, I fully expect that a few years hence we shall know much more about Northwest Coast subsistence than we know today. I have several reasons for this optimism. First, contrary to gloomy predictions by colleagues that I'd find all was lost, when I began working with the Coast Salish I discovered that it was still possible to do ethnography and to get much new data on subsistence. I am sure that my experience could still be duplicated in other areas, if for no other reason than that some activities survive yet in modified form. Second, data from the related fields of linguistics, archeology, and ethnohistory and from the ethnography of other areas can be increasingly used in interpreting the ethnography of one's own area. For example, some of my informants and the informants of others have believed that the gill net is not aboriginal in the Salish area. However, a comparison of native terms for the gill net and the record of an earlier observer suggest that it probably was, in fact, aboriginal. I expect that further probing will settle the matter. Third, the growing body of biological and climatological knowledge can be used to interpret the ethnographic data. For example, the testimony of informants that their ancestors

---

can only conclude that the question should be left open.

I agree with Lee that shellfish gathering has more in common with the gathering of plant foods than with fishing. Both plants and shellfish are immobile and were collected (on the Northwest Coast) mainly by women using digging sticks and baskets. They differ only in food value. But sea-mammal hunting and fishing can present a similar case. The difference between catching a 5-pound salmon in a net and harpooning a 20-ton whale seems clear enough, but what do we do when we find the same Coast Salish "sea-food producer" (a Native category) harpooning at one time a 200-pound seal and at another a 1,000-pound sturgeon? The difference, as it was with roots and shellfish, is simply a matter of food value, and not a very great one at that. The Coast Salish also harpooned salmon and netted seals, ducks, and deer. If we base our taxonomy on implements and activities, we have to ignore the taxonomy of biology, and vice versa. If we set up a category of activity based on either type of implement (as "net") or biological taxon (as "fish"), we will still be ignoring two other variables, specialization and cooperation, which may be more pertinent to the questions we are asking than are types of implements or animals.

fished by trolling in winter as well as spring is supported by the work of researchers in fisheries (for example, Rounsefell and Kelez 1938:749-50). Their work indicates not only that spring salmon are present in winter but that Indians did troll for them. Also, other biological work shows that herring spawn in this area in winter and early spring (Clemens and Wilby 1946:79-80) and would therefore be available [for bait] during times of the month when tides are low. Finally, meteorological data could undoubtedly be obtained indicating average number of days during winter months when weather would permit trolling in each of several areas.

When I express this optimism about the possibility of increasing our knowledge of Northwest coast subsistence, I do not mean to imply that we shall surely be able to reconstruct the quantitative data. But what we surely can do is define more narrowly the requisites and limits of each technique so that we can make some estimates of the relative effectiveness of the different techniques under similar conditions and the same technique under different conditions.

Food-Storing Methods

The techniques for preserving food are certainly as important as those for getting food. Thousands of salmon swimming upstream in September would not make winter a time of ceremonial activity if people lacked the means of preserving them, nor would several tons of blubber on the beach. No doubt some people would not have survived some winters without storage methods.

A few foods do not keep well at all. Mussels and salmonberries, for example, seem to be too soft and watery. But most fishes and meats, some shellfishes, and some berries can be preserved by drying, either with or without smoke. Clams and some meats were steamed and salal berries were sometimes cooked before drying.

Whether fish or meat can be dried outside in the sun or must be smoked indoors depends of course upon the season of the catch and the climate of the area. In the Central Coast Salish area, where summers are relatively dry and sunny, summer catches of sockeye and humpback salmon, as well as halibut, lingcod, and other fish, were generally dried on outdoor racks at summer fishing camps, where the fishermen could live in mat shelters. Fall runs of springs, cohoes, and dog salmon, however, usually had to be smoked indoors because of the danger of rain. Occasionally separate structures may have been built for smoking fish, but evidently the usual "smokehouse" was the ordinary winter plank house and in local English usage this is what it is still called. The importance of this difference in preserving methods for social relations is easily seen. In the drier season a nuclear family, on its own, could store up a considerable amount of food with a minimum of shelter, but in the wetter season it would be bound to the plank house of its extended family. Because of its use as a smokehouse, the plank house is thus an important instrument of production, and the ownership or control of a house at the site of a fish weir used in the fall may have had as important social and economic consequences as ownership or control of the weir itself. In the Salish area, weirs were in fact usually public property but houses were not.

In many other parts of the coast, climatic conditions probably did not permit as much preserving of food outside as in the Salish area. During the three months of summer, Victoria (in the Salish area) gets an average of 14 days of rain (out of an annual total of 133) while Port Hardy (in Kwakiutl country) gets 38 (out of a total of 204), Masset (Haida) 41 (out of 210), and Prince Rupert (Tsimshian) 46 (out of 215). During an average year Victoria gets a total of 2,092 hours of sunshine while Prince Rupert gets 1,019, or roughly half (figures from Kendrew and Kerr 1955). Precipitation is also greater on the outer coast to the south than in the central coast Salish area. These differences certainly have implications for food preserving and possibly for social relations.

It should also be noted that not all species of salmon, perhaps not even all populations of the same species, keep equally well. My Salish informants say that fatter fish last longer and thus sockeye and dog salmon are their favorites. Other species may not last through the winter months.*

Another very important method of storage is rendering of fat into oil, which can then be kept in such containers as seal bladders (in the Salish area), kelp bulbs (Kwakiutl), or wooden boxes (Chinook). Throughout most of the coast, dried fish or meat was eaten after being dipped in oil; sea-mammal oil was used from the Salish and Nootka southward, and eulachon oil was used from the Kwakiutl northward. On the Fraser, where seal oil was less plentiful, salmon oil was also used (Duff 1952:66). This constant use of oil seemed excessive to Europeans but it may have compensated for the scarcity of carbohydrates (Drucker 1951:62; Rivera 1949:34; see also note 5 of the present paper).

In the north, oil was also used for preserving some kinds of berries. From the Chinook southward, meat was preserved by pulverizing it and mixing it with grease. Salmon eggs were first allowed to get "high" and to form a kind of cheese-like substance, and eulachon were also allowed to decay before rendering; however there was evidently no general practice of allowing fish to decay. Storage pits are reported for a few areas and so are raised caches, but probably throughout most of the area preserved food was stored in boxes, baskets, and bags placed on racks inside the dwelling house.

---

*[I was quite wrong about this. As Curtis (1915:28) reported for the Kwakiutl, it is the leaner fish that preserve longer. Sockeye are relished for their fat but do not last as long; "dog salmon" (now called "chums") are lean and last longer. For a detailed study of salmon preservation, see Romanoff 1971.]

A number of foods, such as dog salmon, must have required far more effort in the storing than in the taking. Thus limits in the exploitation of times of abundance may have been set less by the people's capacity to *get* food than by their capacity to *store* it. How much of a very heavy fall run of dog salmon could be stored must have depended on the number of hands available for the work of cutting and skewering, the drying-rack capacity of the houses at the site, fuel for smoke, and finally the number of containers available. As Gould has stressed, preserving food was largely the work of women and for this reason rights over women and bride prices were so important in the economy of the Tolowa. The role of women in subsistence no doubt deserves reappraisal elsewhere on the Northwest Coast. But it must be remembered that women need not be wives; they may also be slaves.

Values and Social Organization

Of course the possibilities offered by the environment and the techniques of food-getting and food-storing could be realized only through the work of people organized by their social systems and motivated by their value system. To survive the occasional period of scarcity, people had to have not only the earlier periods of abundance; the weirs, nets, etc., to take food with; and the drying racks, houses, etc., to preserve and store it with; but they also had to have a reason for doing it and the ability to mobilize the labor for it.

Probably the knowledge that there is an occasional period of scarcity is not reason enough to make most people store up food for every winter. But the Northwest Coast peoples had "better" reasons. From the Yurok and Tolowa northward there was the ultimate goal of prestige, into which food was eventually converted. From the Chinook northward there was also the cultural definition of winter as a ceremonial season, when people should not have to seek food. (This last reason for storing food was also found through much of the Plateau as well.) Swan's account of sorcery among the Makah (1870) suggests that some people did not expect random variation in their environment anyway; they attributed bad weather to human malice and coped with it by threatening the supposed sorcerer. If the people stored food for "cultural" reasons rather than the rational recognition of possible failure in the environment, this may explain why they sometimes did improvidently eat up all their stores in feasting, as Poole reported for the Haida. Nevertheless, the "cultural" reasons may have enabled larger populations to survive in this habitat than rational planning alone would have done.*

---

*[Anastasio (1975:139) refers to this attitude as one of optimism about natural resources and discusses its implications.]

In social organization, there seems to have been a rough sort of south-to-north gradient of increasing tightness of structure and size of social unit. Kroeber found the Yurok so individualistic that he declared:

> Property and rights pertain to the realm of the individual, and the Yurok recognizes no public claim and the existence of no community. His world is wholly an aggregation of individuals. There being no society as such, there is no social organization. Clans, exogamic groups, chiefs or governors, political units are unrepresented even by traces in Northwest California (1925:3).

Nevertheless, Kroeber's data suggest possibly three kinds of social groups engaging in social activities: the members of the household, the joint owners of a fishing place, and the large group from several villages that built the Kepel weir. The last group is an example of what Anastasio (1955) has called a "task grouping," in which members of social units defined by other criteria come together for a particular purpose at a particular time and place. These task groupings are generally under the leadership of a person who has the requisite technical and/or ritual knowledge. Treide (1965) has recently analyzed the function of such "salmon chiefs" as the ritual director of the Kepel weir for much of western North America.

Northward, on the Oregon coast the village seems to have consisted of an unnamed patrilineal kin group formed by patrilocal residence and to have functioned as a unit under some circumstances (Barnett 1937:elements 1345, 1400). Among the Chinook at the mouth of the Columbia, there was a village chief (who may have been simply the head of a patrilocal kin group) who evidently exacted tribute from his villagers and redistributed it (Ray 1938:56).

The Central Coast Salish social organization was seemingly looser than that of the Chinook. Village exogamy was preferred but residence was ambilocal so neither the household nor the village formed any kind of definable kin group. There were, however, cognatic kin groups perhaps best understood as "stem kindreds," that is, the personal kindreds of successive generations of "owners" of certain ceremonial rights and one or more of the more productive natural resources. One of these men might tend to dominate a village but there was no village chief as such. The village was recognized as a unit when it came to certain types of sharing and certain ceremonial activities, but in general the household was autonomous. Task groups were directed by the "owners" of resources, such as fishing sites and clam beds; by owners of special gear, as the net for a deer drive; or simply by skilled specialists in the activity. Such subsistence activities often brought together people from several villages over areas which crossed dialect and even language boundaries, but there were no structural principles that allowed for the definition of discrete social units.

Wakashan (Nootka and Kwakiutl) social structure seems to have been similar to that of the Salish in that both lacked rules of unilocal residence and unilinear descent. The Nootka and Kwakiutl, however, were much more structured through the principle of ranking of titles in series. Within the cognatic kin group, individuals, at least the more important ones, held positions ranked in relation to one another. Within the village (or "tribe"), kin groups were so ranked. In a few areas "tribes" formed confederacies through the same principle. Among the Wakashans, as among the Chinook, "chiefs" (in fact, kin group heads) evidently received tribute and acted as redistributors. (For the Nootka, see Drucker 1951:especially 220-21, 251-57.)

The highest development of formal organization with permanent discrete social units was that found among the northern peoples. The Tsimshian, Tlingit, Haida, together with the Haisla (the northernmost Kwakiutl), had a system of matrilineages, sibs, and phratries or moieties. The largest of these kin groups were the phratries of the Haisla and Tsimshian and the moieties of the Tlingit and Haida. These were simply exogamous units and served to classify every person in the whole northern area for marriageability. Except for the Tsimshian, the largest unit with economic and political functions was the lineage. But the Tsimshian of the lower Skeena and Nass rivers went farther and acknowledged the chief of the leading lineage of a village as the village chief. Garfield believes that this probably occurred early in the eighteenth century. Then, early in the nineteenth century, villages up the Skeena established colonies near its mouth and these each remained under the authority of the chief of the mother village, who in some cases also moved to the colony. "At this stage," writes Garfield, "tribal chieftainship emerged and the tribal chief was regarded as the active leader of his tribesmen regardless of where they lived." The village chief and the tribal chief, like the earlier lineage chief, received tribute and made decisions regarding moves to fishing sites and other subsistence activities (Garfield 1951:34-35).

The greater development of formal organization in the north was probably accompanied by more effective control of larger labor forces. This difference in turn may account for the remarkably different views we find on the economic importance of slavery on the Northwest Coast.

Barnett, writing primarily of the Kwakiutl and Coast Salish, suggests that slaves were "in bondage . . . as much a liability as an asset and . . . useful primarily as overt demonstration of the ability to possess them" (1938b:352). Drucker, writing about the area in general, says

> It is difficult to estimate the slave population of the area, but
> it was certainly never very large, for slave mortality was high.
> Slaves' economic utility was negligible. They gathered firewood,
> dug clams, and fished, but so did their masters (1965:52).

Kroeber, listing exchange values among the Yurok, expressed mainly in strings of dentalia, writes:

A slave was rated at only one or two strings. Evidently the Yurok did not know how to exact full value from the labor of their bonds-men, not because the latter could not be held to work, but because industry was too little organized (1925:27).

The Yurok did not take slaves in war nor buy them from other peoples; all Yurok slaves were fellow Yurok enslaved by debt. The greatest number of slaves held by one man did not exceed three (1925:32).

On the other hand, Garfield (1945:628; 1951:30) has strongly opposed the view that slaves were kept merely for prestige value and argued that their contribution must have increased the productivity of their owners' households. A potlatching Tsimshian chief was not expected to mention what his slaves contributed in labor, but if he gave them away he boasted of what he had paid for them. During the nineteenth century a slave was worth from two hundred to a thousand dollars. They were mainly war captives and their descendants. The numbers held were much higher than among the southern tribes.

Ten to twenty slaves are reported as belonging to each of the nine tribal chiefs of Port Simpson in the middle nineteenth century. Each of approximately fifty Port Simpson lineage heads is also reported to have owned from two to as many as ten slaves (Garfield 1951:30).

It does seem that the mere fact that slaves performed the same task as their masters does not rule out their being of economic importance. If adding a wife or daughter-in-law can increase the productivity of a Tolowa household and give additional economic advantage, as Gould reports, why not adding a slave to a Tsimshian household? Kroeber may have been correct regarding the organization of labor among the Yurok, but can't we expect more from the Tsimshian? Driver (1961:245-46, 387-88) has pointed out that at the southern end of the Northwest Coast a master could not kill a slave nor did he have sexual rights over a female slave, while in the north he held both these rights. This too suggests the possibility of greater control over their labor in the north.*

---

*[Ruyle (1973) interprets Northwest Coast social systems as having rigid class distinctions with slaves playing an economically important role, but not all of the comments published in *Current Antropology* with his article agree with him. Donald (1983) also argues for the economic importance of slaves.]

Slavery may also be seen as one of several possible ways of making the human population fit the resources. The most drastic of these is infanticide in times of scarcity. As far as we know this was not practiced on the Northwest Coast. The least drastic is fluidity of social groupings, allowing "surplus" people at a place with poor resources to move in with those at more favored places. This fluidity was a prominent feature of the Coast Salish social system. With local exogamy, a man's four grandparents were likely to have been from four different villages; at each of these he had residence rights and he also had the option of living with his wife's people. For men of property it was certainly preferable to stay in one's father's village, but no rule required it. The Wakashans also seem to have been flexible in the residence of lower-ranking people. For the northerners, the sib system may have facilitated the mobility of sib-identified groups. But for northwestern California and the Oregon coast we get consistent reports of patrilocal residence and also of impoverished parents selling their children into slavery. Perhaps if residence rules are rigid, selling "surplus" children is the only peaceful alternative to infanticide.

Finally, in looking at social organization in relation to subsistence, we should note that the local group was not simply a task force for the exploitation of resources. In one season it could function as a producer and distributor of surplus *and* in another season as an absorber of surplus produced by other groups. Elsewhere (Suttles 1960a, 1962), in discussing the Central Coast Salish socioeconomic system, I have pointed out how the preference for local exogamy and the exchanges that occurred between affines in different villages may have been adaptive under conditions of variable occurrence of natural resources. A man with a temporary abundance of food had three choices: (1) he could share it with his fellow villagers, if they could consume it (which they could not if they too had the same abundance); (2) he could preserve it, if it was preservable and he had the labor force and time before the next harvest of fish, berries, etc., was due; or (3) he could take it to his in-laws in another village (where this particular food might be scarce) and receive in return a gift of wealth, which he might give later to in-laws bringing food to him. If he got more wealth than he gave, he could always potlatch and convert the wealth into glory, which of course might attract more prosperous in-laws. Thus, exchange between affines made it possible for a household *not* to store food and still take advantage of times of abundance.[6]

---

[6]Exchange between affines may also have served simply to keep more people busy. Woodburn states (Lee and DeVore 1968:ch. 17c) that a skilled Hadza hunter could not control the number of his hangers-on. I suspect that a good provider among the Coast Salish had the same problem, an increased number of less productive resident kin. But this was offset by his obligation to take food to his in-laws, who were honor-bound to repay him with wealth, which he did not have to redistribute. A man's affines in other villages may have been his covert allies against potential spongers at home.

Vayda (1961a) and Piddocke (1965) have suggested that the Kwakiutl pot-latch system may also be seen as an adaptation of a fluctuating environment rather than the "absurdly wasteful" epiphenomenon it has sometimes been labeled. From Piddocke's review of the data, it appears that the Kwakiutl converted food into wealth by selling it to those in need (somewhat as Gould reports the Tolowa having done) and then (unlike the Tolowa) converted the wealth into prestige through competitive potlatching. Piddocke argues that the entry of new wealth into the system and the reduction of the population through disease increased the size and frequency of potlatches to the "fan-tastic" level of classic descriptions.

Weinberg (1965) has criticized and expanded on Vayda's suggestion and worked out a model of Kwakiutl culture as a self-regulating adaptive system in which the stability of culture is dependent on fluctuation in the environ-ment within certain limits. When, in the nineteenth century, the limits were exceeded in the direction of surplus, the spectacular growth of the potlatch that followed was essentially an effort to maintain the stability of the culture (cf. "Romer's Rule" of Hockett and Ascher 1964).

It has been implicit in the previous discussion of the Coast Salish that items of "wealth" (blankets, canoes, hide shirts, etc.) did not constitute all-purpose money. As in several other parts of the world, there were restrictions on the occasions when wealth items could properly change hands. These restrictions seem to have been less severe among the Tolowa, but still present in that only exchanges that related to marriage and litigation were publicized, while those that were purely commercial were not, hence the appearance of a separate "prestige economy." Among the Kwakiutl, too, giving was certainly more honorable than selling. The areas where commercial transactions were most open and honorable seem to have been the north and, most especially, the lower Columbia. But even here commerce was not wholly free, for it is reported that chiefs (lineage heads?) held monopolies over trade in their territories. It seems possible that such monopolies may have had their origins in exchanges between affines in areas of different resources. In both cases the most impor-tant trade was between the coast and interior—the Tlingit with the Athapaskan hinterland and the Chinookans with the Plateau Sahaptins. Perhaps the most important question, at present unanswerable, is: *Why didn't* a market econ-omy develop and spread out from these areas? Or were these commercial developments so recent that there was no time left for further growth? This may be, yet archeological evidence suggests that some form of trade goes back to the early occupation of the area.

Conclusions

I am afraid I have raised more questions about the Northwest Coast than I have been able to answer. If I can offer any conclusion it can only be this:

The Northwest Coast material suggests that where people are faced with great seasonal and local variations in the amount of food offered by their habitat, their success in exploiting the abundance depends on more than technology alone. They must also have: (1) the organization of labor for getting and storing food (marital rights? kin obligations? property rights? monopoly of technical and/or ritual knowledge?); (2) some means of redistributing population on the habitat (wide kin ties and fluidity of residence? slavery?) and/or redistributing the bounty of the habitat among the population (barter in foods? exchange of food for durable goods? markets?); and (3) some motivating value (prestige?). It seems to me that these factors together with an adequate technology, are necessary conditions for coping with abundance, regardless of whether it appears in the form of fish, sea mammals, land game, or even vegetable food.

From the data presented on the "simpler" hunters by other members of the symposium, it appears that those hunters often are capable of organizing drives and other activities that would take quantities of animals if available. They also seem to have, and necessarily so, a fluidity of organization that permits redistribution of population and at least rudimentary trade. Perhaps the greatest point of contrast is that the simpler hunters lacked the characteristic Northwest Coast feature of motivation to achieve and maintain superior status through the production of surplus. For this reason it seems to me that the "hunting ideology" or nomadic style (Lee and DeVore 1968, Chapter 1) may turn out to be well worth the attention it seems to have attracted. Finally, I would ask, when we find archeological evidence of unexpected cultural complexity and population density, is it altogether hopeless to seek ethnographic parallels from the Northwest coast? This is not to say that I believe the Upper Paleolithic Europeans held slaves and gave potlatches.* But I expect that some day we will be in a position to say whether they possessed the functional equivalents.

[POSTSCRIPT, 1987

I did not mean, as one reader seems to think, that a once-a-generation hardship sent people scurrying off for prestige. I meant that a system of exchange powered by a desire for prestige (whatever the ultimate origin of the desire) would have had a selective advantage over a system of village self-sufficiency even if hardships came only once a generation. Nor

---

*[I believe that the suggestion that prehistoric Western Europe might be seen as comparable to the Northwest Coast is one that I first heard from Melville Jacobs. See Jacobs and Stern 1947:88, Jacobs 1964:51-52.]

have I ever argued, as Piddocke seems to do concerning the Kwakiutl, that shortages led directly to invitations to potlatches. For the Central Coast Salish, I know of no evidence that the news of another village's hardship prompted a potlatch, and I see no reason to suppose that it did. The argument was (and is) that the system was adaptive because it promoted a continuous exchange among villages, increasing the variety and quantity of available food and promoting intervillage ties. I do suppose (with some evidence, I think) that blood kin and affines helped each other in time of need with gifts of food. The gifts of wealth received at a potlatch would not have been as immediately useful. Lastly, I did not suppose that the system worked so well that all were equally well supported and nobody ever went hungry. Adaptation does not mean perfection.]

Part II

Knowledge, Belief, and Art in Historic Culture

5. Space and Time, Wind and Tide— Some Halkomelem Modes of Classification*

In Halkomelem, the Coast Salish language spoken on the Lower Fraser and the shores of Vancouver Island directly across Georgia Strait, relationships in space and in time may be expressed by the same grammatical means and even by the same words. An article system used with nouns and nominalized verbs distinguishes three positions differing in nearness, visibility, and certainty of existence; reference seems primarily to position in space, but in certain usages it is to time. Two stems used in ways resembling the use of auxiliary verbs in English seem basically to express notions of "be here" and "be there" but also often seem to imply "be now" and "be then." However, as in English, past time is most clearly indicated by a suffix and future time by a modal particle. Location and direction of motion are expressed by a series of stems and their derivatives having reference to shoreline, flow of water, fire, house, canoe, etc. Common elements occur in the expression of motion in relation to flow of water, fire, and center of house. Time is not involved in these, but in indicating sequence, words like English "before" may refer to both space and time. Units of both space and time are counted with the same numerals.

Cardinal directions are not named in Halkomelem. It is easy to elicit wind names identified as "north wind," "south wind," etc., but checking usage shows that direction, which is quite variable, is only one component of

---

*[Abstract submitted for the 17th Northwest Anthropological Conference, Pullman, April 1964.]

meaning, others being season, temperature, and precipitation. However, the region as a whole has an axis in that the northwestern end of Georgia Strait seems to be equated with "upstream" and the southeastern end with "downstream." Time is reckoned in months and years, but it is not altogether clear how in earlier times intercalation was achieved to make a properly functioning calendar. Astronomical observations were certainly made, but it is also likely that certain annual regularities in the tidal cycle were used as checks. Thus the flow of water may have been important in reference to time as well as space.

All considered, the data do not seem to permit any conclusion that Halkomelem speakers keep categories of time and space any better separated than do speakers of English, or that Halkomelem gives its speakers any different view of time from the view English gives us. Greater differences exist in what the two languages require us to express when we talk about location or direction.

Time and Tide*

The Coast Salish of the Fraser Delta and the shores of Vancouver Island directly across Georgia Strait formerly practiced a food-gathering way of life in an environment of considerable spatial and temporal variation in the abundance of natural food resources. The evolution of Coast Salish technology in this area was surely influenced by these environmental conditions and so probably were features of Coast Salish social organization. To gain the greatest reward from nature, men had to be at the right place, at the right time, with the right equipment, and with the right complement of personnel. It would be unwise to suggest that this always happened or even that it ever happened with the greatest possible reward. But it does appear that the Coast Salish of this area were sufficiently well equipped and well organized to have multiplied and prospered for many centuries and to have become the possessors of a value system powerful enough to survive to the present day. It also appears that they must have had, besides technology and organization, sufficient means of describing and interpreting what we call space and time in order to be—

---

*[The paper as presented at the 17th Northwest Anthropological Conference. As it must often happen, I wrote the abstract before writing the paper and then discovered I could not cover the whole ground in allotted time. The abstract and the paper seem complementary and so I include them both.]

68

often enough—in the right numbers, with the right gear, at the right place, and at the right time. It was originally my intention to make this paper a kind of preliminary exploration of that means. However, restrictions in the temporal dimension in relation to reading papers at meetings require that I concentrate on one or two points. Therefore I shall not cover everything I implied in my abstract but speak only of time reckoning and the tide. Native terms cited will be in the Musqueam dialect of Halkomelem.

Speakers of the Halkomelem language have terms for day, night, and several segments of the day, for lunar months, for the year, recurring periods of time within the year, and even recurring kinds of years. Also, for longer than the lifetime of any living person, it has been possible to talk about time by the clock, the day of the week, and important dates in the Western calendar. This last fact has made it difficult to get very clear information on aboriginal time reckoning.

It seems very unlikely that the aboriginal Coast Salish knew the number of days in the solar year or the exact number of lunations in the solar year. But they had names for months and kept some count of them. However, as Leach has pointed out (1950, 1954) with regard to primitive time-reckoning generally, a series of moon names is not a calendar and counting moons endlessly would result in chaos; to allow prediction there must be some means of intercalation. Evidently one such means used in several parts of the world is to begin a moon count from some event occurring at a regular time in the solar year, count ten moons from this time, and then stop counting until the next occurrence of the annual starting point; this allows the intercalary period to vary—as it must—between two and three lunations, whether the users of the calendar are aware of this or not. Leach infers that the Trobriand Islanders' calendar was of this type and suggests that the earliest Roman calendar was the same.

This also appears to have been the type of calendar used by at least two Halkomelem-speaking groups on the Lower Fraser, the Chehalis (Hill-Tout 1904b; data given in Cope 1919) and the Katzie (Jenness 1955, and Suttles field notes), by many of the Interior Salish (Teit 1900:237-39; 1906a:223-24; 1906b:517-18; 1930:95-96, 247; Cline 1938:180-81; only Ray 1932:222-23 is exceptional), and by the Quinault (Olson 1936:175-76). For example, the Thompson started their moon count from the rutting season of the deer or some other animal in the fall, counted through eleven months (other Interior counts used ten), and then left a period as "the rest of the year." As Teit says (1900:239), "This indefinite period of unnamed months enabled the Indians to bring the lunar and solar years into harmony." The Quinault counted ten months beginning with the southward migration of geese in the fall (Olson 1936:175-76). The Chehalis and Katzie counted ten months with an intercalary period in the summer but it is not clear what observation was used as a starting point.

As far as I have been able to look in a rather hasty survey, I have not found as clear an indication of this principle of intercalation among the nearer neighbors of the Salish. It is not reported for the Northwest Coast northward until we reach the Tlingit, who numbered some months, as did the Kodiak, Aleut, and others, according to data compiled by Cope (1919). But it is not clear to me how they achieved intercalation. Southward, Ray reports numbering of months for the Klickitat (Ray 1942:189), Spier for the Klamath (1930:218-19), Barnett for the southern Oregon coast (1937:176). Kroeber (1960:26) describes the Yurok use of two conflicting systems. The scattered distribution outside the Salish area and the occurrence of the principle in clearest form on the western and eastern ends of Salish territory—Quinault and Coeur d'Alene—suggest that a ten-month count with a late summer or early autumn intercalary period may have been a part of proto-Salish culture.

However, the salt-water people on Georgia Strait and Puget Sound did not seem to use this principle, or if they used it, they did so inconsistently: moons were not numbered at all but simply given descriptive names and, while some lists leave gaps in the summer, others run throughout the year. Statements differ as to when the year begins, but most say fall or winter (Gunther 1927:228; Ballard 1950; Barnett 1939:287; Suttles field notes). If the Coast Salish of this area once had a moon count like that of the Quinault or Thompson, capable of predicting, it seems unlikely that they would have abandoned it, unless it was made less useful by the presence of other means of reckoning the passage of the year.

It is clear from the data from salt-water Halkomelem-speaking groups that people took note of a variety of regularly occurring phenomena. The month names themselves refer to seasonal habits of animals, changes in vegetation, and human activities related to natural events. Also there is evidence that people observed the solstices and the changes in positions of certain constellations, especially the Pleiades. These astronomical observations would provide the most precise points in time to start a month count from—and their use for time-reckoning has been reported for the Yurok, the Kwakiutl, and others. But these observations also require clear enough weather for the sun or the Pleiades to be seen, conditions not always present on the Northwest Coast.

There is, however, another phenomenon that occurs in a cycle that shows certain regularities with the solar year and yet is observable throughout much of the area in any kind of weather—the tide. As Arthur Ballard pointed out regarding his Puget Sound informants' vague references to tide in relation to calendar, this is a phenomenon that deserves much more attention by anthropologists than it has received. I offer what I have discovered here, admitting that the data are still fragmentary.

There is no term in Halkomelem corresponding precisely to the English "tide," though qá? "water" may often be translated thus. The following more specific terms occur: sqə́məl "flooding tide," qəqə́məl "be flooding" (with

70

such a verb the noun subject, if any is used, would be simply θə qá? "the water"), sźém? "ebbing tide," żéżəm? "be ebbing," sələlí'c "high tide" (from a stem lə́c "full"), lə́clə́c "be just high water," sxə́m?xəm? "low tide," k̓ʷik̓ʷéyəm "be in a period of half tides," xʷƛ̓ə́nəxʷəm "be slack water," i.e., at the turn of the tide.

The tide was of great importance not only to the people of villages on the salt water, but also to those on the Fraser for some distance up from its mouth. At times when the tides are running strongest and when the river is low, the flood tide is said to produce slack water as far up as Mission, which is about fifty miles from the mouth and is, perhaps significantly, about at the boundary between the upriver and downriver dialects of the Halkomelem language. The downriver speakers, including the Katzie on Pitt Lake (which has a tide), were within the area of tidal water. The Musqueam, at the mouth of the Fraser, when they wanted to travel upstream, whenever possible simply caught the upbound tide. Under optimum conditions—as in December when the river was lowest and the tides were highest—it is said that on one flood tide you could make it to the Katzie village at Port Hammond, which, perhaps also significantly, is the site of a large shell mound. During the summer freshet, however, the water slacks to New Westminster only.

Tide conditions on the river were important for fishing as well. Nets are most effective when the water is muddy. Thus the best times are when the tides are running strong or when the river is high. In winter when the water is low, during periods of half tides, the water is too clear to use a net. I need not dwell on the importance of the tide for salt-water fishing and shellfish gathering.

The Coast Salish were of course aware of the co-occurrence of the greatest highs and lows with the dark and full moon, a co-occurrence that is not as precise in this area as on the open ocean, by the way. They were also aware of an annual cycle in the tides, since this too had some importance for subsistence activities. On Georgia Strait and Puget Sound the highest highs and lowest lows usually come within a month of the summer and winter solstices (Pickard 1963 communication) and these lowest lows come during the middle of the night in winter and the middle of the day in summer. This fact seems to have escaped notice in the anthropological literature on this area, possibly because our formally learned notions about tides may still be based on the Atlantic tidal system, wherein the two lows each day are of about equal height and so there is likely to be one low in the daytime and one low at night throughout the year. Here we have two lows of great inequality, hence the annual cycle through the twenty-four hour day. The economic significance of this cycle lies in the fact that the summer lows are most used for shellfish gathering, when people can camp and dry clams away from home—especially at the June low, while the winter lows at the dark of the moon are used for waterfowl hunting with flares, some species not even being present in summer.

Four terms describe these phenomena: *wéyəlcəm* "shift to daytime," which begins about March; *nə́tcəm* "shift to night-time," which begins about October; *θaʔtə́łcə* "dark tide," i.e., a low at the dark of the moon (from *θéʔt* "dark" and *-əłcə* "low tide"); and *łqəlčə́łcə* "moon tide" (from *łqəlč* "moon" and *-əłcə* "low tide").

This annual cycle of tides thus also provided not as precise a series of points to count from as the astronomical observations but a more readily and continuously observable phenomenon that already relates lunations with the solar year.

In concluding, I would like to suggest that, among the Coast Salish of this area, men specializing in different sorts of activities may well have used different observations from which to count moons in order to make different kinds of predictions. Also several ethnographic works (e.g., Elmendorf 1960:27) mention arguments over what month it was. Sapir (cited in Cope 1919:131) reports that Nootka hunters even tried to deceive one another about the correct month. This jibes with the Coast Salish practice of keeping some kinds of technical knowledge as individual or family property.

Finally, I would like to suggest that with the diversity of kinds of resources and spatial and temporal variation mentioned in my opening remarks, a rigid calendrical system based on a single precise astronomical observation could have even been maladaptive. For those whose subsistence activities were closely linked with the tides, knowing what to expect of the tide was likely of greater importance than knowing precisely when the winter solstice occurs. Any reckoning from this event would have to take the tide into account anyway.*

---

*[For an example of the Kwakiutl use of combined astronomical and tidal observations see Boas 1938:274.]

6. On the Cultural Track of the Sasquatch*

John Green (1968:67-68) has criticized anthropologists for our treatment of Indian accounts of the sasquatch. He suggests that we have failed to recognize that our Indian informants have been talking about real animals because we are predisposed by our professional interests to treat "the Sasquatch by any of its various names" as a mythical being. He also implies, I think, that we must have more data than we have published and he expresses the wish that someone assemble and analyze these data.

Roderick Sprague (1970) evidently suspects Green's criticism is justified and has called for more data and discussion. I agree that we have neglected the subject and I gladly join Bruce Rigsby (1971) in answering the call. I hope that these notes will contribute to the general compendium and analysis that Green and Sprague have asked for.

I will present here data that I have collected among the Coast Salish of southwestern British Columbia and northwestern Washington together with

---

*[From *Northwest Anthropological Research Notes* 6:65-90 (1972), University of Idaho, Moscow, Idaho. This article and others on the same topic published in NARN were put together into a book, Sprague and Krantz 1977, Sprague and Krantz 1979. The title of this essay was based on John Green's *On the Track of the Sasquatch* (Green 1968). I did a second piece on sasquatch-like beings, first as a paper, "Some Questions about the Sasquatch," read at the annual meeting of the American Folklore Society at Portland, Oregon, 1 November 1974, rewritten as my contribution to a conference on "Sasquatch and Similar Phenomena" held at the University of British Columbia in May 1978, and published as "Sasquatch: The Testimony of Tradition" in the volume that resulted from that conference (Halpin and Ames 1980:245-54).]

what I have found in the published works available to me from the larger Coast Salish area. But I should begin with my basic assumptions:

1. I am still unconvinced that there is a real animal there. I must admit that I will be delighted if it turns out that there is, but for that very reason I must be critical in looking at what is said to be evidence. I do not think, however, that scientific objectivity is served by ignoring the question. So if there is evidence in the Native traditions and beliefs, I hope to try to see it.

2. I do not think we can assume from the outset that there is a single image for which "sasquatch" is only one of many names, unless we assume before-hand that the terms do in fact refer to a real animal of wide distribution. If the terms "sasquatch," etc. refer only to imaginary beings then there may be as many images as there are names or even human imaginations. So let us start looking at what attributes have been associated with these various names and see to what extent they may refer to the same being.

3. I do not think we can assume that Indian categories are the same as Western ones. In fact, I see no evidence of a dichotomy of "real" vs. "mythical" or "natural" vs. "supernatural" in Coast Salish thought. There is a dichotomy "myth age" vs. "present age," but the beings seen then were "real" and those seen today are "real" to the Coast Salish. There is also a dichotomy "vision experience" vs. "ordinary experience," but the beings seen in both are equally "real." So I do not think that informants' statements on this matter are relevant to our enquiry.

I will develop this last point shortly and then go on to the variety of names for sasquatch-like beings and the attributes ascribed to them. Finally, I will consider the question of what these names may refer to. But first let me begin with the now-famous name "Sasquatch" itself.

The word "sasquatch" is an anglicization of the word *sésq̓əc*, which occurs in the mainland dialects of the Halkomelem language. This language, a member of the Salish language family, is spoken in southwestern British Columbia in the Lower Fraser Valley from Yale to the mouth of the Fraser and on southeastern Vancouver Island from Nanoose Bay to Malahat. The word occurs in all of the mainland dialects I have data for but not in the island dialects. Phonetically, the Halkomelem /s/ is quite close to the English /s/; the Halkomelem /ɛ/ varies between the English /æ/ of "bat" and /e/ of "bet"; the Halkomelem /q̓/ is a glottalized uvular stop closest to English /k/ but produced farther back toward the throat and with the explosive quality of the glottalized sounds of Northwestern languages; the Halkomelem /ə/ is like the English unstressed /ə/ in "aside;" and the Halkomelem /c/ varies from the /ts/ of "gets" to the /č/ of "church." It seems to me that the Halkomelem *sésq̓əc* should have produced an English /sæskəts/ or /sæskəč/ rather than the existing /sæskwač/; possibly the current spelling is based on a misinterpretation of an anthropologist's or linguist's phonetic transcription rather than a direct perception of the Halkomelem word. Morphologically, the term *sésq̓əc* cannot

74

be analyzed in Halkomelem; I have suggested to my Musqueam teacher James Point a possible connection with *sə́q* "get split, get torn," but he doubts the possibility. The term refers, of course, to a great, hairy, man-like creature said to live in the mountains.

The term may have been introduced into English as "sasquatch" in the 1920s. John Green (1968:1) identifies the source as J.W. Burns, "who was for many years a teacher at the Chehalis Indian Reserve, on the Harrison River near Harrison Hot Springs." Burns wrote articles in the 1920s and 1930s that "achieved wide circulation in newspapers and magazines in the United States and Canada." Burns introduced the "Sasquatch" to the public but at the same time, by quoting Indian stories with supernatural elements, stigmatized it as an "Indian legend." This was unfortunate, Green believes, because scientists in particular are inclined to dismiss the subjects of Indian legends as purely imaginary.

It is certainly true that we anthropologists have generally dumped sasquatch-like beings into a category "supernaturals" and let it go at that. We may have done this because we are professionally interested more in Native culture than in the facts of zoology, but I think it is more because we are operating with too simple a version of the Western dichotomy. In fact, if we were true to our earlier, Boasian objective of decribing the Native culture as seen by the participants, we ought not to categorize so freely the creatures our informants tell us about.

Let me explore this problem. The *sésqəc* is one of many creatures the Lower Fraser people believe (or used to believe) exist (or once existed) in the wilderness around them. Most of these creatures can, from Indians' descriptions of them, be matched with animals known to Europeans. A few, however, cannot. Since we Europeans, scientifically trained or not, operate with a dichotomy real/mythical or natural/supernatural, we are inclined to place these creatures that are not part of our "real" world into our category "mythical" or "supernatural." As Green has pointed out, most of us have done this with the *sésqəc* and we may be wrong.

But I believe we would also be wrong to imagine that the Indians have (or had) the same dichotomy and that they would simply draw the line differently, putting the sasquatch in the category "real animals" and leaving other, to our minds more fanciful, creatures in the category "mythical animals" or "supernatural beings." In fact, I see little evidence for any such Native dichotomy at all.

Once years ago I was eliciting ethnozoological information from an aged Lummi friend, Julius Charles. I had gone through Dalquest's *Mammals of Washington,* asking about everything from shrews to elk, and when I had finished Julius said something like: "There's another animal you haven't got there. They used to be around here but they've become pretty scarce and the white people have never caught one and put it in a zoo. It had a big body in the middle and two heads, one at each side. It lived in swamps where it swam about. But it could turn into a couple of mallards and fly away. It had three kinds of noises—one was like the laugh of a loon, one like the hoot of a hound, and one like the hissing of a mallard drake. It was a great thing to get so you'd become an Indian doctor.''

This "animal" was called a sʔinəɫqəy. Such fierce and powerful things that were seen by men "training" to become "doctors" (in anthropological jargon "questing for shamanistic visions") were sx̌élaqəm. Grizzly bears and killer whales were also good to get a doctor's power from. But any "animal" might be referred to as a sx̌élaqəm.[1]

Evidently to Julius the two-headed serpent sʔinəɫqəy was just as much a "real animal" as the rest of those on my list. It belonged to a class sx̌élaqəm that included most or all of my animals. For Julius, as for other Coast Salish I have worked with since, a distinction between "real" and "mythical" or "natural" and "supernatural" beings just is not there. Thus a description of Coast Salish culture that is truly "emic"—that is, organized by Native categories—should describe whales and bears, sasquatches and two-headed serpents, all under the same heading as part of the "real" world of the Coast Salish.

But this is not to say that they ought to have the same kind of reality for the Western scientist, who surely ought to go on seeking evidence and doubting what evidence does not support. But rather than trying to sort out the beings Indians talk about into the "real" and the "mythical," it might be better to apply our dichotomy to the attributes that Indians ascribe to these beings.

For example, the creature called sqəléw̓, translated by our informants as 'beaver,' is said to fell trees and build dams. Although on the face of it this seems to be an unlikely thing for an oversized rodent to do, we can see evidence of it and are inclined to believe it. Old Coquitlam William was said to have once sneaked up on a beaver colony at work and discovered that as beavers fell trees to build dams they whistle signals and shout instructions at each other like human loggers and teamsters. Without corroboration, some of us may doubt this, but since some kind of signal that a tree is falling should have survival value for the beaver, perhaps we should suspend judgment. Old Pierre, the Katzie shaman, told Jenness (1955:51) that beavers and muskrats will respond to an incantation and change cold, icy weather to rain. Most of us would doubt this and give the label "supernatural" to the relationship Old Pierre asserted exists between beavers and the weather. But we would have to admit that we have not tested the relationship; we doubt it because it is contrary to empirical evidence about causes of changes in the weather and because of a more general proposition that incantations only work

---

[1]Werner Cohn (1962) has also used this incident to question the universality of our dichotomies.

on people who believe in them, a proposition that is also untested. (Old William might have argued that since beavers talk they should respond to incantations. Unfortunately, it is likely that no one today knows the incantation and so we cannot know what responses beavers may once have made to it.)

As a second example, the creature called šxʷəxʷáʔas, translated as "thunder," is described as a huge bird that lives on high peaks, makes a great noise with its wings, and either hunts the sčinkʷaʔ, a snake-like creature identified with lightning, or uses the sčinkʷaʔ as a weapon in hunting whales. Since Ben Franklin's kite experiment, we Europeans have had an explanation of thunder and lightning that does not require birds and snakes (though most of us might find it harder to explain to an old Coast Salish how electricity does it) and so we are likely to doubt the existence of these creatures. Recently, however, it has been suggested (Holmes 1971; Ott 1971) that the thunderbird had a "real" basis in the California condor, a huge bird that once lived as far north as the Lower Fraser, nested on high crags, made a great noise with its wings, and fed on stranded sea mammals. So perhaps we will be left, as with the beaver, doubting only the supposed relationship between the animal and meteorological phenomena.

As a third example, the creature Julius Charles called sʔinəɬqəy seems wholly constructed of attributes we are inclined to doubt. Yet two-headed snakes do exist, as occasional viable mutants. So even this "animal" in the native bestiary may have some basis in our real world. I am not arguing, however, that all of the beings the Coast Salish talk about must have some basis in our reality. My point is simply that we cannot easily sort these beings out into "real" and "imaginary" and that the Coast Salish do not try to. But let me get back to the track of the sasquatch.*

Or are there several sasquatches? In the beliefs of the Coast Salish in the area where I have worked, the sésqəc is not the only being that seems not really human and yet has a human shape and other human attributes. Speakers of the island dialects of Halkomelem and of Straits tell about the žáməkʷəs or čáməkʷəs, which may or may not be identical with the mainland Halkomelem sésqəc. For some there are also čiétkʷ and stítəɬ or stéyʔtəɬ, which may sound like the sésqəc or simply like feral men. Then there are wild women or ogresses who catch children and eat them. These are known especially from a Hansel-and-Gretel-like story where the ogress is outwitted and roasted in her own fire pit. The story is usually given a specific locale, but most people know more than one such story and assume that these refer to different ogresses

---

*[Marjorie Halpin disagrees with my position and after examining Coast Salish data concludes (Halpin 1980:16): "Sasquatch was no more a mundane or ordinary animal to the Coast Salish than it is to us." I am unconvinced. Marie-Françoise Guédon (1984:139-140) has also argued against a natural/supernatural dichotomy for the Tsimshian. For a classic discussion see Durkheim 1915:24-29.]

and give evidence that formerly there were several or perhaps a whole population. There are also forest beings who knock down trees. And there are sea beings, also known especially from localized stories, who have taken human wives, as some say an occasional *sésqəc* has done. Finally, beings that usually have animal forms may appear in human form in the vision experience. If there is a real non-human primate here, his cultural track is obscured by a variety of semi-human footprints.

In the following pages I will present what I have discovered of Coast Salish beliefs that might refer to a real non-human primate, proceeding area by area on a linguistic basis.

Mainland Halkomelem: Upper Stalo

The Halkomelem-speaking people of the Lower Fraser Valley sometimes call themselves collectively Stalo (*stáʔləẃ*, "river") people. Wilson Duff (1952) used the term "Upper Stalo" for the people from Chilliwack upstream, with whom he worked in 1949 and 1950. He gives (1952:118-19) informants' descriptions and accounts of two man-like creatures, the sasquatch (Duff recorded the Native term as *sésxač*) and the cannibal woman (*θúxia*).

"Sasquatches," Duff reports, "are usually seen singly. They are described as men, covered with dark fur, more than 8 feet tall, who leave footprints about 20 inches long." Duff gives two older accounts of experiences with them and two more recent accounts with a generalized version of them. In the first, a "typical" older account (given by Adeline Lorenzetto of Ohamil), the sasquatches caused a person they touched to become unconscious; they stole women whom they kept as wives, had half-human children, and stole food from people for the women and their children. They had a language, which the women learned. When a woman escaped and re-entered human society, she became unconscious again "because she had been with the sasquatches and wasn't like a person any more." She had forgotten her language and hair was starting to grow all over her body, but Indian doctors worked on her and she became normal again. Many years later the sasquatches returned, but she could no longer communicate with them; however, she asked hunters not to shoot them because they might be her relatives. In the second older account a sasquatch murdered a group of women but left their children unhurt. In the accounts of recent encounters, Duff says, a person usually sees a sasquatch on a moonlit night, runs, is followed, but not overtaken, and escapes. In one account given, a man shoots a sasquatch. In the second, which is a brief version of the famous Ruby Creek incident, the sasquatch breaks into a house to steal dried fish.

The cannibal woman was described as a short, stout woman who caught children, gummed their eyes shut with pitch, carried them off in a basket, and ate them. She lived in a cave above Yale, which was blasted away when the railroad was built and the White people may have captured her; at any rate a picture that looked like her appeared in the paper.

Mainland Halkomelem: Katzie

In 1936 Diamond Jenness worked with Old Pierre, a famous shaman at Katzie, near Port Hammond, in what in Duff's terms would be Lower Stalo country. In describing the creatures that might be encountered in guardian spirit vision experiences, Old Pierre mentioned two creatures that Jenness identifies as "timber giants." One is the *sésqəc*, which anyone, even a White man, might meet but which does him no good since the *sésqəc* "was an ordinary creature unable to confer any power." But the other was the *šiyéýə*, which "always carried a small stick, one stroke of which would topple down a small tree, three strokes the biggest tree in the forest." Old Pierre said that a Katzie man named *sɬə́məxʷ* had obtained *šiyéýə* as a guardian spirit and could therefore perform great feats of strength (Jenness 1955:61).

It is not clear in what sense the *sésqəc* is "an ordinary creature." Other creatures that Old Pierre said might become guardian spririts include a number of mammals, birds, fishes, reptiles, and even insects, as well as inanimate things, all of which are "real" to Europeans, and also a number of beings that are "mythical" to Europeans; these last include beings that have human form but live far away where they are encountered by the wandering "vitality" of the power seeker (Jenness 1955:48-64). Perhaps what made the *sésqəc* "ordinary" to Old Pierre was its being human in attributes and nearby. Old Pierre evidently did not mention any cannibal ogress at all in this connection.

In 1952 I worked with Old Pierre's son, Simon Pierre. Information I got from Simon differed from what Jenness was told by Old Pierre in several respects. Simon knew four terms for creatures of the sort Jenness identifies as "timber giants": *sésqəc*, *šiyé·ýə*, *stíʔtaʔaɬ*, and *θáməqʷəs*. But he identified the last two as just being something like the first. He described all four as being able to disappear suddenly. Once up on Pitt Lake an old woman had a sturgeon hanging in front of her house; she saw a *sésqəc* wading toward it and so fired a rifle into the water ahead of him—and he was gone. Simon described the *šiyé·ýə* as his father had, as a creature that knocks down trees, and added that it was "the meanest of them all." But in another context he mentioned, contrary to what his father said, that the Katzie man *sɬə́məxʷ* (a famous outlaw discoverer of a lost gold mine) had obtained power from the *sésqəc*. Simon also knew of the cannibal ogress, called *qəlqəlíɬ*. She caught children and took them home in a basket and ate them. There were perhaps only one or two of these, he thought, one of which had been overpowered at Musqueam and drowned in the middle of Georgia Strait. Simon identified the cannibal ogress as a "spirit" (a word few of my informants have ever volunteered); he also said that the *sésq̓ac* can disappear "like a spirit."

Mainland Halkomelem: Musqueam

The Musqueam live at the mouth of the North Arm of the Fraser River, in what is now the city of Vancouver. I have been working on the Musqueam dialect of Halkomelem, as I have had the time, since the late 1950s, principally with the late Andrew and Christine Charles and with James Point. The term *sésq̓ac* is well known at Musqueam as the name for a large, hairy, man-like creature that lives in the woods and mountains. My informants identified this word with the *ƛ́aməkʷas* of the Cowichan of Vancouver Island. They also identified the mainland *qəlqəlíɬ* (from *q̓al*, "bad," possibly "evil seeker"), the cannibal ogress, with the *c̓awx̣éʔlac* of the Cowichan.

James Point (born 1881) dictated a text in 1963 that consists mainly of a version of the story of how the cannibal ogress was roasted in her own pit. But as an introduction he explained that the *sésq̓ac* is the male and the *qəlqəlíɬ* the female of the same species. A translation of the introductory part of the text follows:

> It must have been long ago when there were still only Indians here and everywhere on up the river too there were only Indians. There were none of those who are called "White people" but only Indian people. According to the old people, walking in the woods, everywhere away from the water, were what are called the *sésq̓ac*. They were big, resembling a person but tall, far taller than the biggest people here. And it is said that their wives were what the people called the *qəlqəlíɬ*.

> It must have been that (now deceased) *qəlqəlíɬ* who was the one who came down to the shore when it became evening and was nearly dark, carrying on her back what was called a *ƛ́pét* [identified as an open-work basket] as a container for everything that she was getting in the ground as she roamed all over the woods. These were all sorts of lizards [the word includes salamanders], frogs [including toads], and snakes, just all sorts of things like that. They were inside the basket that she carried on her back when she was going around doing that. Whenever it had become evening and nearly dark, she went from one to another of the houses of that time, sort of sneaking after the people, when the Indians had nearly gone to bed. And sometime she would catch a small child who was still outside. She would quickly jump to grab it and

80

put it into the basket that she carried.

In the rest of the text the ogress speaks, dances, and sings possessed, activities that are to some extent required by the plot of the story.

Another Musqueam text, dictated by Andrew Charles in 1960, tells how he and two other men were hunting in the Gulf Islands when they heard noises that they took to be sounds of the *k̓ʷak̓ʷəqʷnəcí·ls*, translated by Christine Charles as "The Little Choppers," felling a big Douglas fir. No description appears in the text. But James Point describes the *k̓ʷak̓ʷəqʷnəcíls* as follows:

> It's supposed to be an animal that has the habit of knocking down dead trees. It has only one leg and something in its hand to strike dead trees with. You could hear it. It's gone out of existence. You don't see them any more.

When I asked him, in another context, about the term Simon Pierre had used for the tree-striker, James Point gave it as *syéʔ·λɛʔ* and said it was "some kind of a monkey or something."

Island Halkomelem: Cowichan

There are two main dialects of Halkomelem on Vancouver Island, Nanaimo and Cowichan. I have no data from the Nanaimo, but for the Cowichan area I have several taped texts as yet untranscribed of accounts of encounters with the *żámək̓ʷəs*, identified by my Musqueam informants as the Cowichan equivalent of their *sésq̓əc*, as well as stories of the cannibal ogress. In a Cowichan story known to my Lummi informant Patrick George, the cannibal ogress was originally the daughter of *syálaċa*, the "first man" at Duncan.

Straits: Lummi

The Straits language is or was spoken by the Semiahmoo, Lummi, and Samish on the mainland between Boundary Bay and Anacortes, by the Saanich, Songhees, and Sooke on southeastern Vancouver Island, and by the Klallam on the northern shore of the Olympic Peninsula and at a colony on Vancouver Island at Beecher Bay. I did ethnographic work with Straits informants in the late 1940s and early 1950s.

At Lummi I obtained information on sasquatch-like beings from Julius Charles (born c. 1860, spent some of early years at Semiahmoo) and Patrick George (born c. 1875, spent some of early years at Cowichan and some with the Samish on Guemes Island). Both knew the *ćámək̓ʷəs* (recorded variously), which seems identical with the Cowichan *žámək̓ʷəs* and the Fraser *sésq̓əc*. I give my field notes almost verbatim:

The *čáməqʷəs* is a great tall animal or whatever it was that lived in the mountains. It was like a man but shaggy like a bear, like a big monkey 7 feet tall. They went away when the Whites came. (The Indians never killed any; it was a pretty wise animal, or whatever you call it.) If you saw one it made you kind of crazy. They throw their power toward you.

Over 40 years ago some fellow across the line went hunting deer early one morning when snow was on the ground. He saw one and followed it to the edge of a lake where it had disappeared. He went home and got kind of crazy. His wife put him to sleep by the fire (they were living in a kind of smokehouse) and while she was out getting wood he rolled into the fire and died. (He was a half-breed named Arthur—lived up toward the Fraser.) [JC]

The *čámək̓ʷəs* are big, 7 to 8 feet tall. They whistle only, can't talk. They whistle when you go out in the evening. Once some White people caught one and tried to feed him. They gave him potatoes. He picked them up, looked at them, and threw them away. They gave him meat, and he did the same thing. I guess some make you crazy. They are real *sƛ̓éləqəm*. They grow hair on the body. There are none here any more, but I guess there are some up in the mountains around Chilliwack. If a person could get one for *xʷné?m* I guess it would be pretty tough. (No, I never heard of one with it. I don't know what they eat.) [PG]

Patrick George also distinguished the *stéy?təɬ*, which look like the *čámək̓ʷəs* but are smaller, and the *čiétkʷ*, who were simply "wild Indians." Accounts of encounters with these follow:

The *stéy?təɬ* are like *čámək̓ʷəs*, but are not as big, and can talk. Once we were camped at Warner's Prairie picking hops. We were camped there about a week and one night we heard "wã·· wã·· 'ã···." When you see them, it makes you crazy. Lots of fish there, and they must have been fishing. People from the hop-fields were fishing and one man went fishing up where the dam is. He went up on horseback with a hook and got his two saddle-bags full of fish. (He was greedy.) Coming back, he heard these people and whipped his horse to go faster, but the two saddle-bags slapped the horse and he couldn't run fast. These people got him, put him unconscious, ripped the saddle-bags and all off, breaking the bellybands, and the horse came home alone. The people at the hop-yards went up to look for him with horses and buggies and found him and brought him back. An Indian doctor worked on him. At first he couldn't talk at all, he just sat and turned his head from side to side. Later he talked slowly, just a little, and told what had happened. After about a year he got worse and died. (I went up to Warner's Prairie [on the Samish River] once or twice while I was married at Guemes.) [PG]

David Crow, *sk̓ʷtá*, was a slave. Nobody knew where he came from in the first place. He was raised here and he just spoke Lummi. Once when he was a young man, he was sold from here, south, perhaps to Squally people. He didn't like it there so he ran away. On the way he was caught by *ćiétkʷ*. These were wild Indians who had some kind of poison which they could throw at a person and make him crazy. They also had whistles with which they were able to make noises like the calls of various birds. They wore no clothes but had guns. They killed beavers and dried the skins and sold them to the Whites. They left broken twigs along the road as a sign that they were out. They carried bags over their shoulders in which they had kept their equipment—the poison, which they threw by hand, and the little whistles made with two pieces of wood tied with cherry bark. They caught Crow and kept him by their campfire, but in the evening he got away and hid a short distance away in a willow tree that hung over the water. They looked for him and all night long he heard the calls of various birds which they made with their whistles. He kept thinking he was going to go out of his mind, but he would put his hand down into the water and after a bit it would revive him. In the morning they were gone. And soon an Indian with a survey party stopped and used their fireplace. Crow came out of his hiding place and spoke with the Indian in Skagit language: the Indian explained to the Whites about the *ćiétkʷ*, saying that this was the month that they came out, and that you could tell when they were about by the broken twigs along and across the road. They directed Crow to where some other Indians and Whites lived. He went there and he was given a canoe and some food and directions as to how to get back to Lummi. [PG]

Both of these informants also knew *ćəwx̣éʔləc*, a cannibal ogress who is clearly the same as the Cowichan *ćəwx̣éʔləc* and the Fraser *qəlqəlíł*. Julius Charles described her as a huge fat woman who stole children, put them in a basket she carried on her back, took them off and roasted and ate them. One place where she "napped kids" was at a stream on Birch Bay. When he told me this, early in my field work, I assumed that it was just a story told to children to keep them quiet, but both Julius and Mrs. Charles insisted that this had really happened. As proof, they said, there is a place on Vancouver Island where the ogress cooked the children; there were a lot of stones and a big pole she used that lasted many years without rotting so that it was pointed out as a local wonder. The ogress was finally killed, they said, by a number of people from several tribes armed with arrows and spears. It was not clear from this whether there was one ogress or several, but another Lummi I only worked with briefly, Elizabeth Malenberg, told two ogress stories; one accounted for how the ogress was destroyed at Lummi and the second for how she was destroyed at Guemes Island. Patrick George knew a Cowichan story accounting for the origin of the ogress and gave an account of how an ogress was captured.

Once we heard of it, it might be just a story. They were fixing the railroad tracks, slashing. [This was the Esquimalt-Nanaimo RR.] There were lots of tents. Every time they came home, and there was no flour or bacon, so they got more. This happened again. So someone got a rifle and waited by a hollow stump. An old woman came with a big sack on her back. She ate the flour, sometimes 2 or 3 bags, or she shook her back and a bag opened up and she put it in there. They followed her to a cave in the mountains. A blacksmith made a trap and they set it with a sack of flour for bait. It caught her with a sort of handcuff. When she pulled away, 10 men pretty nearly got beat, holding the line. One half-breed there claimed to understand her and said she said, "*kʷés, nəʔiŋəs*" [let me go, grandchild?]. After that they got her locked up in a wire wagon. She bent it trying to get out. Then she started to cry. It rained a heavy rain. They got her down to camp and put her on a train for Victoria. They claim they sent her over to old Queen Mary [Victoria?] but they got tired of it, because it eats too much. After that she got tame. Maybe this is just a story. I heard it at Cowichan when I was growing yet. It was supposed to be *čəwxéləč̌*. It was a little woman but awful strong.

Patrick George also told about a tree-stalker:

There is a kind of person you sometimes see in the woods. He is a short and hairy man with a cane. He walks with it and hits trees with it. When he hits a tree it falls over. He is called *šəčəčičələ* in Lummi.

Once a Matsqui man named *sxʷəcsé·nəm* went out to *k̓ʷčást* [seek a vision] and saw a big tree fall with its top coming toward him. He saw something moving in the thick branches of the top and so he jumped in among them and caught the thing. It put him to sleep right away. When he woke up he was sitting nicely with his head against a log. It became his *xʷné?m* [shaman's guardian spirit].

Finally, Julius Charles and Patrick George each knew a story about a woman who married a man-like sea being and became a sea being herself. One was a Semiahmoo legend set at Point Roberts, the other a Samish legend set at Deception Pass. In the latter the woman gradually acquired the non-human attributes of her husband and so was told by her family not to return.

Straits: Saanich

At East Saanich, Louie Pelkey (born c. 1870) told me about the *ẑáməkʷəs*, the cannibal woman, and the tree-stalker.

The *ẑáməkʷəs*, he said, were wild Indians who lived on the high mountain behind Malahat. They look like people but they cannot bend their legs; they hop but they cannot go very fast. They "belong to Malahat." The Saanich used to call the Malahat people *ẑáməkʷəs* because they were husky and tall; perhaps the Malahat were partly the descendants of *ẑáməkʷəs*. On the mountain behind Malahat they threw rocks at strangers. Once when he was hunting deer there rocks came down into camp. There is a hole in the mountain above and that must be where they live.

While the *ẑáməkʷəs*, in Louie Pelkey's view, may have become human, the ogress was a woman gone wild. He gave the following account of her:

Once a woman was lost up in the bush. She was gone a long time and people thought she was dead. But pretty soon they saw that woman in the bush. She was small, but normal size, but she had turned into something like an animal. She must have had a place two miles or so away up from here. Pretty soon there were two of them. They came into houses and took things. People here saw them. They would come into the house and you wouldn't think they would be dangerous.

This sort of person is called *čuxélič*. They took dry salmon. Sometimes they made themselves very small and very old. At other times they were big, tall as the ceiling. They watched people fishing and when they saw them come back they came and loaded up their baskets with fish. They also came to the spit for crabs. Sometimes

85

they heard talking and came like ghosts. They had a roasting ground up there but you can't find it.

They must have been killed out. They came from Saanich but they got wild. They ate persons too. They got children and took them up there. They got soft pitch and pitched the children's eyes shut in order to roast them. Once there were ten kids going to be roasted. One bigger boy closed his eyes very tight, I guess it was his help came to his mind to do that. The fire was red hot then. In a few minutes' time they were going to roast those children and eat them. All the other children were small and could not see. The one opened his eyes and the pitch was on his lids so he could see. There he saw čuxéličʼ dancing in front of the fire. He saw a stick lying there so he raised it up between her legs and tripped her. Then with the stick he pushed her into the fire. The boy worked at his eyes so that he could see well and went down and told the people to bring up oil, ratfish, or dogfish oil, to rub the kids' eyes with. They got the oil, came up, and saw čuxéličʼ burned there.

That's how one was killed. There must have been more since one was drowned off D'Arcy Island. A young man was out one fine day spearing crabs and flounders, singing as he went along. He saw a woman walking way up here [south of the spit]. He knew it must be čuxéličʼ. (The beach was clear then, no logs and drift-wood.) The woman hollered, "What are you doing?" He kept on singing. "You better come over here; I'm going with you." He thought what should he do. Pretty soon he thought, "I'm going to get her." When he came close, she said, "Where are you going?" He said, "To D'Arcy Island to catch fish. You can go along." She got in. The young man was getting crabs with a spear. He told the old woman to lie flat with her arms and legs spread so as not to rock the canoe. The crabs piled up beside the young man. The young man said to the crabs, "Go bite her behind." (Of course you know they didn't wear much clothes.) She said, "What did you say?" He said, "I told the crabs to be quiet." When he got way out he told the crabs again to bite her. They did so. She howled and turned over so he was able to push her out and under, crabs and all. That was way out past D'Arcy; that's why we call that rock čuxéličʼ. That was the last one.

The two stories of the destruction of the ogress are very like the two Mrs. Malenberg told at Lummi. I asked Louie Pelkey if this account was a sxʷiyém, a myth. He said no, it was not, and then told me a Star Husband story as an example of a sxʷiyém.

Louie Pelkey also knew of a tree-striker. He had once seen a tree fall and asked his uncle Harry what had happened. His uncle said it was "a person that you don't see" called šəččəlísələ, who hits trees and knocks them down. There were many, he said, on Pender Island, and he told of an encounter with one.

> Once on Narvaez Bay Harry wouldn't make a fire on the beach. He hung onto the kelp in a dark place and covered himself with a dark blanket. The moon shone. He never slept. His wife was along. He looked at the hill and pretty soon he heard a deer coming down. He watched with a Kentucky rifle.Then he saw a man coming. The man walked with a cane and came down towards him. About fifty feet above him was a tree. The man looked down and Harry thought, "The man must know we're here." He was almost going to shoot him, then said, "I'll wait," and told his wife to let go of the kelp, and they pulled up the bay. Then the tree came down right where the canoe had been. Harry looked to shoot but saw the man no more. (When a tree falls it means a close relation will pass away.)

Straits: Klallam

The only Klallam person I have worked with any length of time was Henry Charles (born c. 1875) of Becher Bay. He told me briefly of two beings of man-like appearance, čiétkʷ and stítəɬ.

> The čiétkʷ are giants. They have no joints in their legs so they are stiff. They are seen in the mountains on Vancouver Island and on the mainland. If they chase you, climb up because they can't go uphill fast; if you go down they would catch you in a few jumps.
> The stítəɬ are like us but wild. They make you sleep. When the Klallam went fishing on Hood's Canal, they made people sleep and took their fish away. They can talk like an eagle, owl, screechowl, and bluejay. They say there are some yet there on that side [on the Olympic Peninsula] but they are hard to find.

These have the same names as two of the three beings described by Patrick George at Lummi, but Henry Charles's čiétkʷ has the gait of the žamakʷəs of Louie Pelkey at Saanich.
  The Klallam also told stories about a cannibal woman, named slápu (Gunther 1925:148-51).

Puget Sound

The Puget Sound language is (or was) spoken in several different dialects from the Samish and Skagit valleys of Northwestern Washington southward to the Puyallup and Nisqually drainages at the head of Puget Sound itself. I have no field notes from Puget Sound speakers on sasquatch-like beings, but there are references in the published works on the area that relate to the data I have already presented.

The speakers of Puget Sound seem to have known three kinds of—or known three terms for—man-like forest beings or "wild people." The terms are something like: 1) čyátkʷuʔ, 2) qəlúsabš, and 3) stítał. One source goes back to the middle of the last century.

George Gibbs collected information on the Puget Sound area in the 1850s that was published in his *Tribes of Western Washington and Northwest Oregon* in 1877. In the body of this work there is no mention of sasquatch-like beings, but there is in the appended "Dictionary of the Niskwalli." In the Niskwalli-English section (Gibbs 1877:305), is the entry: "Tsi-át-ko, *a race of spirits who haunt fishing places.*" And in the English-Niskwalli section, under the heading "Mythological Characters" (Gibbs 1877:308), there are mentioned as belonging to the myth age the "Ke-ló-sumsh *or* ke-ló-sām-ish, *giant hunters of the mountains,*" and there is the further note: "Tsé-at-ko are a race supposed still to exist, haunting fishing-grounds and carrying off salmon and young girls at night."

Hermann Haeberlin worked in the central Puget Sound area in 1916-17 and his work was augmented and edited by Erna Gunther in the 1920s and published as *The Indians of Puget Sound* (Haeberlin and Gunther 1930). In this work, under "Intertribal Relations," we find the following:

> The Sound tribes seemed to have some knowledge of the people of the interior. They mentioned the stē'tał, identified by Teit as the Thompson. He believed that these tribes lived on the Fresh River [Fraser River?]. They called these people "wild tribes" who traveled by night and attacked lone wayfarers. They were cowards, never attacking larger groups, so they had no real wars with the Sound Indians. They spoke a language unintelligible to the Snohomish. The Sound Indians said that the stē'tał used to be savages but they had become civilized now.
>
> Another tribe they mentioned are the qlō'sabc, which has not been identified. These people were supposed to be "savages" living in underground houses.[18] The Snohomish did not know exactly where the qlō'sabc lived permanently, for they roamed over the country most of the time. They were supposed to be "built like giants" and were noted for their thieving. [The footnote reads,

"This fact leads one to believe that this was an Interior Salish tribe, if it is not altogether mythical."]

An amateur folklorist, Nels Bruseth, also believes that beliefs about the stítał were based on experience with real people. Bruseth collected folklore among the Stillaguamish and the Suiattle and Sauk of the Upper Skagit area, evidently beginning around 1910. According to Bruseth (n.d.:14-15) the "Steetathls" were regarded as

> . . . strange and ghostlike Indians, who traveled about and had to be appeased or guarded against, to prevent thievery or murder. There were certain trails that were unsafe; strange tracks had been seen on them. There were noises in the night, chirping and whistling, not of birds. There were disappearances of Indian children, all charged to the Steetathls.

Bruseth finds the source of these beliefs in traditions of real conflict, which he estimates occurred around 1800, between the Skagit people and "King George Indians" over hunting territory above the mouth of "Steetathle Creek." Bruseth gives an account of the conflict based on several versions. The creek he refers to is probably Stetattle Creek, which flows into the Skagit just below the present Diablo Dam. This area was very likely used by hunting parties of Thompson and perhaps other interior Salish (Spier 1936:39).

On the other hand, Marian W. Smith, who worked in the southern Puget Sound area in 1935-36, seems to have seen no real basis to similar beliefs. In her ethnography *The Puyallup-Nisqually* (1940:129-30), under the heading "Mythological Beings," she describes a "race of tall Indians, called 'wild' or 'stick' Indians . . . said to wander through the forests." These were usually referred to as "tsiátko" though also as "stetá'ł, from ta'ł, spear." It was said that they were about mainly at night, they lived by hunting and fishing; their homes were like the dens of animals; their language was a kind of whistle, often heard when they could not be seen; they could not travel by water; they stole fish from Indians' nets and drying racks; they could paralyze human beings with their whistle and so could play tricks, such as removing a man's clothes and tying his legs apart; if harmed they would kill a man with their arrows; and they sometimes stole children or adolescents for wives or slaves. Smith gives an account of one giant boy that was captured and another of one that was killed. She also quotes a similar description of this being given by James Wickersham (1898).

At least two of the three terms given above have been in recent use. Warren Snyder (1968) in his dictionary of southern Puget Sound gives the entries čyátko and stétał both glossed as "wild men said to wander in the woods and be dangerous (Smith 1940)." Also, Thom Hess (n.d.), in an unpublished

Stem List of Northern Puget Sound, has an entry *čyátk^wu?* or *či?átk^wu?* 'wild people.'

In Puget Sound beliefs there is also a cannibal woman (*jə́g^wa*), but as far as I know she has not been associated with the "wild people." In a story given by Snyder (1968:61), however, she removes a man's heart, like the sasquatch in one of the accounts Duff gives.

The Puget Sound people also believed in a race of dwarfs called "Little Earths," who could make people crazy and who had to be propitiated (Smith 1940:130-33). They do not appear to be like the tree-strikers of the Halkomelem-Straits area.

Twana

The Twana occupied the shores of Hood Canal and the drainage of the Skokomish River. W.W. Elmendorf, who worked with them beginning in the late 1930s, describes (1960:532-34) sasquatch-like beings as one of several kinds of dangerous beings that were not acquired as guardian spirits.

> Mountain and forest giants (*c'iátqo*) were generally referred to in English as "stick Indians," the Chinook Jargon term stík meaning "forest." These creatures were of human form, taller than normal human beings, lived in the mountains or rough foothill forests, went naked except for a breech clout, had odorless bodies which enabled them to walk up to game and kill it before the animal scented them, and could climb vertical cliffs and leap great distances. They were usually invisible. People feared the *c'iátqo* but seem to have suffered little harm from them beyond occasional thefts of killed game. Henry Allen had heard they could "make people crazy" but did not know how this was done. They did not function as soul stealers.

Other beings of human form were the underwater people who lived in plank houses at the bottom of Hood Canal and who had occasionally taken human wives; the earth dwarfs ("little earths") who lived in nooks, crannies, and forest recesses and could control the game and steal human souls; and possibly (it is not clear how human the shape) the wet-cedar-tree ogre, who could put unsuspecting hunters to sleep and steal their souls.

Quinault

The Quinault are one of several peoples who speak (or spoke) forms of the Olympic branch of the Salish family but they are the only one of this group for whom we have much information. Their villages were nearly all on the Quinault River, which flows into the Pacific about half way between the Columbia River and Cape Flattery. Their closest contacts were with their neighbors facing the open ocean but they also had some contact via the Chehalis River with the peoples of southern Puget Sound and Hood Canal, with whom they shared some notions about "giants." Ronald Olson worked with them in 1925-27; his oldest informant, Bob Pope, was born in the 1830s. Of the "giants" Olson (1936:170) says:

> In the mountains live many giants, called *tsadja'tko* or *tsa'áloh*, who look almost the same as humans. On their right big toe a long quartz spike grows up to six feet long. If a human is kicked with this he will likely die. They are great thieves. People avoid the creeks on which they live. Some still come around the village at night and borrow a harpoon or a drift net, but usually return it before morning. They are fond of playing tricks on humans, such as sneaking up and kicking them, tying them to trees with thongs lashed to the genitals, etc. Some even married humans, and even today there are people living who are half *tsa'áloh*. The giants can often be heard at night. Even if their whistling sounds far off it is certain that they are close.

Olson adds two narratives, one telling of an encounter where a man managed to surprise a giant, described as having a hornlike growth on his head with a light at the end, and frighten him away; the other telling of a giant who murdered five men and was killed in a mass attack by the men of several villages.

The Quinault term Olson recorded as "*tsadjátko*" is almost certainly identifiable with the Puget Sound term Hess recorded as *c̓yátkʷuʔ* and its Twana and Straits counterparts. Most of this description, except notably the toe spikes and the headlamp, sound like attributes of the *c̓yátkʷuʔ*. The term "*tsáaloh*" may have actually referred to a different being since it occurs again in another context.

Earlier in his ethnography, Olson (1936:145-50) gives his informants' descriptions of various beings that may become guardian spirits, some of which were referred to by the Chinook Jargon word *skukúm*, "strong," "powerful being," "dangerous being." But Olson says (1936:146) "there was no sharp distinction between the 'real *skukúms*,' who were cannibal women named *oéh* and those called *skukúm mátikulc* or *hecáitomixw* (devil of the forest), who live in the high hills and mountains.'' Some of these *skukums* appear as men or women and may marry human beings. (Once near the mouth of the Hoh a female *skukum* even came into a White man's cabin and climbed into bed with him; he had sexual relations with her but ''at the moment of orgasm he fell dead'' and she died too.) In this context Olson gives an informant's account of a *''skukum* spirit'' called *''tsáãloh''* (one of the two terms later identified as ''giants'') who had icicle-like toenails that he kicked people with; he was once a man, had become a monster, and was ultimately killed by human beings.

Squamish

The Squamish live north of the Musqueam, formerly occupying the shores of Howe Sound and the valley of the Squamish River. They tell about a kind of wild people called *smáy?it*. Aert H. Kuipers has recently (1969:23-28) re-elicited a story, originally recorded by Charles Hill-Tout before 1900, accounting for the origin of these wild people, and he has recorded two more stories of encounters with them. These people are said to be the descendants of a chief's daughter and a slave who were abandoned but escaped into the mountains. They are described as big, but otherwise there is nothing in the stories suggesting the *sésq̓ǝc* of their neighbors to the south.

I have presented data on the beliefs of a number of Coast Salish peoples, but this is certainly not an exhaustive study. There are no doubt published sources that I have missed within the area I have tried to cover, and there is unpublished material—even in my own possession in the form of untranscribed tapes. Also, I have covered only a fraction of the territory that might be covered in the pursuit of Native traditions about sasquatch-like beings.

I said at the beginning of this paper that I could see no real/mythical or natural/supernatural dichotomies in Coast Salish thought. I believe this view is supported by the material I have presented and also by the problems some ethnographers have had in presenting their data when they have tried to use these dichotomies. But there is in Coast Salish thought, I believe, a largely implicit dichotomy of human vs. non-human. I will return to this later.

I also suggested at the beginning that we cannot simply assume that the various terms for sasquatch-like beings refer to the same entity but must demonstrate it. How many sasquatch-like beings do the data suggest? Here is a tentative taxonomy:

I. The *stítǝł* as described by all or nearly all sources appear to be unfriendly strangers. Smith derives the term from 'spear' (harpoon?), which could imply the strangers were fishermen, but I suggest that it is identifiable with Halkomelem *stéytǝł* 'from upriver' and that it originally simply referred to the direction the strangers came from. The *ċyétkʷ* of the Lummi informant Patrick

George sound like his *stítəɬ* under another name. The Squamish *smáyʔiɬ* are also simply strangers.

II. The Halkomelem and Straits tree-strikers, though called by various terms, sound somewhat similar, and I would be inclined to equate them and suggest a common source for the belief, though not necessarily a real animal.

III. The Puget Sound and Twana "Little Earths" resemble each other but differ, I think, from the more northerly tree-strikers. (I should mention that throughout the whole area covered another dwarf people, called *qʷiqʷəstáy-məxʷ* or something of the sort, are known, but only in a story in which they live far to the north or off in the ocean.)

IV. The cannibal ogress has pretty nearly the same image throughout the area, stabilized no doubt by the roaster-roasted story. It seems that only James Point at Musqueam has explicitly connected her with any of the other beings.

V. If we subtract all of these, we are left with: 1. the Stalo *sésqəc*, 2. the Cowichan and Saanich *žáməkʷəs*, 3. the Lummi *čáməkʷəs*, 4. the Klallam *čyétkʷ*, 5. the Puget Sound *čyátkʷuʔ*, 6. the Twana *čiátqo*, and 7. the Quinault *cəjátko*. Clearly 2 and 3 are cognate terms and so are 4, 5, 6, and 7. It is tempting to equate them all and conclude that they are simply different words for the same thing. However, the descriptions we have of them do not really give them many common attributes.

All are giants, human in form but bigger than ordinary human beings, and all live in the woods and mountains. But beyond these attributes there is not another thing mentioned by all accounts. The next most common attribute is nocturnal habits, mentioned by all but the Saanich and Klallam informants. Since their descriptions were brief, this may be simply an accidental omission. All but the Lummi, Saanich, and Klallam informants mentioned stealing food from people, which might also be an accidental omission, except that Patrick George at Lummi ascribed theft of food to the other two kinds of beings that sound like real human beings. Only the Stalo and Lummi accounts describe their giants as hairy. The Twana account, moreover, says their giants went naked except for a breech clout, which suggests to me that they were no different from ordinary human beings in pelage. Only the Saanich and Klallam accounts mentioned abnormal walking, but the Stalo and Twana accounts mentioned unusual speed. Lummi, Puget Sound, and Quinault accounts mentioned whistling; Stalo, Puget Sound, and Quinault the theft of women. Other attributes appear less often. I have tentatively listed them as Table 1. It is quite possible that further investigation would put more plusses on the list. But as things stand it seems we can only say that most if not all of the Coast Salish of this area seem to agree that there are large, man-like beings in the woods and mountains who differ from human beings in various ways.*

---

*[In my contribution to Halpin and Ames 1980, I summarized this as "the Sasquatch-like creatures of the Native peoples have a range of attributes somewhat wider and less

Why should the Coast Salish believe this? Why should they have these traditions about giants in the woods and mountains? I see several possible answers, which are not mutually exclusive:

1. There is a real animal there—a big non-human primate perhaps—and experience with this animal confirms and perpetuates the tradition.

The existence of a large non-human primate would account for the image of big, hairy *sÉsqÉc*, the big footprints, the frightening encounters, possibly the theft of food, and the whistling. But a large non-human primate would not really steal women—though the gorilla was once accused of this, nor trick people by tying them up, nor kick them with spiked feet, nor have some of the other attributes ascribed to one or another giant.

If there is a real animal, shouldn't there be better descriptions in the ethnographic literature? Not necessarily. Anthropologists do not consciously suppress information, but they sometimes do not know what to do with it. There are ethnographies of peoples whom I know to have traditions of sasquatch-like beings that make no mention of such traditions; I suspect that these omissions occur not because the writers had never heard of the traditions but because they did not know how to categorize them.

If there is a real animal, why should it be given fanciful attributes, like unbendable legs or odorless bodies? Because people make things up? Well, if people could have made up unbendable legs and odorless bodies, couldn't they have also made up seven-foot, hairy sasquatches? Of course they could have, but as I suggested earlier, we might think they made up beavers too, if we did not know better.

2. There were real people there—hostile strangers in the mountains—who were so little known they could be given non-human attributes.

Interior Salish and Sahaptins did cross over the Cascades into the upper drainages of coast rivers. At an earlier time, the ancestors of the Athapaskans who lived in historic times in the hills near the mouth of the Columbia must have passed through Coast Salish country, probably as inland hunters, possibly not inclined to establish friendly relations with the river and salt-water people. Such inland hunters could easily account for the theft of women and children as well as food, perhaps for the mysterious whistling (Patrick George gave them whistles, remember) and even for tying people up. But they would not have been seven feet tall, nor covered with hair, nor leave giant footprints.

---

consistent than what we might expect a real animal to have." I also had to report the discovery that George Gibbs (Clark 1955-56:313-15) had "anticipated me by more than a century in commenting on this variation in attributes."]

Besides, there are names for real people—*stitəł*, etc. as distinguished from giants. On the other hand, if there were several such incursions of real people, then possibly some became better known and recognized as human, while others remained mysterious and non-human.

3. There are natural events that are better explained by the hypothesis of forest and mountain beings than by competing hypotheses.

Rocks fall; trees fall; there are strange noises in the mountains; children and even adults do get lost; women do run away. How are these things explained? Marian W. Smith (1940:131-32) cites Wickersham's (1898) account of how the Little Earths cause a person to get lost and comments to the effect that the belief makes sense in "a culture where accident as such did not exist." Did the Coast Salish have no concept "accident"? I do not believe we can answer the question yet. Native theories of intention, responsibility, causality, etc. are matters for linguistics—grammatical and textual analysis—and currently a number of people are working on Salish languages, so the question may be answered. But it has seemed to me that some of my informants, Patrick George for one, have operated without a concept "natural death." In his narratives (given in English) no one died but what some entity that in my tradition, but not his, would be called "supernatural" had entered or left the body. Perhaps there was simply no theory of deterioration of the body with age; so people just cannot die of natural causes.

Perhaps then in the Native view, trees do not simply grow old and fall; they have to be pushed. Rocks do not simply loosen through erosion and fall; if you are below them, they are thrown at you; if you are above them, they are not rocks at all but beings capable of bounding away at great speed—but only downhill since they cannot bend their legs.

In human relations perhaps sexual attraction and affection between husband and wife do not simply deteriorate through time; love potions, spells, and *skukums* steal them away. For both parties to a separation this hypothesis may be more satisfactory than the alternatives our culture offers.

4. The belief in forest and mountain beings promotes behavior that helps perpetuate the belief.

That is, the beliefs do not merely offer better explanations for observable events (as in 3) but reward the believers with something more than just the satisfaction of their curiosity. This is of course not an answer to the question of how the beliefs originated but only to the question of how they are maintained and modified once they are there.

Do, for example, beliefs in unreal dangers protect people from real dangers? Possibly if there are real people in the mountains who may steal women and children, there is survival value in imagining that they have superhuman proportions and powers.

Perhaps too, beliefs in imagined localized dangers may promote the specialization in subsistence activities that seems to me to have been basic to Coast Salish social organization (Suttles 1960a). I have been writing here as if beliefs were uniform within a village or dialect area, but they probably were not. Within a single village different persons followed professions requiring special skills and knowledge, which they closely guarded. Thus it may be that a mountain-goat hunter knew very well that certain whistling in the mountains came from marmots or pikas (animals that live only at high altitudes) but preferred to let others believe it was sasquatches; at the same time he might subscribe to the sasquatch hypothesis himself to explain less common events such as falling rocks.

As another, I hope not too far-fetched example, the Twana belief in the wet-cedar-tree ogre (who stole the souls of hunters who loitered under wet cedar trees) may have kept some Twana hunters from spending too much time on rainy days under cedar trees and promoted their hunting success. This success gave the hunter an audience respectful of his beliefs, which got perpetuated. In this case the belief also provides an explanation of failure for the hunter who succumbed to the temptation of resting under a cedar tree.

5. The existence of sasquatch-like beings makes the world more intelligible.

This is to suggest that the beliefs do more than explain specific events like the falling of a rock or the loss of a woman but that they are "myths" in the sense that they reflect some fundamental truths about the world.

Two basic truths for the Coast Salish, as perhaps for all non-Western peoples, are: man stands apart from nature and yet man depends upon nature. (For Western peoples it seems to be man stands apart from and must dominate nature.) How can these truths be presented? More specifically, how can we define man as something apart from nature and how can we make his dependence on nature acceptable?

One way the Coast Salish separate man from nature is by showing how dangerous it is to cross the barrier that separates the human from the non-human. Thus the Upper Stalo woman who married a sésq̓əc became unconscious, first when she was captured by her non-human husband and again, after she had developed non-human attributes, when she returned to human society. The Samish woman who married a sea-being under Deception Pass began to sprout sea-weed and could not return at all. And that encounter in the cabin on the Hoh was fatal to both parties.

Perhaps another way of separating man from nature and defining humanity is through images of non-human beings that are minimally different from human beings. Giants, gnomes, etc. around the world may provide these images and our sasquatch-like beings may provide them for the Coast Salish.

Mary M. Young (1970) suggests that belief in these figures is akin to racism, since racism consists of defining other peoples as non-human. In this connection I should point out that although the Coast Salish terms that originally meant "person" or "people" now mean "Indian" as contrasted to "White," it seems that before Europeans arrived these terms were not reserved for members of one's own village, language group, or even the Coast Salish social organization consisting of overlapping networks established by marriage and containing no discrete, bounded social units. Thus the human/non-human boundary was much less restricted here than in parts of the world where there are we-groups who define themselves as the only true human beings. This means that the Coast Salish images of minimally non-human beings were not based on real neighbors of different customs, language, or skin color; it does not mean, however, that they always treated each other humanely.

For the Coast Salish, man's dependence on nature is shown in two ways, which are patterned after human relationships. First, there is the relationship between the individual human being and a non-human being seen in a vision (the "guardian spirit" relationship), which is a kind of partnership. Probably most persons had vision experiences, and in a sense then there was a "myth" for every person. Sasquatch-like beings seem rarely if ever to have become guardian spirits. Perhaps they are too similar to human beings.

Second, there can be a relationship (in the Halkomelem- and Straits-speaking area anyway) between a local group and some non-human being or population, established by a mythical marriage and therefore an affinal relationship. Marriages with sasquatch-like beings establishing such ties seem rare. The Upper Stalo marriage with a sésqəc was not permanent, though the woman did leave a child behind. The Quinault marriages with skukums sound more like guardian spirit relationships. But perhaps the real meaning of that fatal encounter in the cabin on the Hoh is that White men cannot establish affinal ties with nature.

I do not mean to suggest that people consciously invent stories and beliefs to illustrate great truths. I would suggest rather that when the people are presented with alternatives they choose the ones that make the most sense to them. Possibly they have chosen to believe some things about sasquatch-like beings in this fashion.

The problem with the kind of speculation I have just engaged in is that it has some of the same circularity of some kinds of functional analysis, e.g., we observe practice A, we postulate that there is a need X that it serves, we are asked how we know there is a need X, and we answer that it is obvious because there is a practice A to serve it. I may be simply inferring the "basic truths" from the beliefs I see as embodying them. Others may find quite different ones. They may also find the sasquatch-like beings playing a more central role in Coast Salish mythology than I have been able to cast them in.

6. People enjoy believing in scary things.

There seems to be plenty of evidence around that people enjoy talking about scary things and appreciate a well-told story about a frightening experience. Is the esthetic experience of listening to such a story heightened by belief? Are we tempted to believe because it makes life more exciting?

Also, if you are alone in the mountains and something bounds away from under your feet and the hair rises on the back of your neck, isn't it perhaps more comfortable to believe that it was something truly frightening than to admit that you were scared by a mere rock?

I have given all the possible and defensible reasons I can think of for the Coast Salish belief that there are giant man-like beings in the woods and mountains. There may be other possibilities that I have not thought of.[2] It does not seem to me that any one of these reasons is sufficient to account for the diversity of the beliefs. It seems more likely that these beliefs have grown out of several sources and have been maintained in several ways. One of the sources may have been a real man-like animal. But I must reluctantly admit that as I have presented the data and organized the arguments, I have found its track getting fainter. On the other hand, I have had some new thoughts about the Coast Salish, which is reward enough. I must agree with Young (1970) that studying people's beliefs tells us more about the people than about what they believe in. And of course, as Green (1968) was well aware when he challenged us anthropologists, we can neither prove nor disprove the existence of sasquatches by ethnography anyway, any more than we could use it to prove or disprove the existence of beavers.

---

[2] I can also think of a few impossible and indefensible reasons, e.g., a. sasquatches exist but they are supernatural, b. sasquatches exist but they are extra-terrestrial. The latter sort of hypothesis, which I have not yet heard but expect to, seems especially appealing to those who, in the Western scientific tradition, reject the supernatural as such but do not want to give up myths as concretely real. For them, a comet causes the earth to stand still for Joshua at Jericho, angels descend from flying saucers, and Jesus Christ is Commander-in-Chief of Cosmic Affairs. Surely a better way of having your cake and eating it too is to look for truths about ourselves in myths rather than for truths about external reality—providing of course that we know a myth when we see one.

Table 1

	Stalo sésģəc	Lummi c̓amək̓ʷəs	Saanich z̓amək̓ʷəs	Klallam c̓yétk̓ʷ	Puget Sound c̓yátk̓ʷuʔ	Twana c̓iátqo	Quinault c̓əjátko
giant size	+	+	+	+	+	+	+
in woods/mountains	+	+	+	+	+	+	+
nocturnal	+	+			+	+	+
hairy	+	+					
breech clout						+	
stiff legs				+	+		
fast	+					+	
whistle		+			+		+
speak	+	-					
steal food	+				+	+	+
steal women	+				+		+
have half-human child	+						
steal children					+		
cause unconsciousness					+		
make crazy		+				+	
kill people	+						+
trick people					+		+
travel by water	+				-		
odorless						+	
spike on toe							+

99

7. Productivity and its Constraints: a Coast Salish Case*

On the Northwest Coast in historic times the area to the south of the Kwakiutl seems to have produced far less carving and painting than the area to the north. But a number of carvings of high quality—both naturalistic and stylized—produced in a part of the Coast Salish area suggest that neither technical skill nor stylistic tradition was a limiting factor. Why then did Coast Salish carvers not produce more? This is the question asked recently by Bill Reid in a discussion (Holm and Reid 1975:58-61) of an especially fine Coast Salish spindle whorl (Fig. 10a). Reid asked, in effect, when they could produce such a well designed and executed piece as this, why did the Coast Salish not produce more such pieces and more kinds of art? Bill Holm commented that the answer must lie in the whole Coast Salish way of life, as indeed it must. In this paper I shall present an analysis of the art (in the sense of carving and painting) of this part of the Coast Salish area, trying to show what features of their way of life may have limited productivity, and I shall try to show what I think this analysis implies for the reconstruction of Northwest Coast culture history.

*[Read at the Conference on Northwest Coast Studies, 12-16 May 1976, Simon Fraser University, and published in *Indian Art Traditions of the Northwest Coast*, edited by Roy Carlson (Burnaby, B.C.: Archaeology Press, Simon Fraser University 1984), pp. 67-87.]

Historical Hypothesis

But first let me dispose of a couple of answers to Reid's question that might easily occur to anyone who has read the general and popular works on the Northwest Coast. One of these might be: The Coast Salish did not produce much good work because the whole of Northwest Coast art was a northern development that has only recently diffused southward; the peoples living south of the Wakashan were merely imitating Wakashan (Kwakiutl or Nootka) versions of northern art (Drucker 1955a:162,181). But several facts argue against this view. The area in which people decorated some of their containers, canoes, and houses with carvings and paintings representing human or animal forms extended southward at least as far as the Chinookans of the Lower Columbia Valley. There the earliest European visitors, in the late eighteenth and early nineteenth century, saw house fronts "painted in the form of a human-like face with open mouth, or legs, straddling the doorway, holding up the roof" (Siverstein n.d.). In 1846 Paul Kane painted the interior of a "ceremonial lodge" somewhere near Fort Vancouver, showing a house-post carved in the form of a humanoid face and a carved wooden screen topped by confronting animals (Harper 1971, pl. xxxvii). Before the great epidemic of 1830 the Chinookan area was probably more densely populated than the Wakashan area and the Chinookans probably outnumbered the Wakashans (Kroeber 1939:135-36). The Chinookans were probably not in direct contact with any Wakashans, but certainly received from Nootkans, in trade through intervening Salishans, dentalia shells. They may also have received Wakashan slaves and decorated objects, both of which could have been sources of Wakashan influence. But to suppose that a population numbering in the thousands could produce no art that was not mere imitation of Wakashan art is preposterous. Also, there is a prehistoric tradition of stone sculpture on the Lower Columbia (Wingert 1952, Butler 1957) that seems to have a respectable antiquity, perhaps beginning c. A.D. 200 (Pettigrew 1976), which could more easily be the source of historic carving in wood. Moreover, some distinctive styles have been iden-tified in the historical materials from the Coast Salish and Chinookan areas, by Wingert (1949a, 1949b) and Holm (1972), which are clearly not simpli-fied versions of something Wakashan.

Another answer to Reid's question might be: The Coast Salish did not produce much good work because they were "johnny-come-latelies" recently emerged from the interior who had not yet had time to shed their Plateau heritage and acquire a decent foundation in Northwest Coast art from their Wakashan neighbours. Or, considering that art may be old on the Lower Columbia, we might add—from their Chinookan neighbours. But this theory of recent Salish emergence from the interior, which goes back to Boas, has little to support it. The supposed evidence for it from physical anthropology seems to have been an illusion; the archaeological evidence can be read either way (to support cultural replacement or cultural continuity); and the linguistic evidence is, if anything, against it, suggesting rather a homeland for Proto-Salish on the coast and an early movement into the interior. For all we know, the Salishan languages have been spoken on the coast for as long as the Wakashan languages. Without the biological, archaeological, and linguistic evidence for Salish emergence from the interior, the ethnological arguments become very weak. With no proof that there was a time when the Wakashan had plank houses, sea-mammal hunting, and social stratification while the Salish did not, we cannot argue that the Salish got these things from the Wakashans except by begging the question. And if we try to use such supposed borrowings as evidence of Salish emergence, we may find ourselves arguing in a circle—the Coast Salish must have borrowed these features of coast culture from the Wakashans because they came from the interior where they could not have had them; the Coast Salish must have come out of the interior because they have these features of coast culture they borrowed from the Wakashans. This circular argument seems to be supported by presuppositions about Wakashan creativity and Salishan imitativeness. (I am expanding this discussion elsewhere.) Now, I am not saying that the Salish have never borrowed anything from the Wakashans or other neighbours. Borrowing in all directions has probably occurred many times. But in each case only careful study will show which direction the trait went. Art is no exception.

Which Coast Salish?

But before I return to art I must establish clearly *which* Coast Salish I shall be talking about and what position they occupy within the Coast Salish area. This is essential because from the literature one might also easily get the impression, on the one hand, that the whole Coast Salish area was culturally homogeneous, or on the other, that the Coast Salish of Puget Sound were somehow the most typical or true Coast Salish while those living farther north were peripheral deviants. Neither of these impressions would be correct. There were a dozen or more Coast Salish languages spoken through a continuous area extending from Johnstone Strait in the north to the Columbia River in the south. The speakers of these languages seem to have formed a biological and social continuum, which may have extended far beyond in all directions. But within this continuum there were some pretty clear cultural differences, seen especially in the distribution of ceremonial activities (Barnett 1938a, Smith 1941, Elmendorf 1960:298-305).

I am especially concerned with the speakers of two languages, Halkomelem and Straits, who occupy one segment of the Coast Salish continuum, a region extending from the Lower Fraser Valley to the Strait of Juan de Fuca. These people are better known under a number of "tribal" names, each of which designates a village or group of villages sharing a dialect of one of these languages. The Tait, Katzie, Kwantlen and other Lower Fraser people collectively called Stalo, the Musqueam at the mouth of the Fraser, and the Nanaimo and Cowichan of Vancouver Island all spoke dialects of Halkomelem. The Semiahmoo, Lummi, and Samish to the south of the mouth of the Fraser along the mainland shore and the Saanich, Songhees, and Sooke of the southeastern end of Vancouver Island all spoke dialects of Straits. Clallam, on the southern shore of the Strait of Juan de Fuca is either a divergent dialect of Straits or a closely related language. The Nooksack, inland to the south of the Fraser, and the Squamish, to the north, spoke their own separate languages but culturally seem to have been somewhat closer to the speakers of Halkomelem and Straits than to their neighbours beyond. In spite of this linguistic diversity, the absence of any formal political organization, and occasional conflicts, the people of this region were linked together by continual inter-village marriage and participation in economic and social activities and the exchange of foods, goods, information, and personnel. Such ties extended beyond this region, of course. But the Halkomelem and Straits people shared patterns of subsistence activities relying especially on salmon runs ascending the Fraser (see discussion in Mitchell 1971:19-29). And within the region, I believe, certain concepts and values were held and expressed more frequently than they were outside it.

It would be useful to have names without linguistic connotations for culturally distinguishable regions within the Coast Salish area. Elsewhere (Suttles 1968a:58) I have used "Central Coast Salish" for the Halkomelem-Straits region. Geographically, Straits was at the very centre of the total Coast Salish area. Demographically, Straits and Halkomelem territories together seem to have been a peak, perhaps the most densely populated region on this part of the Northwest Coast. Mooney's (1928) estimates, accepted by Kroeber (1939) and not yet superseded, give it more people than the rest of the Coast Salish area combined and also more than the entire Wakashan area. Thus "Central Coast Salish" might be justified on two grounds. I should note that in using the term I do not mean to imply that other Coast Salish were peripheral deviants nor that the people to whom I apply the term were a unit in all things. I do think we can make some generalizations about these people and we need a collective name.

Art, Power, and Prestige

During the nineteenth century the Central Coast Salish carved and/or painted ceremonial paraphernalia of several kinds, house posts and (in some places) house fronts, grave monuments, and several kinds of implements of practical use. Discovering what this art meant to the people who made it and used it is now very difficult. But perhaps we can make a start by sorting it out by its association with some Native concepts. It seems to me that, while some Central Coast Salish art may have been purely decorative, much of it can be related to four sources of power and prestige—the vision, the ritual word, the ancestors, and wealth. (I believe I have considered most of the available ethnographic data—works by Boas, Hill-Tout, Jenness, Barnett, Duff, and others, but inevitably I have been guided most by my own field experience, which began in 1946 and has continued now and again over the years.) I shall discuss these four sources of power and prestige first and then return to the kinds of things that were carved and painted.

The *vision* was the unique experience of the individual, the source of his or her skill at subsistence activities or crafts, and the essential basis of professional status as warrior, seeress, or shaman. In theory, though not always in practice, the exact nature of the vision experience was something one ought to keep secret, perhaps until old age. The vision experience inspired a unique individual performance in the winter dance, but its nature was only hinted at by the words of the song and the movements of the dance (Jacobs 1959:13 on Clackamas Chinookan, Collins 1974:145-46 on Upper Skagit, Barnett 1955:146 on Georgia Strait secrecy). Any other representation of the vision experience we might expect also to be vague, ambiguous, or covert.

The *ritual word* was for some purposes more important than the vision. It too was an aid in subsistence and crafts and was the basis of a profession, that of "ritualist" (Barnett's term; Jenness says "priest"). The ritual word was the heart of the first salmon ceremony, of incantations to quell wounded bears and sea lions, and of the "cleansing rites" used at life crises and to wipe away shame. These cleansing rites included the use of masks, rattles, and several illusions—one in which stuffed animals appeared to climb a pole, another in which a basket appeared to float in the air, etc. The ritual word was also associated with designs, which the ritualist painted with red ochre on those he protected or purified (see especially Jenness 1955:37-39). The rites and the designs were the property of individuals, who kept to themselves the knowledge of the ritual words that made them efficacious, but they could be used on behalf of descendants, descent being reckoned bilaterally, of an ancestral owner.

The *ancestors*, for the Central Coast Salish (perhaps with a few exceptions), had always had human form. Some of these first humans dropped from the sky at the beginning of the world. Others seem simply to have been here. In a few myths they were created by the Transformer. Some animal species are the descendants of people, as the sturgeon in Pitt Lake came from the daughter of the first man there; some are the affines of people, as the sockeye salmon are for the Katzie through a marriage of another first man (see Jenness 1955:12, 18-21). But people are not the descendants of animals. In the most common kind of myth, when the Transformer came through the world and brought the Myth Age to an end, he transformed some of the First People into animals but left others, who pleased him, to become founding ancestors of villages. Some of these founders received, from the Transformer or from other sources, the ritual words, incantations, and ritual paraphernalia of the cleansing rites, which have been transmitted generation after generation to their present owners.

The value of the vision, the ritual word, and the ancestors was reflected in *wealth*. In Native theory, they were responsible for one's having wealth, and so having wealth demonstrated their presence and efficacy. Giving wealth, as Barnett (1938b) and others have pointed out, was a necessary step in validating claims to status, ultimately confirmed by being given wealth. Wealth for the Central Coast Salish included slaves and dentalia obtained from elsewhere but consisted mainly of items made within the area by skilled craftsmen and, more importantly, craftswomen. Probably the most important item of wealth was the blanket woven of mountain-goat and/or dog wool. These blankets had several advantages as wealth; they were made of materials of practical value and available in large but finite amounts and they were divisible and recombinable, since they could be cut up or unraveled and the material rewoven into new ones.

When I began work on this paper I did not see wealth as something I might discuss in relation to art in the same way I saw the vision, the ritual word, and the ancestors. But I have come to see it this way, for reasons I shall return to later. But now let me go on to the art itself, taking up in turn each of the main classes of things that were carved and painted.

Ceremonial Paraphernalia

The Central Coast Salish did not have very much in the way of decorated ceremonial paraphernalia associated with vision power. Shamans evidently had little or nothing of the sort. Winter ("guardian spirit") dancers of a few types had a few items. In recent years, and perhaps earlier, dancers with the type of song called "male," once sung by the professional warrior, have induced possession by shaking staffs that are often decorated with animal forms (see Stern 1934, frontispiece; Hawthorn 1967:214, fig. 250, centre). These forms may have vision-related meanings, but I have no information on this. There were also men and women, perhaps mainly among the Samish and Lummi, with the vision-empowered boards, poles, and duck-shaped floats that were used more often in the Northern Puget Sound region and generally known by their Lushootseed (Puget) names, respectively *sgʷədílič*, *tə́stəd* and *čáju* (Suttles 1951a:370-78; Jenness 1955:61-64; Lushootseed orthography as in Hess 1976). I have no information on the decoration of these items in the Central Coast Salish area, but on Puget Sound some *sgʷədílič* boards were painted with designs symbolic of the songs revealed by the vision (Waterman 1924, pl. 1) and *tə́stəd* poles were decorated with red ochre, cedar bark, and deer-hoof rattles (Hess 1976:495). While these items appeared in the winter dances, they were also occasionally used in a form of divination to find lost objects or persons, though the owners were not regarded as shamans.

In not having any portable representations of their visions, Central Coast Salish shamans differed markedly from those of two other Coast Salish regions to the south. In the centre of the Puget Sound region the best known works of art are the posts and boards (Wingert 1949a:pl. 8-21; 1949b, pl. 4-6) used in the famous "spirit canoe" ceremony in which several shamans dramatized a trip to the Land of the Dead to recover a lost soul (Fig. 1). This ceremony seems not to have been performed in the Central Coast Salish area and the styles of carving and painting seen on the "spirit canoe" paraphernalia do not closely resemble anything in the Central Coast Salish area. To the southwest, among the Quinault (and others?), shamans used small boards and "wands" carved with representations of their "guardian spirits," the wands with deer-hoof rattles attached (Olson 1936:148-50; Wingert 1949a, pl. 1-7). Again, nothing like these has been reported for the Central Coast Salish area.

In the Central Coast Salish regions the most important decorated objects of ritual use were the rattles and masks used to "cleanse" (*ẑxʷát*, in Halkomelem, Musqueam dialect, orthography mine) persons worthy of that honour. Such a rattle or mask, or perhaps the physical object together with the ritual words and acts that it was used with, is called a *ẑxʷtén*, literally "cleansing instrument." I shall refer to a ceremony in which the rattle, mask, etc. is used as a "cleansing rite" (Jenness 1955:71 calls them "community rituals," Barnett 1955:154 "privileged performances"). These rattles and masks are instruments empowered by the ritual word and used by the ritualist. They belong to a cultural complex that is separate from, though not altogether unrelated to, visions and shamans. The use of the cleansing rites is not confined to the winter dancing season. In fact, at one time they were used most often in the potlatch, which was most often a fair-weather gathering. But recently they have appeared most often at the larger winter dances.

The Rattles (Fig. 2). The ritualist's rattle is called *sxʸélməxʷcəs* in Halkomelem (Musqueam dialect). This word is certainly Salish and specifically Halkomelem in form but cannot yet be wholly analyzed. It may mean simply "something round held in the hand." A number of ritualist's rattles that are known to be old are made each of a sheet of bighorn sheep horn bent over and sewn along the edges to form a bulging triangle (like the pastry called a "turnover"), provided with a wooden handle extending from the apex, and having strands of mountain-goat wool attached to the sewn sides. Both surfaces of the bulging horn usually have incised designs and the end of the wooden

106

handle is usually carved. There are also some uncarved horn rattles and a number made in about the same shape but of metal, said to be a modern substitute. In pre-contact times the California bighorn sheep ranged westward to the eastern edge of Central Coast Salish country (Cowan 1940:554, 558, 574) and so some coast hunters may have hunted it. But the animal is little known among the Coast Salish today and probably most of the horn was imported from the Plateau.

In recent years ritualists with rattles have appeared as participants in the "work" (the potlatch-like activities) that accompanies the winter ("guardian-spirit") dancing. Acting in pairs, they usher into the big house the young people to receive names or the photographs of the dead to be honoured. The audience first hears the chanting of the ritualists, coming faintly and then gradually louder, from outside the house, and then sees them enter, walking slowly and pausing every few steps, chanting with a slow steady beat of the rattles. After the young people are named or the dead honoured, many members of the audience receive blankets or silver coins as thanks for their witnessing the event. Such "work," once part of the summer potlatch, seems to have been only recently inserted into the winter dance and is still only an optional adjunct to it (Suttles 1960b).

But at one time the ritualist's rattle had another use directly related to the winter dance. In a text dictated in Halkomelem, one of my Musqueam teachers describes her great-grandmother's work as a ritualist. That woman had four rattles, one of which she used to induce possession in a person expected to become a "new dancer." She would first simply paint designs directly on the body of the initiate, reciting the proper ritual words. But if that did not work, she would choose the rattle that had a face carved on it, put red ochre on it, and then stamp it onto the body of the initiate, at which point he would become possessed with his song. She used this method to bring out songs of one of the several categories of "spirit songs." She also used a rattle for a girl who had reached puberty. After painting the girl four mornings and four nights, she led her down to the river, recited the ritual words to the water and bathed her.

The designs (Fig. 2) carved on the sheep-horn rattles vary in complexity. But several I have seen appear similar in features of composition and style. Three I have seen have on one side a clearly defined, roundish humanoid face. On one, the face has what seems to be bunches of hair, feathers or rays radiating from it; on the other side are what appear to be fishes. The second has a face with radiating rays and fishes, and on the reverse a bird with fishes. On the third, the face has fishes above it and facing birds enclosing it, while on the reverse another pair of birds face each other to enclose a space in which the features of another face appear. As recurrent elements of style there are circles, concentric circles, crescents, and elongated wedges that I have been tempted to call "cuneiforms." Bill Holm has suggested to me, and I am convinced he is right, that the crescent and cuneiforms are "holes in the donuts" between formlines. Holm's analysis of the northern two-dimensional style seems to work for this style too, yet this style generally lacks the ovoids that are such a prominent feature of the northern style.*

(A rattle of unknown provenience shown in the Art of the North show in 1973—see Collins et al. 1973:262, fig. 341—is clearly the same kind of rattle in form and style, though the design is somewhat more complex than any known Central Coast Salish rattle that I have seen and it seems to contain an ovoid.)

I do not know what these designs represent, nor do I expect to find anyone who does. Forty years ago Diamond Jenness (1955:37-39) learned that ritualists painted the faces of those they worked on, every ritualist having "his own hereditary set of designs that varied with different functions," such as healing the ghost-struck and recovering lost "vitalities" as well as performing puberty rites for both sexes. Jenness worked, in 1936, with Old Pierre of Katzie, perhaps the most famous shaman in the Central Coast Salish region. To Pierre, all power came from "Him Who Dwells Above," and the ritual words, which Jenness identifies as "prayers," were initially addressed to this deity, though they have come to have power of their own. The rattles too, according to Pierre, came from the deity, who gave one with a different design to each of several village founders. However, "No one now knows the meanings of the patterns."

Are the designs on the rattles related to the designs painted with red ochre by ritualists on their patients? It seems reasonable to suppose so, in view of Pierre's attributing them to the same source and the use by one ritualist of her rattle as a stamp. Were the designs the ritualist drew on their patients the formlines or the crescents and cuneiforms—the donuts or the holes? If the unincised surface of the horn transmitted the paint, the ritualists must have been drawing formlines. Holm (1965:92-93) has compared the flow of movement that produced the Northern formlines with the flow of movement of the Northern dance. Did the ritual painting of esoteric designs among the Central Coast Salish provide a link here between dancing and carving?

What about the recurring face on the rattles? Is it "He Who Dwells Above"? Probably not. That name is Jenness's translation of čícəɬ síʔém̓, a phrase that appears to be a loan-translation of the Chinook Jargon sáxali táyi "chief above," perhaps better "Lord Above," used by the missionaries as the term for "God." Similar loan-translations can be found in several other languages along the coast. A "Lord Above" does not play any role in other origin myths collected in the Central Coast Salish or neighbouring regions. So it appears

---

*[For an analysis of this style see Kew 1980 and Feder 1983.]

108

to me that the "Lord Above" is a post-contact concept and that Old Pierre's theology is a synthesis that post-dates the rattles (cf. Suttles 1957b:377-81). But there are at least three other possibilities. First, the face on the rattle may be the face of the Daylight (swéyəl in Musqueam, skʷéyəl or skʷéčəl in some other dialects of Halkomelem and Northern Straits, skʷáčəy in Clallam), seen as something of very great power to which—or to whom—people who knew the ritual words addressed them as spells—or prayers. I have the impression that to some the Daylight was simply a very powerful impersonal force, while to others it may have been a deity-like entity. Second, the face may be that of xé·ls, the Transformer of the mythology of the region and the source, according to some myths (e.g., Stern 1934:107), of ritual words. Third, the rattle may have been used in the first-salmon ceremony, and so the face and the fish on the rattle may represent an ancestor and the species he made a compact with, a compact to be maintained through the ceremony. But this is sheer conjecture. The face on the rattle may represent no particular person or being at all. Perhaps a human face simply symbolizes consciousness and purpose, which are, at least, attributes of the ritualist that should be reassuring to the patient.

The distribution of the ritualist's rattle is not altogether clear. Its centre seems to be the Halkomelem area but some ritualists among the Northern Straits people to the south and among the Squamish and perhaps others to the north also used rattles. The decorated rattles that I know of are from the Halkomelem and Vancouver Island Straits area.

The Masks (Fig. 3). The mask used in one of the cleansing rites is known in the literature under a variety of representations of the Native name, which seems uniform throughout the Central Coast Salish region and which I record as sxʷáyxʷəy and will spell "sxwayxwey." The name appears to be Salish but I can give no etymology for it. I know nothing to justify identifying it with "whirlwind" as did Emmons (Notes in the Provincial Archives and Catalog of the American Museum of Natural History) nor with "earthquake" as Boas (1897:497) did for its Kwakiutl counterpart. Recently Lévi-Strauss (1975:1-39) has followed an earlier suggestion by Codere (1948:7) that there is a relationship between this name and the word used on Puget Sound for "potlatch," but this is highly unlikely.

The name refers, I believe, to the whole character portrayed by the dancer in his costume rather than to the mask itself, which exists in several named varieties. As it appears in a performance, the mask is worn high on the head, surrounded by plumes and a bib-like collar. The dancer's whole "outfit" includes a cape worn over the back of his head and shoulders, lines of large white feathers wrapped around his middle, leggings of downy swan-skin and deer-hoof rattles at his ankles. In his right hand the sxwayxwey dancer carries a rattle made of perforated scallop shells strung on a wooden hoop or pair of hoops.

The mask itself is carved of wood. Most now in existence may be of red cedar but at an earlier time they may have been made of maple. Most are painted with three colours—black or blue, red and white. Masks used in the Halkomelem area, with a few exceptions, conform to a standard pattern. (Squamish and Lummi carvers have produced some different types.)* The mask consists of a fairly round face, the most conspicuous features of which are a pair of projecting cylinders representing the eyes, or more precisely the eyeballs or irises, since the lids appear in low relief around the bases of these stalks, which look like the eyes of a crab or snail. Rising from the top of the head is a pair of horn-like projections carved in the form of animal or bird heads. (I use "animal" in the sense of a creature with a snout rather than a beak; "animals" may include reptiles and amphibians as well as mammals.) With the possible exception of one type, the face seems to lack a mandible, the straight lower margin of the face appearing as a maxilla. Projecting downward from the face is a long, broad, flat, grooved surface that appears to be a tongue. Perforations at the root of this tongue, under the maxilla, allow the dancer to look out. The "nose" of the face and the area surrounding the eyes vary with the type of mask.

Lists of types of sxwayxwey given by Jenness (1955:72, 91), Barnett (1955:158), Emmons (n.d.), and my own informants add up to some thirteen names: Thunder, Raven, Sawbill, Snake, Two-headed Snake, Beaver, Spring Salmon, Owl, Ghost, Buzzard, Eagle, Bear, and Clown. The actual number of types may be somewhat less, since "Owl" and "Ghost" may be the same, as may "Bear" and "Clown." Some of these named types are identifiable with masks in museum collections; some are not. I will not try to present all of the data here. I will describe briefly only the most clearly identifiable types.

One type (Fig. 3a) was identified at Musqueam, by Mr. and Mrs. Andrew Charles from photographs, as "Sawbill-Face" ($x^w\acute{a}\cdot\mathring{q}^w\mathfrak{s}$, from $x^w\acute{a}\cdot\mathring{q}^w$ "sawbill, merganser, fish duck," -$\mathfrak{s}$ "-face"). This name appears in every other list that I have. On the masks so identified, a fully carved head of a merganser forms the "nose" of the mask as a whole, while the rest of the bird may be shown in low relief, the wings and feet appearing around the eyes of the mask and the tail on the forehead. There are variations: on several Sawbill-Faces the "horns" are birds, but on one so identified they are animals; and while on several the body of the merganser is shown in a clear though stylized fashion, as just described, in one mask the body of the bird is much less clearly indicated.

---

*[All of the Lummi and Squamish masks I know were made, I believe, relatively recently, and primarily to illustrate the old ways rather than for use in traditional contexts.]

In the type the Charleses identified as "Snake-Face" (Fig. 3b) (x^wʔə́ɬqəyəs, from ʔə́ɬqəy "snake"), an animal head facing upward forms the nose of the mask. In some examples, two feet extend upward from the head toward the eyes of the mask. In all, ridges I take to be the snake's body extend from the head in an arc up and around either side of the face of the mask. A spiral or set of concentric circles appears on the forehead of the mask. The horns are animal heads.

In a type identified as "Ghost-Face" (Fig. 3c) (pəlq^{w}əẑáyəs, from spəl-q^{w}íẑeʔ "ghost, corpse, screech owl") the nose of the mask is neither an animal nor a bird head but a simple triangular projection with an inverted V incised in the flat end, which looks (to me, anyway) like the nasal aperture of a skull. If the identification with a skull is correct, the lines on either side of the nose may represent the sutures. In two masks but not in a third, the upper jaw seems to be painted with teeth.

Photographs of two masks with similar triangular noses were identified as Ghost masks by the Charleses but one was identified as a Beaver by Emmons. The latter identification may be correct, since they have nostrils cut in a different form and they have pairs of wide incisors projecting downward from their upper jaws.

On a mask Emmons identified as a Raven (Fig. 3d), the nose is the bird's head, facing downward, with its mouth extending nearly across the width of the mask. If we focus our attention on the Raven's mouth, it may appear that it is also the mouth of the mask itself. But the Raven's eyes are not identical with the eyes of the whole mask and so I am inclined to think that the Raven's mouth is still the upper jaw of the whole mask. On this type of mask, the Raven's mouth is cut all the way through the wood, providing a slit the dancer may see through, which suggests that this mask was worn a bit lower on the face than the others.

In style, most of these masks share two organizational principles with the art of the more northerly Northwest Coast peoples: the bird or animal (the snake, anyway) is spread out and wrapped around the space available to it; and a part of one creature may be simultaneously a part of another, as when the head of the sawbill is also the nose of the mask (a relationship Laura Greenberg and Bill Holm have called "visual punning"). Also, elements of the northern style are present; we can certainly see formlines created by the cutting away of the "holes in the donuts." But just as in the ritualist's rattles, the incised elements are cuneiforms, crescents, circles and arcs; rarely, if ever, ovoids.

When the sxwayxwey mask is worn, various things are attached to it. In the top of the mask there are holes into which are thrust large feathers (golden eagle tail feathers?) or Chinese feather dusters. (Photographs dating back to the turn of the century show that the latter have been in use at least that long.) Behind the top of the mask is attached a roll of rushes into which are thrust a number of flexible stalks, earlier sea-lion whiskers but now usually (I believe) wood and wire, tipped with tufts of white down. The bib-like affair that surrounds the rest of the mask consists of a fan of feathers cut evenly at the perimeter and covered with patterned or embroidered cloth. A mask in the American Museum has a carved wooden attachment projecting from either side, perhaps originally to hold up the "bib." The British Columbia Provincial Museum has a pair of slender "wands" (Fig. 4) said to have been attached to a sxwayxwey mask; the end of each is carved in the form of an animal and very much in the style that appears on the ritualist's rattles and, as we shall see, on the spindle whorls.*

The sxwayxwey, like the ritualist's rattle, is a cleansing instrument. And like the rattle, it was formerly used in the summer potlatch but has recently been used in the "work" accompanying the winter dance and for the same purposes. An even number of sxwayxwey dancers, usually four or six, dance around the person, persons, or photograph for which they have been hired. The owner of a mask may dance with it himself or may engage someone else to wear it. Men only dance with sxwayxwey masks, in contrast to the winter dance (the "guardian-spirit" dance), in which both sexes participate equally. However, women are hired to sing as the dancers perform. A sxwayxwey dancer moves with high, short steps, raising the right arm with the right foot and the left with the left ("like a pacer"). The style of dancing does not resemble those of the winter dancers. At one time, it is said, the different types of masks were used with appropriate movements. I have also been told that at one time the masks were much heavier and hard to breathe through so that the dancers engaged in a kind of endurance contest. Two kinds of songs are associated with the sxwayxwey. In the past, at any rate, at dawn on the day of the potlatch when the sxwayxwey was to be used, the owner beat a box drum and sang an incantation (sźélǝm) that announced the event and, I believe, empowered the sxwayxwey with the ritual word. Later, as the sxwayxwey danced, the chorus of women sang a "song for a person" (stǝlǝméyǝł), which is either an inherited song or one composed for the occasion in order to wipe away an insult.

The box drum used for the sxwayxwey was another piece of decorated ritual paraphernalia. A Lummi man who saw one used at a Quamichan (Cowichan) potlatch said that it had animals on the front of it but he could not make out what they were. The Field Museum's box drum from Cowichan that has four little human figures on it (Wingert 1949a, pl. 44) may have been used for the sxwayxwey.

---

*[As Ailsa Crawford has suggested to me, one of the animals has scales and is probably a lizard; the other seems to have costal grooves and so may be a salamander. When the wands were attached, these two creatures must have appeared to be springing out of the mask.]

Two generations ago a Musqueam man, and perhaps no one else, owned the $q^{w}\acute{i}\hspace{1pt}?niye$ (probably "hairy thing") identified as a "clown." This character appeared with the sxwayxwey dancers, wearing a somewhat different type of mask and a costume of cured bearskin. The "clown" chased the sxwayxwey, poking at their eyes with a stick, and threatened the women in the audience. The owner of the "clown" is said to have lost the costume and so abandoned the practice. Old photographs (e.g., Barnett 1955, p. XIX) show it as having less projecting eyes than the sxwayxwey proper and a single "horn" on the head. (Barnett 1955:178-79 discusses the clown. See also Stern 1934:57-59.*) This figure of the "clown," with its dark fur and audience-oriented behaviour, contrasts sharply with the figure of the sxwayxwey, with its white feathers and down and behaviour oriented toward the subject of its purifying power.

What does the sxwayxwey really represent? I do not really know. The myths that account for its origin usually identify it as a mask and costume worn by a human being or human-like being. There is no evidence that I can see that it represents a "spirit" (there is no equivalent of "spirit" in Halkomelem) or some non-human species of bird or animal (cf. Suttles 1972 on "natural" vs "supernatural" in relation to the "sasquatch"). Perhaps the question is misguided. Feathers are themselves a ritual substance, like red ochre and hogfennel seeds. Central Coast Salish ritualists scatter feathers as they purify dance floors. The purification would not be effected, I believe, without the ritual words used by and known only to the ritualist, but the feathers evidently help make them efficacious. Perhaps the sxwayxwey is no more than an elaborate use of the magical powers of feathers and patterns, which increase the efficacy of the ritual word. If so, it need not represent anything. It is just what it is called, a "cleansing instrument."

The sxwayxwey has a much wider distribution than the ritualist's rattle, but it too may have been spreading, on the coast at least, from the Halkomelem area. It has been used northward as far as the Kwakiutl and southward as far as the immediately adjacent Saanich and Lummi. But the conclusion that it originated in the Halkomelem area or more specifically among the Lower Fraser people, reached by Barnett (1955:167, 178-79), Duff (1952:123-26), and Lévi-Strauss (1975:1-44), is based largely on judgements about the historicity of myths and traditions of who got the sxwayxwey from whom (especially in Duff's case) or on a structuralist theory of myth applied to insufficient data (as in Lévi-Strauss's cases). I see serious problems here but cannot go into them at this time. The sxwayxwey may indeed be old in the Upper Stalo

---

*[Stern's work should be used with caution because he occasionally ascribed to the Lummi a practice of a neighboring group (for instance, sea-lion hunting) known to his Lummi sources but probably not Lummi.]

113

area. But I do not believe that myths and traditions prove it. Some ethnographic evidence seems to support it. Inland neighbours of the Upper Stalo used carvings of the sxwayxwey as grave markers; this is reported for the Nooksack by Fetzer (n.d.) and for the Lower Lillooet by Teit (1906a:272-73). Teit also reports (253-54) that both the Lower and Upper Lillooet used various kinds of masks. But most important is the archaeological evidence. Among materials taken from a prehistoric site at Chase, in the middle of Shuswap country, Sanger (1968) discovered pieces of scallop shells used as rattles and a broken mask that looks like a sxwayxwey. A scallop-shell rattle was also discovered in the Lochnore-Nesikep locality (Sanger 1970:94, 101). In both places there was other evidence of trade with the coast. This does suggest that the sxwayxwey was in use on the Lower Fraser in prehistoric times.*

Another object that must be mentioned in this context of art relevant to the ritual word is the stone bowl. Wilson Duff, in his thorough treatment of these bowls (Duff 1956), has summarized the scant ethnographic evidence that they were used by ritualists in historic times. I have nothing at this time to add to what Duff has said. Still other objects that we may be able to consider in this context when more is known about them are the paraphernalia of the Nootka-style secret society that has flourished at the western end of Straits country. Whatever members think, non-members have seen it as a kind of cleansing ritual. Finally, among decorated ceremonial objects we should include painted drums. These used to be less common than unpainted drums, but are fairly often seen today at big dances. I have no information on the meaning of the designs.

Houses

The Central Coast Salish house was a long, shed-roofed structure consisting of a sheath of huge planks over a frame of posts and beams. The posts were often decorated and in rare cases so were the beams. Also, early European observers saw decorated house fronts on the Lower Fraser. In 1808 Simon Fraser saw one in what may have been a Kwantlen village. The 640-foot long house he visited had, in "the chief's" section, a post with an oval opening serving as a door, above which on the outside "are carved a human figure as large as life, with other figures in imitation of beasts and birds" (Masson 1889-90:197). Fifty years later, in 1858, Charles Wilson saw decorated houses in the same area. He wrote (1866:287-88):

---

*[As Ailsa Crawford has suggested to me, one of the animals has scales and is probably a lizard; the other seems to have costal grooves and so may be a salamander. When the wands were attached, these two creatures must have appeared to be springing out of the mask.]

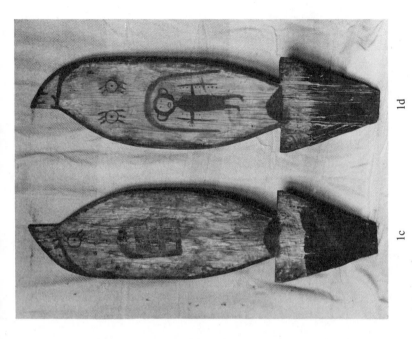

1a   1b

1c   1d

Fig. 1. Carved figures and boards used in the spirit canoe ceremony by shamans in the Southern Coast Salish region. 1a and 1b, spirit canoe figures, Snoqualmie. 1c and 1d, spirit canoe boards, Duwamish.

2a

2b

2c

2d

Fig. 2. Mountain-sheep horn rattles used by ritualists as cleansing devices in the Central Coast Salish region. 2a and 2b, Cowichan, purchased in 1929. 2c and 2d, Cowichan.

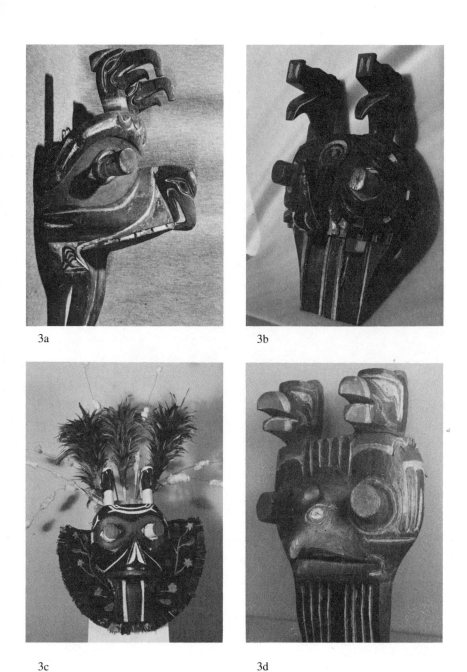

3a   3b

3c   3d

Fig. 3. Sxwayxwey masks used as cleansing devices in the Central Coast Salish region. 3a, sawbill-face, Katzie, collected by Harlan I. Smith in 1898. 3b, snake-face, Musqueam, purchased in 1954, said to be four generations old. 3c, ghost-face, with plumes and ruff, Quamichan (Cowichan). 3d, raven-nose, Cowichan, collected in 1912.

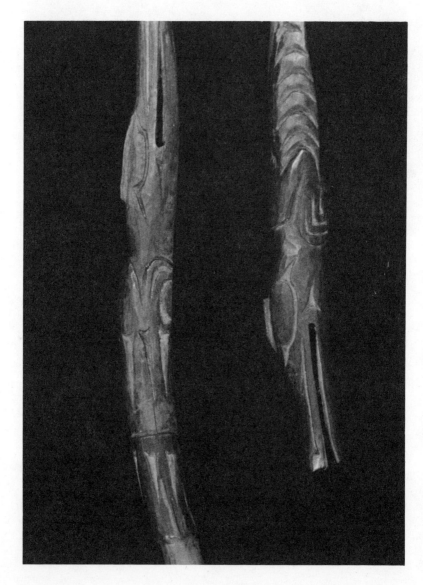

Fig. 4. Wands used with a sxwayxwey mask, probably to hold the roll of matting into which feathers are stuck.

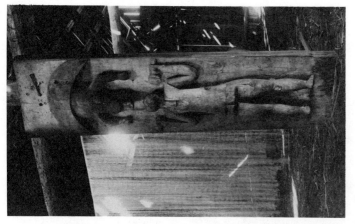

5a

5b

Fig. 5. Houseposts representing ancestors, at Musqueam. 5a, post representing qiyəplénəxʷ (Capilano I), still standing after most or all of the rest of the house had fallen. 5b (taken 1898), post representing čsimlénəxʷ, said to be a replica of the original, here fastened to a central post in a late-style gable-roofed house. Both posts are now at the University of British Columbia.

Fig. 6. Houseposts. Cowichan village of Quamichan, near Duncan. A photograph taken about 1897 shows that these posts (probably originally a set of six) once stood inside a house, holding the transverse beams. They were later used to decorate the outside of a newer house, shown here. They are now at the British Columbia Provincial Museum. The animals held by or on the body of the human beings depicted by the posts probably represent stuffed fishers used as a cleansing device.

7a

7b

Fig. 7. Houseposts, purchased by Harlan I. Smith at Musqueam in 1898, said to have stood in the house of Capilano II, now at the American Museum of Natural History. 7a shows (top to bottom) a pair of animals (probably fishers), a face with extended tongue (probably a sxwayxwey face), a pair of two-headed creatures (probably $s^{\text$?}\!i\!\cdot\!tq\partial y$), and a disk. 7b, above, shows three disks, a circular shape with a human figure squatting in it, and a human figure from the waist up holding a pair of bird-like creatures by their necks. A catalog note, presumably by Smith, says the disks represented stars, sun, and moon, and the humans represented ancestors who taught about them. 7b, below, shows a winged bird-like being with a human face holding a two-headed creature in its claws. These carvings seem to combine inherited privileges (the fishers and masks used in cleansing ceremonies), representations of creatures seen in visions (two-headed serpents and bird-like beings?), and perhaps ancestors as well.

121

Fig. 8. Housepost photographed at Musqueam in 1898 by Harlan I. Smith, present location unknown. This post seems to represent a man being attacked by a giant salamander or lizard.

Fig. 9. Musqueam mortuary box with carved fishers, collected in 1930 by Harlan I. Smith.

10a

10b

10c

10d

Fig. 10. Central Coast Salish spindle whorls. 10a, whorl with human figure between facing birds (compare design on rattle in Fig. 2d). 10b, bird with outspread wings, collected by W.A. Newcombe in 1929. 10c, Cowichan whorl with fish. 10d, bird and beast in mutual pursuit.

The buildings at Langley and Chilukweyuk are the only ones on
which there is any attempt at ornament, the former being adorned
with some curious pictographs, in which a bird something like
a crow figures conspicuously; the latter with some grotesque
carvings, apparently representing tortoises, large snakes, and some
animal of the crocodile type.

In his journal (1970:37) he mentions not being able to copy the "pictographs
on the lodges because of the rain," so we can assume they were on the outside. In the same year (1858) James Madison Alden visited the same area
and produced a series of watercolours of the country, several of which show
native houses with large circular designs on their fronts, but at too great a
distance to give any details (see Stenzel 1975, pls. 37, C-21, and 40). Alden
also produced a watercolour of the village at Nanaimo (pl. C-24), which does
not show any external decoration. Probably features of structure and use
worked against the decoration of house fronts. The heavy wall planks were
held horizontally, overlapping, between pairs of upright poles. The planks
covering a section of a house might be owned by the family occupying it.
They were easily removed so that they could be laid across a pair of canoes
as a "raft," taken to cover a frame at a summer fishing site, or taken to another
village by a family changing residence. It seems likely that houses with decorated fronts would be only those whose owners would not have to remove
the planks seasonally or could be assured of getting them back in the right
order. Perhaps there was less moving of planks on the Lower Fraser than
elsewhere in the area, where decorated house fronts have not been reported.
Paul Kane in 1847 sketched two carved house entrance posts he must have
seen at or near Victoria (Harper 1971:260, fig. 195) but shows no decorated
house fronts in his scenes of villages (e.g., p. 254).

The posts that stood inside the house, holding the beams and constituting
part of the frame, were often decorated. In the Northern Straits area, it seems,
they were decorated with representations of vision powers. One that survives
(at the Whatcom Museum of History and Art in Bellingham) is as stark as
a Puget Sound shaman's figure. It belonged to Chowitsut, who was the wealthiest Lummi in the early 1850s, and it is an incised pair of concentric circles
linked with two smaller circles. In the 1940s my oldest Lummi teacher
identified this design as representing one of Chowitsut's wealth powers—
"the sun carrying two valises of expensive things." Other posts with carvings representing visions stood in Victoria, and Boas tells us (1891:564) that
the Songhees owner kept them covered except during festivals because he
did "not like to be constantly reminded of these his superhuman friends and
helpers."

In the Halkomelem area, it seems, house posts were carved to represent
ancestors and ancestral heritages related to the ritual word. A post at Musqueam

(Fig. 5 left) represented the famous warrior named *qiyəplénəxʷ* ("Capilano"). Another Musqueam post represents *c̓simlénəxʷ* (Fig. 5 right), a descendant of the man who bore that name, according to Old Pierre, at the beginning of the present world, who became the founding ancestor of a Musqueam village, and received a ritualist's rattle, a sxwayxwey mask, and the empowering incantations from the Lord Above. On this post the bearer of this famous name is seen quelling a bear by shaking the rattle and chanting the incantation (cf. Barnett 1955:54). The post honours both the ancestor and the heritage.

A house post that once stood in a Nanaimo village (now in the Field Museum and illustrated in Wingert 1949a, pl. 40) portrays a sxwayxwey dancer and thus illustrates that a house post can represent a cleansing rite alone.

A cleansing rite is probably also the source of a number of animals that appear on house posts (and also grave monuments) in museum collections, several from the Cowichan village of Quamichan but others from Musqueam, Saanich, and Songhees. On some posts there are only animals; on one set of posts there are six to a post. On other posts the animals appear on the fronts of large human figures, two or four to a post; on still others a large human figure holds a small animal (Fig. 6). Recent informants have identified these animals as some kind of mustelid (member of the weasel family)—minks, otters, or fishers. Early collectors recorded a name for them as "scowmidgeon" or "sqa-mit-chen" (Wingert 1949a:39; Barbeau 1950), which must represent the Halkomelem *sx̌ʷə́məcən*, "fisher," an animal that does not live on Vancouver Island (Cowan and Guiguet 1965:308). I have been told of cleansing rites using several kinds of stuffed animals. But the most detailed information was given to Jenness (1955:72-73) by Old Pierre on the use of stuffed fishers. In this rite they cleansed a dead youth by climbing up a pole set up to represent him or cleansed a pubescent girl by climbing up and down her body. Thus the posts show the animals only and those that show them climbing on a human figure may both commemorate a cleansing rite. The posts that show a human being holding a single animal may have some other significance.

At Musqueam there were once posts that are much harder to interpret. In 1963 I showed photographs of them to older people at Musqueam but could learn nothing about them. These are posts (Fig. 7) that were collected at Musqueam in 1898 by Harlan I. Smith for the American Museum of Natural History. According to a note in the museum's catalogue, three stood in the house of "Kaplänux, the old chief." The people I talked with thought this most likely; that would have been Capilano the Second, the son of the First who was the famous warrior portrayed by the post mentioned earlier. A catalogue note that may refer to post 16/4652 reads:

> Top row of circles they say represents stars, then moon, sun, then row of stars. Then sun with moon in it. Below represents ancestors who taught them of sun, moon, and stars—a carved woman.

126

Perhaps somewhere a Smith journal note will tell more. Two other posts (16/7947 and 16/7948) that evidently came from the same house portray, among other things, two-headed creatures that are probably the s?í·ɫqəy or s?ínəɫqəy, the two-headed serpent, which is as important in Coast Salish traditions as its Kwakiutl counterpart is in theirs. It is a very important source of vision power for a shaman. But it also appears in a Musqueam legend that accounts for the winding stream that ran through the village and the growth of rushes that gives the village its name and symbolizes the capacity of the Musqueam to multiply again after a catastrophe. The being holding the two-headed serpent (on 16/7948) may be thunder, also an important figure in Coast Salish tradition and a source of shamanistic power. But in view of the absence of representations of shaman's visions generally in the Halkomelem area, it seems more likely that these represent something else.

Another post that Smith photographed at Musqueam with the previous three seems to have disappeared, perhaps through someone's censorship (Fig. 8). It was a striking piece of sculpture that, informants agree, must have represented a man being attacked anally by a giant "lizard." In Central Coast Salish belief, this "lizard" (to judge from one description, probably really a salamander, the Pacific newt), if stepped over in the woods, will follow you home, creep into your bed and attack you in this fashion, ultimately destroying you from within. But why should this kind of attack be portrayed, with a giant "lizard" as the attacker, on a house post? Did this post belong to a shaman or ritualist who could remove the intrusive amphibian? Or did it belong to someone who could direct one to attack an enemy? And did the owner have this post covered except on festive occasions?

Grave Monuments

At the time of first contact with Europeans, the Central Coast Salish disposed of the dead in wooden coffins and in canoes set up in graveyards. In some places, at least, the coffins were decorated with carvings and in some places carved figures were set up as monuments. As Duff (1952:51) points out, in 1808 Simon Fraser saw "tombs" carved with "figures of birds and beasts" near Yale, where the Halkomelem and Thompson met. In 1847 Kane sketched a single human figure standing beside a group of graves at Port Angeles in Clallam country (Harper 1971:251, fig. 179). In 1854 Alden sketched a group of grave posts near Victoria. The sketch (Stenzel 1975:33, pl.9) shows five human figures, two of which hold each a pair of animals and look very much like the house posts that seem to show purifying mustelids, while another is holding what looks like a cedar-bark hoop. (What appear to be the identical grave posts are shown in a watercolour, pl.23, but the location is given as Departure Bay.) Photographs taken by Harlan I. Smith in the late 1920s at Saanich and at

Musqueam show grave carvings of animals and men holding animals. A carving that stood at Patricia Bay is described as a "grave figure of a man holding a scowmidgeon" (National Museum Neg. No. 72,843, caption on back of print). If this is the s̆xʷə́məcən used as in Old Pierre's description, the carving must represent a man being cleansed by having a stuffed fisher climb up his body. A grave box at Musqueam (Fig. 9) had four animals on its front and is probably the one mentioned by Jenness (1955:73); according to Old Pierre, the ancestor of a village that merged with the Musqueam was given a fisher cleansing rite by the Transformer, but

> The last priest [ritualist], having no descendant to whom he might impart his knowledge, hired a skilled wood-carver to make him a coffin showing on one face four fishers in full relief. This coffin is now in the National Museum of Canada.

Above the slab with the animals, on this coffin, is a board decorated with concentric circles and cuneiforms, while below it is a longer board carved with a head at each end, forefeet, and a scaly body; both boards are done in the style that appears on rattles and spindle whorls.

Another grave at Musqueam had on the upper part of its face a large board carved in low relief with a pair of sturgeons flanked by two larger creatures with snouts and ears, short legs, fish-like tails and dorsal fins and what seem to be fish-like backbones. I was told at Musqueam that the grave of a famous sturgeon fisherman had a sturgeon on it; this may be it. But I do not know what the flanking creatures might be.

Could some grave carvings represent visions? A few statements in the literature suggest it. Jenness (n.d.:66) says that the National Museum has "a carved wooden coffin depicting a man's guardian spirit flanked by two wolves," the coffin of a famous Saanich warrior who died early in the nineteenth century. But I have no indication of what the "guardian spirit" (vision) looks like. Hill-Tout, writing on the Chilliwack (1902:364-65), says

> On the exterior of this [coffin] were painted the family crests or totems, called salúlia (collective of súlia) = "the dream objects." Among these figured the bear, goat, and beaver. Human effigies roughly carved in wood were also sometimes placed nearby, similar to those found among the N'tlakápamuQ [Thompson].

When Hill-Tout writes "family crest" he is usually referring to the sxwayxwey or some comparable possession but the Native term he gives is "vision," which is puzzling, but in general it is hard to disentangle Hill-Tout's ethnographic data from his theorizing about "totemism." Writing on the Chehalis of the Harrison River (his "StEélis"), Hill-Tout says informants told him that grave boxes were "never decorated with paintings or carvings of the *súlia* of the owner." But he supposes this to be because they had only recently adopted the practice of putting the dead in boxes or slab shelters.

As noted above, the Nooksack and the Lower (Douglas) Lillooet both set up grave monuments carved to represent the sxwayxwey. One of Fetzer's informants at Nooksack, a woman originally from Matsqui on the Fraser, said that "high-born" families had "totem-poles" called "*sx^wáyx^woi*" (and described as sxwayxwey-like) set up at their graves, while other families had "totem-poles" with other things—"sometimes animals were used, especially those that are scarce (among these *šx^womə́ċəl*, 'like otter but walks in the woods')." This animal would be the fisher. The informant did not mention any purifying function for either the sxwayxwey or the animals. But she told a myth accounting for the origin of the Matsqui "totem," presumably the sxwayxwey, unlike any other I know of: the people of a certain house swept it out with hemlock boughs; after many years a great pile of debris had accumulated away from the house, and the "totem" emerged out of this pile of sweepings. A purifier out of impurities? A cleanser to reward the cleanly?

Implements

The tools, weapons, canoes, etc. made by men and used by men seem to have been usually undecorated or decorated sparingly, e.g., an adz handle might bear just the suggestion of an animal form. Perhaps this was because of the association of skill and success with vision power and the dangers inherent in revealing or calling up the source of that power.

Household equipment of wood, such as boxes, buckets, dishes and spoons, things that were used by both sexes, were also usually undecorated. (The Museum of the American Indian has three decorated dishes, but one is said to have been used at a wedding; perhaps none is an ordinary household utensil.)

In contrast, implements made by men but used by women, such as mat creasers, spindle whorls, swords for beating wool, the posts of weaving frames ("looms"), etc. were often, though not always, decorated with carving and/or painting. These decorations included both geometric patterns and representations of birds, animals and people. (The women themselves, of course, produced geometric patterns on blankets, mats and baskets.) I have looked at one time or another at seventy or eighty spindle whorls. Some are wholly undecorated. A good many (Fig. 10) are decorated with simple curvilinear designs, either painted or incised in the surface that faces the spinner as she spins. And a number are decorated with incised representations of bird and/or animal figures or human figures with subordinate birds and/or animals. The design may be radially symmetrical or it may consist of a pair or quartet of creatures pursuing each other around the circle, a single animal chasing its

129

tail or a single figure crossing the circle, facing either right or left. The direction of the spinning seems not to be relevant. In both composition and design elements these spindle whorl designs resemble the incised designs on the cleansing rattles. And as we have seen this is a style that also appears on some sxwayxwey masks and grave monuments.

How can we interpret this disparity in the decoration of implements? Why should men, or some men, be more interested in, or more willing to, decorate women's implements than their own? And why should they use what appears to be the most structured style on one particular article, the spindle whorl? Are the designs on the spindle whorls purely decorative, do they symbolize the power of the vision, or do they symbolize the power of the ritual word?

My guess is that the answers lie in the use to which these implements were put, producing that other, essential source of power and prestige—wealth. It seems unlikely that the designs are purely decorative, though the circular form of the whorl may have challenged the artist. It also seems unlikely that they represent vision power, though it is possible that the production of wealth gave the artist the courage to portray something he might not dare reveal elsewhere. Moreover, since he is not doing the spinning, he might portray his "superhuman friends and helpers" without being constantly reminded of them. Could he create something relating to the spinner's vision power? As long as she is spinning it would be an invisible presence for her, reminding her only when she stopped and so driving her on. But I doubt this. The style on the spindle whorls is associated, on the rattles and on the masks and perhaps too on the grave monuments, with the power of the ritual word as used in purification. Ritual words may have played a part in the spinning and weaving processes; for example, the spinner may have recited them to the wool or to the spindle, but I have no information on this. There may, however, be a more direct association between spinning and purification. Mountain-goat wool, one of the substances spun though not the only one, seems to be itself associated with purification; it appears on the ritualist's rattle and on costumes worn by persons undergoing crisis rites, for example, the "new dancer" at the winter dance. It is white, like the feathers and down of the sxwayxwey. And it is the stuff of blankets, which are given out when the purifying rattles and masks are used.

(Laura Greenberg and Marjorie Halpin have suggested to me that a structuralist analysis would show a parallel between the rattle and the spindle whorl: both are involved in transformations, the rattle in the transforming of human beings from one state into another, the spindle whorl in the transforming of wool into wealth.)

Constraints on Productivity

Let me return to the question I started with. Why did the Central Coast Salish produce some great works of art yet neither the range of kinds of things nor the quantities of things produced farther north? Were there constraints at work here restricting and channelling productivity? It seems to me that there were. Clearly there were limits on the representation of visions ("guardian spirits"). In Native theory, everyone (or every male perhaps) ought to "train" and have a vision. But it was dangerous to reveal too much about it. If you talked about it, you could "spoil" it: it might leave you or even make you sick or it could be taken away from you by an enemy shaman. Yet eventually you wanted others to know that you "had something." Probably all of us who have worked in the area have heard hints and half-revelations about what people "have." Possession by a song at the winter dance is, of course, evidence that you "have something" and the words of the song and movements of the dance may hint at what it is. But it must be tempting to hint in other ways, though dangerous to go too far.

Sources vary on the strength of the prohibition. Barnett (1955:146), referring to the whole of Georgia Strait from the Saanich and Musqueam northward, says flatly that visions were not concretely represented in carvings on house posts, etc., though they were portrayed in the song and dance. But this contradicts what Boas says for the Songhees and Hill-Tout for the Chilliwack. It is my impression, from both my own field work and this survey of the art of the area, that all are right. There were very likely differences within the region, perhaps especially between the Halkomelem and Straits areas, not of an absolute sort but statistical differences—in the frequency with which visions were concretely portrayed.

Farther south, in the Puget Sound region, visions were more commonly portrayed but still, I think, with constraints. The Puget Sound shaman's guardian-spirit figure used in the spirit canoe ceremony, that seemingly crude stick of wood, was perhaps deliberately made stark and empty because it only hints at the secret, invisible, unique power of the shaman it belonged to. Probably asking the man who made it, "Why don't you produce the kind of explicit forms the Kwakiutl made?" would be like asking a Protestant who has just set up a rugged cross, "Why don't you decorate your church with all those nice plaster images the Catholics use?" The ideological difference is not really analogous but it may be as great.

The dangers that lie in portraying a vision too clearly may have affected artistic expression generally unless it was clearly identifiable with some other source of power. It may be that men refrained from decorating tools and weapons in order not to suggest even falsely the source of their vision powers. Or if they did decorate things they may have done so vaguely and ambiguously so that they could hint vaguely about what they had.

With art related to the power of the ritual word, the constraints must be different. The viewers of a rattle or mask know that its efficacy depends not on the private experience of a vision but the private knowledge of ritual words that have inherent power. That power cannot be diminished by concrete representation. You can lose it only through revealing (or forgetting) those carefully guarded words. Yet you may want to suggest their power or that you are the possessor of esoteric knowledge. The style that appears on the rattles and in the masks may be a useful medium for expressing this. (I am following a suggestion that Wilson Duff has made about the Northern art in supposing that it may imply esoteric knowledge.)

In the portrayal of ancestors there may have been a still different kind of constraint—fear of ridicule. When the man carved the house post at Musqueam portraying the ancestor confronting the bear, a Musqueam friend told me recently, he introduced something into the carving that was a covert insult to the subject. Whether this is true or not I do not know. Nor is the truth important for my argument. Covert insults were certainly a part of Native life. When the sxwayxwey is dancing, an old Lummi friend told me years ago, if the dancer shifts his scallop-shell rattle even for a moment to his left hand it signals to the spectators who have received the proper "advice" that the person for whom they are dancing has some lower-class ancestry. In the old days, I suppose, a man thinking of having a carving made of an ancestor must have had to consider whether he had the wealth or influence to protect that carving from slurs. Probably no one was permanently safe from such slurs. In Native society, leadership was specific to an activity; there were no all-purpose leaders and no great concentrations of authority. Perhaps few men could live without fear of ridicule.

Implications for Prehistory

I have tried to show how the people of one region had different forms of art related to different concepts and limited by different constraints. It appears to me that within the region there were local differences in the degree to which each of these concepts might be expressed, depending on the strength of fears about the harmful consequences of concrete representation versus desires for the useful consequences. These constraints are such that they may have varied in intensity through time and so may account for variations through time in kind and amount of artistic output. We need not, therefore, interpret qualitative or quantitative changes in prehistoric art as evidence of cataclysmic culture change or population replacement. They may have been the result of shifts in importance, back and forth, between the power of the vision and the power of the ritual word or shifts in the concentration of wealth and authority.

I am grateful for comments and suggestions from a number of people, including Harry Hawthorn, Marjorie Halpin, Pamela Amoss, Jay Miller, Darleen Fitzpatrick, Erna Gunther, Bill Holm (with whom I have discussed Salish art at length on several occasions), Randy Bouchard, Doe Kennedy and others, and for help with photographs from the National Museums of Canada, Lynn Maranda and the Vancouver Centennial Museum, Audrey Hawthorn, Madeleine Bronsdon and Carol McLaren at the University of British Columbia, Peter Macnair and Allan Hoover at the Provincial Museum, Barbara Lane and most especially Doe Kennedy of the British Columbia Indian Language Project. I have also had much help from the Audio-Visual people at Portland State University.

PART III

Adaptation and Survival Through the European Invasion

8. The Early Diffusion of the Potato among the Coast Salish[1]*

The first Europeans to observe the Coast Salish peoples of the Strait of Juan de Fuca, Puget Sound, and Georgia Strait were the Spanish and British explorers of 1790-91. Their accounts describe these tribes as hunting and fishing peoples without cultivation of the soil.[2] Fifty years later, travelers, traders and the like report Indian women of nearly every tribe in this area cultivating patches of potatoes with digging-sticks. At this time, in the 1840s, Whites were living only at a few Hudson's-Bay Company posts. Settlers began coming into this area in the 1850s, but the potato seems to have arrived before them. Living informants tell how their people got potatoes from other Indians. Settlement eventually destroyed the old potato patches or Whites taught the Native men farming on reservations.

The cultivation of potatoes during this period between first contact and settlement suggests three problems: First, where and how did the Coast Salish get their potatoes? Second, what is the relation of the sort of cultivation they

---

[1]A condensed version of this paper was read before the Northwest Anthropological Conference, 5 May 1950. The material from field notes was obtained while doing work sponsored by the University of Washington and by the Viking Fund.

*[From the *Southwestern Journal of Anthropology* 7:272-85 (1951).]

[2]I have found no reference to potatoes or cultivation in the accounts of Espinosa y Tello (Wagner 1933), Vancouver (Meany 1942), or Menzies (Newcombe 1923) where they refer to exploration of the Strait of Juan de Fuca, Puget Sound, or Georgia Strait, nor in Fraser's account of his descent of the Fraser River in 1808 (Masson 1889).

practised to pre-contact practices? Third, what bearing does this have on the relation between food-gathering and cultivation in general?

I. THE SOURCE

Historic Evidence

The earliest possible sources of potatoes on the Northwest coast are the Russian settlements in Alaska and the Spanish settlements at Nootka Sound and Neah Bay.

Although the Russians arrived early, their first colonization was at Kodiak in 1783. Here and at colonies established later to the east agriculture was tried but apparently without too much success.[3] Diffusion down the coast may have occurred, but evidence I will give later suggests diffusion in the opposite direction.

The Spanish put in gardens at Nootka, and one account mentions a number of plants, including potatoes, seen growing there in 1791 (Wagner 1933:162). But the Spanish did not stay long, and Jewitt in 1803 found a few European plants seeding themselves on the site of the Spanish establishment. He mentions no potatoes among them (Jewitt 1815:15).[4] I think Nootka Sound may be ruled out as a possible source of potatoes for the Coast Salish. There was also a garden at Neah Bay in 1792, but the settlement was abandoned after less than a year (Wagner 1933:62).[5]

Another possibility is that one or another of the earlier traders planted potatoes simply to create good will among the natives. A Captain Douglas planted some beans for the Haida in 1798 as such a good will gesture (Dawson 1880:159B-160B).

However, the most likely source of potatoes is, of course, the fur companies.

---

[3]Bancroft says that Shelikof, the founder of the colony on Kodiak, planted vegetables but could not persuade the Kaniagmiut even to eat them, let alone cultivate them (Bancroft 1886:227n.). However, he says "Khlebnikov . . . claims that mealy and good-flavored potatoes were raised at Sitka on ground manured with sea-weed, the crop being in some places 12 or 14 to one, but there is no confirmation of this statement." Furthermore, Wrangell states that more than a ton of potatoes were raised in 1831 (Bancroft 1886:687n.). Dr. T.C. Frye has told me that in 1913 he observed the Indians of New Metlakatla growing potatoes, using *Nereocystis* kelp as fertilizer. He believes this use of kelp was unknown to Americans at that time. It seems possible, then, that the planting of potatoes and the use of kelp as fertilizer by Indians go back to the time of Russian occupation.

[4]Sproat (1868:53) mentions potatoes as something obtained within the preceding twenty years.

[5]The account mentions only green vegetables.

The Pacific Fur Company planted twelve potatoes near Astoria in 1811 and three years later harvested fifty bushels of them (Barry 1929b:161).[6] When the Hudson's Bay Company took over Astoria, they continued to farm. Soon after posts were established on the Pacific slope, the Hudson's Bay Company was faced with the need for a supply of agricultural products not only for its own use but to fulfill a contract with the Russians as well (Bancroft 1887:61-62, 80-81). Therefore the Hudson's Bay Company established farms in connection with its forts. Gardens were planted at Fort Vancouver in 1825 (Scott 1917:56), Fort Colville in 1826 (Bancroft 1886:472), Fort Langley in 1827 (McKelvie 1947:46, 48), and at Fort Nisqually in 1833 (Bagley 1915:187). At each of these posts company employees were married to Native women, and it is likely that through them cultivation was spread among the Natives. The Company may have encouraged the Natives to take up cultivation in order to have another source of supply in emergencies.

Potatoes may have come up the coast from the mouth of the Columbia to the Strait, but the Hudson's Bay Company's Fort Langley, founded on the Fraser in 1827, looks like the most probable source of potatoes for the Strait and northern Sound peoples. The testimony of a company officer, the accounts of informants, and linguistic evidence support this conclusion.

James Douglas, in a letter to London in October 1839, wrote:

> I may be permitted to mention . . . as a matter to interest the friends of our native population, and all who desire to trace the first dawn and early progress of civilization, that the Cowegians around Fort Langley, influenced by the counsel and example of the fort, are beginning to cultivate the soil, many of them having with great perseverance and industry cleared patches of forest land of sufficient extent to plant, each ten bushels of potatoes; the same spirit of enterprise extends, though less generally, to the Gulf of Georgia and de Fuca's straits, where the very novel sight of flourishing fields of potatoes satisfies the missionary visitors that the Honourable Company neither oppose, nor feel indifferent to, the march of improvement (Ft. Langley Correspondence, p. 190).[7]

Douglas was, of course, attempting to refute accusations that the Hudson's Bay Company was determined to keep the country in a state of savagery,

---

[6]According to Barry the first Whites to plant in the Oregon country were the crew of the *Ruby*, near Ilwaco, in 1795. Barry (1929b) and Scott (1917) give considerable information on early White farming, especially in Oregon.

[7]Also quoted in McKelvie 1947:57. "Cowegian" is an old spelling of "Cowichan." Actually the name Cowichan belongs properly only to the villages on the Cowichan River, Vancouver Island, but it has been used by several writers as a general term for the Halkomelem-speaking peoples. Here Douglas simply meant Lower Fraser tribes.

so he may have exaggerated the role of the company in the spread of cultivation. However, Fort Langley looks like the best possibility for the northern Sound and Strait.

The next earliest report of potatoes grown in this area I have discovered is that of Father Blanchet, who visited the Skagit in 1840.[8] In 1841 Wilkes found them grown also by the Port Discovery Klallam and the people of Port Townsend (possibly Chemakum). The same year some Indians at Point Roberts offered some to George Simpson. In 1842, while reconnoitering the site of the future Victoria, Douglas found the Songish growing potatoes, and the next year he reported them for the Dungeness Klallam. In 1843 Father Demers was given potatoes by the Snohomish.

During the 1850s potatoes were reported for the Duwamish, Skagit, Makah, Cowichan, Nanaimo, Samish, Nuwhaha, and Semiahmoo. And I am sure I have not exhausted the literature.

Fitzhugh's description of the Nuwhaha (whom he calls "Neukwers") and other interior groups of northern Puget Sound deserves to be quoted in full because of the cultural and historic context in which potatoes appear. This was written in 1857.

> They have very little intercourse with the Saltchuck Indians, and never had seen a white man in 1852, when the first settlers came to this bay [Bellingham Bay], and did not even then come down for a year after.
> They dress in skins and blankets, made of dogs' hair and feathers, of their own manufacture. They have had no muskets until the last three years. They cultivate small patches of potatoes but subsist principally on elk, deer, fish, and berries (Fitzhugh 1858:326).[9]

From this one may infer that the Nuwhaha had potatoes before they had any direct contact with Whites.

Outside the Sound and Straits area the situation was the same. Potatoes were raised among the Haida by 1841, the Lower Thompson by 1847, the Kalispel by 1841, the Copalis and the Quinault by 1854, and the Umpqua by as early as 1834.

---

[8]This and the references immediately following are included in Appendix 1.

[9]The Nuwhaha lived in the Samish Valley and have sometimes been called "Upper Samish." This is a confusing term, however, since they and the Samish were different in orientation and in speech. The Nuwhaha were an inland people who spoke Puget Sound Salish; the Samish were a salt-water people who spoke *lək'oŋe′nəŋ*, the language I have called here "Straits Salish" from its distribution on both sides of the Strait of Juan de Fuca. The term "Nuwhaha" I have taken from the native name which appeared in the Point Elliot Treaty of 1885, "Noo-wha-ha."

It is possible, of course, that the word "potato" does not always refer to the white potato, *Solanum tuberosum*. One, perhaps several, native plants have been called "Indian potato." The plant most frequently so called was *Sagittaria latifolia*, called "arrowhead" in English, *wapato* in Chinook Jargon. The two plants, *Sagittaria* and *Solanum*, are not closely related, look quite unlike, and have quite different habits: *Sagittaria* has leaves like a calla lily and grows under water; it was gathered by wading and treading the roots loose. But apparently the two taste alike, so Native names for *Sagittaria* came to be used by Indians for the white potato. But the Whites usually used the name "wapato" to designate *Sagittaria*, and when they wrote of large quantities of potatoes of fine quality being raised on the natural clearings called "prairies," it is hard to believe they could have been writing of *Sagittaria*. Several native plants grew on the prairies, the most important being camas. But the early Whites also knew camas and called it that.

Old Indian informants describe the potatoes their grandparents raised as white potatoes and clearly distinguish between them and anything that might be called "Indian potatoes." It seems most probable that although there may have been an occasional confusion with a native plant, when early White accounts say "potatoes" they nearly always mean *Solanum tuberosum*.

Ethnographic Evidence

I first became aware of the early occurrence of potatoes among the Coast Salish while working on the Swinomish Reservation. Here three informants, two Samish and one Swinomish, told me substantially the same story. Potatoes came before the Whites were here. According to one account a man went to New Westminster and brought one sack of them to Swinomish. He gave the informant's grandmother about a dozen, told her to cut them into pieces, one eye to a piece, and plant them in the spring. She planted them, using a digging-stick such as women used for camas bulbs or clams. According to another account, potatoes were brought by Sechelt who came in big canoes and gave one bucket to each person. The informant's grandmother got one bucket. The Skagit chief *ní·x̌əm* came and got some to take back to Whidbey Island.

It was while he was on his way to meet a chief Netlam on Whidbey that Father Blanchet stumbled onto a Skagit potato patch. This was in 1840. When Wilkes came by the following year he found the Skagit growing potatoes and beans, and reported "the priests are inducing the Indians to cultivate the soil." Since Blanchet was the first priest to visit the Skagit and he found them growing potatoes already, he cannot be responsible for them, though he may have introduced the beans.

Informants from the Lummi, Saanich, and other groups also report potatoes being grown in their grandparents' time. One variety, possibly not the first to arrive, was called "ship potato" presumably from its source. The sources of the other varieties were unknown, but a Semiahmoo said that the variety believed to be the first grown used to be obtained from the Snokomish at Boundary Bay.[10]

Marian Smith states that the Nooksack were a center for the early diffusion of potatoes but says nothing as to time, source, or direction of diffusion (Smith 1949:2).[11] It seems quite possible that the Nuwhaha and other interior groups to their east and south got potatoes from the Nooksack, who are of course also interior people. But my Samish and Swinomish accounts suggest that salt-water people got them from other salt-water people. It may be that there were two lines of transmission south, one on the salt water and one in the interior.

Linguistic Evidence

Four Coast Salish languages are spoken in the area I am dealing with: the Vancouver Island tribes from Malahat to Qualicum and the Lower Fraser tribes speak a language they call Halkomelem; the southeast Vancouver Island tribes, the Klallam, and the Semiahmoo, Lummi, and Samish speak Straits Salish; the Swinomish and Nuwhaha and tribes south to Olympia speak Puget Sound Salish; while the Nooksack speak an isolated Salish language. As I have already indicated, over a fairly wide area the Native name for the *Sagittaria* came to be used for the introduced white potato. The Chinook Jargon *wapato*, the Puget Sound Salish *spiəqo'l'c*, and the Straits, Halkomelem, and Nooksack *skä'us*, all came to mean the white potato. Perhaps the transfer was made first in Chinook Jargon on the Columbia. Then when the word *wapato* was brought north as the name for both the native *Sagittaria* and the new plant, this precipitated the same transfer in the Salish languages. Or it may be that the two are so alike in flavor that the transfer of names suggests itself to everyone meeting the potato for the first time. Since Lummi and Nooksack informants knew *Sagittaria* as having been obtained on the Lower Fraser or in Duwamish country, it may be that the name *skä'us* is originally Halkomelem only.[12]

---

[10]Appendix 2 gives the data I have obtained on potato varieties.

[11]The statement appears in the article by Dr. Trinita Rivera, but was apparently written by Dr. Smith.

[12]McKelvie, apparently using McMillan's journal for the fall of 1827, says that at that time as many as 5,000 Indians, on the Lower Fraser for salmon, assembled at Pitt River at the end of salmon season "to dig 'skous,' a tuber that grew in pools and swamps, and which was considered a delicacy" (McKelvie 1947:33).

The word *skä'us* evidently originally meant the tuber of the *Sagittaria*; the whole plant, following the usual Salish practice, was called by a derivative word *skawi'səl'ł*. But when the white potato was introduced and it became *skä'us*, *Sagittaria* retained the name *skawi'səl'ł* only, and while some informants point out what has happened, others are apparently unaware that the two words are cognates. The common root is *ka'uis̯*. (The initial *s* is a frequent Salish prefix; the terminal *s̯* represents a sound which is probably distinct from *s* and sometimes appears as a *θ*.) This root is probably an old one in the Halkomelem and possibly Straits and Nooksack languages. But it has spread in the word for the white potato beyond its original range where it first meant *Sagittaria* tuber.

While the Halkomelem and the northern Straits dialects have *skä'us*, for the southern Straits dialects, Klallam and Samish, I recorded *ska'us* and *ska'wəc* respectively—the difference is probably not phonemic. (The correspondence of *s* of the northern dialects to *c* in the southern is usual.) Swinomish and Nuwhaha, the two northernmost Puget Sound dialects, have *ska'us* for the potato. In other Puget Sound dialects to the south the potato is *spiəqol'c*, the old word for *Sagittaria*. Swan (1870:101) gives the Makah word for potato as "kau-its," obviously the same word without the *s*- prefix and with the southern Straits final *c*. Dr. Morris Swadesh gave me the Alberni Nootka word (if my memory is right) as *ska'wəs*, with the *s*- prefix and with the northern final *s*. It is possible that the Swinomish and Nuwhaha words are old borrowings for *Sagittaria*, but the Makah and Alberni words must have arrived with the potato. And the fact that the Makah and Alberni words are unlike indicates separate borrowings from separate Salish dialects. What is more, Dawson recorded the Haida word for potato as "*skow-shīt*"(Dawson 1880:113B), which looks as if it may be the word *skä'us* plus some Haida suffix.

These terms for potatoes (with the Haida doubtful) then seem to go back to a Halkomelem or possibly specifically Lower Fraser word for the *Sagittaria*. This suggests that the potato itself was carried by Indians from the Lower Fraser.

It seems to me that a similar situation might be discovered elsewhere—lines of diffusion leading out from each early trading post, traceable by the terms used.[13] But what is to me more significant than *where* the Coast Salish got their potatoes is *how*. The inescapable conclusion is that, although in some

---

[13]Another example: Simpson saw potatoes on the Pend d'Oreille River in 1841, learned the Indians had got "the seed and implements" from Fort Colville (Simpson 1847:134), and gives the native word "*patac*" (presumably for potato, p. 146). Dr. W.W. Elmendorf was told by a Columbia that the Columbia and the Wenatchee raised potatoes, called *läptä'k*, before White settlement. In this instance the planting was done by men who broke the soil with large (six feet or more long) digging-sticks. Both sexes harvested.

places they got them directly from Whites, elsewhere they must have got them indirectly and with only the barest instructions as to their cultivation.*

II. The Position of the Potato in the Native Culture

To answer the question on the relation of potato cultivation to Native cultures, I shall summarize potato cultivation from early accounts and field notes, then try to show what was involved in the addition of potato cultivation to the Native culture.

Both the early accounts and the word of informants indicate that the labor of planting and harvesting was done primarily by women, using the traditional digging-stick that women used for roots and clams. The Saanich informant, however, said that the chief ləsče·'m at East Saanich owned about ten slaves of both sexes and that they cultivated potatoes for him. They turned the soil with digging-sticks and broke up the clods with their hands. In both the Swinomish and Samish informants' accounts potatoes were brought by men but given to women to raise. A Semiahmoo said his grandmother raised them, and Swan speaks of Makah women raising them. I am not sure ·how to interpret Gibbs' (1855:432) statement about the Duwamish: "Each head of a family plants his own, the quantity being regulated by the number of his women."

Early accounts usually describe the potato patches as small. So do the accounts of the informants: even the ten Saanich slaves cultivated altogether only about an acre.

Potato patches were usually on the natural clearings called "prairies" that used to be found on some of the islands and on some of the upper river valleys. The Samish first planted on a camas-prairie on Fidalgo Bay which was an abandoned village site to which women had habitually come for camas before they got potatoes. Blanchet, Gibbs, and Wilkes wrote of Skagit patches on prairies on Whidbey Island.[14]

---

*[I erred in my transcriptions of some of the Native terms. The Halkomelem for 'potato' is sqə́wθ, the Lummi probably sqə́ws, and the Samish, Klallam, and Northern Puget (Lushootseed) probably all sqáwc. My memory of what Swadesh said must have been dead wrong, for Sapir and Swadesh (1939:292) give the Nootka for "potatoes" as qa·wac. Some new data may be added. Kuipers (1970:65) gives the Squamish for "potato" as s-qawc and the Coeur d'Alene as sqig^wc, noting that the latter probably contains qig^w "dig roots," and he reconstructs s-qawc. If this Coeur d'Alene etymology is correct, perhaps the word was originally a generic term for edible root. Farther afield, a connection between this word and the Interior Salish and Sahaptin words for Lomatium cous (e.g., Turner et al. [1980:65] give the Okanagon as qaws or sqáwqaẁcn) might be worth exploring.]

[14]See Appendix 1 for references.

Simmons (1858:225) wrote in 1858 that the interior tribes raised more potatoes than the salt-water tribes. This may be simply because they had more prairies.

Two exceptions to the usual description of fields as small are those of the Cowichan and the Duwamish. The Cowichan fields which Douglas saw in 1854 were on "alluvial islands near the mouth of the river." He described them (1854:246) as "large and well-kept."

Gibbs (1855:432) says that the Duwamish and some others had about thirty acres under cultivation at the outlet of Lake Washington. In 1854 they raised about 3,000 bushels, an average of one hundred bushels to the acre. "Of these," he says, "they sold a part, reserving the rest for their own consumption." He does not say to whom they sold, but I take it sale was to Whites. He says, "Their potato patches are very fine, although they have used the same seed on the same ground for a succession of years." Elsewhere, referring to Puget Sound tribes in general, Gibbs (1877:223) writes, "Enclosures for garden patches were sometimes made by banking up around them with refuse thrown out in cleaning the ground, which, after a long while, came to resemble a low wall. . . ."

These statements, incidentally, suggest practices of long standing.

In regard to cooking methods, Lummi and Saanich informants say that potatoes were at first only roasted in the ashes and eaten with dried fish. One added that they were boiled only after iron kettles were acquired. Swan (1870:26) says that the Makah steamed their potatoes in wooden troughs by putting hot rocks in with them, sprinkling, and covering them over with mats. Describing meals, he says, "The potatoes are served first, and are eaten with oil, the custom being to peel off the skins with the fingers, dip the potato in oil and bite off a piece, repeating the process at each mouthful."

It is difficult to determine what role potatoes played in the native diet. Marian Smith (1949:21) says, "The potato was so quickly and readily accepted by all the groups of the area, and soon formed such an important item of diet, that one suspects the Indians had previously felt a certain deficiency in starch foods." But Swan (1870:33), writing of the Makah, says, "Potatoes are esteemed by them rather as a luxury than as ordinary food. . . ."

The truth may be that potatoes were accepted quickly and readily because in part they had a cash value at the trading posts, and this in turn gave them a potential value and thus a superior status among roots even at some distance from the posts.

During the period of settlement White needs may have been a factor in increasing Native production. Buying potatoes from Indians seems to have been a common practice among settlers.[15]

---

[15]In 1852 two traders, Cooper and Blankhorn, bought potatoes and cranberries from the Katzie to sell in San Francisco (Nelson 1927:19).

On the other hand, White settlement eventually had a bad effect on Native potato-raising. Without clear title to their lands, the Indians could not hold patches of prairie that they visited only for a few weeks or months of the year. Simmons in 1858 mentions the Whites' practice of taking over the good potato prairies (Simmons 1858:235; and better, Jones in Alvord 1857:9-10). The spot on Fidalgo Bay where the Samish first planted potatoes was, it so happens, the spot where the first settler in that area picked to settle. Even where colonists did not settle on the inviting prairies, they often had loose grazing livestock which soon found the prairies and destroyed the plants. Gibbs (1855:433) speaks of the cattle and hogs of settlers on Whidbey Island destroying not only the Skagits' potatoes but the Native camas as well. Thus it seems likely that the Indians were raising more potatoes before White settlement than after.

III. Possible Significance

The change from a food-gathering to an agricultural mode of life is usually represented as a highly significant one. It *is*, of course, in its ultimate consequences. But here such a change was taking place almost imperceptibly. The institutions and techniques of the Native food-gathering societies were organized in such a way that the cultivation of potatoes was able to enter without any need for a major economic readjustment.

Two things made this possible: first, the existence of a root-gathering tradition; and second, a sedentary life.

A root-gathering tradition implies a division of labor, with some members of the group assigned root-gathering as their regular task. It implies tools and digging techniques. And it implies methods of preparation and possibly of storage. Coast Salish culture assigned to men the task of providing meat and fish and to women the task of providing vegetable food and shellfish. Women gathered, among other things, roots, which they dug with digging-sticks, stored in baskets or bags, steamed with hot rocks under mats, served with fish and oil.

A sedentary life implies opportunities for the revisiting of the same root patches, the tending of the plants, and the development of concepts of ownership. The Coast Salish people maintained permanent dwellings in which extended families lived during half the year and which served as bases for food-gathering expeditions the other half. Their habitat was rich enough in natural foods and their preserving techniques were good enough to allow some members of the group to stay at home at any time if need be. And their means of transportation was fast enough that few expeditions took them more than a day's journey from home base. Thus women were able to return to the same root-patches, year after year, not only at digging-time but at other times as

146

well if they chose to. Concepts of ownership and simple tending of the plants could exist and did.

Ownership of patches may not be necessary to cultivation but caring for plants usually is, and the two—ownership and plant-tending—seem to be related. Among the Straits people, whose territory extended into the San Juan and Gulf islands, families owned not only camas beds but clam beds as well. In both cases they took some care of their property. In camas beds they kept the ground loosened up so as to make digging easier, and one informant spoke of burning off the bed after digging. In clam beds they sometimes took out the bigger rocks; one old Samish woman supervised the digging in her horse-clam bed, not allowing anyone to leave broken shells in the sand. Such beds and patches were the property of upper-class families. Ownership was through inheritance, but I suspect that an investment of labor helped maintain it.

Into this natural background came the cultivation of potatoes. The only new elements that were added were the plant itself and the planting of it. Moreover, this sort of planting does not require as great an understanding of what is involved as the planting of turnips or carrots. The potato-grower does not plant a small seed which sprouts and grows into a plant, another part of which is eaten. The potato-grower simply puts back into the ground a piece of the same stuff he eats.

Diffusion may also have been accelerated by other practices. Local exogamy, especially among the upper classes, and residence with the husband's family mean that women have greater mobility than men, and that women's activities have a better chance of spreading than men's.

Potato cultivation in turn may have had some influence on the uses of native plants. A Nuwhaha informant reported that the Nuwhaha had patches on Jarman Prairie where they raised three kinds of native bulbs. Each woman had her own strip, and around the patches were high fences of upright poles tied with cedarlimb rope. If a woman found good bulbs elsewhere, she brought them to her patch; and when she harvested the roots, she broke off the tops, crumpled them up, and put them back into the holes the roots came from. A Nooksack reported similar practices for her people at Goshen.[16]

How late this was I cannot say. These may have been practices transferred from potato cultivation or they may be older. Haeberlin and Gunther (1930:21) also have a tantalizing reference to the possible transplanting of *Sagittaria*.

The kind of cultivation practiced by these peoples naturally had its limitations. Without further development, either through more contact with Whites or through Native inventions, the potato crop probably could not have been

---

[16]Stern (1934:42-43) reports a similar seeding practice for the Lummi. But since Stern's data include items which are not Lummi but from neighboring groups I cannot be positive that this is a separate instance. [Later work made me think that Stern was in this instance probably right. See Suttles 1957a:164n.]

147

increased to any great extent. The amount of arable land available was limited, since most of the area was heavily forested. The fertility of the land used was limited; without manuring, crop-rotation, or any such means of renewing it, the soil would eventually have become poor. Simple farming peoples who do not practice manuring or its equivalent simply move on to richer soil. This means slashing and burning or actual clearing of land. The Coast Salish might have burned, as they sometimes did to let berries grow, but real clearing requires steel axes.

Another sort of limitation, imposed this time not by the habitat but by the organization of activities within the society, is the limitation of human time and effort. I suspect that women with digging-sticks could not have got much more land tilled than they did, considering the amount of time and effort required of women in their other activities, such as the gathering of other kinds of food and especially the preservation of fish and game brought in by the men. I doubt if potato production would have risen without better tools to till with or a decided shift in emphasis, or both.

But this is simply speculation. White settlement ended the whole Native way of life. The Indian men who were taught to plow and sow on reservations were taking over a new way of life.

Recent workers in this area seem to have ignored cultivation. It is understandable that one might say cultivation is due to White influence, therefore it is not part of the Native culture. But then neither are the products of steel blades a part of northern Northwest Coast culture nor horses of Plains culture.

I think we can learn something from Coast Salish potato-raising. A culture's ability to accept an item presented to it by diffusion tells us something about the structure of that culture. The ability of Coast Salish culture to accept the potato shows that food-gathering societies may be set up so that they can take over food-producing without wholesale change. But what has happened here is that the kind of cultivation which resulted looks quite unlike that prevailing at the source of the plants. Coast Salish cultivation took the form of something rather close to the simplest form of agriculture known elsewhere. The age-area principle applied to a series of peoples like the Coast Salish, marginal to advanced agriculture, could make a story quite different from the truth.

But the study of a number of such cases—food-gathering societies that were able to fit food-producing into pre-existing patterns—would tell us something about the origins of agriculture. What kinds of societies can begin cultivation?

Appendix 1

Tribe or location	Observation	Observer	Source
Duwamish	1855	Gibbs	Gibbs 1855:432
Snoqualmie	1853	Jones	Alvord 1857:7
Snohomish	1843	Demers	Quebec 1843:57
Skagit	1840	Blanchet	Quebec 1842:65
	1841	Wilkes	Wilkes 1845(4):481
	1855	Gibbs	Gibbs 1855:433
Samish	1857	Fitzhugh	Fitzhugh 1858:327
Nuwhaha ("Neukwers")	1857	Fitzhugh	Fitzhugh 1858:329
Semiahmoo	1857	Fitzhugh	Fitzhugh 1858:328
Point Roberts	1841	Simpson	Simpson 1847:183
Lower Fraser, etc.	1839	Douglas	Fort Langley Corresp., p. 190
Katzie	1852	Cooper and Blankhorn	Nelson 1927:19
Port Townsend (Chemakum?)	1841	Wilkes	Wilkes 1845(4):303
Klallam			
Port Townsend	1855	Gibbs	Gibbs 1855:430
Port Discovery	1841	Wilkes	Wilkes 1845(4):299
Dungeness	1843	Douglas	Douglas 1840-41:101
			Bancroft 1887:93
Makah	1855	Gibbs	Gibbs 1855:429
	1855	Gibbs	Gibbs 1877:126
	1868	Swan	Swan 1870:2,11,23,etc.
Sooke	1849-57?	Grant	Grant 1857:283
Songish	1842	Douglas	Bancroft 1887:89
Cowichan	1852	?	Douglas 1852
	1854	Douglas	Douglas 1854:246
Nanaimo	1854	Douglas	Douglas 1854:246-47
Outside the Sound and Straits Area[17]			
Haida	1841	Work	Simpson 1847:232
	1878	Dawson	Dawson 1880:113B
Lower Thompson	1847	Anderson	Bancroft 1887:167
Pend d'Oreille	1841	Simpson	Simpson 1847:143-44
Copalis	1854	Swan	Swan 1857:259
Quinault	1854	Swan	Swan 1857:267
Umpqua	1834	Work	Bancroft 1884:528

Appendix 2

The following are varieties of potatoes said to have been grown before the introduction of those raised in recent years. The descriptions are poor and confusing. It is even possible (though I doubt it) that the first two do not refer

---

[17]For further references to cultivation, especially in Oregon and eastern Washington, see Barry 1929a.

149

to potatoes at all but to other plants, native or introduced. The informants insisted all were potatoes.

1. According to one of the Samish informants, the first potatoes, which were introduced from "across the [Canadian] line," were small, round, and black with white spots. The informant gave no distinguishing name.

2. ƛ́uxʷ k̓ə́kələŋ ("no eyes," from k̓ə́ləŋ "eye"), described by a Semiahmoo as the first potato. They were smooth ("dirt didn't stick"), with thin ("thin as cigarette paper"), light orange skin and white flesh, and the size of prunes. Each hill produced a large cluster. The informant saw his grandmother dig these in her patch near White Rock, B.C., when he was a child. Although he is unsure whether they really had eyes or not and did not see the tops because they were dried up, he is certain that this was a variety of white potato. This potato had been replaced by other varieties by the time the informant (now in his 80s) was grown. He does not know anything of its origin, but remembers his grandmother saying that the Semiahmoo used to get them from the Snokomish at Blackie Spit, Boundary Bay. The Snokomish were wiped out by an epidemic, possibly that of 1852. They were in direct contact with Fort Langley via the Nicomekl River.

The name "no eyes" must have been given to this variety to distinguish it after the deep-eyed variety was introduced. It may have been merely a shallow-eyed potato, but if it were actually without eyes it could not have been a potato at all.

3. šə́pəɫ skä́us ("ship potato," from šə́p "ship"), described by a Saanich as bluish and as big as one's fist. They were raised by chief ləsčé·ʼmʼs slaves before White settlement although the name indicates that they were introduced from a ship.

The Semiahmoo believed that this variety had been introduced by a United States government ship before the Indians had any other contact with the government. He described them as similar to the present "red rose" variety. They came after the "no eyes" variety.

A Lummi knew vaguely of this variety and believed it was long, white, and with deep eyes. This sounds like the Saanich informant's kʷiʼtələs (No. 4).

4. kʷiƛ́ʼələs (meaning not known), described by the Semiahmoo informant as a big potato, raised by an uncle on San Juan Island during the informant's childhood.

The Lummi informant described potatoes of this variety as almost round, heavy, with reddish skin, white flesh, deep eyes and therefore hard to peel, slow to cook. They were also called xəmxəmíʼkʷən skä́us, "heavy potatoes."

kʷiʼtələs (wrongly recorded?), described by the Saanich informant as white, long, with lots of eyes. It was also planted by ləsčéʼmʼs slaves in pre-settlement times. They kept the two varieties separate.

5. xʷəŋxʷəŋəl skä́us ("early potatoes," from xʷə́ŋ, "fast"), described

by the Lummi informant as small, crooked (kidney-shaped?) and white, with good dry flesh.

Obviously more information is needed on early varieties of potatoes and native plants with which they may have been confused. It is possible that some early varieties still exist and may be collected: Dr Erna Gunther has told me that the Makah still raise a small white "finger potato," which they have had longer than other varieties.

The presence of several varieties of potatoes here soon after the first White contact would not be surprising. It is possible that different Whites introduced different varieties. It is also possible that new varieties were produced naturally from the variety or varieties introduced. Potatoes are usually grown from tubers, and that is the way the Indians learned to plant them. This involved no genetic change from one crop to the next. But let potatoes seed themselves and something different is bound to show up. The difference can then be preserved simply by planting from tubers again. The Saanich kept their two varieties separate. This is easy when one plants from tubers, since cross-fertilization is not a problem.

9. The Plateau Prophet Dance among the Coast Salish[1]*

The subject of messianic movements, revival cults, and related phenomena has continued to hold the interest of students of cultural change. The occurrence of these movements among American Indians has been best documented for the Basin and Plains areas, but they are also known from the Southwest, the Mackenzie, and the Plateau. In fact, Spier (1935) has presented good arguments for deriving the Basin, Plains, and Mackenzie movements from an underlying stratum of religious activity in the Plateau, which he has called the "Prophet Dance." He has also presented evidence that a form of the Plateau Prophet Dance reached the Northwest Coast by two routes, down the Skeena River to the Tsimshian and Haida, and down the Fraser River to the Coast Salish.

Since the appearance of Spier's paper twenty years ago, so far as I know, no further work has been done specifically on the occurrence of the Prophet Dance on the Coast. But several publications have contained material on it not fully recognized as such. And in addition, in the course of my own field work with the Coast Salish I have obtained several accounts of Prophet Dance

[1]I am grateful to the Western States Branch of the American Anthropological Association for financial aid in the publication of this paper and to W.W. Elmendorf, Walter Goldschmidt, Leslie Spier, and to my colleagues at the University of British Columbia for their helpful criticisms and suggestions.
*[From the *Southwestern Journal of Anthropology* 13:352-93 (1957).]

phenomena.[2] In view of the continued interest in such phenomena and their theoretical implications, it may be worthwhile to assemble this new material and look again at the westward extension of the Prophet Dance. In this paper I shall first summarize Spier's analysis of the history of the Prophet Dance in the Plateau, then present the data I have collected on its occurrence among the Coast Salish, and finally try to reconstruct the history of several of the elements of the complex.

The Coast Salish data should demonstrate that a form of the Prophet Dance was carried westward from the Plateau to the Coast, where it spread to all or nearly all the tribes of Puget Sound and Georgia Strait. The nature of the movement, moreover, suggests that the distinction between the "Native" belief system and Christianity may not be as clear and simple as most ethnographers have implicitly assumed; contemporary Coast Salish religion must be seen as the result of not one but a series of compromises and reinterpretations. Also, the early occurrence of this movement suggests that it may not be explained by hypotheses invoking conflict of cultures or deprivation.

The Prophet Dance of the Plateau

The Prophet Dance is reported ethnographically for most of the Plateau tribes for which there are data. Teit usually refers to it as the "religious dance" or "praying dance." Typically the ceremony was held under the direction of an inspired leader who interpreted portentous signs and direful events. This man had visions or even experienced a resurrection from the dead. The ceremony itself was a dance, usually circular, or series of dances in which a whole village or more participated and which included the worship of or appeal to a deity sometimes identified as the Transformer of mythology. Among some tribes the dances included one in which the participants confessed their sins; among some they included a dance in which the unmarried men and women might choose mates by touching one another. The doctrine behind the performance was one of imminent world destruction and world renewal with a return of the dead led by the Transformer. All were urged to join in the ceremony because it was believed "that intense preoccupation with the dance would hasten the happy day." Interest in the ceremony periodically declined when the day did not come, only to be stimulated again by new portents and new prophecies.

---

[2]I have done ethnographic work with the Coast Salish during several periods between 1946 and the present. This work has been supported successively by the Department of Anthropology at the University of Washington, by a Wenner-Gren Pre-doctoral Fellowship, and by the Carnegie Grant to Anthropology at the University of British Columbia.

Spier sees the roots of the Prophet Dance in Plateau and Northwest Coast culture, particularly in beliefs about the dead and in burial practices. These beliefs are seen in numerous myths and tales of visits of the living to the land of the dead, the fact that the dead may steal the soul or the guardian spirit of a living person, and the shamans' treatment of this type of soul-loss or spirit-loss by making a trip to the land of the dead. Also among several tribes preparations for burial are made immediately upon the death of a person, so that several instances have been reported of seeming resurrections that were evidently the result of premature burial. In some instances the resurrected person reported experiences clearly based on current beliefs about the dead. Spier notes that the interest shown by the Plateau and Northwest Coast tribes in the relation of the living to the dead is not shared by the tribes of the Basin or the Plains apart from the Prophet or Ghost dances.

The historical evidence for the Prophet Dance, Spier shows, can be sorted out into three periods:

(1) Before 1820 observers saw no Christian practices but did see dances of worship and evidence of the Indians' belief that a great change was to take place. A Kootenay woman seems to have transmitted these practices and beliefs to the Northern Athapaskans.

(2) During the 1830s several observers reported Christian worship among groups of Indians who had little contact with Whites. After examining the data Spier concludes that what had been observed was the aboriginal Prophet Dance to which had been added such elements as the observance of a Sabbath and the sign of the cross. These, he suggests, were probably introduced by a band of Iroquois who settled among the Flathead about 1820. (There is another possible source of Christian elements. Two Indian youths, Spokane Garry and Kootenai Pelly, were taken to Red River in 1825 where they received an education in English and instruction in the Anglican faith. They returned to their homes in 1829, after which Garry is said to have taught Christianity among the Plateau tribes. See Jessett 1951:226-31.) The Christianized Prophet Dance that developed among the Flathead after 1820 spread throughout the Plateau and northward where it may have been the impetus of the movement among the Carrier led by the prophet Bini.[3] This movement spread down the Skeena River and even reached the Haida in the Queen Charlottes.

(3) From about 1850 onward several clearly defined cults arose in the Plateau, probably as a result of more direct contact with Whites and perhaps aggravated by some warfare with them. The best-known example is that of Smohalla, who preached among the Sahaptins of the Columbia River. His doctrine was that the world, and particularly the Whites, would be destroyed and the old way of life would be restored complete with the resurrection of

---

[3]Since the publication of Spier's paper considerable data on Bini have been published by Jenness (1943).

the dead. In preparation for this event he warned his followers to adhere strictly to Native dress and customs. For his ceremonies he had built a building resembling a church and erected a flagpole on a parade ground resembling a military establishment. The ceremony consisted of a dance with bells and drums, recitation of doctrine with questions by the leader and answers by the followers, a ritual meal of water and salmon, more dancing, and individual accounts of vision experiences.[4]

Spier suggests that the Shaker Church that was established on Puget Sound in the 1880s was possibly inspired by the Smohalla movement, which was undoubtedly known on the Sound. The Shaker Church was established after the resurrection of John Slocum of the Squaxin tribe near Olympia in 1882. It differs strongly from the Smohalla movement in having more of Christianity in it and in lacking any anti-White feeling. Spier says of it, "Nominally Christian, in actual practice it is an extraordinary blend of old shamanistic performances with Catholic ritual and Protestant doctrine." The Shaker Church has made converts as far north as southern British Columbia and as far south as the Klamath Reservation in Oregon.[5]

From this third phase in the Plateau Spier derives the Ghost Dance of the Paviotso in 1870 and 1890, the last leading to the great spread of the Ghost Dance through the Plains.

Early White Contact with the Coast Salish

Before I discuss the appearance of the Prophet Dance among the Coast Salish it might be well to review briefly the history of the earliest European contact with them, particularly the first missionary activity. The first recorded contact was in 1790-93 when the Spanish and British explored the Strait of Juan de Fuca, Puget Sound, and Georgia Strait. The accounts of these expeditions give no indication of any sort of cult activity nor of any great awe on the part of the Natives, such as Thompson met with among the Interior Salish two decades later.

Contact with later maritime fur traders was probably only sporadic and of not much importance since the Coast Salish had less to offer than the people on the outer coast; the most valuable fur animal, the sea otter, was rare inside the Strait of Juan de Fuca.

In 1805-06 Lewis and Clark passed by the southern end of Coast Salish territory, but the first land expedition to reach the center of the territory was that of Simon Fraser, who descended the Fraser River in 1807. Further contact by land, however, was probably negligible until the establishment of the

---

[4]For a somewhat late cult among the Sanpoil see Ray 1936; see also DuBois 1938.

[5]The most recent discussion of the history of this sect is Gunther 1949. [See also Barnett 1957.]

Hudson's Bay Company posts. The first post in Coast Salish territory was Ft. Langley, established on the lower Fraser in 1827. In 1833 Ft. Nisqually was established near the head of Puget Sound and in 1843 Victoria was founded. It is worth noting that these posts were established somewhat later than those on the lower Columbia and in the interior.

While it is quite likely that the Native peoples learned something of Christianity from the fur traders, the first recorded contact of any Coast Salish with missionaries was in 1837. In that year two Catholic priests, Fathers F.N. Blanchet and M. Demers, arrived on the lower Columbia and established a mission on the Cowlitz River in Coast Salish territory. In the spring of 1839 several Indians from Puget Sound, including a Suquamish chief, journeyed overland to Cowlitz to see the priests, so Demers went to Ft. Nisqually near the head of the Sound, met these Indians again and others of twenty-two different nations (Blanchet 1910:32), and distributed among them "Catholic Ladders," which he explained in Chinook Jargon. The "Catholic Ladder" was piece of wood with groups of notches and symbols carved on it to represent the passage of time and the principal events since Creation. In the spring of 1840 Demers again visited Nisqually where he instructed chiefs of the Skagit, Suquamish, and Snohomish. Later in 1840 Blanchet was taken by the Suquamish chief to Whidbey Island, where he was pleased to meet a large gathering of Skagit, Suquamish, and Snohomish, and to find that they had already learned the Chinook Jargon prayers and hymns that Demers had taught their chiefs at Nisqually. His presence also had some political consequences since he helped settle a dispute between the Klallam and the Skykomish. In 1841 Demers again visited Whidbey Island and probably passed through Samish and Lummi territory to go to Ft. Langley on the Fraser where he baptized several hundred children. In March of 1843 Father J.B.Z. Bolduc accompanied Douglas to the site of Victoria, preached to the Songish and others there, then returned southward by way of Whidbey Island, where he met the Klallam, the Skagit, and an unnamed group from the mainland. In May of 1843 Bolduc and Demers again went to Whidbey where they continued to have contact not only with the Skagit but also with the Suquamish, Snohomish, Klallam, and even Makah. First Blanchet and then Bolduc had hoped to establish a mission on Whidbey but by the end of Bolduc's second visit, to judge from his own statements, the enthusiasm of the Indians for the new faith had waned and he himself had become discouraged.

The Coast Salish north of Nisqually apparently had little or no contact with the missionaries between the early '40s and the early '50s. In 1847 Demers was appointed Bishop of Vancouver Island but he was not able to reach Victoria until 1852. When he did, he discovered to his dismay that an inexperienced priest had just preceded him and had baptized many Indians without giving proper instruction in Catholic doctrine, thus making future work more difficult. This priest, Father H. Lempfrit, may have been the first to visit the Saanich and Cowichan, although many of these tribes may have seen Demers earlier on the Fraser. Regular contact with priests began only after the arrival of the Oblate Fathers, who established their headquarters at Esquimalt in 1857. The most influential of these men on the American side of the boundary was Father E.C. Chirouse, who established a mission at Tulalip on the Snohomish Reservation in the same year, 1857. During the next few years chapels were built for most of the tribes in the Straits area. Chirouse was especially active among the northern Puget Sound and Straits tribes.[6]

Thus the Coast Salish of Puget Sound and Georgia Strait had their first direct contact with Christian missionaries only in 1839, after which some, such as the Skagit, had fairly close contact for three or four years. This was followed by a period of ten to fifteen years during which there was little or no contact. The first appearance of the Plateau Prophet Dance on the Coast occurred, according to Native tradition, before the first priest arrived. If tradition is correct this would be before the period of mission activity from 1839 to 1843. It seems probable that some of the phenomena described in the following pages did exist before 1839. Other developments probably occurred during the later period of little contact, when some of the elements of missionary teaching were put to use for Native ends.

The Coast Salish Data

In the present section I have tried to extract from the data at hand, both published and unpublished, all references to elements that seem to be manifestations of the Prophet Dance. These elements include principally (1) the marriage dance, a dance during which young people were able to choose spouses by some gesture such as placing something on the person of another; (2) the worship of a deity, usually identified by a term meaning "Chief Above"; (3) prophecy, especially foretelling the coming of the Whites, and the prophet as a leader in Native society. In the published material all three of these elements are nowhere presented as part of a single complex. Yet the accounts given by some Coast Salish informants make it seem probable that they did form a single complex. The sum of the data presented here and comparison with the Plateau material lead to the conclusion that the Coast Salish area has experienced a series of developments parallel to that outlined by Spier for the Plateau. It appears that, as in the Plateau, there was some basis in Native culture for the rise of prophetic leaders, that somewhat before much

---

[6] For the history of the missions I have used mainly Blanchet 1910, Jennings 1937a and 1937b (translations of Bolduc's letters), and Morice 1910 (the English edition). It should be noted that Morice 1923 (the French edition) contains material not given in the earlier work.

157

if any missionary activity had occurred prophetic leaders introduced a form of the Plateau Prophet Dance having the marriage dance as a rite of worship, and that later prophets, as in the Plateau, incorporated more clearly Christian elements into local cults.

But before I go into the material itself I must first dispose of the possible northern route of diffusion from the Plateau to the Coast Salish. Spier suggests that the Prophet Dance spread down the Skeena to the Tsimshian, to the Haida, and then southward along the Coast to the Salish. Evidence for the spread of the movements down the Skeena and to the Haida seems clear enough, but Spier's assumption that it came southward as far as the Nanaimo is based entirely on his interpretation of a statement by the Rev Thomas Crosby. Crosby writes (1907:18-19) that "at the time of the great revival on the North Coast, in 1875," he had been told of much earlier religious excitement due to news brought from down the Skeena and from Alaska of what sounded like Christian worship. But while Crosby's book mainly describes his work among the Coast Salish, especially at Nanaimo, this statement appears in the introductory chapter with nothing in its context to suggest that its locale was Nanaimo. On the contrary Crosby's "North Coast" must mean the north coast of the province, not of Vancouver Island, since Crosby was in fact preaching there among the Tsimshian in 1875 (Crosby 1914:29ff.; Arctander 1908:245).

The data are presented tribe by tribe in roughly geographical order.

Lummi

The first account that I obtained anywhere of the Prophet Dance-like activity was from Julius Charles, a half-Semiahmoo half-Lummi born about 1865. The account came spontaneously after a question on the Native word for "prayer":

> "Pray" is *t'i'wyəł*. The old prayer was started by the leader. It went: "*aa t'iwyəł aa t'iwyəł aa šišəkəli.*" The whole tribe came together. They danced circling around like a square dance. If a young man loved a girl he stuck a feather on the girl's head. If the girl kept it they were engaged. A girl could do the same. This was just called *st'i'wyəł*. All danced, married and unmarried, all that believe there is a *xé·ls* [Transformer]. That's all they do. It's any time of year; don't know how often. Some don't care and stay away but most believe that. Davy Crockett was the leader. He did that before the priest came. It was done way before that. Davy Crockett was the first one to believe in *xɛ'els*, so the old folks said.*

---

*[In this article, Native terms stand as originally published.]

158

This informant later added that Davy Crockett ($x^way l\varepsilon'n\partial x^w$) not only led the marriage dance "before he know there was a priest in the world," but also after the priests did come he was the first convert and helped convert the others. It is a matter of record that David Crockett was the chief in the 1860s and that he led the Lummi in Catholic worship.[7] This informant also gave the words of the Chilliwack song and said that the Saanich and Cowichan also had the same practice.

Another informant at Lummi, Patrick George, a man born about 1877, gave a description somewhat different from that of the first informant; since this man said that he heard about the practice both from his mother, who was a Semiahmoo, and as a boy while staying at Cowichan, it seems probable that his description refers to other than the Lummi practice. Also he did not relate the dance to Davy Crockett.

> The people stood in a circle and sang. The leader called out and the people raised their hands and repeated. Then they danced in a circle and a boy threw his handkerchief (?) to the girl he wanted. She threw it back or kept it. If she kept it they were married right away. I don't know how that came to the Indians . . . . The first part of the song went, "*t'i'wyəɬ əkʷə si'səɬ siɛ'm*," and the second part went, "*həy' kʷəntɛ'ləs əkʷə si'səɬ siɛ'm.*"

This informant translated *si'səɬ siɛ'm* (literally "above chief") as "God," but also equated the term with *x̣é·ls*, the Transformer.

The marriage dance had already been reported for the Lummi. In the chapter on marriage in his ethnography of the Lummi, Stern (1934:29) gives a brief description of a marriage dance in which a boy or girl could choose a mate by placing a hand on the shoulder of the other. If the proposal were acceptable the couple locked arms and were considered betrothed at that time. Later there might be the customary proposal by the boy's family and exchange of property.

Stern presents this without comment as if it were part of the aboriginal culture, which he doubtless took it to be. He also says that the performance took place "in the 'humpbacked year' only" a statement which calls for a comment. I once discussed the dance with Stern's principal informant, Joseph Hillaire, a well-educated man in middle age. Hillaire compared the dance to the White's notion of "leap year" as a time when women may propose marriage and said that it must have been held at some fixed interval marked by some event such as the biennial run of the humpback salmon. Older

---

[7]See McKenny 1868:93. Roth (1926:974) quotes a local historian to the effect that Crockett was chosen chief about 1859 after he had embraced the Catholic faith. See also Suttles 1954:67-71.

informants' statements give no indication of such an interval for the dance. Moreover, they make it clear that the marriage dance was not an ordinary practice but part of an introduced cult and was accompanied by the worship of a deity identified as x̣é·ls (the Transformer) or as si'sət siɛ'm (Chief Above) and by the assumption of some authority by the cult leader.

Lummi informants also believe that this cult occurred also among several other tribes; they named the Chilliwack, Swinomish, Snohomish, Saanich, and Cowichan. Data collected since have borne out their statements.

Upper Stalo

The term "Stalo" was recently revived by Duff for the Coast Salish of the lower Fraser River, the groups whom Hill-Tout called "Mainland Halkomelem." The first is an anglicized form of the Native word stá'ləw, "river," by which these groups are often collectively designated; the second is an anglicized form of the Native name for the Native language hɛl'k'ʷəmi'ləm in the dialects spoken above Matsqui, hən'k'ʷəmi'nəm below Matsqui and on Vancouver Island.*

Duff uses "Upper Stalo" for the three groups nearest the Interior, the Chilliwack, Pilalt, and Tait. He notes (Duff 1952:93) a marriage dance, described by a Chilliwack informant as,

> a "marrying party" which was held once every few years and at which young people got the chance to choose their marriage partners. To the constant rhythm of a song, the words of which seem to have been "who is going to take this woman," etc., couples paired up on the floor, dancing. Then the speaker had each couple take hands and repeat vows, witnessed by the other people present.

Duff adds that a Tait informant denied that the Stalo had this "marrying party," but believed the Thompson may have had it, and he notes that Stern reports it for the Lummi. Duff evidently got no association between the marriage dance and any form of worship. One of my Lummi informants, however, stated that the Chilliwack had the same dance as the Lummi and gave as the Chilliwack words to the song "hay kʷət ƛ̓at sə stɛləy," which he translated as "Go get the girl." This is probably the same song that Duff's Chilliwack informant gave.

But Duff has discussed at length (1952:119-22) the concept of a Supreme Being as he found it among the Upper Stalo. All of his informants believed

---

*[More correctly hɛlq̓əméyləm upriver, hənq̓əmínəm downriver, and həlq̓əmínəm on the island.]

160

that their ancestors knew, as čícəɬ siɛ′m, the same God that the missionaries talked of; however, they only introduced the concept when discussing the first salmon rite and certain persons whom they called "prophets." The first salmon rite included prayers addressed to the Supreme Being but otherwise resembled the first salmon rites of other peoples in this area. The term "prophet" was his informant's English translation of a Native term *alia*. Ordinarily *alia* (ʔə′lyə) as a verb means "to have a vision" and the noun derivative *sʔə′lyə* means "vision" or "guardian spirit"; this is the case in both Upper Stalo and Lower Stalo dialects. But Duff's Upper Stalo informants also used *alia* as a noun for a type of dealer in the supernatural distinct from the *sxʷəlɛ′m* ("shaman") and *se′uwa* ("fortune-teller"). Two such persons were described in detail.

One was a man named *skəlbɛ′xəl*, who lived a few miles above Agassiz and flourished, Duff estimates, about 1840. It was said that this man had a vision in which three men appeared and bade him kneel, make the sign of the cross, and worship God. Then they showed him the inside of a great church, they taught him rules of moral conduct, they described the coming of the Whites and their technology, and they warned him that the priests to come would be half good and half bad. After his vision *skəlbɛ′xəl* preached to his own group and to others who came to hear, and he enabled them to see his vision of the church. Later he travelled and preached as far up the Fraser as Lytton, in Thompson country. When the first priests came he was an old man. According to a second account the prophet's church was a cave in the mountains. A third account described what must have been the same person under the name *tawqpa′mət*, but had him bringing writing, which he preached from, and metal tools from his cave in the mountains.

A second *alia* was a man from Seabird Island named *kʷələs*, who had a vision a few years after the first one died. He also preached, practiced clairvoyance, and performed miracles, such as curing with medicine that he produced magically from a bottle.

Some of Duff's informants believed that there had been other *alia* before these two. Duff concludes that the belief in a Supreme Being was a result of White contact and that it was introduced by the *alia*, who may have existed in pre-contact times as a type of seer or miracle-worker.

The prophet *skəlbɛ′xəl* described by Duff's informants is probably the same person as the "Skilmaha" about whom Densmore (1943:86-87) obtained some information in the course of collecting Coast Salish songs.

> This man lived near Hope "about a century ago, before the coming of the white man." He "foretold the coming of a different people and had many followers." He also was said to be subject to trances of a cataleptic nature.

161

Densmore's "free translation" of the words of the prophet song reads: "I would believe you if you would destroy us by fire." The analysis of the music suggests that there were also other verses. She believes that the words show a knowledge of the New Testament, disproving the statement that the prophet lived before the Whites came. She also suggests that this man was the same as the Interior Salish* prophet Smohalla, but this is undoubtedly incorrect.

Teit (1900:366), after discussing several Thompson prophets, states that a prophet from the Fraser Delta had appeared at Lytton "in the last fifteen or twenty years," that is, not earlier than about 1880. He preached through an interpreter, prayed a great deal, and performed sleight-of-hand tricks. Duff's *skəlbɛ́xəl* also preached among the Thompson, but if both Teit and Duff are correct in their dates, their prophets could not have been the same man.

Duff concludes that the concept of the deity was probably the result of "early borrowing," despite his informants' opinions that it was aboriginal. However, some of the Chilliwack would agree with Duff; Jenness (1955:88) says that a Sardis (Chilliwack) man "emphatically insisted" that the name "Chief Above" was introduced by White missionaries and that before this his people had prayed only to the sun, forces of nature, and the spirits of animals.

Hill-Tout's work on the tribes of the lower Fraser contains some material on the Chilliwack. He speaks (1902:357) of the Chilliwack chief having priestly functions, but it is not clear whether he refers to aboriginal conditions as well as post-missionary conditions.

Chehalis

The Chehalis of British Columbia (not to be confused with the Chehalis of southwestern Washington) are a small group on the Harrison River below Harrison Lake. They were in an especially good position to receive any influences from the Interior since they were on friendly terms with the Douglas Lillooet at the upper end of Harrison Lake (Duff 1952:22).

As Spier noted, Hill-Tout (1904b:529) reported Prophet Dance phenomena among them. According to Chehalis tradition, the people used to come together every seventh day for dancing and praying. They assembled at sunrise and danced till noon. At this time of the day they believed that everybody stood on his head till the world rolled around again. This topsy-turveydom took place during the middle hours of the day. When the world had come round again, they all fell to dancing and praying again till sunset.

---

*[Correction: Smohalla was Sahaptin (Mooney 1896:716).]

162

Spier (1935:62) observes that "both the seventh day performance and the interruption of the dance by a period of rest have parallels in the Thompson practice." Hill-Tout only concludes that neither the practice nor the concept of the deity to whom the prayer was directed was Native. I will return to his opinions on the matter later.

It will be remembered that the Upper Stalo deity appears in relation to the first salmon rite. Hill-Tout (1904b:331) describes the first salmon rite of the Chehalis, during which all persons were forced to shut their eyes while the chief prayed, and mentions a ceremony held for the first green shoots eaten in the spring. But he takes the position that these ceremonies were not addressed to any higher deity but rather had as their object the propitiation of the fish and the plants themselves. This interpretation of the salmon rite seems quite in line with Gunther's interpretation and with my own impressions. Gunther (1928:116) writes "In every salmon ritual it is clear that the welfare of the animal is most important and these taboos regulate conduct that his spirit may not be offended."

Kwantlen

In pre-contact times the principal villages of the Kwantlen were at New Westminster, at the head of the Fraser Delta. However, after the Hudson's Bay Company established Fort Langley, in 1827, the Kwantlen moved upstream and established themselves near the fort, where their descendants have remained, to be known as the "Langley Tribe." From all accounts the Kwantlen were the most important of the Stalo tribes, evidently even in pre-contact times, though their position was undoubtedly later strengthened by their alliance with the Whites at the fort.

As Spier noted, Hill-Tout (1902:410-11) also gives an account of a sort of Prophet Dance among this tribe. He does so in discussing the functions of the chief, who was "the tribal high priest," necessary for every religious ceremony, but with functions quite distinct from those of the shaman.

> On the occasion of any public calamity, such as a wide-spread sickness, times of famine and want, during meteorological phenomena, such as violent storms, prolonged droughts, earthquakes and eclipses, it was he who led and conducted the prayers and confessions of the people, and invoked the pity of tᴇ tcĩtcil siä'm, or "the Sky Chief", whom he addressed as cwai'ᴇtsᴇn, i.e., "parent", or "Father", or "Creator". He would bid the people come together on these occasions and pray and dance; the latter action being regarded as propitiating and honouring in their estimation. As they danced the people would hold their hands aloft.

At the close the chief would bid them place them on their breasts and repent of their evil deeds and thoughts.

Hill-Tout notes that the element of confession suggests Roman Catholic influence, but concedes that it may be "genuinely" Native. Spier (1935:62) observes, however, that there are parallels here to the Southern Okanagon form of the Prophet Dance.

Although Hill-Tout (1902:414) clearly indicates, in discussing the Chehalis, that he does not regard the concept of a deity as Native, when discussing the Kwantlen he says that "Qäls [xɛ'ɛls], the Transformer" was invoked as a deity and was believed to have instituted the first fruits rite, taught people to pray, and taught the shamans their songs. He adds that "Qäls" was not a single character but rather eight brothers.

Katzie

The Katzie are a small group whose territory lay principally on Pitt River and Pitt Lake. Jenness (1955:10-34) presents a myth of nearly epic length that he recorded from a shaman of this group. This myth or cycle of myths and the practices and beliefs described by the informant reveal a rather well-integrated concept of a Supreme Being called ci'cɛł siɛ'm which Jenness translates as "He Who Dwells Above." In the view of the Katzie informant, xɛ'ɛls (the Transformer) was a single person who came transforming, accompanied by several animal characters; he was sent by ci'cɛł siɛ'm, to whom he was subordinate. Jenness indicates that informants elsewhere regarded the concept of the deity as a recent introduction, but after some hesitation he concludes that it may have been aboriginal among the Katzie, especially because of the existence of parallel beliefs among the Bella Coola, the northernmost tribe of Salish speech.

Jenness gives nothing on the Katzie suggesting any marriage dance, or prophet-like leaders among this tribe. In his appendix, however, there are several notes on other tribes, which have been introduced in their proper places here.

Nooksack

The Nooksack (xʷsɛ'ʔɛq) live in the valley of the Nooksack River south of the Matsqui and Sumas and inland from the Lummi; to their south are the Upper Skagit. They spoke an isolated Coast Salish language called łə'čələsəm. The late Paul Fetzer spent several periods working with Nooksack ethnography and linguistics from the summer of 1950 until his unfortunate death in January of 1952. From his ethnographic notes, now on file at the University of British Columbia, I have extracted the following:

Indian Church—in the winter-time, or any time, maybe once a month—the people of a village would gather around a fire in a longhouse and dance around it, singing a song in which "thanks is given to God." The arms are held up at an angle and the hands palms upward. [diagram] Then if a woman wants a man or vice versa, she comes up to the other and hooks arms and dances with the chosen partner. This act signifies that she wants to marry the other. If the other doesn't want the first, then he or she tries to shake him or her off, but the other must hang on tightly and continue to dance. No one could break this, for they were married right there, while they were dancing and singing the praise of God. If the person who is hooked onto doesn't want the other person, he or she can't do anything about it as long as the person hangs on.

The Lummis and Skagits used to come up to Nooksack to attend the Nooksack Indian Church, because they heard it was a great thing.

The Indian preacher in the Indian Church—There was a regular preacher for the whole tribe. He received his message in a dream from God. He was from *spɛ·'t̓xən* [Goshen]. (Doesn't remember his name or family.) He would go from village to village and the people in each band area would know when he was due and would assemble to dance and sing.

The informant who gave this note was Agnes James, a woman born about 1885; she states that she had heard Charlie *ɛdɛ·'s*, a man a generation older, tell this. Another note, presumably supplied by Fetzer's principal informant George Swaniset, adds the opinion that parents could nullify selections made in this manner but usually felt obliged to permit the marriages.

Samish

The Jenness (1955) work on the Katzie contains an account given by the informant of a case of return from the dead. A relative of the informant's Samish grandmother, identified as a Guemes Island Samish, was said to have died and come back to life. He claimed to have been taught moral principles by the deity and he took a new name *čəwa'yəs* meaning "returned to life." But the account contains no indication that any ritual practices were developed from this experience. My own Samish field notes contain no information on this person at all. Actually I am not at all sure that this man was Samish;

the Katzie informant's Samish grandmother was evidently also of Skykomish ancestry and the relative may have been from one of the tribes farther south.

Upper Skagit

Collins (1950:340) discusses the appearance of several religious leaders among the people of the upper Skagit valley. These leaders, she believes, were men who had contact with Christianity at the first mission west of the Cascades and returned to their homes to institute cults combining Native and Christian elements. One such leader was a man named Slabebtikud, who organized ceremonies with Catholic elements, such as the sign of the cross, around Native practices such as the first salmon rites. He also handed down moral rules and appointed officers to be responsible for enforcing the rules with such punishments as whippings and exposure. Collins points out that in Native practices there was no comparable formal organization or concentration of authority. The earlier first salmon rite was practiced separately by each household; during Slabebtikud's ascendance he supervised one rite for the whole Skagit valley and saw that those who took fish beforehand were punished. Such authority aroused resentment and in the end Slabebtikud was assassinated. Collins does not mention any sort of marriage dance.[8]

Snohomish

An informant at Tulalip, Mrs. William Shelton, gave an account of the marriage dance among the Puget Sound tribes. Mrs. Shelton believes she was born about 1858. Her father was a Klallam and her mother a Nuwhaha ("Upper Samish"); she regards herself as a Klallam but spent most of her childhood in the Bellingham area and has for more than half a century lived in Tulalip. Her husband was one of Haeberlin's principal Snohomish informants. A question on the marriage dance elicted the following:

> That was called just sə́xəb, "dancing." It came from eastern Washington, down the Skagit River, and spread all around the Sound. They believed in the Creator. They danced in a circle, like the Shakers do now. If a man put a feather on a girl's hair and she left it there that meant that they were married. If she threw

---

[8]Sally Snyder has unpublished material on the political organization of this cult; she also found no indications of a marriage dance associated with it (personal communication).

it away she refused him. This came to the Stillaguamish and to the Snohomish and went all around the Sound to the Klallam. Couples were getting married by it; sometimes, a lower-class man would get an upper-class girl. When it came to the Klallam the Klallam accepted it, but then the chiefs saw lower-class men proposing to upper-class girls. They had to let it go because they had said that they would do it, but they said, "What are our descendants going to be like? All lower class!" In those days they tried to keep their blood pure. So the chiefs got together and stopped it. After the Klallam stopped it, it was stopped all over. It got as far as the Lummi to the north, maybe farther but I never heard of it.

Mrs. Shelton said that she had heard of this from her mother and from an aunt of her husband at Tulalip. Her husband said, "They got drunk on that." Further reflection on the subject reminded her that when she was young she had seen a Swinomish couple who were at that time old, "she was high class and he was low class—not slave, but they were married that way." In another context she mentioned being at Swinomish in the 1870s; a couple old at that time might have been married in the 1830s, about when Smith (see below) calculates the marriage dance struck the Puyallup-Nisqually.

Mrs. Shelton also recalled that some years ago some of the Swinomish had put on a mock marriage dance at the "Treaty Day" celebration, putting feathers in their wives' hair "just to show the young people." I later questioned one old man at Swinomish; he knew of the marriage dance, but could give no further information.

Puyallup-Nisqually

Smith (1940:170) notes a marriage dance ceremony. It was said to have been a new custom, popular, she reckons, about 1830.

> The men danced in a circle with the women around them. A woman chose a husband by placing a little stick on the preferred man's shoulder. These marriages were often followed by the usual exchange of property. The dance was said to have been introduced from the Plateau, but one informant thought it may have been brought back by an Indian who had been by ship to California and who pretended to be able to read.

Smith does not mention worship, prophecy, or any of the other elements of the Prophet Dance.

Twana

Dr. W.W. Elmendorf has given me several items from his field notes.

Two informants described a prophecy of the coming of the Whites: A man at a power dance prophesied the coming of the white men. This was before the people here had heard of whites. The man said they would be strange people, with birds like grouse, and some kind of ducks and deer around their houses, not wild in the woods. They would paddle sitting backwards. The man's name was *waɬa'č'a·ləq*. He made his prophecy at Port Madison. Some people from here (Skokomish) were there and heard it. The man was *swayu'c?d*, getting his power to dance, when he made the prophecy. Anybody might prophesy coming events at scc'u'ctab (Twana, power dance), when they were showing their *təmä'nəməs*.

Henry Allen, born about 1865, described the "marriage dance": We (Twana) had a word *sqʷi'c*, means "dance" of any kind. The Puget Sound word is *səxəb*. This word got used for the "marrying dance," a kind of religion that came here in the generation before me. The parents of Old Man Loojay (probably born in the 1850's) were married here at Skokomish by this dance.

In this dance men and women lined up in two rows, parallel, facing each other. They would dance up and down. Then a man or woman would dance forward and choose a partner from the opposite row. The idea was, the spirit moved you to choose the right person. When the couple met in the dance they shook hands. I also heard they went around in a circle, singing and dancing. When somebody took somebody else, a man or a girl, by the hand, then they were married right now.

They had a poor little song that went something like *ay? he? ha'y? ya ha*. They were a kind of a religion, but I don't know their beliefs, or what they were against. Curtis (the informant was E.S. Curtis' interpreter) worked on this; he traced them clear from Syracuse, New York. The religion came to this country from outside, long before the Shakers. It died out while I was a boy.

Henry's older brother Frank Allen gave the following: Way back, before my great-grandfather(!) a man came along here and preached. The people danced in a circle and married by choosing a man. They confessed sins. Wa'qəblu, the Skokomish woman with power for getting men, broke a stick every time she had intercourse during the week, and burned a great pile of them every Sunday. The man who preached was Skokomish. He had been captured and taken way east years before, and now he came back here.

Klallam

I have no information of the occurrence of any Prophet Dance elements among the Klallam other than the account give by Mrs. Shelton, quoted above, telling how they rejected the marriage dance, and the reference in the Cowichan account given by Jenness (see below). Henry Charles, an excellent informant from the Becher Bay Klallam of Vancouver Island, had never heard of the marriage dance. This man also knows the Klallam of the Olympic peninsula well, having spent part of his youth at Jamestown. Gunther (1927) does not mention the marriage dance.

Songish

Nothing exists in the ethnographic literature or in my own field notes indicating any Prophet Dance phenomena among the Songish. Nevertheless the missionary Bolduc, preaching to a gathering of Indians at Victoria in 1843, had a young man rise up and tell him that nearly ten years before he had heard of the same God and that the coming of the French priests had been foretold. Of the Christian God he said "I have also heard it said that He came to these men here on our land" (Jennings 1937b:14). The youth need not have been Songish. And any time after 1827 he could have heard of Christianity and French priests from the employees at Fort Langley. But the sentence quoted suggests a local re-working of Christian ideas.

Saanich

I have questioned only one Saanich informant on this matter; this was Louie Pelkey of East Saanich, born about 1870. This man responded to a question on the term for "prayer":

The word t'i'wyəł means "to pray." Before the Whites came, the Indians heard they were coming and heard they were going to pray. They all gathered and sang, first one then another. Then one man said, "I think we're making a mistake; this is not praying, only dancing." (This was like the Shakers now. It was here at Saanich.) Finally ministers and priests came with different kinds of religion. When the priests prayed for them it was all in one thing [i.e. a ritual act for the whole group, not individual dancing?] . . . . The people were surprised to see the Catholics. It would have been good if they hadn't gone too far. The man who said to the old Shakers, "That's wrong," said, "Now we've seen the real thing," when the Catholics came.

This informant did not mention any marriage dance. The gathering referred to above suggests something closer to the ordinary spirit-dancing session. This informant also mentioned in a different context several persons who prophesied the coming of the Whites through spirit songs. One woman sang *"waihee,"* which was later interpreted to have meant the Hawaiians brought in by the Hudson's Bay Company.

Cowichan

The term "Cowichan" has often been used for all the speakers of Halkomelem, or for all those on Vancouver Island, that is, all the communities from Malahat to Qualicum. The Nanaimo have been singled out in the literature occasionally, but even the existence of the communities now called "Chemainus" between the Nanaimo and the Cowichan proper of the Cowichan River has rarely been recognized.

My informants at Lummi believed that the marriage dance was practiced "at Cowichan," that is, among the villages along the Cowichan River, but I have no information from any Cowichan informant. However, Jenness (1955:88) records cult-like activities:

> The Coast Salish Indians on Vancouver Island also maintained that the doctrine of a Supreme Being was of recent introduction. Like the Sardis Indians, they directed their prayers to the rising sun (only sorcerers prayed to the setting sun), to animal spirits, and, in some places, to Khaals, who was not the messenger of a Lord above, but a mighty trickster and transformer. The word *ci'cəɬ siɛ'm* reached them a few years before the arrival of Europeans, through contact, apparently, with Indians from the State of Washington. An old Cowichan native said that his people learned its use from the Port Angeles (Klallam) Indians, who themselves derived it from the following incident. One of their villagers dropped out of a fishing party and paddled ashore in a trance. When he reappeared a few days later, he told his people that he had climbed a rope to the sky, and, gathering them inside his house, he bade them sing and dance to *ci'cəɬ siɛ'm*, their "father above" whom he had visited.

Nanaimo

A Nanaimo informant gave Jenness (1955:88) the following incident:

Shortly before the first whites arrived, he said, some one visited his people in the middle of each summer, gathered them into a circle, and bade them point upward to the sky and sing "Don't do anything until the Lord (*siɛ'm*) tells you." He then went to Chemainus, Duncan and other places and taught other Indians to worship the Lord in the sky.

Squamish

Hill-Tout gives no data on any cult-like phenomena among the Squamish. However, two Squamish informants described different activities at two Squamish villages. Dominic Charlie of the Capilano Reserve volunteered the information that his grandfather, named *sixʷa·'ltən*, was a "prophet." He lived at *iłe·'xʷ* (Ashlu) up the Squamish valley. There he called a meeting to pray every seventh day, reckoning time by breaking a stick into a basket each day. He prayed holding up his hands, singing and dancing. He also prophesied that the Whites would come and that everything would be different; people would get their food right at home (through cultivation, etc.). The informant believed that it was Jesus to whom his grandfather prayed, but said he called the deity *čə'ł siʔa'm*, "high chief."

A second Squamish informant, Louie Miranda, of Mission Reserve, told that at a time before the first Whites had come the people of *yu'k'ʷc*, the village at the mouth of the Cheakamus River, gathered every spring for a dance during which they prayed to a Supreme Being and betrothed their children. They addressed the deity as *čɛ·'łi siʔa'm* (people now say *čɛ'ł siʔa'm*), asking for his help and kindness. They blessed themselves with the sign of the cross, saying "*tə sna's tə ma'ns, i tə mə'n's, i tə səntəspri', hiyo'y'əm tiʔma'*" ("In the name of the Father, the Son, and the Holy Ghost, Amen." The modern version is the same except that the last line now goes "*haʔł kʷəs tiʔma's*"; both are good Squamish for "So be it.") They used no visible cross. At this gathering, during the dancing, a parent might hold up a baby of the opposite sex to indicate acceptance. Children pledged in this manner were married when they grew up. The bond established between families in this manner was a strong one; if, for example the boy died before reaching maturity and marrying the girl, the boy's family addressed the girl as *sləqʷa'ił* (deceased child's spouse).

This informant had heard of the dance itself from his stepfather, who said that it had been practiced in the time of his own grandfather. The informant had heard of the older form of the blessing later; when the Shaker Church was established among the Squamish one of its oldest members, Jimmy Jimmy, had used the older formula instead of the newer one and had explained its source.

Sechelt

Hill-Tout (1904a:51-52) gives a text and translation of a Sechelt story of a prophet who was said to have lived "some generations ago before the coming of the priests." This man told about an "unseen power above," who made the world; and he also foretold the coming of the Whites, which the people did not believe. He also foretold the approach of enemies. Barnett also (see below) mentions the Sechelt when giving an account of a Slaiaman practice.

From a Sechelt, Basil Joe, who was born about 1884, I obtained notes on three examples of prophecy. One was an old man who used to get up early in the morning before daybreak and lecture his people on how to be rich and happy. He was a *siyu'ʔwa*, a seer. One morning he made a fire, wrapped his goat-wool blanket around him, and giving a jerk, said, "White man coming across; too much!" This was before anyone knew of the Whites. He also foretold of stoves, kettles, dishes, etc. The other two examples of prophecies were women who had *sʔəlyu*, visions, that made them sing and dance. One had a vision of God; she said *ší'šikle*, meaning "God" (actually "Jesus Christ") and *kʷa·ʔam saʔam*, meaning "Heaven." This last person was an old woman when the informant's father was young.

Slaiaman

Barnett (1955:206) reports that the Slaiaman, the Sechelt, "and probably other mainland groups" had a marriage dance. He was unable to learn how often it was held but found that it was a round dance, conducted under the direction of some prominent man, and all who wished could participate. The singing accompanying the dance was addressed to "the one above," identified by the Slaiaman informant as God, who was known to the Indians "before they learned about Christianity." While the dance went on a man could touch the hand of any woman and when it was over take her to sit down with him. This made them married but later there were the usual exchanges of gifts and so forth. Theoretically any man was free to choose any woman, but Barnett suggests that in practice a poor man would probably not have been willing to accept the consequences of selecting a rich man's daughter—possible ridicule as a social climber and the responsibility of providing the wealth required to maintain the position.

Kwakiutl

While I am concerned here primarily with the Salish, I cannot overlook the occurrence of cult-like phenomena among the tribes to the north and west. So far as I know, the voluminous literature by Boas and Hunt contains nothing on anything resembling the Prophet Dance among the Kwakiutl. However, Curtis (1915, 10:244-45) has the following:

> There is a tradition that long ago a rumor was spread among the tribes of Vancouver Island and the opposite mainland to the effect that a new dance was coming from Sa'hali-qa'ntlun which is said to refer to the region of the upper Columbia. In anticipation of its arrival the people cleaned out their houses and kept their persons clean. The dance came first to the tribes at Victoria harbor, then to the Cowichan, the Comox, the Lekwiltok, even to Nass River and Stikeen River, and finally southward again to the northern and western coasts of Vancouver Island. The same songs accompanied the dance from tribe to tribe. . . .
>
> This is said to have happened before the time of the father of a Nawiti man born about 1814. There were three waves of this religious fervor, the last coming in the boyhood of this Nawiti traditionalist, that is, about 1820. Old men among the Clayoquot on the west coast say that the first dance reached them seven generations ago. The people in dancing stood in a row shoulder to shoulder, held palms turned toward the sky, and looked at the sun until they fell into a trance. When anyone fell, the others gathered around him in a circle, still dancing, and when he recovered his senses he rose and told what he had seen in his vision. They pretended thus to foretell events. The essential identity of this cult with the hypnotic features of the ghost dance and the sun dance of the Plains tribes is strikingly evident.

Curtis gives a footnote on the term Sa'hal qa'ntlun (in modern transcription sa'xali kʷa'nƛən?) saying, "Sa'hali is Chinook Jargon for 'above,' or 'upper.' Qa'ntlŭn has the unmistakable ring of a Salishan word." The latter word ought to sound Salishan since it is the name of the Stalo tribe at Fort Langley. And since Fort Langley was well known to the Southern Kwakiutl from its foundings in 1827, it seems likely that "Upper Kwantlen" or "Above Kwantlen" means "up the Fraser." The words to the song, omitted above, Curtis explains as meaning "Now tell Gwasila; now tell Gwasiya," followed by meaningless syllables; "Gwasila and Gwasiya are said to be the names of the spirits to which the song was addressed." For Curtis's somewhat different account of the Clayoquot Nootka tradition that appears in his Nootka volume see below.

Before I had discovered Curtis's account, I questioned Mungo Martin, a Fort Rupert Kwakiutl, on the possibility that the Kwakiutl had received anything of the Prophet Dance from the Salish. He said that he knew of such a tradition. A *na'ʔnǝlči* (Salish) dance was "relayed" from tribe to tribe up the coast. The Kwakiutl proper received it when they were still on Turnour Island, that is, before Fort Rupert was built in 1849. People danced for four days and four nights, never lying down. They made up Kwakiutl words for the song. It was used once a year but at no particular time. He did not know how long it was practiced, since it had ceased long before his time.

Nootka

Evidence for the early occurrence of the name "Jesus Christ" among the Nootka is supplied by Boas and by Curtis. Boas (1895:115-16) recorded a Nootka tradition in which a being named *"Cíciklé"* appears as a boy and instructs him to pray to him with hands stretched upward. In *Indianische Sagen*, where this tradition appears (1895:340), Boas suggested that *"Cíciklé"* was a name for Twin Transformers derived by reduplication from the Chinook Transformer's name "Cikla."* In an earlier paper Boas (1891a:585) mentioned the tradition and identified *"Cíciklé"* with a deity whose worship was taught by the Twin Transformers. But the name *"Cíciklé"* (in modern transcript *ši·'šikle*) or variants of it appear as the Indian equivalent of "Jesus Christ" among both the Coast and Interior Salish; the Nootka name must be the same. Curtis identifies it as such.

Curtis (1916, 11:179-80) recorded the name in a song that accompanied the performance referred to in the Kwakiutl data given above. He writes:

> A dance obtained from Christian sources is thus described by an old Clayoquot man: "About 1840 or 1845 when I was a boy, a danced called húhltsumis ('dance going around the world') came to the Clayoquot from the people beyond Cape Scott (probably Nawiti). The chief would hold the white tail of an eagle in his hand and make sweeping motions with it, while the people of both sexes and all ages stood in a row beside him. All were silent. Then

---

*[According to Dell Hymes (personal communication), the Chinook name *šikla* consists of the dual prefix *š-* and a root *-ikla*. Thus there is probably no connection between this name and name *šišikli* and other forms derived from the French pronunciation of Jesus Christ.]

the chief sang a song in some foreign language. They danced, and during the second repetition of the song some would fall in a faint, and the others would gather around and continue to sing until the unconscious ones rose. No visions were related.''

Curtis adds the words of the song, meaningless to the Clayoquot except for the name "*Shíshiguli*," which he identifies as "the native pronunciation of 'Jesus Christ'.'' He gives no evidence other than the name that the dance was "obtained from Christian sources," but the other details in this and in his previous account certainly suggest the Prophet Dance, though not specifically the Coast Salish form.

Bella Coola

McIlwraith (1948; 1:588-91) reports that the Bella Coola recognized a special type of shaman who received power directly from the supreme god, *Aɫquntäm*. One of these persons is said to have lived on the lower Fraser before the Europeans arrived. This man had a vision in which *Aɫquntäm* revealed the coming of the Europeans and told him to transmit the message to other tribes. To do so he travelled to the sites of Seattle, Comox, and Nanaimo. He also performed miracles. McIlwraith believes that the account has some historic basis and calculates that the news of the vision reached the Bella Coola about 1800. He also recorded a song that the prophet is said to have sung but which is meaningless to the Bella Coola. A few Bella Coola prophets also foretold the coming of the Whites. McIlwraith does not question the position of the supreme god in Bella Coola culture but suggests that the concept of obtaining power directly from him reached the Bella Coola from Christian sources.

The Elements of the Complex

It should be clear that some sort of Prophet Dance activity occurred among perhaps a majority of the Coast Salish tribes. But is it possible to say whether it was a single movement or several separate movements and when it occurred? To attempt an answer I will examine in detail several of the elements that have entered into the complex.

Assuming that both Native culture and Christianity are fairly well known, logically we ought to be able to distinguish between Native and Christian elements and to say these are clearly Native and those are clearly Christian elements and therefore introduced. But in fact the distinction is not at all clear. As I see it, the only element that is clearly Native and *not* Christian is dancing as a religious activity and the only elements that are clearly Christian and *not* Native are the Sabbath, the name "Jesus Christ," and the use of written

175

or carved symbols representing the history of the world. A few elements, such as prophecy and belief in resurrection, probably occurred in Native culture as well as in Christianity. Several, such as belief in a Supreme Being, group worship, and confession, may also have been Native as well as Christian. At least one element, the marriage dance, is neither Christian nor Native Coast Salish, but is probably native to the Plateau.

The Marriage Dance. This element seems to have been the most widespread and most important one in the Coast Salish complex. Or at least it is the element that has stood out in the minds of most informants. Its distribution on the mainland was probably continuous from the northern end of Georgia Strait to the southern end of Puget Sound. And it may also have been practiced on the Olympic peninsula and on southeastern Vancouver Island. It may have been remembered by informants best because it is so clearly at odds with the usual Coast Salish marriage practices. The usual marriage was an arrangement between families of relatively equal status accompanied by exchanges of food, wealth, and privileges, and establishing a permanent economic relationship between them. Mrs. Shelton's story of the ultimate rejection of the marriage dance because it permitted lower-class men to marry upper-class girls may not be correct in its details but it is certainly a plausible story. The aberrant Squamish practice of betrothing children must have been a local adaptation, a compromise between a marriage dance and marriages arranged by family. Barnett's comments on Slaiaman theory versus practice also indicate the conflict.

We must look to the Plateau for the origin of the marriage dance and for the route by which it came to the Coast. It is widely reported for the Plateau. Among the Flathead it is associated with a camas dance (a first roots ceremony?), among the Coeur d'Alene and Kalispel with a scalp or victory dance (a purifying rite?), and among the Kootenay with a praying dance that had hunting luck as its object. Among the Northern Okanagon, Shuswap, Thompson, and Lillooet, the marriage dance was a part of the Prophet Dance, usually so among the Thompson, occasionally so among the Lillooet, and at the specific instruction of a woman prophet among the Shuswap. Ray (1942:210, element 5422) indicates an absence for the Umatilla and Tenino and no information for the Lower Chinook, Klickitat, Kittitas, Wenatchee, and Sanpoil. Cline and Spier do not mention it for the Southern Okanagon. Teit (1928:128) mentions it for the Middle Columbia Salish but apparently it was separate from the "praying dance." Thus it seems likely that the marriage dance was absent among the Sahaptin, present but not integrated with the Prophet Dance among the southern Salish tribes, and present and integrated with the Prophet Dance among the northern Salish tribes. This distribution makes it probable that the form of the Prophet Dance having the marriage dance as an important element reached the Coast Salish from the Lillooet, Thompson, or Northern Okanagon.

The ultimate origin of the marriage dance and why it should have become attached to the Prophet Dance is another matter. Spier (1935:15) suggests that it is a formalization of the practice, which is fairly widespread in the Plateau, whereby a man forced a girl to marry him simply by touching her. Such forced marriages are not reported from the Coast. Spier suggests that the incorporation of the marriage dance into the Prophet Dance among the Thompson and their neighbors may have occurred only because the gathering of the Prophet Dance offered the opportunity for the marriage dance, but he also asks if it may not have been related to the sexual interests shown by some of the later Plateau prophets. It seems to me, however, that missionary influence is not altogether out of the question. The early missionaries sometimes blessed the unions of a number of couples in a single ceremony. This association of the marriage of a number of persons with a religious ceremony invoking a deity could have provided a stimulus for the association of the marriage dance with the "praying dance." Yet I must admit that the latter association did not occur in the southeastern Plateau where the indisputably Christian elements were evidently introduced, but in the northwestern Plateau. At any rate, what may have been only a casually-associated element in the Plateau seems to have become a central element on the Coast.

The Worship of a Deity. The association of a Supreme Being identified with the Christian God is clear for the Lummi, Nooksack, Snohomish, Squamish, and Slaiaman, and probably for the Twana. The absence of a record of any such association for the Chilliwack and Puyallap-Nisqually may be only because it was not sought after. In my own material the association appeared when I tried to elicit information on "prayer."

The terms for the Supreme Being that I obtained from informants from several tribes, both in connection with the Prophet Dance phenomena and with Christianity, were identical with the terms given by Hill-Tout, Jenness, and Duff. These terms are: Puget Sound *šə'q sia'b*; Straits (Lummi, Saanich, etc.) *si'sət sie'm*; Halkomelem (Stalo, Cowichan, etc.) *ci'cət sie'm*; Squamish *čə'ł si?ám*. (The only term used by the Sechelt informant in this connection was *ši'šikle*.)

The term *sie'm* (and variants)* is often translated as "chief." It did not, however, mean "chief" in any political sense in pre-reservation times, but rather indicated the social status of the person so labelled. It was used for persons of both sexes of upper-class status. As a term of address it was the equivalent of "Sir" or "Madam" or perhaps "My Lord" and "My Lady," and was used as such not merely by inferiors addressing superiors, but also by anyone addressing another formally, by lovers and spouses speaking to

---

*[The term is *si?ə́m* in most dialects of Halkomelem and Northern Straits.]

each other, and one informant illustrated the noble and gentle nature of her grandfather by saying that he even addressed his slaves as *sie'm*. Formerly the most prominent man of a household or village was evidently called the *sie'm* of that house or village and in the case of a larger aggregate the term "first *sie'm*" was used, to judge from some accounts. After a system of "chiefs" with responsibilities toward the White governments was imposed, the term *sie'm* came to mean "chief" in this sense.

The term *ci'cət* (and variants) means "above." The Straits form *si'sət* means "above" in a simple locative sense; I recorded it in the text of a folktale in which two boys were captured and confined in a box, which was raised *si'sət*, "aloft." The term *si'sət sie'm*, *ci'cət sie'm*, etc., thus means literally "Chief Above," with reservations about the word "chief," or perhaps better "My Lord Above."

This term is identical in meaning and structure with the Chinook Jargon *sáxali tayi'*, usually spelled "Saghalie Tyee," which means "God." The trade language called Chinook Jargon evidently developed on the lower Columbia and was introduced among the Coast Salish by the fur traders and early missionaries. According to Northern Puget Sound tradition the Indian named John Taylor, who interpreted for the Indian side at the Treaty of Point Elliot in 1855, was the first local Indian to learn Chinook Jargon. However, the missionary Demers learned Chinook Jargon while at Fort Vancouver on the Columbia in the winter of 1838-39 (Blanchet 1910:25) and presumably used it in instructing the Puget Sound tribes in his first contacts with them. But he and the others also made an effort to learn the true Native languages. Blanchet says in fact that Bolduc was sent to spend the summer of 1843 on Whidbey Island "in order to learn the idiom." But in a letter written at Cowlitz in March of 1843, Bolduc gives a short vocabulary of "Some Tchinouc and Senehomish Words" (i.e. Chinook Jargon and the Snohomish dialect of Puget Sound). The first pair of words recorded (Jennings 1937a:115) is: "God Sakale-Taye (Chief of the heavens) shoc siab (Chief of the Heavens)." So far as I know this is the first recording of the term.

In view of the diversity of terms for other religious concepts among the various Salish languages (only the words for "shaman's spirit" and for "holy" seem very widespread), it seems unlikely that if the concept of a Supreme Being had existed in pre-contact times he would have been everywhere designated by the same compound term "Chief Above" or that this term should be identical with the Chinook Jargon term. It seems much more likely that this term was spread with Christianity. Indeed, Teit asserts that the term was introduced among the Lillooet about 1830 along with the observance of a Sabbath and that it is the missionaries' term (see below). It may be that the term "Chief Above" was aboriginal on the lower Columbia and was translated, perhaps by Demers or Bolduc, into Puget Sound Salish, or it may be that the term originated with the introduction of Christian concepts at an earlier

Fig. 11. Julius Charles. At home at Lummi, April 1950. He was a real *siʔéṁ*, a dignified aristocrat, concerned that I understand the workings of Native society as well as the details of fishing and hunting.

Fig. 12. Patrick George. Singing, in front of his house at Lummi, September 1950. He was funny, dramatic, and ready to talk about the work of Indian doctors and sources of extra-human help.

Figure 13. Louie Pelkey. On the beach at Tsartlip, Saanichton Bay, July 1949. A practical, skeptical man, he was especially interested in technology—both Native and introduced.

Fig. 14. Simon Pierre. At home at Katzie in the summer of 1963. As a young man Simon was an interpreter for the Salish chiefs who went to London to argue for Native rights, but he still seemed to stand in the shadow of his father, Peter Pierre (''Old Pierre''), the famous Indian doctor.

Fig. 15. Christine (Mrs. Andrew) Charles. At Musqueam in the summer of 1963. Mrs. Charles was a superb teacher of her language, patient with my ignorance but intolerant of my mistakes. She and her husband dictated accounts of Native practices and historic events.

Fig. 16. James Point. At Musqueam in the summer of 1965. One of the kindest and most even-tempered men I have ever known, he dictated myths and tales and patiently went through my lexical file with me, inventively illustrating the usage of words and supplying missing forms.

time, perhaps in the Plateau, and was already present on the Coast by Demers's time.

But if the term "Chief Above" for a Supreme Being is not Native, need the concept be ruled out? This is of course another question. Most Coast Salish today believe that the concept is Native; however, a century of missionary work may determine their opinions. The data available on Coast Salish culture that might reveal the concept are of two sorts: myths, and statements about prayer and worship.

The central figure in Coast Salish mythology is the Transformer. He is called χέ·ís in the Halkomelem and Straits Languages, du'k^{W}ibəł in the Puget Sound and Twana languages; both terms contain roots meaning "to change." The Coast Salish Transformer appears as the purposeful creator of a new order: he transforms dangerous beings into stone; he transforms some of the "first people" of the myth age into animals that will be useful for the people to come; and to the "second people," man, he teaches the basic arts. The "second people" may be his creation or may be from another source. Most of the Halkomelem-speaking groups had traditions of first ancestors who dropped from the sky and later received gifts from the Transformer. As Boas (1898:9) pointed out, the character of the Transformer among these groups, as among the Kwakiutl, is more clearly that of a benefactor and has little of the Trickster like the Raven of the Northern Coast tribes or the Coyote of the Plateau. The Coast Salish Transformer sometimes appears accompanied by Mink and other characters of a Trickster type, but he himself is rarely concerned with anything but his mission as the creator of the present world.

In view of his character it is not surprising that some Coast Salish of today should identify the Transformer with the Christian deity. Several of my Straits informants state that χe'ɛls was God or was "Jesus Christ when he came to this part of the world." Elmendorf (personal communication) indicates a similar identification by some Twana.

Yet there is little evidence that the Transformer was addressed in prayer or worshipped in strictly pre-contact times. In fact there is little evidence for the worship of any deities. Gunther (1927:289) writes of the Klallam that there was no feeling of reverence for the Transformer and that the only deity to whom all the Klallam occasionally prayed was "Seqwa'tci," conceived as earth, sky, or dawn, and as female. Gunther also quotes the missionary Eells to the effect that the Klallam formerly worshipped the sun, which some identified with the Transformer, but she suggests that this was a confusion for "Seqwa'tci." Elmendorf writes (personal communication) that the Twana had two Native deities said to have been addressed in prayer, Sun and Earth, but they were "weak concepts, not associated with other bodies of belief or with any ritual system."[9]

---

[9]See also Olson 1936:141, on the Quinault.

My own data on the Straits tribes gives no evidence for the Transformer as an object of worship except in relation to the Prophet Dance. But there is some indication of a situation like that described for the Klallam. It was felt that the "daylight" (skʷɛ́yəl or skʷɛ́čəl, probably the same term as the Klallam "Seqwa'tci," i.e. skʷa'čəy) had enormous power, and people are spoken of as addressing it. Yet it is not clear to me whether it was addressed in an attitude of prayer or merely addressed with spells (syəw'i'n'). In some instances informants have certainly spoken of persons addressing spells to the daylight, particularly just at dawn, yet the attitude might well have been different from that of a person addressing spells to a cedar tree so that it might not split or to a hunter's feet to make them swift. Spells used for these purposes are clearly verbal formulae of magical efficacy and not prayers. But spell and prayer may only be end points in a continuum.

What the word t'i'wyəɬ meant before it became the term for the marriage dance is not clear. Comparative Salish linguistics should reveal, in time, the nature and distribution of the concept if it is indeed aboriginal.

Another term that is used in the Straits language as an adjective applied to the Christian deity is xɛ́xə. This term in Native contexts seems to mean both "holy" and "tabu," or "in a dangerous condition," as that of a girl at puberty. In the Interior the same term is used among the Thompson for the supernatural or a supernatural being; Teit sometimes translates it as "mystery" (for example Teit 1898:117, note 264; Teit 1912:253n). This is also probably the "mystery" of Teit's "Great Mystery" as a term for the "Old Man" of Thompson mythology (for example, Teit 1898:48). Here, too, comparative linguistic work is desirable.

The area of most conflicting opinion on the deity is the lower Fraser. As we have seen, Jenness hesitatingly concludes that the Katzie ci'cəɬ siɛ'm is aboriginal, and indeed there is nothing in the Katzie material itself to suggest otherwise. Yet in Hill-Tout's material from the neighboring Kwantlen, who have lived on both sides of the Katzie on the Fraser, the same "Chief Above" is clearly associated with a Prophet Dance sort of worship. Also it may refer to the Transformer, while among the Katzie the two are distinct. And in Hill-Tout's later report on the Chehalis the concept is clearly associated with something like the Christianized Prophet Dance of the Plateau. There Hill-Tout emphatically declares that the concept of a Supreme Being "is entirely foreign to the native mind, and is in direct conflict with the democratic genius of Salish institutions, and with the ideas embodied in their myths." In the most recent work on the area, Duff concludes that the concept is probably introduced.

Turning again to the Plateau I find that some of the Interior Salish tribes seem to have had deities who were both characters in mythology and objects of worship. Ray (1932:179) identifies Sweatlodge of the Sanpoil as both the Transformer who put an end to the Myth Age and a deity who is available to all men through sweating and prayer. Teit (1930:184ff.) reports that the

186

Coeur d'Alene worshipped a deity called "Amo'tqɛn" and also the sun and the day; the first is the deity addressed in the Prophet Dance, but he was evidently prayed to on many other occasions as well. The Old One of the Thompsons seems to have been either a chief Transformer or the one who sent Coyote and other Transformers into the world to change it; Teit (1900:337, 344) is not certain whether he was addressed in prayer. The Lillooet also had an "Old Man" as chief Transformer and a "Chief of the Dead" to whom the worship of the Prophet Dance was addressed (Teit 1906a:274, 278, 284). The Northern Okanagon addressed the "Old Man" also as "Chief," "Chief Above," "Great Mystery," and "Mystery Above"(Teit 1930:284). But, writing of the Lillooet, Teit (1906:289) says that the term "Chief Above" was introduced about 1830 along with a Sabbath, and a footnote (possibly added by Boas) states of the term "Chief Above," "This is the Indian term for 'God,' as taught by the priests."

I conclude that among the Coast Salish in pre-contact times the principal character of mythology, the Transformer, was not worshipped. I conclude that attitudes of worship directed toward the sky or daylight may have occurred but they were not frequent enough and their manifestations were not well enough organized to warrant our speaking of a "sky-god." And I conclude that the term "Chief Above" must have been introduced.

Religious Functionaries

Among all Coast Salish groups for whom there is information, any person may in theory acquire one or more spirit helpers and certain of these helpers may bestow the power to function as a shaman. The shaman's power enables him to perceive and to manipulate spirits and human souls. He may use this power either to benefit or to harm others; there is nothing inherently good or bad in it.

Beside the shaman there are among the Straits and Halkomelem tribes several other functions that are made possible by the possession of guardian spirits. A person, usually a woman, called *siə'wa* functioned as a seeress, foretelling the approach of enemies, divining lost objects, etc. The possessor of the *sk*ʷ*ədi'ləč* spirit power of northern Puget Sound had similar functions. Also among the Straits and Halkomelem tribes there was a spirit power that made its possessor able to deal with ghosts.

Besides these functions derived from the possession of individually acquired spirit power, there was also a function derived from private knowledge, learned from older kinsmen or even purchased from non-relatives. This was the knowledge of spells (*syəw'i'n'*), the use of which I have already mentioned. Specialization in the use of spells as a ritualist (*yəw'i'n'mət* or *sɫθi'ʔθə*) was particularly well-developed among the Halkomelem tribes of the lower Fraser, where there seems to have been two grades of specialization. These persons used their knowledge of spells to aid individual hunters, craftsmen, etc., and also to aid persons undergoing crisis rites. The person officiating at a crisis rite was often a ritualist (that is, a master of spells); his or her function at this time was probably twofold—to protect the person in the dangerous (χεʹxə) condition and to protect other members of the group from possible contamination.

The first salmon rite was also conducted by someone with knowledge of spells. Among the Straits tribes the rite was performed for sockeye salmon caught by reef nets; it was performed at each gear and conducted by the owner of the gear or by someone more proficient with ritual practice. Elsewhere the rite is often said to have been conducted by the "chief" of the local group. Whether ritual knowledge was necessary is not always clear, but such was probably the case. In pre-contact times the first salmon rite and such rites as the purification of mourners after a death were probably the closest Straits society came to religious ceremonies for the benefit of a group, though the group was a small one. The spirit dance gethering was essentially a series of individual performances, where spectators might as easily be secretly working against a dancer as supporting him. The potlatch was perhaps for the benefit of the group as a whole, but it was essentially a secular affair.

It will be seen that the initiator of any sort of Prophet Dance phenomena would have to resemble the shaman or other possessor of spirit power in that he would have derived his status from a personal experience with the supernatural. In fact the Twana, Saanich, and Sechelt data provide examples of the foretelling of the coming of the Whites through spirit songs and by a seer. But the real prophet is something more because, like the ritualist, he conducts a ceremony for the benefit of the group.

The only term recorded for a "prophet" is Duff's Upper Stalo term *alia*. As Duff points out the term means "to have a vision." But Hill-Tout (1902:365) seems to equate the term with the ritualist, the user of spells. He found the term, which he gives as "olia," used among the Chilliwack for a type of religious practitioner whose functions were curing wounds, interpreting dreams and visions, reading omens and portents, preparing the dead for burial, and protecting people from the evil influence of ghosts. The "olia" was believed to hold nightly communion with the dead at the burial-grounds.

I find it difficult to explain this association of the term "vision" with these functions, which are mainly derived from ritual knowledge rather than contact with spirits. It may be that the Chilliwack ritualist acquired his knowledge of spells through visions of ghosts. Or it may be that Hill-Tout recorded a late usage that was influenced by the combination of vision and rite found in the Prophet Dance. But Hill-Tout makes no mention of any cult-like phenomena in relation to the "olia," but instead relates them to the chief.

The association of the cult and chieftainship is a persistent feature. The initiators about whom there is some information—Duff's Upper Stalo prophets, Collin's Upper Skagit cult organizers, and my Lummi leader Davy Crockett—all seem to have been men whose objectives were to dominate their groups; it is perhaps not going too far to say that they had political ambitions and that they found the Prophet Dance activities a useful means to that end. This certainly seems to be Collins' view. From the Plateau accounts it would also appear that the Prophet Dance leaders were identical with "chiefs," that is, persons who had what little political authority there was.

Public Confession and Punishment

The belief that sin causes misfortune which may be relieved by confession may be old in Native North America, since it is found in several areas—among the Central Eskimo, the Algonkians of the Northeast, and the Yurok of northwestern California, for example. There is little evidence for the belief in aboriginal Coast Salish culture; however, it seems to have been present in the Plateau. Ray (1942:214, elements 5605-6) reports individual confession before death for several Plateau groups and the denial in all cases that the practice was due to Catholic influence. Spier (1935:8) reports for the Southern Okanagon a separate confession dance, which he believes must have been part of the Prophet Dance complex. In the Coast Salish data on Prophet Dance phenomena, confession is mentioned for the Kwantlen, where, according to Hill-Tout, the chief "led and conducted prayers and confessions of the people" at times of crisis, and again to the south among the Twana. As noted above, Spier sees this as parallel to the Southern Okanagon practice.

Rules of good behavior are no doubt a prerequisite to the existence of any society, but they need not be made explicit in formal instruction. In Coast Salish society, to judge from the accounts of Straits informants, insofar as they were made explicit, it was mainly as part of the "advice" that "upper-class" families gave to their children in private. No doubt moral principles were not in fact private knowledge to the few "better" people, but it may have been useful to a society that stressed private property to pretend that they were. The overt public concern with morality implied by the public confession mentioned for the Kwantlen and the Twana may have been a new feature in Coast Salish culture.

The only instance of the enforcement of rules by corporal punishment by an initiator of Prophet Dance phenomena is that given by Collins for the Upper Skagit, where one prophet appointed officials who punished those who broke the rules by whippings and exposure. This degree of authority and type of punishment is paralleled elsewhere on the Coast only by the post-Christian rule of "Native priests" acting on behalf of the church. It seems unlikely that this sort of thing could have developed on the Upper Skagit before it had already come into being among other groups directly under the rule of the church. Collins, in fact, says that the Upper Skagit phenomenon occurred after the first priests were on Puget Sound. This development must therefore have come somewhat later than the marriage dance movement, which is generally said to have come before the priests, unless the practice reached the Upper Skagit from the Plateau.

One historically documented example of the rise of a "native priest" is that of the Skagit chief called "Netlam" by the missionaries Blanchet and Bolduc. This man was undoubtedly *ni'ƛ'əm* (or *di'ƛ'əb*) of the Lower Skagit, whose village was at Coupeville on Whidbey Island and for whom Snakelum Point was named. Netlam was among the people who received instructions at Nisqually in 1839; he may also have been among those who went with the Suquamish chief "Tslalakum" to Cowlitz to find Blanchet and Demers earlier that year. At any rate when Blanchet visited Whidbey Island for the first time in 1840 and found that the Indians assembled there already knew the Chinook Jargon prayers and hymns that he proposed to teach them, he attributed this knowledge to the zeal of the Suquamish chief Tslalakum, the Snohomish chief, Witskalatche (also called "Le Français," because of his dress), and the Skagit chief, Netlam. Later he visited Netlam at his home and when he returned to Nisqually he left to Netlam the great Catholic Ladder that he had used. The following year, 1841, Demers also preached at Whidbey Island (Blanchet 1910:40-42, 47).

Two years later, in the spring of 1843, Bolduc travelled in the Hudson's Bay Company Steamship *Beaver* from Nisqually to the site where Douglas was establishing the fort that became Victoria. Returning, Bolduc stopped at Whidbey Island. Jennings' translation of his journal reads (1937b:18-19) in part:

> Many Klallams and Skadjats came to the seashore to receive me. I knew Netlam, chief of the Skadjats by reputation so I inquired for him and was told he had gone to Vancouver Island to meet me. However, his two boys were presented. One pressed my hand and said to me, "Netlam, my father, is not here; he has gone to see you at Camosun [Victoria]. However, when he learns you are here, he will come in haste. He will be very happy to have you stay here for he is tired of saying mass and speaking to the people."
> I did not know what to think of this mass. This Netlam is an eccentric of the first class who *already had compelled the savages to confession and was concerned principally about enforcing punishment* [italics mine, W.S.]. If he had thought of imitating the ceremonies of the mass, he certainly would have done it. Later I learned that the mass said consisted of an explanation to the savages of his tribe, of the historical, chronological religious ladder,

the making of many signs of the cross and the signing of a few canticles and the ''Kyrie eleison'' of the second class of masses in which Father Blanchet had instructed them in 1840.

Since Bolduc had not yet met Netlam, he must have known of his activities through Blanchet's or Demers's visits of two or three years before. It is probable that the other chiefs mentioned were engaged in the same kinds of activities and that this was the source of the cult activity that went on a few miles up the Skagit River as suggested by Collins.[10]

Turning again to the Plateau, we find the use of corporal punishment widely recorded, but with no great agreement as to its history. Ray (1932:112-13) reports it for the Sanpoil as if it were aboriginal. He writes of open hearings held by chiefs and punishment dealt out by appointed ''lashers.'' Crimes so punished were stealing, perjury as a witness, assault, improper sexual relations, and abortion. On the other hand, Walters (Cline 1938:94) writing on the Southern Okanagon, says that Catholic priests are said to have introduced a simple, judicial system with policemen, trial, witnesses, a judge, a whipper, and a counter of strokes. She adds that as part of the new system each week people confessed their sins to the chief. A third version is given by Curtis (1911, 8:75), who states that whipping as punishment for such offences as adultery, theft, drunkenness, and murder was introduced by the Spokane chief Garry after his return from the Red River School and that it later spread among many Interior Salish tribes.* The development of political and juridical institutions in the Plateau seems to be a matter that needs further research.

Indisputably Christian Elements

In this category are only the observers of a Sabbath, the use of written documents or other records, the sign of the cross, and Christian terms. One of these elements that appears in association with the circle marriage dance is the name šišikli´, which is undoubtedly a Native version of the French pronounciation of the name ''Jesus Christ'' (žezükri´). This term is widely used. Teit identifies ''cicikli'' in Interior Salish traditions as ''Jesus Christ.'' Coast Salish informants from several groups gave variations of the same as ''the Indian word for Jesus Christ.'' And the Kwakiutl did not learn this term

---

[10]Netlam was otherwise known as an innovator; he was among the first to obtain potatoes from the Whites and to spread their use among the Native tribes (see Suttles 1951b:276).

*[Garth (1965) finds that whipping was practised on the Plateau by 1800, and he suggests that the practice had spread there from the Southwest.]

from the English-speaking Protestant church from which they received their present form of Christianity. They must have learned it either from the earlier Catholic missionaries or from other Indians. The term appears in the marriage dance song given by one of my informants at Lummi. Since other informants did not mention it, I would be inclined to doubt it as an element of the marriage dance but for its occurrence in the Nootka traditions given by Boas and by Curtis. It seems probable that these traditions refer to pre-mission times. The French form of the name might have resulted from the teaching of the first missionaries, who were French-speaking priests; but if the term was used before their coming, it may have been learned from the French-speaking employees of the fur companies, or even from the group of Iroquois from whom Spier derives the earlier Christian elements of the Christianized Prophet Dance.

The observance of a Sabbath is reported for the Chehalis, Upper Skagit, Twana, and Squamish; and preaching from writing for the Upper Stalo and Squamish. The Sabbath and the sign of the cross may have been introduced from the Interior as part of the Christianized Prophet Dance.[11] But the preaching from writing, especially the Squamish prophet's "map," strongly suggests the Catholic Ladder introduced on the Coast by Blanchet in 1839. It may be of some significance that the tribes among whom these distinctly Christian elements (excepting the wider occurrence of the name Jesus Christ) are reported are tribes who were somewhat removed geographically from the first missionary activity. The Squamish were up Squamish River beyond the head of Howe Sound, the Upper Stalo and Chehalis were up the Fraser, the Upper Skagit up the Skagit River, and the Twana tucked away in Hood Canal. Christianized cults may have developed here while Christianity itself was being introduced on the shores of Puget Sound and Georgia Strait. The only association of any of these elements with the marriage dance was among the Twana and the Squamish. The Squamish form of the marriage dance is one that must have been a local development, again suggesting a later date than that of the earliest occurrence of the marriage dance on the Coast.

---

[11]Waterman (1924:501) notes that the Shaker prayer ends with the Puget Sound words for "in the name of the Father, the Son, and the Holy Ghost, it is well" and that the term for the Holy Ghost, "Santu Splay," is from the French "Saint Esprit." He writes: "This phrase (in the name of the Father, etc.) was the first element of Christianity to reach the Indians of the Northwest. It came to them, passing from tribe to tribe, and was used by them as a new and powerful 'medicine,' long before the first missionary came to them."

Conclusions: Historical Reconstruction

In view of the data given and the points raised in the preceding discussion, the following sequence seems probable:

(1) Pre-contact Coast Salish culture included power through visions, prophecy, and control of rite through knowledge of formulae, but had little development of rite for the benefit of the community, probably little approaching worship as a recognized technique of dealing with the supernatural, and no concept of a supreme deity.

(2) The Prophet Dance first came to the Coast Salish in pre-mission times, i.e. before 1840, with the marriage dance as its central element. It spread rapidly and widely in Coast Salish territory but it did not persist. The important elements of this movement that were new were the marriage dance itself, worship, the deity worshipped, status of leader held through a combination of vision experience and ritual knowledge, participation by the whole community in a single rite. Possibly the only early Christian element in this movement was the use of the name "Jesus Christ."

The source of this movement is quite clearly the Prophet Dance of the Plateau. Moreover, it very probably came from the northern Plateau where the marriage dance occurred in association with the religious dance. Possible routes of diffusion are down the Fraser from the Thompson, down Harrison Lake from the Lillooet, or across the Coast Range from the Lillooet to the Squamish. A fourth possibility is a route via the Upper Skagit; however, relations between the Upper Skagit and the Thompson hunting parties whom they occasionally met were usually hostile. Relations between the upper Skagit and the Chelan via the Suiattle and Sauk Rivers were good but this is a less probable source of the Prophet Dance. The Fraser was probably the main channel of communication and therefore the most probable route by which the Prophet Dance reached the Coast.

The movement may have been at first accepted because it satisfied a spiritual need, or it may have been accepted because it provided a new basis for leadership and group unity, or both. It may have failed later to take root because, as one tradition has it, the implications of the marriage dance were not acceptable. Or it may have failed because the Native basis of leadership and group unity through the potlatch permitted no other system (until it was upset by direct contact with Whites). Or the movement may simply have come too late and did not survive because genuine Christianity shortly replaced it.

It is also worth noting that the Coast Salish did not take over the Plateau movement intact. There is little evidence in the Coast Salish data for any importance attached to portents or any doctrine of imminent world destruction and world renewal with the return of the dead led by the Transformer. Spier holds these elements, portents and doctrine, to be of central importance in the Plateau Prophet Dance. Admittedly there is little material of any sort on the reasons why the Coast Salish performed the ceremony, but if portents and this doctrine had been of any great importance it seems probable that there would have been some indication of it. Instead the concept of a deity and act of worship seem to have been more important on the coast. The deity, Spier (personal communication) suggests, was relatively less important in the pre-Christian Plateau movement and thus the importance of the concept on the Coast lends support to the conclusion that the source of the Coast Salish movement was the Christianized Prophet Dance of the Plateau, from which the Coast Salish borrowed selectively.

(3) A second development took place among the Squamish, Upper Stalo, Upper Skagit, and possibly the Twana, of localized cults with more Christian elements. This development came after the first Christian missionaries were on the salt water, i.e. after 1840. It may be that they developed among these upstream groups because of their relative isolation from missionaries or it may have been because of their greater exposure to Plateau influences.

In particular the 1840-43 mission work on Whidbey Island and the role of such men as the Skagit chief Netlam suggest how a Native leader might derive secular authority from religious functions. Such partial conversions probably formed the basis of independent cult developments among the Upper Skagit a few years later. As Collins suggests, the organization of rites brought a new kind of authority.

(4) Some elements of the Prophet Dance were passed on to the Nootka, Kwakiutl, and Bella Coola, though these tribes may have received elements of the complex from other sources as well. The marriage dance, so prominent among the Coast Salish, does not seem to have been accepted at all.

(5) The Shaker religion, which began about 1882, probably had stronger roots in these earlier movements on the Coast than in the Smohalla cult of the Plateau.

As I conclude this paper I am keenly aware of its deficiencies. Much of my reconstruction depends upon negative evidence. I infer that the Prophet Dance came from northern Plateau because the marriage dance is not reported in association with a praying dance in the southern Plateau. I infer that the worship of a deity appeared on the Coast for the first time with the Prophet Dance because there is little evidence for it in any other context. Yet it is possible that these are not real absences; only a matter of not enough data may be involved. Certainly in most of the published ethnographic works on the Coast Salish there is little that has any bearing on pre-contact or early-contact religious movements. Still the sum of the data that I have been able to gather and present here should be enough to show that there was indeed such a movement, identifiable with the Plateau Prophet Dance, even though the details of its history may not be as clear as we would have them.

But why has this movement been so largely ignored? The reason may lie in the nature of the traditional ethnography, which attempts to give a timeless, impersonal description of the culture of a Native tribe. It may be that ethnographers have tended to assume that they are dealing with two mutually exclusive systems, "Native" and "Christian," and (except for the relatively late Shaker Church) these two systems only, and thus have exercised too great a selectivity in collecting and reporting "Native" religious practices and beliefs. Data relating to the Prophet Dance may have been ignored because they do not fall into the neat categories "Native religion" and "Christianity" or into the historically-documented Shaker movement. But actually the earlier movement, with its mixture of Christian ideas and Plateau practices, probably had an influence upon both Native religion as it survived and Christianity as it was accepted. To understand contemporary Coast Salish religion we will have to be able to evaluate that influence. Moreover, we should not ignore expressions of Christianity as taught by the first missionaries. The Coast Salish texts of hymns and prayers should reveal some of the means by which Christian concepts were introduced into Native thought. Coast Salish versions of Christian cosmology and historic accounts (such as Teit collected for some of the Interior Salish) should reveal the extent to which Christian concepts were understood. Practices that are apparently purely "Native," such as spirit dancing and shamanistic curing, still flourish in a number of Coast Salish communities. Surely these practices can best be understood in the total context of Coast Salish religious expression.

Conclusions: Theoretical Implications

It may now be worth considering where this material fits into existing theoretical treatments of related phenomena. Herskovits (1938:75-103) summarizes some of the papers on cults as examples of "acculturation" studies. Defining "acculturation" as the result of "first-hand contact" of "groups of individuals having different cultures," he sees the late Plains Ghost Dance as a phenomenon of acculturation and as a "contra-acculturation movement" due to White contact. But he agrees that the earlier Prophet Dance of the Plateau preceded any great amount of White contact and that it rose from Native roots and spread through "intertribal acculturation." He finds (1938:10, 12, 16, 76) that Spier's Prophet Dance paper sharply challenges the view that such movements are "cults of despair" and "reactions against social and political forces with which the natives could not cope." And he regards the paper as a corrective to the "too facile approach" that derives everything that resembles European custom from European sources; the paper presents rather an instance of intertribal acculturation.

Herskovits notes that a paper by Nash (1937) on "religious revivalism" on the Klamath reservation takes an opposing point of view, seeing "nativistic cults" as arising among "deprived groups." Herskovits (1938:89-90) criticizes Nash for undue stress on White influence and not enough attention to intertribal relations and suggests that the case for religious revivalism as an invariable response to deprivation has not been made.[12]

Deprivation was again suggested by Barber (1941) in a paper "Acculturation and Messianic Movements." Barber uses the term "messianic movement" for the sort of phenomenon, like the Ghost Dance, which he describes as a proclamation of a golden age or at least a stable order for the immediate future. As his title implies he sees such movements as occurring in the context of acculturation, which I take to mean Indian-White acculturation, and he suggests that such movements are correlated with the occurrence of widespread deprivation, but as only one of several alternative responses.

Linton (1943) uses the term "nativistic movement," which he defines as "Any conscious, organized attempt on the part of a society's members to revive or perpetuate selected aspects of its culture." He suggests a fourfold typology of "nativistic movements" based on whether the aims of the movement are "revivalistic" or "perpetuative" and whether the means are "magical" or "rational." He also suggests that nativistic movements arise in situations of culture contact, where the groups in contact are of unequal status, and where this had led to dissatisfaction. He names as frequent causes "exploitation" and "frustration."

The two most recent theoretical papers are those by Voget and Wallace. Voget (1956) discusses the Iroquois "Great Message," Peyotism, and Shakerism as examples of "reformative nativism," which he defines as "a relatively conscious attempt on the part of a subordinated group to attain a personal and social reintegration through selective rejection, modification, and synthesis of both traditional and alien (dominant) cultural components." He sees as major characteristics: prophetic revelation from a Creator-God; concern for legitimizing beliefs vis-à-vis the dominant group, for healing the body, and for mortality; proselytizing; and the creation of new statuses. He recognizes that anti-nativism, in the opposition to earlier curing or other practices, is also inherent in these movements and that schisms, representing different levels of acculturation, may also be inherent.

Wallace (1956) proposes a concept "revitalization movement," which he defines as "a deliberate, organized, conscious effort by members of a society to construct a more satisfactory culture." He sees such movements as attempts to bring reality into congruence with a changed "mazeway," by which term he means "nature, society, culture, personality, and body image as seen by one person." Revitalization movements, he says, constitute a large class of phenomena divisible by several criteria into such subclasses as "nativistic

---

[12]Herskovits also discusses examples of similar phenomena in Melanesia, but without much comment as to underlying causes.

movements," "revitalization movements," "cargo cults," "millenarian movements," "messianic movements." Using the mazeway concept Wallace outlines the process by which a revitalization movement is formed and the varieties it may take.

From what we know of the content of the Coast Salish Prophet Dance we can identify it as a member of, or at least closely allied to, the class of phenomena discussed by Barber, Linton, Voget, and Wallace. Prophecies of the coming of the Whites and of a new way of life suggest that Barber's term "messianic" (proclaiming a golden age) is applicable. Using Linton's criteria of ends and means we might classify the Coast Salish movement as "magical-revivalistic." Of the major characteristics of "reformative nativism" outlined by Voget, prophetic revelation from a Creator-God, concern for morality, the creation of new statuses at least that of the Prophet or leader), and proselytizing seem to have been present in the Coast Salish movement. Wallace's concept, by the very range of examples he lists (1956:264), would have to include the Coast Salish movement.

But Barber, Linton, and Voget all see "messianic" or "nativistic" movements as responses to direct contact with a dominant alien society and consequent deprivation and frustration. Here the Coast Salish movement does not fit the concept. The Coast Salish movement, like the Prophetic Dance of the Plateau, occurred before there was much direct contact with White society. Until the 1840s contact was only with the fur traders and was not characterized by any great inequality. Widespread first-hand contact and serious deprivation began for many Native communities only when the area swarmed with would-be miners attempting to get up the Fraser in the Gold Rush of 1858. The first appearance of the Prophetic Dance was long before this.

One or two causes of social disruption may have occurred, however, even before much direct contact with the Whites. Epidemics of smallpox and other diseases swept across the continent, the earliest according to Mooney (1928:13, 26) about 1782, a decade before the first recorded exploration of the Coast Salish area. According to traditions I have recorded in the Straits area, whole villages were wiped out by an epidemic that occurred before the first Whites arrived. This experience must have had a serious effect on the lives of the survivors.

The fur trade, while not accompanied by much external pressure, may have led to some internal causes of social disruption. It permitted hunters and trappers to accumulate wealth more rapidly than before and probably enabled them to rise socially at the expense of the hereditary owners of fishing locations and other productive sites. This increase in social mobility may have stimulated others to seek other sources of prestige and authority. Collins has pointed to the growth in political authority in relation to cults among the Upper Skagit. This relationship deserves more attention here and elsewhere.[13]

---

[13]Belshaw (1950) and Guiart (1951) have pointed out that the recent cult activity in Melanesia has its political aspects.

But aside from causes of social disruption resulting indirectly from the presence of small numbers of Whites, there may have been causes within the Native society itself. It seems to me rather probable that Coast Salish society suffered chronically from a need for more bases for leadership because of its poverty of political institutions. This need may have led to occasional internal crises that permitted the rise of prophets who used religious concepts and ceremonies to exercise more than usual authority. This argument provides one more reason for concluding, as Spier did on the basis of underlying religious concepts, that such phenomena may have been endemic in northwestern North America and not merely a response to the presence of Europeans. Herskovits' criticism of too much stress on White influence and on deprivation seems justified. Moreover, the term "nativistic" can hardly be applicable in a so-largely Native setting. Wallace's more inclusive concept "revitalization movement" seems to be a more useful one.

One difficulty with the definitions offered by Linton, Voget, and Wallace lies in the element "consciously organized." We may infer that some of the Coast Salish prophets were quite conscious that they were attempting to change their culture. Yet one informant's account was that the Klallam at first accepted the marriage dance and then rejected it after they saw it resulted in marriages ,across class lines. The Klallam were evidently not at first conscious of the social implications of the new religious ceremony. In using the concept "revitalization movement" it may sometimes prove difficult to distinguish between a genuine movement and the mere diffusion of a new ceremony that happens to imply religious concepts and social relationships that are new but not clearly perceived by the recipients. Again I suggest we look here and elsewhere for a relationship between poverty of political institutions and readiness to accept new ceremonies.*

---

*[Aberle (1959), referring to this article, argued that it is less likely that Prophet Dance phenomena occurred under purely aboriginal conditions than under conditions of deprivation brought about by White influence or contact. His article prompted Spier to enlist Herskovits and me in a joint reply (Spier, Suttles, and Herskovits 1959), essentially asking for more evidence for deprivation. I would now allow for more and earlier White influence than I did when I wrote this article, but I still think it possible that Prophet Dance phenomena might have arisen under purely aboriginal conditions. Could not deprivation have occurred aboriginally?]

10. Spirit Dancing
and the Persistence of Native Culture
among the Coast Salish*

At present there are nearly seven thousand Coast Salish Indians living in a number of small communities on Southeastern Vancouver Island and the adjacent mainland from the Lower Fraser Valley southward to the Skagit River. Like their neighbors to the south in Washington and to the north in British Columbia, these people might appear to the casual observer to be almost wholly acculturated. In their housing, dress, diet, automobiles, and television sets many of them are hardly distinguishable from their White neighbors of similar occupations—fisherman, loggers, longshoremen. If some of them are in their way of life distinguishable from Whites, it is mainly because they have less well-kept houses and yards, have larger families, and depend more on seasonal work such as berry-picking—but these are differences that one might easily attribute to lack of education and poverty rather than to the persistence of cultural difference.†

Somewhat closer acquaintance would not change the image. All but the very oldest people speak English, many of the middle-aged are literate, most of the

---

*[Read at the 6th International Congress of Anthropological and Ethnological Sciences, Paris, 1960; published in abstract only, not previously published in full.]

†[As indicated in the Postscript to No. 1 in this volume, I would now substitute "settlement" for "community." See Knight (1978) for the history of Indian participation in commercial fishing, logging, and other industries in British Columbia.]

young are in school, many in public schools along with White children. Most people are baptized and buried as Roman Catholics. Except for a number of large barn-like structures most of which were once used as dwellings, there is little of Native material culture visible. In the summer several communities have carnivals that include canoe-racing and dancing, but the dancing is often performed in Plains Indian costume and in Plains style. Tipis and feather war-bonnets are symbols of Indian-ness that must be presented to a White audience, but they are far removed from the cedar-plank houses and shredded bark skirts and ponchos of the earlier Coast Salish. Even a fairly careful observer, visiting these people during the summer months, might see very little that would suggest any significant survival of Native culture.

However, a night spent at one of the barn-like "smokehouses" in winter or early spring might give one an entirely different impression. During these months, the Coast Salish of this area are participating in a vigorous Native ceremonialism, known in the ethnography of the area as "spirit dancing."[1] Let me describe a "big dance" that I attended on the 26th of March of this year [1960] at the Penelekut Reserve on Kuper Island, a few miles south of Nanaimo.

The dance was held in a house built in a modified version of the old style, with tiers of benches around the walls, an earth floor, and when in use two great open fires in the center. By evening the house was filled with six or eight hundred people from various Salish communities on Vancouver Island and the Mainland. Each community was assigned its own section of the house. All were dressed in ordinary working clothes except for six "new dancers," xəwsá'kʷɫ, who wore headdresses of long strands of wool and carried staffs decorated with more wool. These were people dancing this year for the first time and therefore undergoing a period of ritual care. They and perhaps seventy or eighty "old dancers" were here to dance and sing their syə́wən, the songs that come to them in winter and possess them so that they must míɫə or become sick.

The smíɫə had already started by mid-afternoon though most of the guests were still arriving. From time to time a man or woman would cry out, people with drums would gather round and take up the beat of his song, and he would

[1]Aboriginal spirit dancing within the area considered here has been described by Barnett (1955:272-88), Duff (1952:103-12), Jenness (1955:41-47), and Stern (1934:61-69). Gunther (1927:289-95), Haeberlin and Gunther (1930:289-95), and Smith (1940:100-107) refer to groups living south of those considered here, but their data are relevant. Modern spirit dancing has been described best in two unpublished works, Wike 1941 and Lane 1953. I am indebted to all of these works, particularly to the last two; however, the present paper is largely the product of my own observations made in the course of research on Native culture and language. This research has been most recently supported by a grant from the Leon and Thea Koerner Foundation.

rise and without moving far sing with his mouth taut and his eyes shut. These were the dancers who could not control their songs until the dance proper, which was to come much later, and so had to let themselves be possessed long enough to dance for a minute or two at their places. Meanwhile, the guests were gradually being served a meal of venison, salt-water ducks, potatoes, and coffee.

About nine o'clock the portion of the program called the "work" began. Mrs. Angus Edwards of Kuper Island had three tasks to perform. First she gave inherited names to her brother and niece, for which purpose she had hired two $sx^wáyx^wəy$ dancers from Nanaimo. These appeared with their characteristic bug-eyed masks, suits of feathers, and scallop-shell rattles, and danced before the person to be named. The ritual purpose of the performance is purificatory; the right to have it performed is hereditary. A speaker then explained the family's right to the names and fifty-cent pieces were given to leading men from other communities, who spoke in response. Next Mrs. Edwards displayed a photograph of her deceased sister. Someone carried it around the house with a lantern, while she walked beside it crying "oh, my poor younger sister," and handing out fifty-cent pieces to her invited guests. Finally she had a group of her own people display her deceased father's dance costume and sing his song. During this she gave a fifty-cent piece each to a number of women from other communities so that they would walk around the house thanking the people for listening.

These events occupied about three hours. They proceeded slowly and were occasionally interrupted by a dancer who could no longer resist the possessing song and had to be placated. Around midnight we were served another meal. This was followed by another naming with more masked dancers.

The last major event was still another naming ceremony. The speaker, a Nanaimo man, announced that the two sons of Basil Charley of Kuper Island were taking hereditary names. A sister of the men, a woman now married at Saanich, then had someone bring out a large native blanket of mountain-goat wool and throw it down on the ground in the center of the house between the two fires. Several flannelette blankets went down on top of that and it was announced that this pile was to be the "mat" for her brothers, and that the gift was not to be returned. Two masked dancers from Nanaimo then led the men out, had them stand on the "mat," and danced around them while others, hired on the spot, sang an hereditary song suitable to the occasion. The dancers and singer were paid with kerchiefs and flannelette blankets tied about them. Then from away outside we heard the sound of a low chant. It gradually grew closer and finally eight people appeared, six of them shaking rattles fringed with mountain-goat wool. These, like the masks, can be used only by families with the hereditary right. Next the speaker called up a row of older men who spoke each in turn to the two young men, addressing them as "$si\cdot\,?ém$ nəstətíwən" ("Chiefs, my nephews") and urging them to remember the solemnity of the occasion and the value of the names they were receiving. At about this point, someone from Nanaimo gave the young men $10, and since nothing was said about not returning it, presumably the giver expects to see the gift again. Finally the young men gave away the "mat." The Native blanket was presented to someone from Chemainus Bay and the flannelette blankets were simply thrown to the crowd.

These events were also occasionally interrupted by possessed dancers. Moreover, during lulls in the major "work," other persons took advantage of the situation and with their speakers stepped out onto the floor and made some announcement to be witnessed by the recipients of fifty-cent pieces. More than once there were two such speeches going on simultaneously in different parts of the house, while participants in the major "work" stood waiting to proceed with their next act.

At last, about three o'clock in the morning, the dance proper began. The old dancers brought out compacts and suitcases and put on face paint and costumes. A few, however, who had already had paint on their faces were now too tired and took it off. Depending on the type of song, the paint is red or black, and the costume may be merely a kerchief added to one's working clothes, or a cedar-bark headdress, or a full suit. The style of dancing also varies. A man with a *wəẏqéꞏn* song generally wears a headdress of human hair topped with two twirling feathers, a shirt with rows of little wooden paddles suspended from it, and leggings with deer-hoof rattles. He also has a short staff decorated with deer-hoof rattles, which he holds between his legs and shakes furiously as he becomes possessed. And when he dances he may leap high with arms alternately straightened and flexed, fists clenched and teeth bared. When the dancer comes back to his place he may have to be held and placed in his seat, where he may continue to groan for several minutes while another near him becomes possessed and begins to dance. Thus one after another perhaps fifty people danced, always moving counter-clockwise around the house between the drumming, singing crowd and the fires.

The dancing continued till daybreak and long after. There were no speeches to interrupt it, but other activities accompanied it. Nearly every time a dancer moved out onto the floor, some member of his family walked around the house handing out fifty-cent pieces to selected persons asking them to help the dancer regain his seat. Often more persons were asked than possibly could have helped and so the "help" was merely a gesture. Meanwhile the new dancers were passing out apples and oranges to everyone. Before the dance was over all six of the new dancers were made to run around the house together to the rapid beating of the drums while their attendants held them from behind with cedar-bark harnesses. As its final act of hospitality, the host community distributed three hundred pounds of sugar.

The ceremonial gathering that I have just described is not at all unusual. The description would be different in details but true in general outline for "Indian dances'' held in a number of communities on southeastern Vancouver Island and the adjacent mainland. In most Indian communities in this area there is some ceremonial activity each winter, if only a ''small dance,'' that is, an intra-community gathering for dancing only. If a community has a new dancer this may mean small dances nearly every night for some weeks. The larger and more active communities, like Cowichan, Saanich, or Lummi, also usually have one or more ''big dances'' to which they invite a number of other communities or even the whole dancing area. This may mean that a ''big dance'' is being held somewhere nearly every Saturday night for several months. These ''big dances'' may be sponsored by individuals, families, or whole communities. The dance on Kuper Island this year was a ''company dance,'' that is, given by the whole community. Not every member of the community is a dancer and not all participate in the ''work,'' but nearly all give some help in providing food for the guests or fuel for the fires. So the number of people who participate at some time in some way is almost the total Indian population.

In the communities on Vancouver Island and in some on the Mainland, interest in these gatherings seems to be growing. Four communities have built new smokehouses in the last five years or so. Two communities have had dances in the last few years after a number of years with none. Every year there are several new dancers, often young people.

It should also be noted that the Shaker Indian Church, a blend of Christian and Native religion that originated on Puget Sound in the 1880s, is still active over much of this area. Also, at Esquimalt and Sooke the x̣ənx̣ənítaʼl, the Klallam-Songish secret society, is still very much alive—and very secret.

Thus, in spite of a century of White settlement, the presence now of White cities next door to Indian reserves, and the almost complete disappearance of Salish material culture, Salish ceremonial life is flourishing. Moreover, and this seems equally surprising, nothing like this degree of constant activity has been reported for any other part of the Northwest Coast in recent years.

This calls for an explanation. What does this Coast Salish ceremonialism really consist of? That is to say, how much of it is a direct survival from aboriginal culture, how much is revival, and how much is something newly developed in response to modern conditions? And why should any Native ceremonialism at all persist so vigorously among the Coast Salish here and not among any other group in the area?

First, the sort of ''spirit dance'' that I have just described is not exactly like any ceremonial gathering of the time before the coming of the Whites. The contemporary ''big dance'' seems to be built around a framework of an earlier spirit dancing but to have a good deal of the content of another, more famous institution, the potlatch. To clarify this statement let me describe briefly the pre-White ideology and its expression in ceremonial gatherings as they can be reconstructed from the ethnographic data. (By ''pre-White'' I mean here before White settlement, which occurred in the 1850s.)

In aboriginal society, to have high status, a man had to have birth in a "good family," which gave him a respected name and privileges, and he had to have the material possessions, food and wealth, needed to assume the name and exercise the privileges. To produce either food or wealth, a man had to have one of a number of special skills which, it was believed, were acquired and practised with the aid of the supernatural.

The most important source of supernatural help was the *s?á/yə*, the vision, sought, especially during adolescence, by fasting and bathing in remote forest lakes or along lonely shores. During the vision the seeker encountered some animal—real or mythical—which conferred upon him a particular skill and became, in anthropological language, his "guardian spirit." The seeker also usually received a *syə́wən*, a "spirit song," which came to him some winter later in life and made him sick. A shaman or ritualist recognized the sick person as a *xəwsá′kʷɬ*, a "new dancer," and helped him learn to control his song and to *mɨ́tə*, to dance with it in a state of possession. Spirit songs also came unsought to persons suffering from grief. They could also be induced to possess persons by means of a ritual abduction and isolation resembling the Wakashan secret society initiation. Each winter persons with songs acquired in these various ways danced possessed at public gatherings held for the purpose.

The Native languages distinguish two main types of ceremonial gathering, the "feast" (*sƛ́éxən*) and the "potlatch" (*sƛ́ə́nəq*). For a "feast," guests were invited from one's own and perhaps immediately adjacent communities and given *mə́qa?θ*, portions of food to take home. Its purpose might be simply the distribution of a sudden oversupply of food. Or it might have the further purpose of marking some life crisis, or, if in winter, to provide an occasion for spirit dancing. The spirit dance was thus only one, though very important, kind of "feast."

The "potlatch" was a much larger, intercommunity gathering. It lasted several days or even weeks, it was held in late spring or early fall—when travelling was easy, and its principal overt purpose was the validation of claims to high status through the giving of wealth. To accumulate the large amounts of wealth and food or credit in wealth or food for a potlatch usually required several years. The leaders of a community intending to potlatch could work at this in several ways. They could produce wealth directly or could acquire it through war, gambling, or payment for services. They could also "paddle" (*?ə́xəl*), that is, take gifts of food to affinals in other communities and receive gifts of wealth in exchange. Moreover, they could "put away" (*lə?éls*) wealth on hand by giving it to relatives or affinals with the understanding that it would be returned, if possible with an additional amount, when needed. They could also "put away" food for later return. This last was no doubt particularly important since a single community would probably have found it very hard to feed several hundred extra people for a period of a week or two from its own resources of that time alone. Having made such preparations, the potlatchers then visited as many communities as possible, inviting important members of each, including relatives and affinals with whom they had "put away" wealth and food on previous occasions.

The potlatch itself consisted of a fixed sequence of events. On the first day, relatives and affinals paid their debts to the hosts. This greatly increased the hosts' already large accumulations of wealth and gave them the food with which to support the guests during their stay. During the next several days the hosts celebrated various life crises, changes of status, memorials to the dead, all events being enhanced by the display of hereditary masks and other privileges insofar as possible. Persons other than the principal potlatchers took advantage of the occasion to seek similar recognition. On the last day, each potlatcher, standing on a platform built out from the roof of his house, gave lavish gifts of blankets and other items of wealth to each of his invited guests as he called each of their names and finally "scrambled" his remaining property by throwing it to the crowd.

It will be seen that the potlatch and the spirit dance were quite distinct. They differed in season, size of gathering, and purpose. They were not, however, entirely unrelated. The would-be potlatcher found the spirit dance a convenient occasion for "putting away" food. During the winter dance season he had members of his household hunting deer, waterfowl, etc., which he could take to relatives and affinals. These people received the food and used it for their feasts for spirit dancing, knowing they would have to return in kind when the giver potlatched. Thus the spirit dance provided a link in the economic process of which the potlatch was the dramatic climax.

As I have argued elsewhere (Suttles 1960a), the total socio-economic system, in which the "function" of the potlatch was the redistribution of wealth, seems to have been adaptive under certain conditions of Coast Salish environment— spatial and temporal variation and fluctuation in natural resources.

Having now looked at the aboriginal institutions from which the modern ceremonialism is historically derived, let us look again at the form and content of the modern "big dance." By informants' definitions and in total form it is still a *sƛéxən*, "feast," for spirit dancing. It is held in winter, for one night, it begins with spontaneous possessions, its climax is dancing, and it ends with a distribution of *mə́q̓aʔθ*, food to take home. On the other hand, the "work" that is inserted into the middle of the "big dance" is quite clearly the sort of thing that went on in the middle of the potlatch. Moreover, some of these events, like the naming of the Charley boys on Kuper Island, even have something of the form of the total potlatch—beginning with gifts brought to the principals by relatives and affinals and ending with the distribution of these gifts. Thus the modern "big dance" is a sort of potlatch within a spirit dance feast.

Elements of the potlatch have also entered spirit dancing itself. The initiation of a new dancer requires payments to the shaman or ritualist and his assistants and the distribution of oranges or apples to the audience. Some dancers add deer-hoof rattles to their costumes in their third year of dancing, with payments to witnesses. These practices may be old, but some costs are said to be rising. On the other hand, the initial burden has been somewhat alleviated by a practice, spreading on the island, of sharing the costs.

One definitely recent practice is that of paying persons to help the dancer regain his seat. I have myself observed the growth of this practice within the last ten or twelve years. It is said to have originated at Saanich when a man who was ashamed because a young relative had tripped when returning to her seat paid two friends to help her the next time she danced. Being ashamed, he should have given away money somehow, and so he simply chose this way of doing it. The practice was quickly taken up by others and within a few years had spread throughout the area. As one informant put it, "it was like lighting a match to a pile of kindling." Its effect was such that the dancer's family paid so many persons to help that they could in fact not all get near enough to him to do any good, their presence on the floor merely obscuring the audience's view of the dancer. But the feeling of obligation has become so strong that a dancer may now try to inhibit possession if he knows his family cannot afford to pay anyone to seat him. Two years ago at Lummi it looked as if the practice might go even further; the last dancer of the evening was the chairman of the smokehouse committee and while he danced his wife handed out—not fifty-cent pieces—but blankets. My Musqueam friends immediately said, "Oh, this is going to spread." But as yet it has not. Moreover, this year on Vancouver Island the practice has been limited to the extent that the dancer's family pays other dancers only, rather than any one in the audience. While this does not reduce the amount a dancer's family might spend, it serves to increase his chance of getting his money back when others dance.

In preparing for participation in the modern "big dance," many people also still "put away" (ləʔéls) both food and wealth by giving a few dollars or a box of fruit at a dance sponsored by others with the expectation of having the gift returned, perhaps with "thanks" (xčíətíət), that is, with a bit more added to show gratitude for the "good feelings" of the giver.

The modern "big dance" is thus an alliance between two separate Native institutions. But it is an uneasy sort of alliance. Interest in religious expression through dancing and interest in improving status through gift-giving are at times clearly in competition, as when dancers become possessed and interrupt the "work," or when the "work" drags on until the dancers are too weary to dance, or when a dancer will not dance because he cannot afford to. This conflict of interests, moreover, is recognized by many of the participants themselves, a few of whom have even suggested in conversation that the work and the dancing should be confined to separate occasions.

How did this modern mélange come to be formed? And why do the Coast Salish continue to participate in all these activities? The answers to these questions may perhaps be found in a combination of legal, social, and economic factors. The earlier missionaries among the Coast Salish opposed Native ceremonial practices, especially those they saw as implying beliefs contrary to Christian teaching. One of the early missionaries is said to have confiscated spirit dance costumes and then desecrated them by dressing his pupils in them for a show in order to make money for his school. Later civil authorities in both the United States and Canada opposed various Native ceremonies. The potlatch especially was prohibited, though in Canada the law was evidently not effectively enforced until between 1910 and 1920. Within the area now being considered, the last potlatch on the U.S. side of the border was about 1905 and on the Canadian side about 1915. Spirit dancing, however, continued to be practiced, though for a period semi-secretly in the face of opposition from many Indians as well as White authorities. At Musqueam, for example, for perhaps a generation the community was split between the families of dancers and the families who regarded dancing as ''the work of the devil.'' By the time the potlatch had ceased to exist as such, however, the non-dancers had gone back to dancing and the split in the community had healed. Other communities evidently went through similar experiences. Moreover, about this time several winter gatherings of potlatch proportions were held. These perhaps established the pattern of combining the two institutions. Two other influences entering about this time were the Shaker Church, which had successfully defied White religious opposition, and the automobile, which brought communities closer in winter weather. Though I do not yet have full documentation for this history, I judge that the present pattern was established by about 1920.

The disappearance of the old potlatch as such cannot be entirely due to opposition from religious and secular authorities, since these opposed spirit dancing as well. Nor can it be due simply to the decline of Native culture, since Native culture has not simply declined. According to some informants, another important cause besides White legal and social pressure was the increasing importance of summer work in berry fields, canneries, etc., which made long summer gatherings less convenient. I suspect that still another reason was the decline, not of the whole of Native culture, but of the Native economic system within which the potlatch played its key role as a regulating mechanism.

The persistence of spirit dancing in spite of opposition from outside and even from within the Indian communities is harder to explain. At present, most dancers get their songs through an initiation rite which may induce a vision in some but probably not in all. Others get their songs through mourning. Few if any endure any prolonged spirit quest. At present most songs are not associated with specific skills or professions still practiced. A great many dancers have, in fact, songs which once would have been associated with the professional warrior. In spite of these changes in the relationship between a dancer and the

207

supernatural source of his song, the state of possession in most dancers seems nevertheless genuine. But what can this deep feeling, which once meant, "I am a great hunter, or a great canoe maker, or warrior," mean today? I believe it can only mean, "I am an Indian." I suggest, then, that the modern ceremonialism insofar as it has a religious content is comparable to "nativistic" or "revivalistic" phenomena observed elsewhere in North America and in other parts of the world.

But as we have seen, spirit dancing is not all that there is to the modern ceremonialism. Spirit dancing has become the vehicle for the survival of a good deal of potlatch behavior, if not the total potlatch. For now, I can account for this only by suggesting that it is evidence for the survival of Native social as well as religious attitudes and that this survival implies much more cultural isolation than casual observation would suggest.

I would like to be able to explain the survival of some of the Native economic processes such as the "putting away" of boxes of oranges, but I am not satisfied with my knowledge here either. I can only suggest that "putting away" food or money on hand by giving it to remote relatives or affinals is a way of putting it out of the reach of close relatives and one's own weaker self, and that the survival of this practice implies a failure to adopt the good Western virtues of banking, budgeting, and being miserly with all but first degree relatives.

Finally, we may ask, why has Native ceremonialism shown such vitality among the Coast Salish and nowhere else on the Northwest Coast? There are several possibilities. It may be a matter of size of population and mobility. The Coast Salish are a larger group than say the Kwakiutl or Haida, and they are now united by modern highways and ferries. Or it may be a matter of time and intensity of contact. Perhaps the conflict between pressures to assimilate and barriers to complete assimilation often related to nativistic and other such phenomena is felt more acutely by the Coast Salish than by more isolated groups farther north. If the reasons are either or a combination of these, then perhaps we can expect a revival of Native ceremonialism farther north in a few years when Native population has increased, roads and ferries are established, and contact with unfamiliar and unsympathetic Whites has increased. But perhaps more important yet are differences in structure among the Native cultures and in the way the Native peoples have been able to adapt Native institutions to preserve ethnic identity. The looseness of organization and individual religious expression of Coast Salish spirit dancing may have provided a better vehicle for the expression of "nativism" and for the persistence of other features of Native culture than the more highly organized and more secular ceremonialism of the Kwakiutl or Haida.*

---

*[I would now write "winter dancing" instead of "spirit dancing" (as indicated in note 7 of No. 11 in this volume). More recent works on winter dancing include Amoss 1977, 1978; Collins 1974; Jilek 1974, 1982; Kew 1970; Suttles 1963 (No. 11 in this volume), 1977. The dancing has continued to spread among the Coast Salish. And farther north, Native ceremonialism has indeed reemerged; see Blackman (1977) for examples and discussion.]

11. The Persistence of Intervillage Ties among the Coast Salish[1]*

Native tribes in much of northwestern North America seem, by Anglo-American standards, beset by social problems but slow to develop the organization and leadership that might help solve them. It has been assumed that one of the causes of this has been a weakening of Native social ties under the impact of Anglo-American society and culture, among the most important of these being those that united the "community" in a self-contained, self-sufficient social unit. This assumption is one made by a major work on contemporary social problems in this area by Hawthorn, Belshaw, and Jamieson (1958:36, 225, 411-13). In this work "community" appears generally equated with the "reserve" or "band," the modern counterpart of the aboriginal village (pp. 17, 41f., 438ff.). Programs of "community development," which the authors see as the best solution to Indian problems (pp. 428ff.), would presumably start with these units. However, the authors also recommend allowing greater mobility between reserves and, pointing to the isolating effect of the reserve system and the need for a common set of interests with other Indians to support Indian self-respect, they suggest (p. 443) that "the Indian concept of community is too limited and needs widening."

---

[1]This is a somewhat revised and expanded version of a paper read at the Sixteenth Northwestern Anthropological Conference held at Reed College, Portland, in April 1963.

*[From *Ethnology* 2:512-25 (1963); reprinted in *The Emergent Native Americans*, edited by Deward E. Walker, Jr. (Boston: Little, Brown 1972), pp. 665-77.]

But perhaps it is rather *our* concept of "community" that is too limited. I stress the "our" because I too have used the term "community" for the aboriginal village and for the modern reserve. The term itself, however, is not important. What matters are the features we ascribe to the unit in our interpretation of the total social structure. I shall try to show here that, in a part of the area covered by the work cited above, the village was not aboriginally a self-contained or self-sufficient social unit. Further, in spite of a century of missionary and government policies that have indeed tended to isolate Indian villages—now reserves— from one another, Native principles of social organization persist in systems of intervillage ceremonialism. The area of this ceremonialism is, in one sense, the modern "community" and it may be the larger unit the authors of the work cited appear to be seeking. Finally, I shall consider possible reasons why they neglected this unit, and offer a suggestion for future research.

The people I am concerned with are the Coast Salish of the lower valley of the Fraser River, the southern shores of Georgia Strait, and the northern shores of the Strait of Juan de Fuca in southwestern British Columbia and northwestern Washington. Portions of this area have been described ethnographically by a number of writers beginning with Boas and including, most recently, Barnett and Duff. However, what follows is based mainly on my own research (see Suttles 1960a, nn. 1 and 2). My interpretation of certain aspects of Native culture may differ somewhat from those of other writers, but I do not believe there is any contradiction between their material and the view of the village given herewith.

It appears that at the time of White settlement the whole area formed a social continuum within which the village was only one of several equally important social groupings. On the basis of winter residence, we might distinguish four levels of discrete units: families, each occupying its own section of a cedar-plank house and maintaining its own domestic economy; house groups, each composed of several families (related through either males or females) occupying a plank house and co-operating as hosts of feasts and other ceremonies; villages, each composed of a group of such houses occupying a short stretch of beach or river bank and sharing a common name and identification with territory; tribes, generally composed of several villages occupying a longer stretch of shoreline or a drainage area and sharing a common name and, to some extent, forms of speech, subsistence methods, and ceremonial procedures. On the basis of kinship, however, we can distinguish at least one other kind of group: a nondiscrete, nonlocalized, property-holding kin group.[2] It was this group or

---

[2]The kinship system of this area has several of the features of Murdock's (1960b) "Ambilineal (Polynesian)" type of cognatic system: ambilineal kin groups, ambilocal residence, incest taboos extended beyond second cousins of all kinds, and Hawaiian cousin terms. Small domestic units (within the big winter house) and lineal kin terms in the parental generation are features of his "Bilateral (Eskimo)" type.

Fig. 17. The afternoon before a big dance. The two houses ("smokehouses" or "big-houses") had been used as dwellings during the first decade of the century, but were now used only for winter dancing, the farther one for the dancing itself and the nearer one for cooking and serving meals to the guests. The cooks are already at work. "Chemainus Bay" (Kulleet Bay), Vancouver Island, February 1962.

211

Fig. 18. Abraham Joe with the thunderbird and whale device that he has painted to go over the entrance to the new Duncan big house. Cowichan Reserve, summer 1960. This new building was one of the first of a number built during the resurgence of winter dancing.

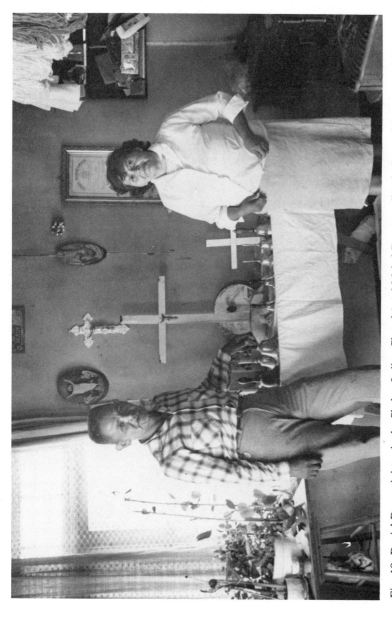

Fig. 19. Daniel Dan, minister in the Shaker Indian Church, and Mabel Dan, standing in front of the prayer table in their home at Musqueam in the summer of 1963. Though never great in numbers, the Shakers have had a powerful influence on Coast Salish life.

Fig. 20. "The Children of the Setting Sun." A Lummi dance troupe, using largely Plains style costumes but many traditional Coast Salish songs and dances, performs at an annual festival with canoe races and carnival rides. Gooseberry Point, Lummi Reservation, near Bellingham, Washington, June 1950.

Fig. 21. Lummi dancer. He is wearing the costume of a winter dancer who has a *wəẏqéˑn* song. Women in the troupe wear Plains-style dresses. Capilano Indian Centennial Pow-wow, 26 July-3 August 1958, Capilano (Squamish) Indian Reserve, North Vancouver.

Fig. 22. West coast (Nootka) dancer. The tipis belong to visiting Cree people. Capilano Pow-wow, August 1958.

Fig. 23. Canoe race. Cultus Lake Indian Festival, 2-3 June 1962. The eleven-man dugout canoes are made in a style that has been in use since the 1930s, perhaps for much longer.

Fig. 24. Joe Washington and his Lummi dance troupe, Cultus Lake Indian Festival, June 1962, using winter dance garb at a summer gathering to remind the audience of the value of their Native heritage.

its head, rather than any of the residential groups, that owned the most important ceremonial rights and the most productive natural resources. Finally, on the basis of participation in the yearly round of subsistence activities and periodic ceremonial activities, we might distinguish a number of other social groupings, none of them necessarily identical with the residential units or the kin groups, some of them necessarily differing from them.

Within this whole, the village was certainly not a self-contained social unit. Individual and family ties were as strong between villages as within the village. Individual and family status was as dependent upon ties of marriage and kinship with other villages as upon economic rights and traditional identity with one's own village. Within the village, people might co-operate in food-getting, exchange labor, and join in potlatching and mutual defense, but they were not obliged to do so by any formal village organization. There was no office of village chief and no village council. Co-operation was ad hoc. Leadership was for specific purposes and was exercised by virtue of specific skills, property rights, or supposed superhuman powers (see Barnett 1955:243; Duff 1952:81-82). Moreover, recognition of leadership came as much from outside the village as from within.[3] Conflict within the village was often resolved by one party's leaving it.

Marriages were often arranged between families in different villages. The couple usually resided with the husband's people but fairly often resided with the wife's. Children could ultimately reside in whatever village any grandparent came from and no choice was permanent. Barnett (1955:182) stresses the value placed on "many homes."[4] Members of different villages who were united by ties of marriage and kinship also co-operated in the food quest or shared access to each other's resources. Summer fishing camps often included families from several winter villages. Formal exchange between affinals in different villages provided a means of converting a temporary surplus of perishable food into nonperishable wealth. An accumulation of wealth was dissipated in the potlatch, at which members of one village played host to members of as many other villages as social ties and means allowed. Probably on this occasion

---

[3]Gunther (1927:262) reports a post-settlement example from just south of the area, describing an agent-supervised selection of a Klallam village "chief" at which not only members of other Klallam villages but non-Klallam as well, who were related to one of the candidates, stood up and were counted.

[4]Although Barnett suggests that marriage alliances between distant villages may have increased after White settlement, genealogies indicate that they go back to pre-settlement times. Perhaps the best example is provided by Boas (1894). His Tables I and II give the genealogy of a Scowlitz (Harrison River) informant about 50 years of age, i.e., born about 1840. In the fifth, sixth, and seventh ascending generations, and thus presumably in the eighteenth century, marriages are recorded with Kwantlen, Cowichan, Songish, Puget Sound (probably Skagit), and even Makah. In later generations there were also marriages with Lillooet and Thompson.

219

more than on any other the village appeared as a social unit vis-à-vis other such social units, but even then unity was not much more than a spatial and temporal juxtaposition of members. Individuals or kin groups performed their ceremonial acts and gave their gifts one after another as the assembled guests moved from house to house. The fact that gifts did not go to fellow villagers was perhaps what most clearly set them apart from outsiders.

I have argued elsewhere (Suttles 1960a) that these intervillage relations formed an exchange system that was adaptive (i.e., increased chances for survival) under the particular environmental conditions of the region. If this view is correct, then it seems likely that tendencies toward village economic self-sufficiency or village endogamy would have been, in the long run, disadvantageous. It is therefore possible that a moderate amount of intra-village friction may have contributed to village survival by pushing each family into alliances with families elsewhere. Evidence that intra-village rivalry did exist may be found in many Coast Salish villages today in the form of gossiping and subtle or even open accusations and counter-accusations of low-class ancestry, all of which appears to go back several generations (see Suttles 1958 on gossip as a part of "advice").

Members of villages allied by marriage and kinship also occasionally co-operated in warfare under the leadership of recognized professional warriors. On a few occasions, after the introduction of firearms, nearly the whole Coast Salish area co-operated in fighting the Kwakiutl. However, this co-operation did not result in the emergence of any permanent political units, though perhaps White settlement followed too soon after these events to have permitted it.

Let us return to the concept "community." If we define the term using "co-residence" as our only criterion, then perhaps the village is our "community." But if we consider other kinds of social ties, then we must look further. I suggest that we adopt as criteria those social ties that define and maintain status. Among the Coast Salish, the minimal unit for the definition and maintenance of status—even within the village—was not the village but the area of intervillage marriage and potlatch relations.

This intervillage "community" may have been different for each village or even different for the same village from one generation to the next. Its boundaries did not coincide with dialect or even language boundaries, so that it is not identical with the "tribe" as defined above. There does seem to have been some correspondence in this region between linguistic and ecological boundaries (see Suttles 1962), but marriage ties and consequent exchange between affinals were perhaps more valuable when they crossed ecological boundaries, as they often did. Overlapping groups of villages of this sort bear the same relationship to organizations of discrete units like the Nootka confederacy of tribes, as, among kinship structures, kindreds bear to lineages; they are not delimitable in any permanent way, and they are not mutually exclusive, but they are nevertheless real. The first clear identification of social units of this

220

sort was made by Elmendorf (1960:296-305) in his analysis of the culture of the Twana, a Coast Salish group in western Washington, south of the area discussed here. It seems likely that such units occurred throughout the Coast Salish area and perhaps more widely in northwestern North America.[5]

Lastly, considering what the concept "community" may imply to those concerned with social welfare, we should note that there is no reason to believe that either the aboriginal village or the intervillage "community" automatically looked after everyone residing within its limits. The Native theory of social stratification seems to imply that some people may not be worth bothering with, and the working of the social system perhaps even promoted some human wastage.

In the preceding paragraphs I have attempted a sketch of some of the features of Native social organization as it must have been at the middle of the last century. During the second quarter of the century most of the Coast Salish had only occasional contact with White fur traders; from the 1850s on they had continuous contact with settlers, miners, loggers, missionaries, administrators, and all the rest of North American society. A sketch of earlier Native society is necessarily based on inferences from more recent practices and from traditions surviving a century of extensive contact.

It is doubtful whether the earlier White authorities clearly understood the nature of Coast Salish intervillage relations. Possibly some did and were consciously attacking Native culture by restricting relations between villages. But it is more likely that major policies were made at a higher level for a variety of Indian groups at once and without much knowledge of local conditions. Some policies, too, were designed to promote the growth of self-contained Indian communities, either as a means of containing the Indians as a whole until their supposedly inevitable extinction or as a means of setting them on the proper path toward assimilation. Governmental authorities established "reserves"— "reservations" in the state of Washington—and thereby instituted the special legal status of "Indian" and the legal basis for the separation of Indians from

---

[5]Elmendorf speaks of intervillage social units of this sort as "community groups." The people of a Twana winter village are a "winter-village community," except for the several settlements on the Skokomish River, which form an extended winter-village community." All the Twana-speaking villages, however, are called a "speech community." I believe that in none of these usages is the term intended to convey any notions of social self-sufficiency. Since such notions seem often to be implied by the term, however, it might be better to avoid it in cases where self-sufficiency does not exist. I suggest that "village" is adequate to designate a local settlement. For the overlapping intervillage social units we may really need a new term. The word "tribe" will not do, since it implies a discrete unit. On the analogy of the "kindred" among kinship units, I further suggest, with some misgivings, an analogic coinage from "kith," originally meaning "country" or "neighbors." Overlapping groups of neighboring villages or other local groups might be called "kithreds."

non-Indians and from each other. In Washington, a treaty signed in 1855 established reservations within the territories of some of the tribes but not of others. Those without reservations were expected to join their neighbors with reservations; generally, however, they refused to move. In British Columbia there were no treaties. The land was simply declared property of the crown, and, in time, every village site in use and nearly every fishing camp became a "reserve" and nearly every village became a "band." The law then prescribed band membership by patrilineal descent unless otherwise specially granted. Instead of attempting, as did the American policy, to throw people of several villages together with no basis for intervillage relations, the Canadian policy gave each village its own territory but imposed restrictions on the ambilineal descent and ambilocal residence pattern of Native social organization. In some places, however, religious authorities persuaded members of several villages to come together to form little theocratic states. Governmental authorities in both countries tried to convert seasonally mobile fishermen into sedentary farmers. Both religious and governmental authorities in both countries tried to put an end to the potlatch and the winter dance. Residential schools, operated by the churches, separated children from families and gave them full-time instruction in Western living habits, Christian beliefs, and the rudiments of Western learning. Arranged marriages and living in multi-family dwellings were discouraged in favor of marriage by individual choice and residence in houses of European style on individual allotments. Reserve land and other band property became the responsibility of officially created band chiefs and councils—under official guidance.[6]

But the Coast Salish were not to be made over to conform to the model of the Old World peasant village—ideologically homogeneous, economically self-sufficient, social self-contained—a model we may suspect some of the authorities had in mind. The theocratic states had some success at the northern end of the Coast Salish area (see Lemert 1954), but it did not endure much beyond the beginning of the present century. The agricultural programs had some success at Lummi (see Suttles 1954), Cowichan, and elsewhere, until commercial fishing, cannery jobs, berry picking, and other seasonal work proved more attractive, partly perhaps because they promoted intervillage contact. The residential schools, simply by bringing young people together, have also encouraged continued intermarriage. Today, in spite of an almost complete replacement of native material goods and a century-long conflict between White and Native beliefs and practices, basic features of Native social organization remain.

The village is not yet a "community." Some time ago Leacock (1949:194) pointed this out very clearly regarding a reserve on the Lower Fraser River that was originally settled by families from several villages:

---

[6]See Hawthorn, Belshaw, and Jamieson 1958 on the effects of official restrictions and paternalism.

222

On Seabird Reserve local contiguity over several generations has not furthered the conversion of formerly like interests into common interests, the process by which community is formed. Seabird has no "community" in this sense of the word. The people living near each other do not form a single social unit, despite the pressure of outside forces in this direction.

In the most usual situation, where the reserve has continuity with a single aboriginal village, the ties among neighbors may be somewhat closer than at Seabird, but only because the kin ties are more numerous and closer. Nonkin or remote kin on the same reserve may see little or nothing of each other. Near kin on different reserves may be in close contact—made even closer by modern means of transportation and communication.

Moreover, an intervillage "community" is still very important in the lives of several thousand Coast Salish Indians. I am not referring simply to the facts of interband or intertribal marriages or movements but to organized systems of intervillage relations. There are today two major systems, the winter dances and the summer sports events, and at least one minor system, the Shaker Church.

The winter dances are held in most Coast Salish settlements on southeastern Vancouver Island and on the mainland from the Fraser River southward to the Skagit River. These gatherings are occasions when dancers become possessed and sing the "songs" they first learned to control as "new dancers" during their ceremonial initiation.[7] There are in the whole area several hundred dancers. During the winter of 1962 there were 26 new dancers. Each of these required a four-day initiation period, during which he was helped by a dozen or more experienced persons, and in addition each required as many occasions to dance during the rest of the season as possible. The ceremony is held, with few exceptions, in a "smokehouse" or "big house" built in a modification of the style of the aboriginal dwelling. The new dancer must stay in this building for the rest of his first season. Caring for him and providing fuel for the house means an additional effort from several persons. He must also attend as many big dances as possible.

---

[7]This is the activity called "spirit dancing" or "power dancing" in regional anthropological usage. The Coast Salish themselves, when speaking English, generally say "Indian dancing" or "powwow dancing" (with the latter apparently gaining ground among the younger people). Since there is no precise Native equivalent of "spirit," and since possession is only a part of the whole activity, it might be better to speak simply of "winter dancing" or "winter ceremonies." Aspects of the contemporary ceremonialism have been described by Wike (1941), Lane (1953), and Suttles (1960b). I have attended the ceremonies now and again over a period of years, but continuous study was made possible during the winter of 1961-62 by a fellowship from the American Council of Learned Societies and the University of British Columbia. My understanding of the ceremonies owes much to Wilson Duff. My thinking on both the winter ceremonies and the summer sports events has also been stimulated by discussion with Sarah Robinson.

In addition to the small dances which go on nearly every night in smoke-houses with new dancers, there are during each winter a number of big dances. Some of these are gatherings to which either all the Island or all the Mainland people are invited; others cover the total area of winter dancing, both Mainland and Island. Some are sponsored by one or two families, others by a "company" that includes most of the reserve or local group. The big dance gives the dancers an occasion to dance possessed, but its sponsors' principal concern is with their "work." This consists of the bestowal of hereditary names, display of pictures or other mementos of the dead, wiping away of shame, etc., and for each of these purposes there will be speech-making, exercising of hereditary privileges such as masks or rattles, and the giving of wealth. Families of dancers also take this opportunity to pay others for recognition of new dancers and help for old dancers. At such a big dance on the Mainland the hosts serve a meal to their guests both before and after the main events. On the Island they serve a meal before the dance starts and as a final act they distribute sugar—generally ten hundred-pound sacks when the whole area is invited. During the winter of 1962 there were twelve big dances held in nine different places and taking up nearly every Saturday night for three months. The attendance on several occasions must have been up to a thousand persons.

The contemporary big dance thus combines most of the features of the aboriginal "guardian spirit dance," which was held in the winter, and the central features of the potlatch, which was aboriginally a more prolonged summer-time gathering. I have discussed the conflict between these two aspects of the big dance elsewhere (Suttles 1960b).

Today's summer gatherings exist ostensibly for the canoe races. These events are held in fewer places than the winter dances because of the requirements of the sport, but the area from which crews and spectators come includes the whole winter dancing area plus a few reserves in British Columbia where there are a few dancers but dances are not usually held. These summer gatherings are usually sponsored by a band or tribal council or by a local committee. They are held on weekends during May and June, though sometimes later, and the races are usually run on both Saturday and Sunday. In some places the intention is in part to make money through paid attendance by and the sale of refreshments to non-Indians, and so there are concessions, carnival activities, and dances put on by Indians dressed as the public expects Indians to dress—in Plains costume with feathers and beadwork.

However, this was not the sort of gathering I attended at Cultus Lake with an Indian family last June. The local interband committee of Chilliwack Indians had engaged a whole camping resort with numerous cabins for the weekend. Two or three White families who happened to be there stayed, but no further rentals were made to non-Indians. Indians from the whole area, Mainland and Island, rented cabins or pitched tents for the weekend. In addition to the canoe races there were: on Saturday afternoon, the crowning of an "Indian princess"; on Saturday night, a modern dance with music played by an Indian band, a lacrosse game in nearby Chilliwack between an all-Indian and a White team, and a slahal (bone) game; on Sunday morning, Catholic mass on the lake shore, a football game, and a demonstration by a drill team from one of the residential schools; and on Sunday afternoon, a series of speeches and a performance by a dance troupe from one of the United States reservations, dressed mainly in costumes worn at the winter dances. Throughout this period, various functionaries were busy barbecuing salmon, managing cabin rentals and flow of traffic, operating the public address system, and judging the races. All functionaries except the priest who said mass and one of the guest speakers were Indians. Very few of the hundreds of spectators were non-Indians.

There was a time when I was inclined to regard the winter dances as genuine aboriginal culture and the summer shows as commercial frauds. But it is not as simple as this.

The meaning of the dancing can hardly be the same as it once was when the dance and song represented a successfully quested vision that was the source of skill at hunting, woodcarving, weaving, or fighting. Now the dancers are commercial fishermen, cannery workers, loggers, housewives, and persons dependent on government assistance. Their songs come unsought and bear no relationship to their professional roles. Nor can the economic consequences of the distribution of wealth at the big dances be the same as they once were in a relatively closed economy, when wealth and food were exchanged among affinal relatives. Now the money comes in from a variety of external sources and may leave by even more routes and faster.

However, dancers still perform possessed; Native theories of psychology and pathology are still fairly prevalent; several shamans and ritualists are still active in the area; and, as in the past, the initiation of a new dancer is a form of shamanistic treatment. After initiation, the dancer who fails to continue dancing may again become ill. The dancer's "song" may thus insure his general well-being without conferring any special skill as it would have in the past. Also, initiation as a new dancer is sometimes used as a means of controlling a difficult young person, and so dancing may imply moral well-being as well as physical. Perhaps most importantly, being a dancer is the most unequivocal symbol of being Indian.

Today, the wealth in money distributed at the big dances may indeed soon be lost to the Coast Salish as individual items, but the distribution commands recognition and obliges an attempt at repayment even though it does not insure it. The symbolic value probably remains the same; giving wealth means regard for status and, by implication, for Native moral values. I have discussed elsewhere (Suttles 1958) the relationship between status and morality in Native ideology.

Both the dancing itself and the potlatching that forms a part of the big dance may thus be seen as attempts by individuals and kin groups to maintain psychic integrity and social status. Underlying both dancing and potlatching is the theme of reaffirmation of shared identity as Indians. This is made most explicit in the speeches that accompany these activities.

Persons speaking four Salish languages, two of these divided into three or four dialects, attend the dances. On Vancouver Island nearly all of the speeches are in Salish, the majority in the Cowichan dialect of Halkomelem, which some non-Cowichan speakers prefer for public occasions to their own forms. On the Mainland some of the younger men can use only English, but often apologize for it. English is also sometimes resorted to for certain communications between people across the major Native linguistic boundaries.

During the winter of 1962 I attended all the big dances in the area and a number of smaller gatherings. Listening to the many hours of speech-making, though unable to follow much more than the stock phrases of introduction, thanks, etc., I was struck by three recurring references in them—to kinship ties, to respect for the ancestors, and to common cause in maintaining Native traditions.

In the smokehouse the guests from each part of the area are seated as a group in a part of the house reserved for them. If many persons come from nearby settlements, the distinctions in seating are made by village; if there are fewer people from more distant places, several villages may be lumped together. When one of the sponsors of a big dance stands up to name his children, his speaker calls out the names of important persons from each group of guests except his own: "So-and-so of Musqueam, hear what you are about to be told . . . So-and-so of Nanaimo, hear what you are about to be told . . ."—and so on around the house. These persons receive payment as witnesses. The sponsor's speaker then announces that the children will be named such-and-such for certain of their ancestors. Thereupon each of the witnesses makes a speech in response, usually with forms of address that are kinship terms, as to the sponsor: "Oh Chief, my junior cousin, I am happy at what you are doing . . .," and to the young persons: "Oh Chiefs, my nephews and nieces, it is a serious thing that your father is doing for you; bear these names so that no disgrace comes to those who bore them in the past . . ." The next speaker may address the sponsor as "uncle," the children with sibling-cousin terms, and so on. The specific relationship is probably not important; since the terms other than "parent" and "child" are classificatory and extended indefinitely to collaterals, the precise genealogical connection may not even be known. The point is that some relationship can be named, and thus through the sponsors of a big dance most or all of the groups of guests are linked. After several hours of this, one begins to see the whole area as one great kin group embracing several thousand people.

When a speaker is addressing the whole house he may use the phrase: "Oh Chiefs, my friends/relatives" (there being no distinction between "friend" and "relative"), or "Oh Chiefs, my fellow Indians" (probably a modern term). In addressing the whole house, speakers frequently give praise to those who are following the ways of the old people and urge others to follow. In speeches made in English by some of the Mainland people, the speaker often states explicitly: "The White people have taken away our land, our game, our fish, but this is something they cannot take away." In 1962 on Vancouver Island, I twice caught the Halkomelem phrase "White enemies" or "enemy Whites." Getting fuller translations from informants, I learned that the comments were directed toward individual Whites believed to be opposing the winter dances, rather than toward Whites generally. On one occasion it was the "Indian agent" and his assistants who were the "White enemies" because they were said to be threatening to withhold social assistance from Indians participating in the winter dances. The gist of one speech was that a united effort might get the "enemies" removed from their positions. So far as I know nothing came of it. But on this occasion, for a few moments, the gathering was less a dance than a political rally.

Winter dancing is not a gradually declining feature of aboriginal culture. On the contrary, it is very much alive. In three places new smokehouses have been built in the last ten years or so, and elsewhere there is talk of building others. In small but potentially significant ways the area itself is expanding. A part-Cowichan family with dancers now lives on the Snoqualmie River but continues to attend dances. In 1962 a young Cowichan woman living in Seattle attended a dance at Lummi, saw her younger sister dancing as a new dancer, returned to Seattle, became possessed, and had to be flown home to Vancouver Island to be initiated as a new dancer herself. In 1962 a young man from Tulalip saw winter dancing for the first time at LaConner, underwent a sudden, powerful emotional seizure, and had to be initiated as the first Snohomish new dancer in half a century. This year the White husband of one of last year's new dancers became a new dancer himself, demonstrating that Indian identity is not wholly biologically determined.

An ideological conflict may be in the offing. Most dancers, when asked "What is your religion?" will answer "Catholic." Dancing while possessed, once defined by the priests as the work of the devil but now viewed more tolerantly, is to most dancers merely an Indian custom, not religion. But the leader of the Lummi show troupe, who dares dress in winter dance costume and appear at summer sports events, also dares to believe that winter dancing is "from God" and loses no opportunity to say so, both in public and when initiating new dancers.

In summary, the contemporary winter ceremonialism of the Coast Salish of this area has some of the features of a nativistic movement.

What of the summer sports events? At first glance they may indeed seem like mere commercial shows bearing little resemblance to the aboriginal summer gathering, the potlatch. But most of our ethnographic descriptions of the potlatch focus on the display of hereditary privileges and the giving of wealth, precisely those features that have now been inserted into the big winter dance. Some of the fuller ethnographic accounts,[8] however, and especially contemporary newspaper accounts of late nineteenth-century potlatches, mention various sports events and gambling as part of the whole affair, which sometimes sounds like a grand extended picnic. The modern weekend of canoe racing certainly has most of the picnic quality of the old potlatch. It is also, like the potlatch and the modern big dance, an occasion when each local group may reidentify itself in relation to other local groups. In fact the local group may emerge more clearly on this occasion because the principal participants are not individuals, for whom identity is only partly a matter of residence, but crews of canoes, which are more readily identifiable with a place. But the individual and the whole are still important at the summer gathering. At Cultus Lake last summer I saw many of the leading figures of the winter dances—speakers and sponsors—attending the canoe races, and I heard some of them repeat in their speeches for this occasion one of the themes of their winter speeches, namely, that this is an Indian tradition we must maintain. That canoe racing is really an old Indian tradition may be doubted. But the intergroup gathering certainly is, and the intergroup ties may well be what the speakers are insisting must be maintained.*

Besides the two major systems of intergroup relations just described, there is at least one other system, the Shaker Church. This cult had its origin on Puget Sound in the 1880s (see Gunther 1949; Barnett 1957) and had spread into this area by about 1910. It is of minor importance today in that its membership includes no more than a small proportion of the people in any one place. Historically it may have been of considerable importance because it was probably the first Native institution that successfully defied White authority, particularly the religious authority of the orthodox Christian churches. It seems also to have provided useful experience in public speaking and conducting organizational business for a number of persons who are now active in the winter dances. Today, while its membership is small, some of its leaders are very active. The leaders on Vancouver Island meet through a good part of the year each week on one of the several reserves that have churches. A similar group on the Mainland has a similar circuit. The congregations in British Columbia hold periodic conventions for the province and send delegates to conventions in the United States. The Shaker area in British Columbia is only slightly less than the area of winter dancing, but is not so limited farther south. In the past the Shaker Church has been important, and may be in the future, since it provides an organizational link between the

---

[8]See Barnett (1955:261:62); *Victoria Daily Colonist*, 20 April 1863, p. 3; 5 March 1891, p. 5; 26 May 1892.

*[Dewhirst (1976) sees these "summer festivals" as a means of "upgrading" Coast Salish identity vis-à-vis Whites.]

Coast Salish of the winter dancing area and the Coast Salish and other Indian groups to the south, including some groups such as the Yakima, who have also maintained more purely Native forms of ceremonialism. It is also worth noting that in the winter dancing area there has been far less conflict between Shakerism and Native shamanistic and dancing activities than there seems to have been farther south.

There may be other forms of intergroup relations present or incipient in this area. During the last year a series of intergroup slahal games was held on Vancouver Island during the fall when other activities (besides the Shaker meetings) did not bring people together. So far as I know these had no permanent organization. But with new smokehouses to meet at and with increasingly better highways and faster transportation, it would not be surprising if other forms of intergroup relations developed.

It seems to me then that, like the ceremonies of the past, both the present winter dancing and the summer canoe racing are meaningful to the individual in that they provide occasions for him to find identity, to establish and maintain status. In the past, identity had to do with economic and professional roles, with hereditary rights directly or indirectly associated with these, and with the value—including implicitly moral value—accorded to those who could provide food and give wealth. Today, all that is left is moral value and this must be found in identity as an Indian.

Also, as in the past, these occasions for finding identity require a unit larger than the village. The individual may not find acceptance and support within his local group in intra-village ties alone (see Leacock 1949 on lack of neighborliness). The survival of Native values as much as modern conditions would make this difficult. The symbols of acceptance and support must be found in intergroup ties.

Aboriginally, the village had its clearest identity vis-à-vis other villages at the potlatch. But this was the time of all times when individuals or kin groups acted separately to establish and maintain status, both in relation to other villagers and within the larger social unit of intervillage relations. The village had no overriding importance. It was simply one component aspect of the identity of the individual and one component unit in the larger social whole. Today, the reserve or local group has an identity thrust upon it by the larger non-Indian society. But this is an identity implying inferior status. Like the individual, the reserve has an identity among equals only in the modern intervillage relations.

In the past the major intergroup gathering, the potlatch, was the most spectacular part of an economic system by which the Coast Salish population survived in a natural environment of fluctuating productivity. Today, in the environment of the modern welfare-state, physical survival is no longer the problem. But today's environment presents social, economic, and legal barriers to free participation in the larger society to all but the best educated and racially least distinguishable Indians. These barriers to assimilation, while in part caused by cultural differences, inevitably maintain some of old cultural differences

229

and create new ones. All Indians may survive in the modern environment, but most must survive as Indians. Under modern conditions, for many Indians the alternatives may be reaffirmation of the value of Indian identity—or apathy. For the individual the problem is psychic integrity, not physical survival. But his survival as a whole person must surely contribute to his cultural reproductivity and thus influence the continuing evolution of Indian culture.

I began with a reference to the assumptions by the authors of the Hawthorn report that the Indian "community" was once a self-contained unit but has been weakened by the impact of non-Indian society, that the "community" is identifiable with the aboriginal village and the modern reserve, and that "community development" might find solutions to Indian problems but with a widened Indian concept of "community." Now I would ask why the authors of this work did not consider the possibility that the intergroup relations outlined here define the real self-sufficient social unit—the community they are seeking—and that these phenomena may even provide a basis for the growth of the organization and leadership that is needed? They are certainly aware of winter dancing and summer sports events and do make passing reference to them. Their failure to consider them relevant may be in part due to their need to generalize for the whole province, while these phenomena occur only in a part of the Coast Salish area of British Columbia and in a smaller area outside Canada in Washington. But I believe their failure is also due to defects in both conceptual framework and method.

The authors state explicitly (Hawthorn, Belshaw, and Jamieson 1958:12-13) that acculturation among different Indian groups is proceeding at variable rates but that for many assimilation will not be achieved in the near future. "Acculturation" they define as the process of westernization, a process they regard as irreversible. In this view, the Indians are on a one-way track to North American culture, though they may get stalled indefinitely along the way. There seems to be no room here for the formation of neo-Indian cultures among these stalled groups of Indians. This appears to me to be a serious defect in their framework of analysis. One defect in method I have already alluded to is that the focus of the research for the study was largely on the reserve. Another is that the study was largely synchronic. Failure to look for continuities with the past, failure to look for the emergence of new cultural forms, and failure to look beyond what is largely an artificial administrative unit—all of these have led to the neglect of what may be the most significant aspect of contemporary Coast Salish life, the continuing and perhaps growing strength of the multi-village community.

A major task for anthropology in British Columbia and elsewhere in northwestern North America lies in discovering the systems of social relations operating among contemporary Indians and understanding the processes by which old institutions have persisted and new ones have appeared. Only then can we adequately assess the basis for Indian solutions to Indian problems.

PART IV

Inferences About Prehistory

12. Notes on Coast Salish
Sea-Mammal Hunting*

The technical and ritual elements of sea-mammal hunting provide interesting and apparently fruitful leads in the study of the culture history of the Northwest Coast and its relations with other areas. Sea-mammal hunting may, in fact, be one of the oldest and one of the most influential elements of this area's unique culture.

Whaling has received the most attention. Margaret Lantis (1938) has suggested that whaling practices from the Washington coast to Point Barrow and from Kamchatka to Hudson Bay demonstrate a fundamental unity. Robert Heizer (1943) has shown that Aleut-Koniag technical practices have affinities with Eastern Asia. And most recently, in the last issue of this publication, Charles E. Borden (1951) suggested that the close parallels between Nootka and Arctic Eskimo whaling in technical elements and between Nootka and Aleut-Koniag whaling in ritual elements imply a genetic relationship and indicate that the Nootka must have had contact with the Eskimo stock on the Northwest Coast at some remote time. He suggests that the Nootka are, of present Northwest Coast peoples, the descendants of the earliest people to reach the Coast from the Interior, and that they found on the Coast an Eskimoid people from whom they learned whaling. He presents archaeological evidence for the existence of Eskimoid elements from the Lower Fraser area in what is now Salish territory. The Salish, he believes, are more recent arrivals on the Coast. In this paper

*[From *Anthropology in British Columbia* 3:10-1952.]

233

I shall present some new data on Salish practices and discuss them in relation to these suggestions.[1]

Seals, Porpoises, Elephant Seals, and Whales

Sealing was practised by all of the Coast Salish tribes on the salt water and by those on the Lower Fraser as well. At the southern end of Georgia Strait, seal hunters clubbed hair seals as the animals tried to leave their hauling-out rocks and bars, or netted or harpooned them after they reached the water.

The harpoon used was the familiar double-foreshafted harpoon with two composite toggle heads and trident shaft-butt. The same basic type was used for both sea mammals and salmon, but the salmon harpoon usually lacked the trident butt, since it was more often thrust, not thrown as for seal, and its head was armed with a round bone point set between the antler spurs or valves instead of the flat shell, bone, or stone blade. A feature of the sea-mammal harpoon reported by one informant was an antler ring attached to the shaft, through which the line passed; this allowed the shaft to come sliding back the line after it was separated from the head. Sea hunters used both wooden floats and inflated floats—the first probably mainly as markers, the second to tire the animal.

To take seals in a net, hunters submerged the seal net around the hauling-out site and caught the seals as they were frightened away from it (Barnett, 1939, Element 139 and note). It was not as widely used as the harpoon; possibly it could be used only at certain types of sites.

Sealing in fresh water may seem strange, but it was practised by several, perhaps many, groups. Marian Smith has pointed out that seals come yearly into Harrison Lake and suggests that this may indicate recent changes in the topography of the Lower Fraser (Smith 1947:266). But it is not at all unusual; a recent study by H.D. Fisher states that seals frequent "at least 20 rivers and six lakes" in British Columbia, going as much as 200 miles up the Skeena and up the Fraser possibly as far as the first major rapids at Alexandria (Fisher 1952:12, 56). The Katzie tribe of Pitt Lake clubbed and harpooned seals at a hauling-out site on the lake. The site itself was believed to have been created back at some remote time by a man who received power for sealing.

Taking seals at holes in the ice that occasionally covers the Fraser was not unknown. But before one sees this as a Salish *maupok*, let me relate the only

---

[1]This is a revision of a paper read at the Northwest Conference, May 1952, under the title "Penelekuts Sea-lion Hunting." Where references are not cited, data are from my own field notes. These data were gathered while working with several Salish groups over a period of several years. Work from 1949 to 1951 was supported by a Wenner Gren Foundation pre-doctoral fellowship, work done during the year 1951-1952 by the University of British Columbia.

such incident that I have been given. The informant (Simon Pierre, of Katzie)* explained that the seals that come up the Fraser after fish usually go down in great numbers if the river is going to freeze. Their goings and comings were, in fact, used to predict changes in the weather. However, sometimes seals got caught upstream by the ice and so had to find holes there. People also had to have holes in the ice for bathing, and so it happened that one time a young woman was bathing in a hole in the ice and, feeling something bump against her, turned to find herself face to face with a seal. Thereupon she jumped out of the water and, modestly covering herself, called to the men. Two men came down to the river, and when she told them what had happened, they got a dried salmon and a harpoon. While one of them held the fish in the water to lure the seal, the other stood by and harpooned the animal. The informant believed that seals had been caught more than once in this manner; I give the story mainly because it suggests the absence of any developed ice hunting technique.

The Coast Salish also hunted porpoises, sea lions, and possibly elephant seals. Two-man teams hunted porpoises nearly everywhere on the salt water with the same harpoon used for seals. A Klallam of the Becher Bay group gave an account, from tradition only, that suggests that the elephant seal occasionally came into the Strait of Juan de Fuca and was hunted. But his description of the method sounds somewhat mythical. He said that the "sea-elephant" sometimes came into the strait, and when it did, could be heard snoring from a great distance; thereupon hunters went quietly out to where it lay in the water on its back, carefully lifted the great snout that hung down over its chest, and plunged their "spears" into it.

Evidently only two Coast Salish tribes habitually went whaling. These were the Quinault (Olson 1936:40-48) and the Klallam (Gunther 1927:204). Among both tribes there were only a few whalers, and both tribes presumably learned the art from their immediate neighbours, the Quileute and the Makah. However, an occasional sea hunter elsewhere killed an occasional whale. One was a Saanich harpooner named χa·člénəxʷ from Saanichton Bay, who was said to have had a harpoon so heavy an ordinary man could not use it. He once harpooned a whale in Saanich Inlet just to see if he could do it. A group of hunters from the village of Cardale Point, Valdes Island, are said to have done the same thing.†

---

*[Simon Pierre was the son of Peter Pierre ("Old Pierre"), the Katzie shaman with whom Diamond Jenness worked in 1936 and whose beliefs and practices are the subject of The Faith of a Coast Salish Indian (Jenness 1955). Simon was my source for Katzie Ethnographic Notes (Suttles 1955).]

†[Kool (1982) presents evidence that the whale most commonly hunted by the people of the outer coast was not the Pacific gray, as commonly supposed, but the humpback whale. This species was once abundant, came into sheltered salt water, and was more easily taken than the gray. Perhaps it was the humpback that these Saanich and Chemainus sea hunters tried taking.]

The sea lion was hunted by the ocean tribes, the Quinault (Olson 1936:48-49) and the Tillamook (Barnett 1937, Element 208), as well as by neighbouring non-Salish peoples, and it was hunted by some of the Salish of Georgia Strait. The practices of these last groups have not been fully recorded though; unlike the ice hunting and the elephant-seal hunting, they are recent and vividly remembered.

The Sea-Lion Hunting of the Penelekuts and their Neighbours

The villages that most recently abandoned the hunting of sea lions were three of the division called by the Indian Service the "Chemainus Tribe." These were: (1) *pənéləxəż* (hereafter spelled "Penelekuts") at Penelekut Spit on Kuper Island, (2) *téʔetəqə* at Shingle Point (*léəqsən*) and (though perhaps this was a separate village) at Cardale Point (*čə́xəl*) on Valdes Island, and (3) *scə́mínəs* at Kulleet Bay (*qəlíč*, formerly called "Chemainus Bay" in English) on Vancouver Island. These villages and several others included as "Chemainus" have been either classed as part of the Cowichan or ignored entirely in the literature on this area. However, the differences that seem to exist between this group and the people of the Cowichan River and the frequency with which informants speak of "Cowichan" and "Penelekuts" (or "Kuper Island") as co-ordinates have made me regard them as separate. Data on the sea-lion hunting of these villages come largely from a single Penelekuts informant, Leo Mitchell.[2]

The villages on Kuper and Valdes Islands were within a short distance of Porlier Pass, or "Cowichan Gap" as old-timers call it. This is the pass that separates Valdes from Galiano Island; it is one of the few breaks in the almost solid wall that the Gulf Islands present to Georgia Strait, "the Gulf." Every spring, beginning about March, herds of sea lions came through this pass from "the Gulf" into the narrower and shallower channels among the Gulf Islands. The sea lion that comes into these waters is Steller's sea lion, which is considerably larger than the California species; adult males weigh 1,200 to 1,500 pounds, going possibly up to a ton (Dalquest 1948:244). When we consider that the sea lion is a carnivore, we must regard him as a formidable animal. Informants liken an angry sea lion to an angry bull.

It was in Porlier Pass that the Penelekuts and their neighbours hunted sea lions. A lookout was stationed at the pass day and night at the season when the animals were expected. When he sighted the sea lions, he gave out a call *u: u: u:::*, in a falling and then rising tone, that could be heard across the water at Penelekuts. At this signal, from half a dozen to twenty canoes put out. Their

---

[2]The only published description of Penelekuts sea-lion hunting that I have discovered is a brief one by Densmore (1943:16-17) identified only as of "Cooper" (Kuper) Island.

hulls had been rubbed smooth with dry fish fins and greased with porpoise oil. Each held a harpooner and one or two paddlers and a supply of food and water.

The harpoon used for sea lions was larger than the seal harpoon and had only one foreshaft and head. The blade of the head was of mussel shell and the spurs were of antler. It was pitched and tied in the centre so that it would turn and toggle in the wound. The shaft was held in the same manner as the seal harpoon and had the same separate butt with the grooves for the fingers. The harpoon was thrown as far as 50 or 60 feet. Harpooners usually stood, but one man, George číkʷa ("left-handed"), was so big he could kneel. When he hunted, he was usually first to strike the sea lion.

Sometimes a good man could kill a sea lion with the first strike. Moses Peter (čéiləxʷtən) could do it, and Dick šwəcətə́s did it twice; but usually this did not happen, so several harpooners each struck it in turn. They did not use floats but held their lines and let the animal pull.

Hunting sea lion was a dangerous pursuit which required special knowledge and probably special spirit power. John Peter, one of the last Penelekuts harpooners, had a "blackfish" (killer whale) guardian spirit (sʔáylə), which seems appropriate. I have not yet learned what guardian spirits the other harpooners had.

Apparently all harpooners had ritual knowledge. Before going out for sea lion, both the harpooner and his wife bathed themselves carefully and slept apart. If they did not do this, the sea lion would become angry and attack the hunter, biting the bow of his canoe. Such restrictions did not apply to paddlers.

Moses Peter could bring sea lions in. When they had not appeared for a while, George číkʷa went to him for help. Moses led a boy to the water by the hands and threw him in. When the boy came up, he threw him in again until he had done it four times. Then he said sea lions would come in the next day. And, according to my informant, they did.

Moses and John Peter (šitxálécə) knew spell words (siẃíṅ) to increase the efficacy of the gear and to control the game. They also knew an incantation (ščéləm), which they sang after the first harpoon struck the animal, to calm it so that it could be struck again. It sounded good, said my informant, when you heard it across the water at night. According to others, an enemy could recite spells to make a sea lion more difficult to manage.

When a sea lion dies it sinks. This is supposed to be because it has several rocks inside it to make it heavy. It was hard to pull one up, but Moses Peter could pull four times at the line, saying a name, and it would come up easily.

A sea lion carcass was divided according to a formula following the order of striking. The first man to strike the animal received the rear portion and the head. The second got one flipper, the third the other flipper, the fourth the back, the fifth the neck, and the rest got pieces of the belly. Each harpooner then divided his share with his paddler. Everyone got a piece of the gut, which

237

was stretched, twisted, and dried for cord. The Penelekuts provided their neighbours to the south with sea-lion gut cord for bow strings.

Several families use a myth to account for some of the practices and beliefs associated with sea-lion hunting. A Penelekuts version tells how sea-lion hunters from the old village at Cardale Point on Valdes Island were tricked by the Squamish of Howe Sound. The Valdes people were in the habit of hunting sea lions at Howe Sound, and the Squamish who lived there were jealous. So a Squamish shaman made a sea lion of wood—first he tried hemlock but failed, then cedar, and it swam when he sang to it. On his instruction it swam out in front of the Valdes harpooners until they all had their harpoons in it, then it pulled them off, first toward Orcas Island, then northward and away for days. When the wooden sea lion stopped and released their harpoons, they made for a nearby island. Here they were captured by a race of dwarfs. The dwarfs released them after they saved the dwarfs in a fight against some birds. Then they were captured by a giant, but they escaped and returned to find that they had been gone so long their wives had remarried. John and Moses Peter told this story to their children and said that the incantation they used to control the sea lion was the one used by the Squamish shaman who made the wooden one, and that when a sea lion went down, they had only to call the name of the Squamish shaman, *spétkʷəm*, and it would rise. The Peter brothers had learned the name and the incantation from their father but did not know how he had inherited it.

This version of this story was given by a Musqueam (John Guerin) who heard it from John Peter, his father-in-law. A Katzie (Simon Pierre) gave another version which he said belonged to the Norris family of Valdes Island. In this version the Kuper Island people were tricked by the Valdes people, who were jealous of the success of the Kuper Island hunters in getting sea lions. The Valdes people made a sea lion of arbutus (madrona) wood, it being the colour of a sea lion, and set it out on a rock where the Kuper people could see it. Six canoes of Kuper sea hunters struck it, and it carried them off. When it rose to the surface and released them, they found they were lost. As in the previous version, they were captured by dwarfs but released after killing the birds. They started back by going in the direction from which the sun rose. They were captured by a giant but escaped. The giant pursued them, but three killer whales came to their aid, killed the giant, and led them home. They landed first at Sechelt, then at Nanaimo, and then returned to Kuper Island, where they were hardly recognized. Because of this story, so the informant said, the Valdes people felt superior to the Kuper Island people.

Few other Salish hunted sea lions. Informants from the Nanaimo to the Sooke on Vancouver Island and from the Musqueam to the Swinomish on the Mainland have denied that anyone within this area or to the south hunted sea lions except the Penelekuts and the villages immediately adjacent to them. Yet they all knew something about Penelekuts sea-lion hunting, and probably for this reason the practice has been attributed incorrectly, I believe, to several of these groups. But farther north on Georgia Strait, Squamish and Sechelt informants said that they and the Slaiamon formerly hunted sea lions. Others at the northern end of the strait may also have done so.

The data obtained on Squamish practices are rather vague. Sea lions hauled up on reefs around Bowen Island in Howe Sound. When the Squamish of the village at or near Gibsons Landing heard the roaring of the bulls on the rocks, as many as ten canoes went out, surrounded them, and harpooned them. One informant (August Jack) believed that the harpoon had a single foreshaft and head and that the head was made with mountain goat horn spurs and a blade of a black stone, probably slate. This man did not appear to know anything of the ritual elements involved or of any division of the carcass by formula. His half-brother, however, told the Squamish version of the sea-lion myth and said that it was an ancestor of the other who had made the wooden sea lion. In the Squamish story both the successful hunters and the jealous hunters were Squamish of Howe Sound. A shaman made a wooden sea lion in order to get rid of the successful hunters, and it drew them across the strait to the Gulf Islands, where they stayed to become the Penelekuts.

A Sechelt informant (Basil Joe) gave a somewhat clearer account of sea-lion hunting. Sea lions came every autumn to White Rocks, where they often stayed all winter. One could hear them out there from the shore. The Sechelt hunter used a single-headed harpoon with a stone blade, of ground slate, to judge from the informant's description. The hunter went out alone, except for his paddler in the stern. He harpooned an animal while it was on the rocks, trying to hit the middle of its body, then threw out the line with inflated floats attached, and let it go. Hunters did not co-operate in killing an animal.

Both the Squamish and the Sechelt gave up hunting sea lions before the lifetime of living persons. This information is therefore only traditional and possibly influenced by knowledge of the more recent Penelekuts practices. The sea lions themselves, however, still come into Sechelt waters, though now they prefer Bertha Island to White Rocks because a lighthouse has been built on the latter. The Sechelt informant believed that the sea lions that come for the winter are the same that summer at Danger Rock between the Queen Charlottes and the Mainland. However, Newcombe et al. (1918:14) believed that the sea lions of Georgia Strait are from the rookery at Cape Flattery. This would perhaps account for the yearly spring movement through Porlier Pass. At this time they would be leaving their winter grounds on the Mainland shores of Georgia Strait and coming into the Gulf Islands perhaps in search of herring runs, thereafter to go out the Strait of Juan de Fuca to Cape Flattery.

Comparison: The Technique of Sea-lion Hunting

Sea lions were hunted by perhaps most tribes on the ocean shores from the Tlingit to northwest California, and also by the Yaghan at the very southern tip of South America. The hunting of sea lions is not rare and, like the hunting of other sea mammals, may have considerable antiquity on the shores of the Pacific. The co-operative hunt of the Penelekuts, however, is not the usual method used for sea lions.

It appears that the most frequently used method was that described by the Sechelt informant, harpooning an animal on the rocks and letting it go. In Northwest California the Yurok method was for two hunters disguised as sea lions to wait on the rocks to lure the animals in, whereupon a crew of five in a canoe harpooned an animal and followed it as it towed off a wooden float; after harpooning it a second time, they held the line and allowed the animal to tow the canoe, perhaps out to sea. No mention is made of co-operation among canoes in taking a single animal (Kroeber 1925:86; Driver 1939:380). The Yurok and other Northwest California tribes and some of the Oregon coast tribes also simply clubbed sea lions as they did seals on the rocks (Driver 1939, Element 289; Barnett 1937, Element 210). The Quinault hunter harpooned sea lions at .night as they lay on the rocks or harpooned them from a canoe manned by an eight-man crew as for whaling. He allowed a harpooned sea lion to tow away the line and marking float until it was tired and then seized the line and dispatched the animal with a club (Olson 1936:48).

The Nootka hunter harpooned sea lions with the same harpoon he used for seals, usually throwing out inflated floats, but no other data are available (Drucker 1951:46). Kwakiutl hunters, however, evidently killed sea lions by clubbing them on their hauling-out rocks (Boas 1909:506). It is perhaps significant that two Fort Rupert men (Mungo Martin and Tom Omhid) did not believe it possible to attack a sea lion in the open water, and when I indicated that some of the Salish told of doing so, one of the two suggested that anthropologists should not believe all that they are told. Data on the more northern people are not very specific.

Actually the co-operative hunt of the Penelekuts has a closer parallel in the co-operative hunt for the sea otter practised by the Nootka, which Drucker believes to be recent (Drucker 1951:46), in the co-operation among canoes of whalers among those people who whaled, or in the co-operation of single hunters among the Eskimo.

Comparison: Ritual Elements

Some of the ritual elements of Penelekuts sea-lion hunting are similar to those of whaling among whaling peoples, but these are associated with the hunting of land animals as well, while elements of the "whale cult" itself are lacking. Special knowledge, including spells, belonged to hunters of other animals among probably all of the Salish tribes around Georgia Strait. Among at least one or two Mainland groups similar incantations were used for quelling wounded bears and, as we shall see later, sturgeon. Hunters of land game and even fishermen using certain methods were also advised to bathe and be continent. In the case of sea-lion hunters it was perhaps more important because of the danger that the animal might turn and bite the canoe of the hunter who had broken the rules.

Placing taboos upon the hunter's wife, even seeing a special bond linking her and the game (as in the whale cult), occurred as part of the ritualism of land hunting. For example, the Katzie informant explained that if a hunter's wife scratched her head, the deer's head would itch and it would become rest-less; if she stepped in her husband's tracks, the deer's feet would itch and it would run away; or if she were unfaithful to him, the deer would tell him this by its actions and would not let itself be caught. But the essential features of the whale cult—the use of the bodies of dead whalers, the dramatization of the hunt by the whaler and his wife, the special treatment of the saddle of the whale—are absent.

The myth used here to explain the origin of Penelekuts practices, or of the Penelekuts themselves, is widespread among the Coast Salish, and some of its elements occur in stories farther north. I have collected several other ver-sions, each told to explain a different belief, and shall discuss them elsewhere.*

Comparison: Rules for Dividing the Game

The most interesting element of Penelekuts sea-lion hunting to see in relation to sea-mammal hunting elsewhere is the sharing of the carcass according to a formula. Sharing a whale or lesser sea mammal according to some kind of set rules occurs among both Northwest Coast and Arctic peoples, but with some significant differences. Among most Northwest Coast peoples the parts of the animal go to persons who may have had nothing to do with the hunt but who receive because of and in the order of their rank.

Drucker reports: "Hair seal among the Northern Nootkans had to be divided in accordance with an elaborate system of ownership rules. This was the only game that did not belong either to the hunter or to the chief in whose territory it had been taken. Certain chiefs of each confederacy owned specified por-tions of any hair seal obtained in the confederacy territory. When a hunter brought in a seal these owners had to be invited to feast on it. Either the hunter or his chief might give the feast." As an example, he gives the Kyuquot hair-seal rights. The first chief owned the breast, the second the right flipper, the

---

*[I now have more versions, which I will incorporate in a future article.]

241

third the left flipper, the fourth the right rear flipper, the fifth the left rear flipper, the sixth a strip of blubber cut down the back, and the rest was cut into strips for other guests. Other sea mammals belonged to the hunter so long as he gave a feast with the fat and flesh. Similar rights, however, were owned for stranded whales (Drucker 1951:252-54). The southern Kwakiutl had chiefs' rights for seal and sea lions where they were hunted, although the division was somewhat different, rear flippers ranking ahead of front flippers, for example. Data for people farther up the coast are not so precise. Drucker believes that wherever such rights existed they were based on ownership of territory (Drucker 1950:281-82). Rights to stranded whales were also owned among the Quinault, on the Oregon coast, and in northwest California (Olson 1936:46; Barnet 1937, Element 327; Driver 1939, Element 293).

The division of the carcass of a harpooned whale, however, is something different. Among the Makah the saddle belonged always to the whaler himself, to be treated ritually. Other parts the whaler might promise to the canoes that came to his aid—a strip around the middle behind the saddle together with the jaw and tongue (itself divided according to rules) to the first canoe, a flipper to the second, and so on. When the animal was ashore and being divided, the whaler gave out these awards for help, then gave the rest as he saw fit, keeping the tail for himself. "This distribution," says Waterman, "is the act so very characteristic of the north-western Indians; that is, the cutting-up of the whale and the distribution of the blubber is a form of potlatch. The donor knows to a pound what everybody receives, and expects a return at a future date" (Waterman 1920:45). The Nootka whaler also gave portions to the crews that helped him and to towers. And Drucker's statement parallels Waterman's: "Finally, as the pieces of blubber were cut and laid out on the beach, through his speaker the successful hunter gave them away to his tribe, giving in order of rank, just as in a potlatch" (Drucker 1951:55).

A closer parallel to the Penelekuts co-operative sea-lion hunt and method of division of the carcass may be seen in the Nootka sea otter hunt, which Drucker believes was a recent innovation. More than twenty canoes attempted to surround a sea otter, and when they were near enough, the hunters shot arrows at the animal. The hunter whose arrow struck first claimed the animal as his, but he paid ten pairs of blankets to the man who had hit it second, five pairs each to the others, and five to the one who harpooned it (Drucker 1951:47-48).

A still closer parallel exists among some Eskimo. Weyer, in his summary of Arctic Eskimo practices, indicates that this sort of hunt and division of the game was practised for walrus by the Eskimo of Hamilton Inlet, Labrador, of Southeast Baffinland, and of the west coast of Hudson's Bay. On the last group he quotes Boas: "The hunter who first strikes the walrus receives the tusks and one of the fore-quarters. The person who first comes to his assistance receives the other fore-quarter; the next man the neck and head; the following the belly; and each of the next two the hind-quarters" (Weyer 1932:177). The

Diomede Islanders share a whale according to a formula, but the order is simply that of reaching the whale as it is being towed in. Among some other Eskimo groups the division is just a scramble (Weyer 1932:176).

Possible Relationships

In view of Borden's suggestion that an Eskimoid culture underlies Northwest Coast culture, we may ask how the Penelekuts division of the carcass might be related to similar practices of other Northwest Coast peoples and of the Eskimo.

It may be that the Penelekuts' practice developed independently; it seems reasonable that a division according to order of striking should have developed out of such a communally organized hunt. It may have done so in the case of the Nootka sea-otter hunt. People co-operating in the taking of a creature have to share it somehow. To share it by order of striking seems rather fair. But why then are not other animals shared in this manner? The Penelekuts take deer in drives by netting but do not divide a deer by any formula. Of course, there is not such a clear order established by the means used to take them, and the factor of private ownership of the net may too sharply separate the owner of the net from the other participants. The one type of activity where there is a parallel, among the neighbours of the Penelekuts, is in sturgeon fishing just above and around the mouth of the Fraser.

Both Semiahmoo and Musqueam informants reported that a man who harpooned or gaffed a sturgeon always gave his paddler the rear portion. Above the mouth of the Fraser, sturgeon were taken in nets. Boas's description is worth quoting also for its ritual elements: "Those who go to catch sturgeon bathe in a pond early in the morning. They rub themselves with bundles of a plant called *tsk'utlptie* until they bleed. Then they smear their bodies and faces with red paint, and strew white eagle-down on their heads. Each winds a thread made of mountain-goat wool around his waist. A woven blanket of mountain-goat wool is painted red, and put on. The fish is caught in this manner: two canoes are allowed to drift down river, a net being stretched between them. The oarsmen are seated on the outer sides of the canoes only. A net is stretched between two poles. As soon as a sturgeon is caught, the two canoes approach each other, and the net is wound up by means of the poles. While this is being done the 'sturgeon hunter' sings, and by means of his song pacifies the struggling sturgeon, who allows himself to be killed. The fisherman must distribute the sturgeon among the whole tribe, each person receiving a portion according to his rank" (Boas 1894:460).

The last statement in Boas's description sounds like the Kwakiutl type of distribution. However, my Katzie informant gave a somewhat different account. The sturgeon-net was operated by four men, he said. The owner, who supervised, was in the stern of one canoe with one line (the informant denied that poles were used), another man was in the stern of the other with the other line, and a paddler was in each bow. When they caught a large sturgeon, the owner of the net cut it up while they were still on the river. He gave the rear portion to the other linesman and one side of the section back of the mouth to each of the paddlers. Then, when he got home, he gave a feast with the rest. This feast was probably the distribution Boas is referring to. At any rate, it apears that the taking of sturgeon has more in common with sea-mammal hunting than do other types of hunting and fishing. Some of the elements of sturgeon fishing may have been derived from sea-mammal hunting.

It is also possible that the Penelekuts form of division is a result of diffusion from the nearby Wakashan northern Nootka and Kwakiutl. This is perhaps made stronger by the fact that the Penelekuts' case is isolated and the Wakashan form is widespread, on the Northwest Coast at least. The Wakashan form seems to be associated with concepts of private ownership of beaches. Salish peoples recognized private ownership of particular sites for particular activities, but usually, I believe, there is the element of labour on the site involved, making its ownership possibly an extension of the principle that a man owns the artifacts he makes. The Salish do not seem to have the concept of private ownership of tracts of land or sea as such. Division based on Wakashan principles then would not make sense. They might, upon receiving from Wakashan neighbours the idea of division by a fixed system, prefer to use it in a more democratic manner.

Yet the functional nature of division by order of striking and the arbitrary nature of division by rank make it seem more likely that the Wakashan division by rank is itself a transfer from an earlier division by striking order. If the Wakashan had formerly hunted sea lions co-operatively and divided by striking order, then they might, upon abandoning the co-operative hunt and under the increasing influence of notions of inherited rights, have continued to divide sea mammals according to a set formula but with inherited rights as the basis. Then the Salish might have learned the division from the earlier Wakashan practice. To know whether such a change in the Wakashan basis for division could have occurred requires a better understanding than we have now of the conceptual relationship here between ownership of land and control over its resources. Drucker reports that when a man through supernatural means causes a whale to become stranded, he divides it as a harpooner does. Do inherited rights to portions of sea mammals imply a degree of supernatural participation in their killing?

But if the Wakashan did once divide sea lions and perhaps seals according to striking order, did they invent the practice themselves? Is it not also possible that all three occurrences—Salish, Wakashan, and Eskimo—are genetically related? Looking at their total distribution in the light of the distribution of other sea hunting practices, it seems to me reasonable to assume that they are related, that a division according to a formula arose from the practice of hunting larger animals—whales, walrus, sea lions—by a group of hunters, each with his own harpoon; and that it has survived in this form among the Eskimo and the Salish—both in a sense peripheral to the Wakashan; and that on the Central Northwest Coast and farther south on the ocean shore it became reinterpreted, according to concepts of ownership of waters or beaches, for sea mammals obtained in other ways, such as seals taken by single hunters or whales stranded on the beach.

Summary and Conclusions

The Coast Salish probably hunted hair seals and porpoises wherever they found them, seals even in fresh water on the Lower Fraser and adjacent lakes. A few tribes hunted sea lions, probably no more than two habitually hunted whales, and at least one appears to have known the elephant-seal.

Around the southern end of Georgia Strait the only people who regularly hunted sea lions were the Penelekuts of Kuper Island and their immediate neighbours. Penelekuts sea-lion hunting practices included ritual elements reminiscent of the whale cult, but they also have parallels in the hunting of land game and even in fishing, and, moreover, the unique features of the whale cult are lacking.

The Penelekuts hunted sea lions co-operatively; a group of harpooners, each in his own canoe with one or two paddlers, attacked an animal, and several harpooned it in succession. The first man to strike the animal divided the carcass according to a set formula, a certain portion going to him, another to the second man, and so forth. This kind of co-operative hunt has no parallel in the hunting of seals or sea lions elsewhere on the Northwest Coast. Its closest parallels are in a probably recent form of sea-otter hunt practised by the Nootka, in the co-operation of whalers among the Nootka and others, and in some types of sea-mammal hunting among the Eskimo.

The division of a carcass according to a set formula occurs among both Northwest Coast and Arctic peoples. Among the northern Nootka and the Kwakiutl, seals and sometimes sea lions are taken by single hunters but divided among the chiefs of the community, portions going to them in the order of their rank. Stranded whales are similarly divided on the ocean shores to the south. In both cases these rights seem to be derived from or at least associated with ownership of beaches and waters. However, among the Nootka a whaler might give specified parts of a harpooned whale to those who helped him, and in the Nootka sea-otter hunt the first man to strike the animal bought out the others according to a set formula. A closer parallel to the Penelekuts practice exists among some Arctic Eskimo, where a walrus is divided according to formula following the order of striking in a co-operative hunt.

There are several possible explanations for the similarities between the Salish

(Penelekuts) division of the carcass and that of other Northwest Coast peoples and of some of the Eskimo:—

(1) There may be no genetic relationship between the practice in separate areas. The division by formula and the co-operative hunt seem to be functionally related; division by order of striking may be a natural outgrowth of a co-operative hunt. The recent development of the Nootka sea-otter hunt argues for this, but the lack of a similar division for other game among the Salish argues against it. The one instance of a similar division is in sturgeon-fishing, and in that there may have been borrowing from sea-mammal hunting.

(2) The Salish may have borrowed the notion of dividing by a set formula from the Wakashan and then used the more functional order of striking as its basis rather than inherited rights. The geographic nearness of the Wakashan argues for this; differences in concepts of land ownership make it possible, yet it still leaves the origin of the Wakashan division to be explained.

(3) The practice may have originated with the Wakashan out of co-operative methods of hunting, spread to the Salish in that context, but suffered a change among the Wakashan to become division according to inherited rights. This requires that we assume that co-operative hunting methods for sea lions or seals were formerly in use among the Wakashan but went out of use about the same time that concepts of ownership were becoming more powerful in Wakashan culture.

(4) The division of sea mammals by some set formula among Salish, Wakashan, and Eskimo may be derived from a single source. This last possibility seems consistent with the evidence presented by Borden and others. In the division of sea mammals we seem to have one more link between the Northwest Coast, perhaps on the southern Northwest Coast, and Eskimo culture.

I reject the first two possibilities as being unlikely; of the third and fourth, I favour the fourth, though still consider it only a best likelihood.* But let me at least point out two things that seem certain: First, that any particular form of sea-mammal hunting cannot be separated from the whole complex of sea-mammal hunting, nor this from the hunting of land game or the taking of large fish; and, second, that Coast Salish ethnography can be a valuable ally of the archaeology of the Coast Salish area in attempts to unravel the early history of the Northwest Coast. It *may* be true that the Salish came from the Interior at a later date than the Nootka or Kwakiutl, but they still may have come early enough that their culture contains Coast elements that later disappeared or were

---

*[Not long after this was published someone called my attention to an article on a similar division of the carcass of an animal among Aborigines on the northern coast of Australia. This case suggests that the first possible explanation—that such a division is a "natural outgrowth" of cooperative hunting—is not so unlikely. I suspect now that in 1952 I was inclined to favor the third or fourth possibility because they argued for a respectable antiquity for the Coast Salish on the coast.]

highly modified in the "more typical" Northwest Coast culture of their northern and western neighbours. May I also suggest that more work be done, and I am sure that it can be done, on the division of game and on its possible relationship to property, rank, and even the potlatch?

13. Linguistic Means
for Anthropological Ends
on the Northwest Coast*

Serious anthropological work on the Northwest Coast of North America began with Boas in 1886, and through Boas's influence a knowledge of the Northwest Coast became a part of the professional equipment of the whole generation of anthropologists that followed him. Native cultures of the Northwest Coast became famous for their colour and drama and provided wonderful material for the refuting of easy generalizations about "primitive" peoples, about their mythology, art, social organization, and economy. Northwest Coast examples continue to appear in the most recent textbooks.

The Northwest Coast is indeed well known. But has it really been well studied? I don't believe so. Several of the assumptions made about the Northwest Coast in theoretical discussions are questionable. Some fundamental questions remain unanswered. For much of the area we may still ask about social organization: What were the structural strands in the social fabric, and what, if anything, was embroidery? What was the relationship between kinship and residence in the formation of social units? Were there indeed any discrete social units at all? What was the nature of social stratification? What was the "chief"? Was he the possessor of real authority? Or was he a relatively impotent centre of a redistribution system? Or were there "chiefs" at all? Was the potlatch really mere social striving unrelated to the "subsistence economy," or was

---

*[From the *Canadian Journal of Linguistics* 10:156-166 (1965).]

it part of that system? If the potlatch was made possible by "surplus," how was the surplus actually realized and used? We may also ask about beliefs: Are the supposedly universal dichotomies "natural"/"supernatural" and "sacred"/"profane" really found here? If so, where are the lines drawn? Why does much of Northwest Coast ceremonialism look "secularized"? We may ask about cultural origins: Why the linguistic and cultural diversity of the area? Which groups came earliest into the area? How much of Northwest Coast cultural development is indigenous?

I do not believe these questions are unanswerable. Some of them, such as those on cultural history, will be at least partly answered by archaeology. Questions on aboriginal economy would, I think, be answered by an ecological study. Also, it is still possible in several parts of the area to record materials in the Native languages from participants in living Native cultures. These are certainly modified Native cultures, but they are still very much alive. I believe it is still possible, through the collection and analysis of materials recorded in the Native languages, to achieve a much better understanding of the Northwest Coast social systems and ideologies than we possess today.

Several years ago, after I had already spent some time doing ethnographic work with various groups of Coast Salish, I became convinced that further ethnography through English alone was simply not getting me any closer to Native culture. Accordingly, after experimenting with speakers of several dialects, and having found an excellent informant for the Musqueam dialect of Halkomelem, I began my research. It has been very slow but very satisfying work. I would like to report here on only one problem to which my Musqueam material is relevant, a problem in the study of kinship.

Elmendorf (1961) has pointed out that the Salish languages of the Coast (including Bella Coola and Tillamook) differ consistently from those of the Interior in their kinship terminologies. While the Interior terminologies are "bifurcate collateral" in type, distinguishing paternal from maternal uncles, aunts, and grandparents by different terms, the Coast terminologies are "lineal," like English, making no such distinctions. Also, many of the Interior terms are reciprocal, as when "father's father" is the equivalent of "man's son's child," while Coast terms are rarely so. Elmendorf presents evidence that the Proto-Salish system must have been of the Interior sort. In his conclusions he states:

> Coastal lineal terminologies have been derived from an original bifurcate collateral terminology similar to systems found among some Interior Salish, and perhaps best exemplified by the Spokane, through two main processes: reduction of number of distinctive terms through generalizing meanings; and, restriction of generation-reciprocity by distinguishing ascending from descending generation usage (p. 379).

The change occurred, he also concludes, "through multiple independent but parallel innovations." In discussing possible causes of change, he points to the existence of other languages with lineal terminologies on the Northwest Coast and of other languages with bifurcate collateral terminologies in the Plateau, and suggests that this distribution is related to "the prevalence of ranked status distinctions" on the Northwest Coast and their absence in the Plateau. Finally, he points out that this seems to be a case that supports a general hypothesis proposed by Service (1960) that kinship terminologies become progressively simpler as societies become more complex. Service's hypothesis seems to fit "the smaller number of terminological distinctions for immediate kin and the presumably more complex structure of general status relationships in coastal cultures, vis-à-vis those of the Plateau area" (p. 381).

The Halkomelem language, of which Musqueam is a dialect, belongs to the group of Coast Salish languages having, for the relationships Elmendorf has considered, the smallest number of terms. According to the Service hypothesis, this poverty of kin terms should be compensated for by the use of non-kin status terms. To test this hypothesis, let us look briefly at the Halkomelem kin terms and certain non-kin terms in their native environment—Halkomelem grammar and Halkomelem texts.

Lexical items referring to kinsmen are indeed few. For relatives of second ascending and descending generations there are only two terms—*si*ˀ*lə* "grandparent"/"grandparent's sibling"/"grandparent's cousin" and *ˀímə*θ "grandchild"/"sibling's grandchild"/"cousin's grandchild." Generation is the only principle of classification used. Sex of referent, sex of linking relative, and sex of speaker are irrelevant. Several other Coast Salish languages distinguish by sex of referent in the older generation, that is, there are terms translatable as "grandfather"/"great uncle" and "grandmother"/"great aunt," as well as "grandchild"/"sibling's grandchild," etc. In Spokane, one of the Interior Salish languages showing the greatest contrast, there are four terms that are generation-reciprocal—"father's father"/"man's son's child," "father's mother"/"woman's son's child," "mother's father"/"man's daughter's child," "mother's mother"/"woman's daughter's child." Thus the Spokane terms distinguish grandparents by sex of referent and sex of linking relative but not sex of speaker; grandchildren by sex of linking relative and sex of speaker but not sex of referent. There is an additional generation-reciprocal term, "parent's parent"/"child's child," substituted after the death of the linking relative.

The rest of the Halkomelem terminology is only a little more complex. All consanguineal kin are consistently distinguished as to generation. Lineals are distinguished from collaterals only in reference to parents and children. Sex of referent is used only to distinguish father from mother. Sex of speaker is a feature of one little-used sibling/cousin term; the commonly used terms distinguish by age (between siblings) or seniority of line of descent (between cousins). "Parent's sibling"/"parent's cousin" and "sibling's child"/"cousin's child" are called by one pair of terms during the lifetime of the linking relative, by another pair after his or her death. Third, fourth, and fifth ascending and descending generations are called by generation-reciprocal terms.

Affinal terms form a structure that, unlike English, does not simply reflect the consanguineal structure. I believe this is of considerable significance in relation to the total social system, but since I have outlined this structure elsewhere (Suttles 1960a), and since consideration of it is not essential to the argument here, I will omit affinal terms in the present discussion.

The lexical items referring to kin in Halkomelem are few, as the principles used to distinguish kin are few and unevenly applied. Looking at these items, we might be tempted to conclude that ego is concerned with the sex of no one but his parents (and we might well ask if any human society can be so unconcerned about who is of which sex) or we might conclude that life status is of concern in only one relationship.

But as Kroeber suggested a long time ago (1909), kinship terms are linguistic phenomena and should be seen in their linguistic context. (This is not Kroeber's phrase, but it is surely what is implied, particularly in his reference to Chinook and to Skokomish.) Also, as Elmendorf and I have pointed out elsewhere (Elmendorf and Suttles 1960), this linguistic context in Halkomelem includes a six-slot article (or demonstrative) system that distinguishes two genders (masculine and feminine) and three positions (present visible, nearby invisible, remote or nonexistent). These articles are obligatory with every noun or nominalization appearing as subject or object of a verb. Thus we find *síʔlə* "grandparent"/"grandparent's sibling," etc. appearing in these contexts with these translations: *tə nə síʔlə* "my masculine present visible kinsman of second ascending generation" or, in better English, "my grandfather (or great uncle) whom you see here"; *θə nə síʔlə* "my grandmother (or great aunt) whom you see here"; *kʷθə nə síʔlə* "my grandfather (etc.) who is out"; *ɬə nə síʔlə* "my grandmother (etc.) who is out"; *ƙʷə nə síʔlə* "my deceased grandfather (etc.)"; *kʷsə nə síʔlə* "my deceased grandmother (etc.)." The last two are in free variation with *kʷθə nə síʔlé·ɬ* and *ɬə nə síʔlé·ɬ* in which the deceased status is expressed by a suffix -*əɬ* indicating past time while the article simply indicates absence. However, the obligatory categories are still six. The lexical item *ʔíməθ* "grandchild"/"sibling's grandchild" occurs in the same contexts, as do all others. Thus the article system expresses both the sex and the life status of the referent.

What do we mean by "kinship terms"? I suggest that where obligatory grammatical categories are involved, we should consider the whole unit as the "term." Considered this way, the Halkomelem terms for kin of second ascending and descending generations (ignoring person of possessive) would be not two but twelve. Considered this way, the terminology is not quite as simple as it first looked.

251

Up to now I have been speaking of terms of reference that are used with possessives and articles in phrases translated as "my father," "your son," etc. There are also separate forms of address for most or all of these relationships. They do not take the article and possessive and are generally simply the bare stem, minus prefixes if any, of the term of reference. Both of these forms are the sorts of terms that would be elicited by the genealogical method, which we as anthropologists have been cautioned to use. We ask our informant who his relatives are, carefully going by first-degree steps, as "Does your mother have a brother who has a daughter?" and then we ask "What do you call that woman and what does she call you?" This procedure may be indispensable in order to avoid total misunderstanding.

However, through recording and translating texts I have discovered a third set of forms, which could not have been elicited by the genealogical method for the very reason that they cannot be used with possessives. Thus we find not only ʔéyəɬ "older sibling/senior cousin" (in address) and tə nə sxʔéyəɬ "my older brother/senior male cousin whom you see here," etc. (in reference), but also tə sə́nƛ̉ɛ́ʔ "the (present visible) older brother/senior male cousin" (of two or more persons being discussed). For "younger brother/junior male cousin" the comparable forms are qé·q, tə nə sqé·q, and tə sá́ʔsəqʷt; for "father," mɛ́ʔ, tə nə mɛ́n, and tə cícət; for "son" mə́nʔə, tə nə mə́nʔə, and tə mím̓ʔnɛʔ. The terms of impersonal reference for "senior, junior," and "parent" have different stems from the terms of personal reference for the same relationships. But others recorded, like the term for "child" just given, are based on the same stem as the term of personal reference. These are formed by reduplication in the same way that the continuative aspect of the verb is formed; in fact they appear to be just that—continuative forms of verbs. Verbs appearing with articles and without any nominalizer and possessive are best translated as relative clauses; compare nɛ́mʔ cən "I go," k̉ʷə nə snɛ́mʔ "that I go" (literally, "my hypothetical going"), tə nɛ́mʔ "the one who goes." Thus the form tə mím̓ʔnɛʔ could be translated literally as "the one who is being child" or "the one who is childing," tə ʔəm̓ʔímʔəθ "the one who is grandchilding," and so on.

These are clearly terms that designate kin statuses without any egocentric reference. We do this in English, of course, with the indefinite article (which has no precise counterpart in Halkomelem) in statements like "A grandfather should be indulgent," "A father should be firm," "A child should be respectful." But the indefinite article seems to give the same reality to "grandfather" as it does to "rock" or "man," whereas in truth "grandfathering" is only a social role played by a real man, who has also "childed" and "fathered." It might be expected that the Halkomelem forms, which seem to express the difference between entity and role better than English, would lend themselves to discussion of kinship behaviour in the abstract. But unfortunately I have not yet elicited any such discussion; the terms occur mainly in texts of folktales

252

where the actors are akin to one another but neither to the teller nor his audience. Perhaps, however, these tales are themselves embodiments of principles in kinship relations.

Let me summarize the argument to this point. The lexicon of Halkomelem undeniably has fewer items that refer to kinship than the lexicon of Spokane. However, the Halkomelem speaker can, indeed must, through the grammatical apparatus of the language, make a number of further distinctions. If we count these distinctions, the total number of "terms" in Halkomelem may not be less than in Spokane. The principal difference may be simply that of bifurcate collateral vs. lineal structure.

Now what about non-kin terms and the possibility that they have gained in importance among the Coast Salish at the expense of kin terms? I cannot at this point contrast kin and non-kin status terms in all of these usages. But I can make some estimate of their relative importance as terms of address. I have observed that close relatives of different generations may address each other by kin terms in ordinary conversation. My impression is that those of the same generation are less likely to use kin terms. Women may say ?éy?əs "dear." In greeting non-kin or less closely related kin, the term of address is usually si?ém?, best translated in such contexts as "sir" or "ma'am." This term is often identified with the English "chief" but certainly should not be translated this way in most contexts. In formal speeches, kinship terms are evidently used whenever possible, together with si?ém, as si?ém? nə šxʷəmnikʷ "Sir, my uncle" or perhaps "my honoured uncle," si?ém? nə stiwən "Sir, my nephew," and so forth. But these are haphazard observations. A more objective measure of usage should be their occurrence in texts.

I have now translated and analyzed some five hundred handwritten pages in the Musqueam dialet of Halkomelem dictated by three informants—Andrew Charles, Christine Charles, and James Point—and consisting of forty-two texts of myths, folktales, narratives of recent events, ethnographic descriptions, and speeches. Within all but the ethnographic texts and speeches there are a great many reported conversations. In many of these, people use pronouns only, but in a number there are also terms of address. Kinship terms, however, are rare. In twenty narratives, ranging from myths to recent events, dictated by James Point and totalling about three hundred pages, no kin terms are used in address at all, with the possible exception of the term siyé?yɛ, translated as "relatives and/or friends." In the same twenty texts, the term si?ém? "sir/ma'am" occurs in nine of them, swə́y?qɛ "man" in four, čɫxʷə́lməxʷ "fellow villagers/countrymen" in one, and various derogatory epithets in seven. In a group of six narratives told by Andrew and Christine Charles, kin terms occur in three, si?ém?, swə́y?qɛ, and čɫxʷə́lməxʷ in one each. Both kin terms and si· ?ém? (the plural of si?ém?) occur in three of the four speeches since they are addressed both to individual kinsmen and to the assembled people.

It is not possible within the limitations of this paper to explore each of the contexts of these terms. But in general, kin terms appear frequently in the formal speeches, rarely in the narratives, whether myths or accounts of recent events; where they do occur it is in dialogue between persons of different generations. It appears that men of the same generation or of the same work group, whether related or not, address each other as *si?ém?* if the situation calls for politeness or gentleness or as *swə́y?qɛ* if it calls for action. Here is but one example: two cousins are escaping from the Kwakiutl; the senior, who has been making plans, wakes the junior saying *xʷéyθət si?ém?* "wake up, sir," but when they are paddling for their lives he say *?ə́xəl swə́y?qɛ* "paddle, man!"

Thus there is evidence that in some areas of usage, kin terms are outweighed by non-kin terms. The non-kin terms do not, however, appear in any great variety; two—*si?ém?* and *swə́y?qɛ*—simply appear more frequently than the kin terms. Of these two, *si?ém?* is the more common. Contexts where this term is used descriptively indicate that some components of its meaning are respect of others, leadership in nearly any kind of activity, and, probably, ownership of important property.

We must of course be cautious about drawing conclusions from this amount of material. Properly we should have several times this many texts and from a larger number of informants. (I have, by the way, made a preliminary check through a body of Cowichan texts that I have not yet finished analyzing and have the impression that usage is about the same as in the Musqueam material.)* Ideally, we also ought to have a comparable body of Interior Salish texts. I would fully expect them to show greater use of kin terms, but unfortunately cannot show it.

One might ask why narrative collected in English would not do as well for something as uncomplicated as a checklist and count of terms of address. English would not have done as well in this case because one of the non-kin terms that appear could have easily been taken for an interpolation of the English usage of "man" while the other was translated by my informants in a variety of ways ranging from "chief" to "dear friend." English is simply not adequate for an exploration of Native categories. We need quantities of Native texts.

It may be objected that I am asking for just what Boas did and that the results are disappointing—a "five-foot shelf" of Kwakiutl texts that no one reads. But surely Boas's sketches of Tsimshian and Kwakiutl cultures as reflected in the mythologies (Boas 1916, 1935) were far from disappointing in their time. If they are disappointing to us now it is because we come to them with questions Boas did not ask. If we do not read the texts, it may be because we feel there is just too much and the reward is not worth the effort. If the reward must be quick publication on some fashionable subject, then probably it isn't.

---

*[The Cowichan narratives I tape-recorded in 1961 are now (1986) being transcribed and translated by Arnold Guerin, who combines a Native speaker's knowledge of Halkomelem with experience and expertise in linguistic work.]

But if we want real understanding of Native cultures then we must have more texts and we must use them.

To many of my colleagues in both linguistics and anthropology, my insistence on the need for context and lots of it may sound utterly trite. But I have been shocked by the naiveté about this need shown by some recent graduate work. Also, I am disturbed by what seems like an increasing distance, yet a subtle parallel as well, between the foci of the two disciplines. The objective of both linguists and anthropologists seems to be increasingly economical statements about structure, phonological and grammatical on the one hand, social on the other. Native culture seems to get lost in between. As I pointed out at the beginning of this paper, many problems in Northwest Coast ethnology may be attacked and perhaps solved by linguistic means. But few solutions to ethnological problems will come from strictly linguistic work. Nor will they come from anthropologists who are unwilling to learn something of a Native language and have no time for collecting and working over large quantities of material.

Where can we get the people who will do this? I am beginning to suspect that we cannot recruit such people within existing academic structures, that we will get adequate study of Native languages and cultures only if we can remove this study from both disciplines and establish it as an independent field within the humanities. Here students who would find this study congenial could work in freedom from the increasingly mathematical orientation of theoretical linguistics and the present social scientific pretensions of anthropology. I do not oppose theoretical linguistics or social science as such, but they should not be allowed to inhibit work that ought to be done.

14. The Recent Emergence of the Coast Salish— the Function of an Anthropological Myth[1]*

One of the results of the Jesup North Pacific Expedition, according to Franz Boas (1900:387-88; 1905:96; 1910:15-16), was the discovery that the Salishan peoples of the coast had recently emerged from the interior with a Plateau type of culture and had acquired on the coast (presumably from the Wakashans— the Nootka and Kwakiutl) some of the features of Northwest Coast culture. Boas stated (1910:15) that this conclusion was indicated by archeological work undertaken by Harlan I. Smith, ethnological work by James Teit, and linguistic work by himself. And he regarded it (1910:16) as having theoretical significance because it demonstrated that peoples could go from a simple family organization to a totemic and clan organization, contrary to what was then commonly assumed.

---

[1]This paper, with a few minor differences in wording, was presented at a symposium on Puget Sound prehistory organized by Gerald C. Hedlund for the 28th Annual Northwest Anthropological Conference, at Seattle Central Community College, 27 March 1975. I am indebted to Ellen Robinson for information on Harlan I. Smith and advice on logic, though she is not responsible for any fallacies I may have committed.

*[This remains as written in 1975. It has not been published before now.]

This view of Salish prehistory became widely accepted. It constitutes one of the cornerstones of the major ethnological interpretion of Northwest Coast culture history, that of Philip Drucker, presented in his article "Sources of Northwest Coast Culture" (1955b) and two popular books (1955a, 1965). It appears in the most recent general work on Native North America, William Newcomb's paperback text (1974:208). And it is echoed by art historians, as in a recent PhD dissertation on Northwest Coast architecture (Vastokas 1966:75).

Yet it can be shown that the hypothesis of recent Salish emergence from the interior had little foundation at the time of the Jesup work and has even less today. The alleged evidence from archeology was in fact from physical anthropology and seems to have been an illusion. The actual archeological evidence can be read both ways. The linguistic evidence suggests, if anything, a Salishan movement from coast to interior. And with these supports gone, the ethnological argument for recent Salish emergence can only be circular, based on prejudgements about who is likely to have borrowed from whom.

Why then has such a poorly founded hypothesis persisted? Probably because it fits an attractive theory. This theory combines two models: a) the creative culture center from which culture diffuses outward, permitting age-area interpretations; and b) the stratification of immigrants, permitting the peeling off of newcomers to discover the purest strain of areal culture. One of the attractions of this theory may be that it provides a closed, culture-determinist system, leading away from consideration of possible extracultural determinants of cultural variation. Perhaps this theory is also attractive because it permits, or even encourages, the stereotyping of peoples as creative or imitative, aggressive or passive, allowing us to glamorize those whom we admire and disparage their neighbors. In the present instance, the Wakashans have become the purest strain of areal culture and the creative culture center from which all good things flow— to the Salish and other late-comers into the area. And, it appears to me, the hypothesis of recent Salish emergence has entered into a mutually supportive relationship with a stereotyping of the Wakashans as creative and aggressive and the Salish as imitative and passive.

Having made these rather strong statements, I must now try to defend them.

What kind of evidence did Boas have? First, there is the indisputable fact that the Salishan languages constitute a language family, which implies that there must once have been a common ancestor, Proto-Salish, spoken over a much smaller area than now occupied by its descendants. Second, there are similarities between Coast and Interior Salish peoples in "physical type" (to use Boas's term) and in culture, facts consistent with the notion that the present Salishan-speaking peoples are largely, if not wholly, the descendants of the speakers of Proto-Salish, who have spread out over their present area. The closeness of linguistic relation and the degree of similarity in "physical type" and in culture should reflect the recency of that spread. But neither the linguistic relationship nor the physical and cultural similarities themselves constitute evidence for the location of Proto-Salish and hence for the direction of the spreading.

What Boas needed was evidence for the Salish having replaced somebody else in a part of their present territory. And he thought he had this in the skulls excavated in the area around the Lower Fraser River. In another paper presented in this symposium, Ellen Robinson* discussed the role those skulls played in the interpretation of the archeology of the area, so I will not dwell on them here. In summary, it appears that Boas took what may have been culturally-created variation in head form, in a pretty small sample, first to be evidence of population mixture and later to be evidence of population replacement. And Boas's interpretation of the skulls seem to have persuaded Harlan I. Smith to interpret the archeology as evidence of population replacement. This became the "archeological" evidence that Boas cited for the emergence of the Salish out of the interior.

Boas's later work (1912) that cast doubt on the immutability of the cephalic index might have challenged this earlier conclusion, but it seems that for over fifty years it did not. Drucker continued to cite the evidence of the skulls for Salish emergence in the 1940s (1943:116-17), the 1950s (1955a:18), and 1960s (1965:112). The weakness of this supposed evidence was first noted, I believe, by Mitchell in 1971 (1971:69).

Drucker also uses Boas's work on "physical types," presumably as evidence for the recency of Salish emergence, asserting (1955a:17; 1965:111-12) that Boas found no difference in physical type between the Coast and Interior Salish. But this is not correct. In his concluding report to the British Association for the Advancement of Science committee, Boas (1899:669-70) indicated that while he saw his Kwakiutl and Thompson (Interior Salish) types as distinct, he was uncertain about the Coast Salish and supposed that if more work were done it might show that the tribes of Harrison Lake and the Gulf of Georgia constitute another type. Thus Boas's work does not suggest as recent a separation of Coast and Interior Salish as Drucker's interpretation of it implies. Nor does the evidence of physical anthropology say anything about the direction of Salishan movements.

As for the archeological evidence, it appears to me that here too the question of Salishan movements is still open. In recent years, Borden (1969:257; 1970:109) has interpreted his new discoveries as supporting the hypothesis of Salish emergence, though a less recent emergence now than he once supposed. However, two of his students, Mitchell (1971) and Abbott (1972), have argued for a "continuity model" for the archeological data, suggesting a long occupation of the coast by the Coast Salish. In the Plateau, Nelson (1969) and others

---

*[Robinson 1976. See also Beattie 1985.]

258

have interpreted archeological evidence as consistent with an eastward movement of the Interior Salish. I'll leave these matters to the archeologists.

Let me turn now to linguistics, which is where the problem started. As I indicated earlier, the fact of relationship says nothing about the direction of movement. It says only that some movement must have occurred. Good linguistic evidence for Salish emergence from the interior would be facts of subgrouping and distribution allowing Sapir's "center of gravity" principle to deliver that conclusion. If, for example, the deepest cleavages within the Salishan family were in the interior, especially if the Coast Salish languages constituted simply one division of the family with several co-ordinate divisions in the interior (as Apachean is only one division within the Athapaskan language family, coordinate with several divisions in the north), then we could reasonably infer an interior location for Proto-Salish.

Drucker does not assert flatly that these are the facts, but he does perhaps imply they are when he says (1955a:11) that "the bulk" of the Salish-speaking peoples lived in the interior. It is true that the territory occupied by the Interior Salish adds up to more square miles than that occupied by the Coast Salish, but this implies nothing. In numbers, however, the Coast Salish probably constituted the bulk of the Salish; Kroeber gives them a total of a bit over 32,000 as compared with a bit over 25,000 for the Interior Salish.[2] But this implies nothing.

For the reconstruction of linguistic history, the relevant facts are, as Elmendorf and I have pointed out (Suttles and Elmendorf 1963), that the deepest cleavage within the family seems to be that separating the Interior Salish language from all of those on the coast. The next deepest seems to be that separating Bella Coola from the main body of Coast Salish languages and the next separates Tillamook from them. Bella Coola and Tillamook are, by the way, clearly Coast

---

[2]If we reorganize Mooney's (1928) figures by language, we find that he gives Halkomelem (his "Cowichan"), the Coast Salish language spoken on the Lower Fraser and on Vancouver Island opposite the mouth of the Fraser, a total of 12,600 speakers, more than any other Northwest Coast language north of the Columbia. If we add Straits, the language spoken on the Strait of Juan de Fuca and channels connecting it with Georgia Strait, with its total of 5,600 (I am subtracting 600 for the Nooksack), we get a grand total of 18,200 for those two languages whose speakers depended on salmon runs headed for the Fraser drainage. The rest of the Coast Salish of the sheltered salt water number only 11,100 (4,900 for the Northern Gulf, 600 for the Nooksack, 4,800 for Puget Sound, and 1,000 for the Twana). The whole of the rest of the Coast Salish (including 1,500 Quinault, 1,200 Chehalis and Cowlitz, 1,500 Tillamook, and 1,400 Bella Coola) give us a grand total of 16,700, still less than the number of Halkomelem and Straits speakers. The grand total of all the Wakashans is 15,200. Had Kroeber (1939:135-36) calculated population densities by language within the Salish area, as he did for some other areas, this peak around the mouth of the Fraser would have been conspicuous. [But for another view see Boyd 1985.]

Salish languages.* The diversity within the Coast group is considerably greater than the diversity within the Interior group—perhaps thirteen contiguous Coast Salish languages plus the two outliers (Tillamook and Bella Coola) as compared with seven Interior Salish languages. These facts are more compatible with a location for Proto-Salish on the coast than in the interior, or perhaps most compatible with a location near the deepest cleavage line and on the route by which the earliest split occurred, as in the Lower Fraser Valley or Fraser Canyon.

Joseph Jorgensen (1969:52-53) has reached similar conclusions about the relative diversity of Coast and Interior Salish and suggests that the splitting up of the Coast languages, including Bella Coola, probably occurred on the coast, but he does not suggest any particular homeland for Proto-Salish.

Unfortunately for the understanding of their implications, the facts of Salish linguistic diversity have been obscured by a persistent use of the word "dialect" where the reference is to *languages*. Boas seems to have used the word "dialects" to mean *related languages* or simply *related forms of speech*, i.e., the members of a language family. But for some time the word has been used by linguists to mean mutually intelligible varieties of speech, e.g., the regional forms of a language. This was identified by Sapir in his article "Dialect" in the *Encyclopedia of Social Sciences* (1931) as preferable to the pejorative use for substandard (socially inferior) forms of a language. However, Drucker (1955a:11; 1965:106-7) and Barnett (1942:380; 1955:4) both use "dialects" to refer to forms of speech perhaps as diverse as English, German, and Icelandic.

In Barnett's case it seems to be a matter of simple ignorance. In his paper "The Southern Extent of Totem Pole Carving" (1942:380), after identifying the nearest Salish neighbors of the Johnstone Strait Kwakiutl, he wrote

These latter tribles [the Comox and Homalco] spoke dialects of *the Salishan language*, as did all the rest of the people on both sides of Georgia Strait, and even those beyond around Puget Sound. [emphasis mine—W.S.]

But in Drucker's case the usage looks pejorative. In his 1965 book he wrote (1965:106):

---

*[I was thinking especially of the fact that the contiguous Coast Salish languages, Bella Coola, and Tillamook, have similar elements marking a distinction of gender in their article and demonstrative systems, and that Interior Salish lacks this distinction. But such a shared feature need not imply a closer relationship; it may simply be a common inheritance from Proto-Salish that Interior Salish alone has lost. Current thinking among Salishanists seems to be that Bella Coola is equidistant from the contiguous Coast Salish and the Interior Salish languages, while Tillamook belongs with the Coast Salish languages of Puget Sound and Georgia Strait.]

To the south of the Tsimshian, a considerable number of groups spoke varieties of a language known as Kwakiutl, and an isolated enclave spoke a Coast Salish dialect, Bella Coola.

Wakashans, it appears, have *languages*, which come in *varieties*; Salishans have *dialects*.

Drucker's discussion of Salish linguistic relations in his 1965 book would take too long to cover here. Suffice it to say he offers nothing to strengthen the case for Salish emergence.

But the case against it may be strengthened by Michael Silverstein's recent monograph on the Chinookan languages. Silverstein (1974:598-99) concludes that the Chinookan language family has been expanding upstream on the Lower Columbia and that Proto-Chinookan, presumably spoken in or near recent Lower Chinook territory, must have had contact with Salishan language, from which it borrowed gender as a grammatical category. This puts one or more Salishan languages near the mouth of the Columbia River for as long as it has taken the Chinookan family to differentiate.

Early in this paper I said that when the linguistic, physical anthropological, and archeological props have been removed, the ethnological arguments for recent Salish emergence can only be circular. The point is this: The conclusion that elements of coast culture spread from the Wakashans to the Salish cannot be used as evidence that the Salish came to the coast recently if this conclusion is itself based on nothing more than the assumption that the Wakashans were on the coast earlier and so could have invented (or acquired from other maritime peoples to the north) those elements of coast culture before the Salish got there. That would be assuming at the outset what we had set out to prove.

Drucker's interpretation of the distribution of whaling seems to be a case of circular logic. The facts of distribution are: The Wakashans of the west coast of Vancouver Island and the Olympic Peninsula (the Nootka, Nitinat, and Makah) were whalers while the other Wakashans (Kwakiutl et al.) were not; the Chimakuan-speaking Quileute on the west coast of the Olympic Peninsula were whalers while the Chimakuan-speaking Chemakum on the other side of the peninsula were not; and the Salishan-speaking Quinault and Clallam of the peninsula were whalers while the rest of the Salish were not. For Drucker, since it is axiomatic that whaling was a Wakashan culture complex, the non-Wakashans who practiced it must have acquired it from the Wakashans while the Wakashans who did not practice it must have done so earlier and lost the practice. It is "inconceivable" (Drucker 1955a:189) that the Kwakiutl did not practice whaling at an earlier time. Inconceivable, I think, only if you start with Drucker's presuppositions and perhaps ignore environmental variables like where it might be worthwhile to practice whaling.

261

Of course we may some day have linguistic evidence suggesting that terms associated with whaling, or sea-mammal hunting generally, have a Wakashan origin and have been borrowed by Chimakuans and Salishans. But that evidence does not exist today. Without that kind of evidence, I see no reason why we need give priority to anyone. Perhaps whaling developed more or less simultaneously among those peoples whose habitat made it possible and productive, developing out of the more widespread sea-mammal hunting complex shared by all of the maritime peoples of the area—and perhaps shared by them for millennia.

The fact that adjacent peoples share elements of culture says nothing, by itself, about who got what from whom. If some of the Salish have been on the coast for a long time, as now seems likely, there is no reason to suppose they could not have contributed to the Wakashans as well as received from them, unless we presuppose Wakashan creativity and Salishan imitativeness.

Thus Drucker's identification (1955a:188-90; 1955b:79) of a set of culture traits and complexes—the D-adz, the curved halibut hook, the end-thrown harpoon, and others—as "Wakashan," when in fact they are also the property of the Coast Salish of the Strait of Juan de Fuca and southern Georgia Strait, seems indefensible. The Coast Salish who share these traits were not merely a few groups who were peripheral to the center of Coast Salish population and so especially vulnerable to Wakashan influence. If Mooney's population estimates are not way off the mark, *they were* the center of Salish population and as numerous as all of the Wakashans combined.

Nor can we suppose with Drucker that because the Coast Salish and Interior Salish share such elements of culture as the mat lodge and coiled basketry that these must be part of an inland heritage brought out to the coast by emerging Salish. Without the evidence for Salish emergence, we may as easily suppose that they were taken inland by eastward-moving Salish. Or, if continental distribution patterns suggest great antiquity, as they may, we might suppose that they have existed in northwestern North America since before present language families differentiated. And surely their distribution is determined in part by environmental variables.

Thus through questioning Drucker's assumptions about the movements of peoples and flows of culture I have come to question the way he has divided the Northwest Coast into subareas. A paper presented at the last American Anthropological Association meeting in Mexico by James Coffin and Harold Driver (1974) shows that other taxonomies are possible. Coffin and Driver ignore linguistic relations and find the deepest cultural cleavage within the whole Northwest Coast runs about through the Strait of Juan de Fuca. I was surprised by some of the groupings and suppose I would have weighed the variables differently. But I found the paper a welcome shift away from the older view and I am eager to see more.*

---

*[See Driver and Coffin 1975.]

I also said early in this paper that the hypothesis of recent Salish emergence from the interior has entered into a mutually supportive relationship with a stereotyping of the Wakashans as creative and aggressive and the Salish as imitative and passive. There is no time to explore fully the disparagement (for use of the term cf. Vogel 1972:284-99) of the Coast Salish. But it appears in discussions of ceremonialism, art, and warfare, as well as in areas of culture already touched on.

On ceremonialism—dog eating, says Drucker (1940:227), "does appear in some of the peripheral rites of the Coast Salish which represent dilute imitations of the Nootkan type of ceremony." Drucker may be referring to the "secret society" of the Songhees, Clallam, Twana, and others, which *may* be of Nootkan origin. But Barnett (1939:276) reports dog eating as a feature of a guardian spirit dance among most of the Coast Salish of Georgia Strait and Haeberlin and Gunther (1930:72) report the same practice for Puget Sound. This is hardly peripheral and hardly identifiable as imitative.

On weaving—Drucker says (1965:34) "a few Coast Salish groups had a small, woolly breed of dogs that could be sheared or plucked." But these "few" Coast Salish groups included most of those of Georgia Strait and Puget Sound together with some of the Interior Salish and the Makah, so that all together the dog shearers may have been twice as numerous as the non-shearing Wakashans.

On painting and carving—Barnett (1942:382-83) says that decorated house posts among the Coast Salish of southeastern Vancouver Island were merely recent imitations of Kwakiutl crests, even though Boas had much earlier (1891:564) identified nearly identical posts as representations of guardian spirits, which is consistent with Coast Salish practice to the east and south. Also, in arguing for the recency of Coast Salish house decoration, Barnett cites the failure of the Spanish expedition of 1792 to mention any such at Nanaimo, but ignores the sketch at the end of the translation he uses (Jane 1930:131) of the carved board the expedition found at Toba Inlet on the mainland.

On warfare—Drucker writes (1965:75) of raiders from Southeastern Alaska and the Queen Charlottes who "sowed terror and panic among the groups of the Strait of Georgia and Puget Sound in early historic times, and probably also before white contact." He offers no evidence, and I believe there is none, that the Tlingit or Haida came this far south in pre-contact times; he does not mention the fact that the northerners got muskets before the Salish; and he does not mention the retaliatory expeditions sent north into Kwakiutl country by the Salish after they got guns.

Drucker also follows Boas in supposing that the Tsimshian, as well as the Salish, had an interior origin. In Drucker's words (1965:124) the Tsimshian "fought their way to the outer coast." The Salish, however, merely (1955a:14) "pushed their way out."

In my title I have used the term "myth" in simply the popular sense of a cherished belief that has no foundation in fact. I believe the hypothesis of recent Salish emergence is such a myth. As with other such myths, we can ask why people believe in them. I suspect that sometimes it is because they allow us to limit our horizons and exercise our prejudices.

15. Northwest Coast Linguistic History— a View from the Coast*

This paper is concerned with the relevance of linguistic taxonomy to theories of prehistory on the Northwest Coast of North America. I shall argue that what we know of the relations among the languages of the Northwest Coast is less compatible with the earlier theories of successive migrations into the area than with the current preference for a "continuity model" (Mitchell 1969; Adams, Van Gerven, and Levy 1978). Indeed, the most parsimonious hypothesis may be that all of the languages spoken on the Northwest Coast in historic times are "daughter" languages of the language or languages spoken by the earliest occupants of the area.[1]

Theories of Prehistory

For over 60 years anthropological thinking about the Northwest Coast has been dominated by the image of waves of immigrants coming out onto the coast from the interior. In the most popular version, the first-comers were the Wakashans, who (perhaps with some help from the Arctic or Asia) made the initial adaptation and became the teachers of the later arrivals—Haida, Tlingit, and Tsimshian coming out in the north and Salishans and Chinookans emerging

---

*[Read at the International Congress of Americanists, Vancouver 1979; not previously published.]

[1] I am grateful to W. W. Elmendorf for criticism of an earlier version of this paper.

265

in the south. Variation in culture within the area is said to be largely a result of what traits its peoples brought with them from the interior and how much they acquired from the Wakashans.

The most popular version just referred to is of course that of Philip Drucker of 1955 and 1965. But Drucker's work only epitomizes a general tendency. Early in this century Boas (1905, 1910) announced that the major discoveries of the Jesup North Pacific Expedition were (1) that the Eskimo had moved westward from the Central Arctic into the Bering Sea region, severing an old tie between the Paleosiberians and the Northwest Coast, (2) that the ancestors of the Tsimshian had moved out of the interior onto the northern Northwest Coast, and (3) that the ancestors of the Coast Salish (including the Bella Coola) had moved out of the interior via the Fraser and spread northward and southward along the coast. The first two conclusions were based on folkloristic evidence while the third was based on what Boas identified as archeological evidence, the work of H. I. Smith and the discovery (first made by Hill-Tout) that an early long-headed population had been replaced by a broad-headed population in the Fraser Delta region. By the middle of the century it was clear that the Eskimo had been in the Bering Sea region for several thousand years and so Drucker (1955a, 1955b), following suggestions by Hill-Tout, Borden, and Lantis, postulated an Eskimo source for the earliest Northwest Coast culture, now retained in its purest form by the Wakashans (Nootka and Kwakiutl), who were cut off in the north by migrations out of the interior of the ancestors of the Tlingit, Haida, and Tsimshian and, more recently, nearly surrounded in the south by Salishans pouring out of the interior there. This history, Drucker asserted, is reflected in linguistic, physical, and cultural types corresponding to his Northern, Wakashan, and Coast Salish-Chinook provinces. Others who postulated migrations out of the interior onto the coast were Kroeber (1917), on the basis of linguistic distributions; Jacobs (1937), on linguistic and ecological grounds; Borden (1950, 1951, 1954), on the basis of archeological discontinuities buttressed by linguistic and cultural distributions; and Cressman (1960), considering western Oregon, on the basis simply of earlier dates for sites in the interior.

In the last few years, however, developments in archeology have made this view of the prehistory of the Northwest Coast increasingly untenable. First, archeological discoveries have shown the antiquity of human occupation of the area to be many times what it was formerly thought to be. Second, archeologists are now considering the possibility that humans first entered the area from directions other than the interior. And third, the evidence now seems to point to long in situ cultural development.

It may be forgotten how recently our views of the antiquity of the Northwest Coast have changed. Before C^{14} dates appeared in the mid-1950s, it was generally supposed that the prehistory of the Northwest Coast could be encompassed within a millennium or two. In 1917, Kroeber (1917:391-92) deplored the practice of falling back on hypotheses of migration to account for complex cultural conditions, while excusing his own "moderation" in hypothesizing migrations into and along the Pacific Coast on the grounds that he was allowing "long periods of time" for them—more than a thousand years! In 1947, Martin, Quimby, and Collier (1947:469) stated that "the archeological remains indicate an age of at least five or six centuries for the Northwest Coast pattern of culture".

The change came quickly. In 1951, Borden (1951:44) was still cautiously estimating his oldest sites in the Fraser Delta as 500+ years old. But in 1954 he was able to report (Borden 1954:26) a C^{14} date giving his Locarno Beach site an antiquity five times greater—of around 2,500 years ago. Now, 25 years later, it seems that "the pattern of Northwest Coast culture" was established about 5,000 (not 500) years ago. This is the date of the earliest known large shell middens, which contain ground-stone implements, ornaments, and art work and imply (Fladmark 1975) large winter villages with supplies of fall-caught salmon. But this date is far from the beginning. Human occupation of the Northwest Coast began at least 12,000 years ago, or so it appears from the discovery, at the Manis site on the Strait of Juan de Fuca in northwestern Washington, of mastodon remains associated with evidence of human activity (Kirk and Daugherty 1978). Farther north, on the coast of British Columbia the earliest sites are dated at 8,000 to 9,000 years ago and in southeastern Alaska the earliest is 9,500 years ago (Borden 1975).

We now have several interpretations of the data offering several possible routes for the entry of human beings into the Northwest Coast. For Borden (1975), writing before the Manis discovery, the Northwest Coast was unoccupied before some 11,000 years ago; its northern two-thirds (from Puget Sound northward) could not have been occupied because of glaciation, while its southern third (the ocean shores of Washington and Oregon) has simply yielded no evidence of early occupation and was probably not occupied because it would not have been hospitable to groups moving out from the interior. Then about 10,000 years ago, following the recession of the ice, people moved out onto the coast "from both the far northern and southern interior . . . bearing with them at least two profoundly different cultural traditions" and "expanded southward and northward along the seaboard." The northern immigrants came out of the upper (southeastern) Yukon drainage and were participants in a tradition distinguished by the predominance of a core and blade and burin technology, while the southern immigrants came out of the Columbia Plateau, via the Columbia and Fraser Rivers, and were participants in a tradition distinguished especially by bifaced points and cobble choppers. Borden inferred different subsistence patterns for these two traditions and suggested that the economic basis of Northwest Coast culture developed, about 5,000 years ago, out of a synthesis of the two. Presumably (Borden is not explicit on this) the occupation of the coast south of the Strait of Juan de Fuca had to wait for the

267

development of marine adaptations farther north.[2]

For Fladmark (1975), the essential event responsible for the emergence of Northwest Coast culture some 5,000 years ago was less the synthesis of complementary cultures than the stabilization of previously fluctuating sea levels, permitting the development of the great salmon runs on which the Northwest Coast peoples so heavily depended. Fladmark (1975) also differs from Borden in his view of the sources of the early, pre-midden cultures. He identifies the biface tradition simply as having "its most direct affiliations to the south and east" but believes that the northern, microblade tradition more likely came not out of the interior but from the Bering Sea region along the Gulf of Alaska coast. He considers this route possible because of his revolutionary conclusion, based on a review of the evidence on glaciation and sea levels before 9,000 years ago, that the outer coast was unglaciated and more extensive than it is today and so could have supported a human population. It may be that "several thousand years of regional history have yet to be found." If so, the evidence, unfortunately, would be largely under water.

It may even be, Fladmark also suggested in his 1975 monograph (see also Fladmark 1978), that the Northwest Coast provided a route for the entry of "early man" into the New World. More recently (Fladmark 1979), he has argued that the Northwest Coast route is more likely than the postulated ice-free corridor east of the Rockies, that a northeastern Siberian culture (the Diuktai) provides a source for "all the main elements of early North Pacific assemblages," and that "a common maritime antecedent" can better account for the known distribution of these assemblages than can the hypothesis of successive migrations out of the interior. Thus in Fladmark's most recently published view, the earliest immigrants into the New World were already adapted to life on the coast and had simple watercraft. They moved out of the Bering Sea region eastward along the Gulf of Alaska and southward along the Northwest Coast from refugium to refugium and reached the unglaciated shores of Oregon and California before 15,000 years ago. Later, groups along the Northwest Coast were isolated by rising sea levels, while to the south some groups moved up rivers, such as the Columbia, to develop inland adaptations (Fladmark 1979:63-64).

The implications of Fladmark's hypothesis are enormous. Even if the Northwest Coast was a second route in addition to the eastern corridor, it implies that a littoral hunting-fishing-gathering way of life is as old or older in the New World than an inland hunting-gathering way and that all littoral cultures on the Pacific Coast of the New World may have a common origin rather than being the end products of separate adaptations to life on the shore. A search for genetic relations among even quite distant littoral cultures and languages may then be justified.

---

[2]In a paper published shortly after his death, Borden (1979:965) identifies the Manis mastodon site with the "Protowestern" movement out of the Columbia Plateau.

Also recently, Carlson (1979), without committing himself to Fladmark's route of entry, has suggested that *three* early traditions contributed to the development of Northwest Coast culture—a microblade tradition coming from the north, a biface tradition from the Columbia Plateau, and a chopper tradition from the south.

Even if Fladmark is quite wrong and ice prevented a southward movement along the northern and central Northwest Coast, it seems to me that we must still consider it possible that the Washington and Oregon coasts were occupied before the recession of the ice and that people moved northward along the coast as the ice receded. In rejecting this possibility Borden greatly underestimated the capacity of the southern coast to support early human populations. While there are indeed short stretches of coastline that cannot be negotiated on foot (at present sea levels), there are long stretches of sandy beaches protecting chains of lakes, lagoons, and estuaries rich in a variety of resources. If shellfish-eating people were present on the coast of southern California by 25,000 years ago, a possibility Cressman (1977:206) accepts, I cannot imagine why they should not have, in a few thousand years, expanded their range northward to Oregon and beyond. If there were people with watercraft practicing deep-water fishing on the southern California coast by 10,000 years ago, why not farther north? If no early sites have been discovered on the Oregon and Washington coasts, it may be, as Cressman suggests, because sea levels were lower and sites then on the shore are now under water.

Turning now to hypotheses about culture development on the Northwest Coast, we find the "retreat from migrationism" that Adams, Van Gerven, and Levy (1978) have identified as a general trend in all subfields of anthropology. The trend is certainly a healthy one, reflecting a growing awareness of the danger of multiplying hypothetical entities unnecessarily and an interest in discovering better explanations of culture change.

The former strength of "migrationism" is clearly shown by the nature and longevity of the original "archeological evidence" for the movement of Salishans down out of the interior onto the coast at the mouth of the Fraser. It seems to have been in fact nothing more than a small number of skulls, varying in breadth—partly as the result of artificial deformation, that Boas took as an indication of population replacement. As Mitchell (1971:69) has pointed out, the evidence of the skulls was never very good and has not been confirmed by recent work. Robinson (1976), reviewing H. I. Smith's work, has concluded that he did not see his archeological data as pointing to population replacement until Boas persuaded him with the supposed shift in head forms. We can, I think, discard the original "archeological evidence" as an illusion. One might suppose that Boas's later work (1912) that cast doubt on the immutability of the cephalic index might have challenged this earlier conclusion, but it seems that for over fifty years it did not. The evidence of the skulls for Salish emergence continued to be cited into the 1960s. Its weakness was first noted, I believe, by Mitchell in 1971.

Contrary to what Boas thought, recent work in the Lower Fraser region does not point unequivocally to population replacement. Although Borden saw this as the implication of his work, Mitchell (1971) finds the evidence indicating a continuity of the same population, while Carlson (1970) and Matson (1976) see population replacement as only one possible explanation for the cultural discontinuities they see in the archeological record.

To the north, MacDonald reports (MacDonald 1969, Inglis and MacDonald 1975) evidence from the Prince Rupert (Coast Tsimshian) area for 5,000 years of cultural continuity, with "all of the artifacts relating to economic activities and manufacturing" showing "continuity from the lower to upper horizons" and with ethnographic Tsimshian specimens (MacDonald 1969:242-43). Considering evidence for similar continuity in the Queen Charlottes, he suggests that the ancestors of the three northern peoples—Tsimshian, Haida, and Tlingit—have been participants in a co-tradition going back several millennia.

To the south, on the Columbia at The Dalles, Cressman (1960) showed that human occupation has been continuous for nearly 10,000 years. But downstream, in coast habitat, sites of even half that antiquity have not yet been found. What there is, however, suggests continuity. In a review of data from the Portland Basin, Pettigrew (1977:369) defines a series of phases but sees them as a continuum. "There is no evidence," he says, "suggesting cultural replacement, migration, or any basic changes in the way of life of the people. The pattern of culture of the ethnographic Chinook . . . has apparently existed in the Portland Basin for at least the past 3600 years."

Thus in radical contrast to the earlier view, we now have people on the Northwest Coast for many thousands of years, no unequivocal evidence that there were any movements out of the interior since the earliest settlement, and the possibility that even the earliest settlers were not migrants out of the interior but coast-dwellers from elsewhere, some of whom later moved into the interior.

The Implications of Linguistic Relations

The earlier hypothesis of westward movements was not illogical. A striking fact about the Northwest Coast is the number of languages spoken here and the number of families and (in modern terms) phyla to which they belong. This apparent diversity was a phenomenon that had to be explained. For earlier anthropologists, with their assumption that the area had been settled only recently, this diversity could only be the result of a number of movements into the area. There simply was not enough time for in situ differentiation. (In the same way, of course, they had to suppose that the linguistic diversity of the whole New World implied successive waves out of Asia.) And with their assumptions about how the New World was settled, these movements had to come out of the interior. As we have just seen, the assumption about when the area was settled is disproven and the assumption about where it was settled from is questionable. Just what Northwest Coast linguistic diversity and linguistic relations do imply needs to be re-examined.

Powell (1891) and Boas (1911) following him found that the languages spoken along the coast from southeastern Alaska to southwestern Oregon belonged to ten "families," coordinate units not demonstrably related to one another or to any other "family," Because some of Powell's and Boas's "families" are language isolates (single languages rather than groups of relatable languages), it might be better to call them simply *taxa* rather than "families." They were (to identify them by their current names):

1. Tlingit (a language isolate, mainly in southeastern Alaska).
2. Haida (a language isolate, mainly in the Queen Charlotte Islands).
3. Tsimshian (northern British Columbia coast and Nass and Skeena Valleys).
4. Wakashan (from the central British Columbia coast to northwestern Washington).
5. Salishan (from the central B.C. coast to northwestern Oregon and in the interior in the Fraser and Columbia drainages).
6. Chimakuan (in northwestern Washington).
7. Chinookan (around the mouth of the Columbia and upstream to The Dalles).
8. Yakonan (on the central Oregon coast).
9. Coosan (on the central Oregon coast).
10. Athapaskan (on the southern Oregon coast and southward into northwestern California, near the mouth of the Columbia River, over a vast area in the north embracing most of the Yukon and Mackenzie drainages, and in the Southwest).

And in the valleys of Western Oregon they distinguished three more "families":

11. Kalapuyan (in the Willamette Valley and a bit south).
12. Waiilatpuan (in the western foothills of the Cascades and in the interior).
13. Takelma (a language isolate in the upper Rogue River Valley).

Thus 13 out of Powell's 58 or Boas's 55 language taxa of North America north of Mexico are found along a narrow strip of northwestern North America and most of the 13 are exclusively within it.

Boas himself pointed to resemblances among some of these taxa but believed that such resemblances could be the result of borrowing and doubted that more distant genetic relationsips could be established. However, some of Boas's students proposed more distant relationships. The most famous of these proposals was Sapir's.

Sapir (1929) proposed a grouping of the Powell taxa, which Sapir called "stocks," into six larger groupings, sometimes called "Sapir's superstocks." Three of the six were represented on the Northwest Coast. Omitting some of the details, they were:

a. Na-Dene, composed of Haida and Continental Na-Dene (comprising Tlingit and Athapaskan).

b. Penutian, composed of Tsimshian, Chinookan, an Oregon Penutian group (comprising Yakonan, Siuslaw [separated from Powell's Yakonan], Coosan, Kalapuyan, and Takelma), a Plateau Penutian group (which included Waiilat-puan), a California Penutian group, and a Mexican Penutian group.

c. Algonkin-Wakashan, composed of Mosan (composed of Wakashan, Salishan, and Chimakuan), Kootenay, and Algonkin-Ritwan (Ritwan consisting of Wiyot and Yurok in northwestern California).

Although Sapir clearly labelled this a "proposed classification," it was widely accepted among ethnologists and archeologists as established truth. However, in recent years this proposed classification has been considerably revised by linguists. Of the three "superstocks" just identified, Na-Dene and Penutian seem not wholly secure, while Algonkin-Wakashan has been altogether dismantled, its Northwest Coast components now appearing as "family isolates." (See Elmendorf 1965a; the Voegelins' map [1966] for a revision as of that time, the table for which appears in Driver 1969:43-45; and Krauss 1973 and Thompson 1973 for recent work.)

But while Sapir's proposed wider relationships have not all been supported by further work, the principles he set forth (Sapir 1916) for drawing inferences about the history of a group of related languages from their distribution have endured. These are two. The first asserts that linguistic differentiation is a measure of antiquity and so the more differentiated a group of related languages the longer they have occupied their territory. The second is the "center of gravity" principle (see Na-Dene below for illustration), which asserts that the homeland of a group is indicated by its deepest cleavages.

What follows now is a review of what can be inferred about the history of Na-Dene, Penutian, and the family isolates of the Northwest Coast according to these principles. As will be seen, they seem to point to movements from the coast inland rather than vice versa. But as will also be seen, the case for antiquity on the coast raises a question about Sapir's first (greater-differentiation) principle.[3]

---

[3]Another method once proposed as a tool of prehistory seems to have few supporters today. This is glottochronology, largely developed by Swadesh, an attempt to use lexicostatistics (a count of cognates) to measure time of separation of related languages. Most recent linguistic writing ignores the subject. Krauss (1973:952-53) expressed doubt about its validity, while Kinkade and Powell (1976:83-84) reject it emphatically as based on false assumptions. It is not surprising then that little attention has been paid to Swadesh's (1962) use of lexicostatistics to place all of the world's languages in a vast network of networks. But I find it of some interest that his "Vascodene" (Eurasian-Oceanian) and "Macro-Hokan" (pan-North American) networks are linked on the Northwest Coast.

272

Na-Dene According to Sapir's proposed classification, Tlingit stood coordinate with the Athapaskan Family while Haida stood coordinate with Tlingit-Athapaskan to constitute a Na-Dene group. It now appears that Eyak (unknown to Sapir in 1929), on the Gulf of Alaska coast, stands coordinate with Athapaskan, Tlingit *may* stand coordinate with Eyak-Athapaskan (grammatically it seems relatable though lexically it may not be), while Haida may or may not be a distant relative of this complex (Krauss 1973, Levine n.d.).

Sapir (1916:79-83) used Na-Dene to illustrate the principles mentioned earlier. Considering the Athapaskan family, he argued that it must have a northern origin because the greatest diversity within it is in the north, the greatest diversity indicating the greatest antiquity. Furthermore, it must have a northern origin because it is merely one division of Na-Dene, the others of which are on the Northwest Coast. He reasoned that, in determining where a proto-language was spoken, we must give "equal weight" to the major divisions of the language group. The major divisions of Na-Dene are first Haida versus Tlingit-Athapaskan and second, within Tlingit-Athapaskan, Tlingit versus Athapaskan, and so the "center of gravity" lies there on the northern Northwest Coast, pointing to the northern Northwest Coast as the homeland of Na-Dene. The argument is simply an application of Occam's razor to the facts of subgrouping and distribution; the hypothesis that the homeland of a group is where we find its deepest cleavages requires the fewest hypothetical movements (cf. Dyen 1956, Diebold 1960). Although the facts about Na-Dene seem somewhat different today from what they did to Sapir, they point to the same conclusion. Even if Haida and Tlingit should turn out *not* to be genetically relatable to Eyak-Athapaskan, the center of gravity of this group is still in Alaska, because the deepest cleavage within it is between Eyak and Athapaskan. Also, the greatest diversity within Athapaskan is in Alaska (Krauss 1973:904). Adding Tlingit and Haida to form a Na-Dene phylum would put the center of gravity only slightly farther south but more definitely on the coast, implying that Athapaskan is simply a relatively recent inland offshoot of the phylum.

This conclusion, available since 1916, has been generally ignored. In a rare instance of recognition, Dumond (1969) saw that the internal relationships of Na-Dene imply a coastal homeland but thought it unlikely because of "the rugged nature of the coastline." (Kinkade and Powell's map shows the Athapaskan homeland in the lower Yukon Basin but they are evidently not considering possible wider relations of Athapaskan.) However, if Fladmark is right about the geological history of the northern Northwest Coast, perhaps there was room there for Proto-Eyak-Athapaskan, Proto-Tlingit, and Proto-Haida—or, if there was one, Proto-Na-Dene.

If Athapaskan is an inland offshoot of a language once spoken on the northern Northwest Coast, how did Athapaskan languages get to the southern Northwest Coast? Relations within Athapaskan suggest to Krauss (1973:917-35) two separate movements southward to the southern Northwest Coast, an earlier one bringing the language or languages that became the Pacific Coast group to southwestern Oregon and northwestern California, a later bringing Kwalhioqua-Clatskanie to the Lower Columbia. Krauss locates the closest relatives of the Pacific Coast Group in the western interior of British Columbia but makes no inferences about the route travelled. Golla (1976) thinks it possible, though not certain, that Kwalhioqua-Clatskanie belongs with the Pacific Coast Group and suggests a movement southward through the interior of British Columbia then westward to the coast near the mouth of the Columbia and then southward along the coast. (Both Krauss and Golla derive the Apachean languages of the Southwest from the northern Athapaskan area east of the Rockies and the product of a totally different movement.)

Penutian The Penutian group, in Sapir's classification, included as coordinate branches: Tsimshian, Chinook, Oregon Penutian, Plateau Penutian, California Penutian, and Mexican Penutian. It appears now that, while some linguists have accepted all of these as a "Penutian phylum" and even extended the phylum southward to include more languages in Latin America (Swadesh 1956, Voegelin and Voegelin 1966), others find the relationship of the northern branches "not yet established" (Thompson 1973:987).

The northern end of the putative Penutian phylum is certainly more diverse than Sapir's (or even the Voegelins') classification suggests. Tsimshian, now seen as a family of two (Rigsby n.d.) or three (Dunn n.d.) languages, and Chinookan, a family of two (Silverstein 1974:S50-51), stand quite removed from each other and from the rest. Sapir's "Oregon" and "Plateau" branches are now identifiable as eight or nine units (comprising 14 languages) that do not necessarily form any larger grouping within the rest of Penutian. Specifically, on the central Oregon coast were Yakonan (a family of two languages), Siuslaw (once considered part of Yakonan but now a language isolate), and Coosan (a family of two); between the Coast and Cascade Ranges were Kalapuyan (a family of three), Takelma (a language isolate, possibly with a closer relationship to Kalapuyan), and Molala (a language isolate); and east of the Cascades were (or are) Sahaptian (a family of two), Cayuse (a language isolate), and Klamath-Modoc (a language isolate) (Thompson 1973:987-94). Further work may, of course, suggest some realignment.

Sapir drew no conclusions from his subgrouping and the distribution of the Penutian languages about prehistoric movements, perhaps because he saw no differences in the depths of the major cleavages great enough to permit any. But Swadesh (1956), though he extended the group, under the name "Penutioid," to include such distant families as Mayan and Quechua-Aymara, still found "the great divergences in the extreme north" indicated that "Oregon may represent the center of the ancient Penutioid area." Kinkade and Powell (1976:91) and Silverstein (1976) locate the hypothesized homeland of Penutian in Western Oregon. This choice, rather than Eastern Oregon, seems indicated by the apparently greater differentiation of Penutian languages west of the Cascades.

Moreover, recent work on three Penutian taxa—Tsimshian, Chinookan, and Molala—does not support the old image of Penutian peoples pushing westward to the sea. Working on the Tsimshian languages, Rigsby (n.d.) sees internal and external evidence that the homeland of the language that became Coast Tsimshian and Nass-Gitksan was in the Lower and Middle Skeena Valley and probably the adjacent coast, that the expansion of the family was up the Skeena and thence to the Nass, and that the Tsimshian are "an old coast people" rather than recent migrants from the interior. The evidence includes a contrast between terms for inland and coast fauna, a number of inland terms being identifiable as loans from Athapaskan while the coast terms are identifiable as old Native words. Dunn's discovery (Dunn n.d.) of what seems to be a third Tsimshian language at the southern end of Coast Tsimshian territory strengthens the case for a coastal homeland.

Silverstein (1974) finds evidence in the grammar of the Chinookan languages (which comprise Lower Chinook, spoken around the mouth of the Columbia, and Upper Chinook, consisting of Kathlamet and Kiksht, a dialect chain extending from below the mouth of the Willamette upstream to The Dalles) for an early homeland downstream, where contact with Salishan resulted in features (such as grammatical gender) common to all of Chinookan, and a later movement upstream, during which cumulative changes occurred in the upriver dialects under the influence of Sahaptin. These changes could have occurred in this direction only, not the reverse, and it appears that the family has occupied its present territory "for quite some time." Silverstein does not rule out the possibility of an earlier movement out of the interior, but there is not (as I understand him) any reason for supposing there was.

In the Molala case, Rigsby (1969) has re-examined the evidence for a supposed close relationship, within the Penutian phylum, between Molala and Cayuse (spoken in northeastern Oregon), once said to constitute a "Waiilatpuan Family," and found it unsupported. This conclusion leaves also unsupported the tradition that the Molala are a recent offshoot of the Cayuse, and were still moving westward across the Cascades in historic times. The ethnohistorical and ethnographic data place them along the western slopes of the Cascades. But the linguistic data do indicate some past contact between Molala and Cayuse, and so Rigsby believes that "the territories of their speech communities may have been contiguous in some earlier period." Whether this means an earlier westward movement of the Molala or an eastward movement of the Cayuse or a separation of the two by some intrusive movement is still an open question.

Family Isolates As mentioned earlier, Sapir's "Algonkin-Wakashan" superstock has been taken apart. Until 1964 (Elmendorf 1965a:98) no evidence had been adduced to support this grouping and the short lists of possible Algonquian-Kootenay and Kootenay Salishan cognates that Haas (1960 and 1965) offered then were not enough to establish these relationships (cf. Thompson 1973:1019).

Recently, however, Larry Morgan (personal communication) has been looking again at the possibility of a relationship between Kootenay and Salishan.

The less-inclusive "Mosan" grouping has fared no better. Swadesh (1953) presented what he saw as evidence for it, but Kuipers (1967:401-5) showed that, using the kinds of resemblances between families that Swadesh adduced as evidence for "Mosan," one can make an equally good case for a relationship between Salishan and Indo-European! Meanwhile, Swadesh himself (1962) had broken "Mosan" apart, putting Wakashan (and Kootenay) into his "Vascodene" network and Salishan and Chimakuan into his "Macro-Hokan" network. (See also Klokeid 1969.) Again, however, Powell (1976) has recently presented a new list of possible Wakashan-Chimakuan cognates and so may revive the possibility of a genetic relationship between these two families.

Demonstrable relationships seem to be as follows: There are three family isolates—Wakashan, Chimakuan, and Salishan. Wakashan consists of five or six languages, two or three in the Kwakiutlan Branch, spoken from the north end of Vancouver Island northward to the Kitimat River, and probably three in the Nootkan Branch, spoken along the west coast of Vancouver Island and at the northwestern tip of the Olympic Peninsula. Chimakuan consists of two languages, on either side of the Olympic Peninsula. And Salishan consists of 22 or 23 languages—Bella Coola, isolated on the central inner coast of British Columbia; a continuum of 13 or 14 languages spoken through the Strait of Georgia-Puget Sound Basin and southward, usually called "Coast Salish"; Tillamook, isolated on the Oregon Coast; and a continuum of seven Interior Salish languages extending eastward through the Fraser and upper Columbia drainages to the Rockies. If we are to consider the Plateau, we must add one language isolate, Kootenay, spoken in the upper Columbia drainage north and east of Salishan.

It is remarkable how little notice was ever given to the implications of the postulated "Mosan" and "Algonkin-Wakashan" groupings. In 1917 Kroeber (1917) pointed out that, if a relationship existed between Salishan and Wakashan (as Boas's comments on structural resemblances suggested), this implied a movement of Salishan inland from the coast up the Fraser rather than downriver as Boas had said. But Boas's view prevailed and the inference seems never to have been drawn again. Yet Mosan, with only one branch (Interior Salish) of one of the three main divisions in the interior, has its center of gravity securely on the coast strongly indicating a homeland there. If we add Kootenay as a unit coordinate with Mosan, we must give equal weight to the Northwest Coast and the Plateau for this larger grouping but still put "Proto-Mosan" on the coast. If we add "Algonkin-Ritwan" as a third coordinate member, the center of gravity of "Algonkin-Wakashan" does not move any farther east, since the Ritwan languages (Wiyot and Yurok) are on the Pacific Coast. The simplest hypothesis would put the "Algonkin-Wakashan" homeland on the southern Northwest Coast or in the Plateau and send a later movement eastward across the Rockies to become the Algonquian family. But in this case Sapir's principles were ignored. Instead, archeologists (cf. Cressman 1960:74; 1977:202-3) tended to see "Algonkin-Wakashan" as the antepenultimate wave out of Asia (followed by Na-Dene and Eskimo-Aleut), which spread southward through the center of the continent and then radiated westward and eastward.

But if neither "Mosan" nor "Algonkin-Wakashan" are demonstrably related groupings, the previous paragraph is simply a footnote to anthropological history. Today the most we can say is that the three family isolates seem deeply rooted on or near the coast.

In the absence of external relatives and members off the coast, Wakashan and Chimakuan offer no linguistic basis for hypotheses bringing them from anywhere else. Kinkade and Powell's (1976) view that the original homeland of Wakashan was on Vancouver Island and that of Chimakuan was on the Olympic Peninsula seems indisputable.

Salishan does have members in the interior but internal relations point to the coast. In 1962 Elmendorf and I (Suttles and Elmendorf 1963) showed that the lexicostatistic data used by Swadesh (1950) for subgrouping the Salishan family indicate that the family consists of two language chains, a coastal chain extending north and south and an interior chain running from northwest to southeast, the two adjoining in the Fraser drainage. Relationships measured by lexicostatistics, with a couple of minor exceptions, accord with lineal distance along this pair of chains. Differentiation is greater in the coastal chain. These facts seem most consistent with a homeland west of the Cascades, perhaps from the southern end of Puget Sound northward to the Fraser, an early offshoot pushing into the interior, and a somewhat later expansion northward and southward along the coast. Elmendorf (1965) further developed the argument for the southeastward spread of Interior Salish through the Plateau. Jorgensen (1969), after subjecting both linguistic (phonological and lexical) and cultural data to statistical analysis, reached the same conclusion. Kinkade and Powell (1976), while differing from us to some extent in their view of internal relations, accept our location of the probable homeland of Salishan.

Thus it now appears that, for every group of languages on the Northwest Coast now seen as genetically related, the facts as we see them are more consistent with hypotheses of homelands on the coast than of migrations out of the interior. These facts are not wholly new but their implications have never been squarely faced.

If, then, the proto-languages of the various families and phyla represented here today were spoken here before their dissolution, it is possible or even probable that some or all of these were related on a more remote level. To say that there is no evidence for a genetic relationship between any of the presently distinguished language phyla and family isolates is *not* to say that they are *not* related. It may be that the three Northwest Coast family isolates are in fact related to each other and/or to one or the other or both of the two phyla but that the break-up of the original (proto-proto-) language or languages simply occurred so long ago that the evidence for it cannot now be detected. There has been, it now appears, enough time for such an in situ differentiation.

If the Northwest was first settled by two groups, one coming in from the south and the other from the north, as Borden would have it, perhaps all present Northwest Coast languages go back to two proto-languages. Or if, as Fladmark suggests, the Northwest Coast was a route for the entry of "early man" into the New World, perhaps all of the languages of the Northwest Coast go back to a single dialect chain that developed as the earliest population expanded south-ward along the coast. In either case, the only subsequent movements we would need to postulate would be expansion out of the area by branches of Penutian, Na-Dene, and Salishan; shifting within the area (through expansion and con-traction) sufficient to account for the isolation of Tsimshian from the rest of Penutian (if that is what Tsimshian is), the isolation of Bella Coola and Tilla-mook from the rest of Salishan, and the separation of the two Chimakuan languages; and the reentry into the area of Athapaskan. We could see the majority of languages as either staying in place, as perhaps the Oregon Coast Penutian languages have done, or expanding into areas contiguous to the original base, as Wakashan has probably done.

The hypothesis of in situ development from one or two proto-languages is not only the most parsimonious in the number of hypothetical movements it requires, it also fits what we know about areal features. These are phonological, grammatical, and semantic features shared by languages of an area regardless of their (apparent) genetic relationships, e.g., the category gender, which Boas (1929) found shared by Salishan (except for the Interior Branch), Chimakuan, and Chinookan and which Silverstein (1974, 1976) says Chinookan may have acquired from Salishan. Although they have had much less attention than genetic relations, they (and evidence of lexical borrowing) are equally important for the understanding of the linguistic history of the area, as well as its social and cultural history.

The history of work on areal features has been summarized by Thompson (1973:1021-1024). As he indicates, Boas saw areal features on the Northwest Coast as evidence that not only words but features of phonology and grammar could be borrowed and so concluded "that it was futile to pursue long-range genetic relationships in North America." Data are presented by Sherzer (1973:766-71) and Kinkade (1976). The Northwest Coast and Plateau appear to be a single area, set off most sharply from the Great Basin and Plains, less so from the other adjacent areas. Kinkade finds that the features he has tabulated define "seven or eight (partly overlapping) major sub-areas . . . cutting across language family boundaries, and reflecting (at least in part) ancient diffusion, although the direction of the diffusion cannot always be determined" (Kinkade 1976:5).

Thus areal features suggest that contact among the languages of the area has

278

been going on over a long period of time, e.g., contact between Salishan and Chinookan predates the break-up of Chinookan, and they do not suggest any major dislocations within the area of intrusions into it, e.g., Salishan is as much a Northwest Coast family phonologically, grammatically, and semantically as is Wakashan. All of this is consistent with the data of archeology that suggest long in situ cultural development, the data of physical anthropology suggesting that between areas occupied by different language families there has been "frequent genetic interchange over some period of time" (Cybulski 1975:260-62), and especially with the ethnographic data indicating wide social networks extending right across linguistic boundaries (e.g., Elmendorf 1960:277-305).

But how, one might ask, could in situ linguistic differentiation have occurred in the midst of a network of social and biological ties? In fact, these ties may have contributed to the process. In historic times, at least, local and/or kin groups were exogamous entities, each engaged in maintaining its own status vis-à-vis surrounding groups and thereby maintaining its marital and economic ties with them. As Silverstein (1976) suggests, people may have consciously emulated the speech of higher-status neighbors, now on one side and now on another as fortunes rose and fell. Arguing for the in situ differentiation of Oregon Penutian, he writes:

> If the various indications we have of the sophistication in pinpointing "fashions of speaking" throughout this region are understood properly, speech mannerisms—even including implementation of categorial distinctions in morphological forms—were subject to being talked about, hence used as goods for proper display and bestowal. And such a phenomenon is locked into the regional social systems. I think it is only by such an explanation of shifting lines of influence through time, rather than shifting biological populations, that we can understand how the essentially continuous distribution of supposed Penutian languages in Oregon have come to be differentiated (Silverstein 1976:8).

To this I would add that, because each group (or its elite) was also engaged in maintaining its own integrity and identification with its resources, people may also have consciously tried to maintain some unique features of speech as symbols of that identity. I would conjecture that the game was played by emulating your more prestigious neighbors without merging with them. Thus there may have been both external and internal forces promoting differentiation.

At this point other questions arise. If features of Northwest Coast social organization have promoted linguistic differentiation, then is it not possible that languages have differentiated faster on the Northwest Coast than in the interior, where social organization was different? And if so, does this not vitiate any argument for a coastal homeland for a group of related languages based simply on its having more members on the coast? I believe the answer has to be yes. If social relations of one sort in one area can promote in situ differentiation while those of another sort in another area do not, then we can no longer accept Sapir's first principle "the greater the differentiation the greater the antiquity." That principle must rest on the assumption that differentiation proceeds everywhere at the same rate. If the rate is not the same, the case for a coastal homeland for Salishan, for example, based on two-thirds of its members being on the coast is not very good, though the converse (an interior origin in spite of less differentiation there) is certainly no better.

Sapir's center of gravity principle, however, rests on no such assumption: it relies on established subgrouping implying an order in the splitting up of a group. Thus a coastal origin for Athapaskan seems indicated because it is a subgroup of Eyak-Athapaskan, which in turn is a subgroup of Na-Dene. If we accept Na-Dene in the broadest sense and suppose an inland homeland, then we must postulate a series of movements to the coast, one following each split, for Haida, for Tlingit, and for Eyak. But if we suppose a coastal homeland, we need postulate only one movement inland, for Athapaskan, and so this is the more economical view.

The center of gravity principle, however, cannot yet be applied to the Penutian phylum or to the Salishan family because we do not yet have a clear family tree for either. There would be a strong center-of-gravity case for a coastal homeland for Salishan if we could show that the Interior languages constitute a subdivision of one of two or more divisions otherwise on the coast (as Athapaskan is a subdivision of Eyak-Athapaskan, etc.). But we cannot make such a case with our present knowledge. On the other hand, the Interior Salish languages are said (Kinkade and Powell 1976:91) to form a closely related group and this precludes a center-of-gravity argument for an interior homeland. But the possibility remains that Proto-Salish was spoken in the interior, that it split into two divisions when some of its speakers moved to the coast, and that differentiation was accelerated on the coast as a result of the development or adoption of a coastal social organization. Similar arguments might, I suppose, be made for Penutian—not very convincing, I think, but not utterly impossible.

Unfortunately, the neat family trees that would clear up this uncertainty may never appear. The areal features that show widespread and enduring contact between languages, together with everything we know about the historic Native social systems, argue against the assumptions of the family-tree model (cf. Bloomfield 1933:310-18) of a homogeneous trunk and cleanly separated branches. The wave-theory image of innovations spreading through areas occupied by contiguous Salishan or Penutian languages must be closer to reality. Ultimately, a clearer understanding of Northwest Coast linguistic history will have to come from a combination of the pursuit of genetic relationships and the analysis of patterns of diffusion, pursued with a growing understanding of how the Native social systems worked.

For now, I think that, even with the possible weakness of Sapir's greater-diversity principle, the case is better for an earlier occupation of the coast and later movement inland than for the opposite. I suspect that Sapir himself may have had something like Fladmark's hypothesis in mind when he commented, near the beginning of his 1929 article, on the uneven distribution of Powell's 55 "stocks"—"37 of them are either entirely or largely in territory draining into the Pacific, and 22 of these have a coast line on the Pacific." Only seven had an Atlantic coastline and ten were on the Gulf coast and lower Mississippi Valley (Sapir 1949:169). I find it hard to believe that this distribution is accidental or simply the result of topography. New World distributions need to be reconsidered.

16. Plateau Pacifism Reconsidered— Ethnography, Ethnology, and Ethnohistory*

In his ethnography of the Sanpoil of the central Plateau, Verne Ray (1932:25-27) identified pacifism and the equality of man as the "dominant trends" of Sanpoil culture. From Ray's account it appears that one of the principal functions of the village chief was to express these values in speeches to his people. Moreover, Ray tells us, they were put into practice in Sanpoil political and economic life. There was peace and harmony within the household and village, equal division of fish and game taken by cooperative means, no warfare, and no slavery. In the final paragraph of his description of these "dominant trends," Ray wrote:

> It is interesting to note that here in the center of the Plateau, an area hitherto considered a cultural mixture of Northwest coast and Plains traits, we find one of the outstanding cultural trends in direct contrast to the Coast, the other to the Plains. At opposite poles were the Sanpoil principles of equality and the rigid Coast system of classes and preferences. And the Sanpoil ideal of pacifism was utterly foreign to the central theme of Plains life, the exhibition of bravery in warfare [Ray 1932:26-27].

*[Presented at the 34th Annual Northwest Anthropological Conference, Portland, 27 March 1981; previously unpublished.].

This paragraph became a major theme in Ray's ethnological reconstruction of Plateau culture history, *Cultural Relations in the Plateau of Northwestern America* (Ray 1939). In this work Ray went on to identify pacifism and egalitarianism as ancient Plateau values, overlaid in the eastern section of the area by Plains militarism and in the western section by Northwest Coast social stratification but surviving strongest at the center. Like Leslie Spier before him (Spier 1930), Ray was concerned with demonstrating that the Plateau was not simply an area marginal to the Coast or the Plains but had "a distinctive character in its own right" (1939:145). These values, it appears, were important components of that distinctive character. And so the Sanpoil emerge in Ray's work as having preserved the purest form of Plateau culture.

Recently, however, Susan Kent (1980) has shown that the ethnohistorical data do not support Ray's image of the Plateau in general and the Sanpoil in particular as pacifistic. She suggests (p. 129) that Ray's original study of the Sanpoil was biased and concludes (p. 133) that Plateau pacifism is a myth—perhaps the last remnant of the myth of the noble savage.

There does seem to be a problem. If Sanpoil Indians did indeed occasionally engage in local feuds and in raiding for horses and war honors on the Plains, as Kent's sources indicate, then why did Ray's informants give him the impression that they were wholly pacifistic? Were Ray's informants idealizing the past? Was Ray himself selecting the evidence to idealize the Sanpoil? Or were the historical sources maligning the Sanpoil?

I am going to argue here that it may be possible to reconcile the ethnography and the ethnohistory, that Ray's informants did not misrepresent the importance of pacifism and egalitarianism and neither did the early White observers misrepresent the participation of the Sanpoil in conflict. My argument consists of two assumptions, a prediction, and a demonstration.

Assumption 1: We must suppose that a people can hold contradictory values, such as (a) it's good to live in peace and harmony, and (b) it's good to avenge an injury. In fact, most of the world's peoples may be well acquainted with both of these values.

Assumption 2: We may suppose that if a value such as (a) is more frequently expressed than a value such as (b) it is because (a) promotes, or motivates, or justifies behavior that is more important to the functioning of the cultural (social, socio-economic) system than behavior promoted by value (b). (You'll note that these assumptions contain a lot of other assumptions about the nature of values, motives, behavior, systems, and the like. But I'll ignore those assumptions here.)

Prediction: If Sanpoil chiefs harangued their villagers about the virtues of peace and harmony and social equality, we should be able to discover some institution that works better with behavior consistent with those values.

Demonstration: We do find just such an institution in the most productive kind of salmon fishing practiced in the region occupied by the Sanpoil and their

283

neighbors. This was fishing at the great communal traps. Relevant passages from Ray's Sanpoil ethnography follow. On the implementation of the egalitarian value, he writes:

> Why should one man have more than another? Yet nature was bountiful—was not every man deserving of a living? The solution of these questions was a modified communistic organization. The huge catches of salmon made each summer at the great fish traps were divided entirely equally between all present, foreigners included. A man need have taken no part in the fishing activities to be entitled to a share in the daily distributions (Ray 1932:26).

And we shall see it was not the man but the woman who received a share of the fish. On the seasonal round, Ray writes:

> The summer fishing season began about the first of May . . . Most of the members of each winter village built summer mat shelters at the fishing grounds nearest that village but some preferred to go elsewhere. The largest traps were located at the mouth of the Sanpoil river, the mouth of the Spokane river and at Kettle Falls. These places drew persons from far and near. Like the root digging, the salmon season was initiated with a ceremony, the first salmon rite . . . Social as well as economic life was intense from the opening rite to the end of the season at the end of August. Each day was punctuated with the distributions of the salmon at which time everyone gathered together. Visitors were constantly coming and going and gambling was rampant. The greatest amount of travel occurred toward the end of the season when the fish became scarce. There was always the hope that some distant site might prove more productive. The woman were far from idle while the men were fishing and gambling. Theirs were the tasks of cooking and drying the salmon and of gathering berries in any spare time (Ray 1932:28).

Actually, at Kettle Falls, it appears that most of the men gathered there did no fishing at all, since the traps, once installed, simply had to be protected from driftwood and emptied of fish. The supervision of the trap was in the hands of the Salmon Chief, who was not a village chief and not answerable to the local village chief. In discussing his functions, Ray writes:

> At the communal traps all fish that were taken were distributed equally among all present at the camp, irrespective of whether one was a stranger, a temporary visitor, or a permanent resident. Presentation of the fish was to the women who did the cooking and drying.

The size of the family was considered in the apportionment (Ray 1932:70).

Ray is of course not the only source we have on this. The Columbia Plateau pattern of co-utilization of resources has been described and analyzed by Anastasio (1975) and the role of the Salmon Chief by Treide (1965). Ethnohistorical data on the Kettle Falls area are presented by Chance (1973) and more on the Kettle Falls fishery itself by Bouchard and Kennedy (1975, 1979).

All of this sounds to me as if the organization of the great trap fisheries of the Central Plateau provided a great way of coping with abundance—of getting more out of those great fish runs than a policy of every-village-for-itself would have gotten out of them—as well as having an exciting summer. Let people move freely from trap to trap, gathering where the most fish could be taken—perhaps with the least effort. Give the fish to the women, since after all it is the amount of female effort that determines the number of fish that can be preserved. And leave us men free to gamble. Under these conditions it should not be surprising to hear numerous speeches in favor of pacifism and egalitarianism.

Thus I'm arguing that what Ray identified as the "dominant trends" of Sanpoil culture really were *the values most frequently expressed* among the Sanpoil and that they were most frequently expressed because their expression promoted the smooth operation of the great salmon fisheries that were their most productive resource.

This interpretation does not preclude the expression of other, even contradictory values. When discussing a projected expedition to the Plains to hunt buffalo and fight the Blackfeet, some Sanpoil may quite possibly have spoken about the sweetness of revenge and the glory of war. But probably such occasions occurred less often than occasions for talking about peace.

Note that I am not talking about a contrast between "ideal behavior" and "real behavior" or between "what people say they do" and "what people really do." In fact, I suspect that the concept "ideal behavior" is an empty one—an artifact of anthropology that has outlived whatever usefulness it may have had. I am talking about two kinds of real behavior—people saying what they *ought* to do and people doing it. And I suspect there's no contradiction. When Ray's informants described the speeches of chiefs urging peace, they were reporting real behavior, as they were when describing the organization of the great fisheries. If not all Sanpoil behaved peacefully at all times, we can suspect that occasionally somebody was urging war.

Let's return to the questions raised by Kent's paper. Were Ray's informants idealizing the past? Perhaps only in that they may have reported only the most commonly expressed values. Did Ray idealize the Sanpoil? Perhaps only in assuming that a people can live consistent with "dominant trends." And in that he was consistent with a dominant trend of his time. His Sanpoil ethnography was published the same year as Ruth Benedict's article "Configurations of Culture in North America" (Benedict 1932), which adumbrated her *Patterns of Culture* (Benedict 1934). Did the early White sources lie about Sanpoil conflict? I doubt it.

Finally, while I do not see the discrepancy between the ethnography and the ethnohistory as irreconcilable, I do have trouble with Ray's ethnological reconstruction of Plateau culture history. In Ray's view, remember, the values pacifism and egalitarianism are old and preserved best at the center of the culture area. In Ray's view, presumably, the intergroup egalitarianism of the great fisheries was an expression of these values. The interpretation presented here, however, would suggest something different—that, as the great fisheries developed, the expression of consistent values increased in frequency. If chiefs urged pacifism and egalitarianism to a greater extent in the central Plateau than on the periphery, it is because the Central Plateau is where the great fisheries developed. And this may not be an ancient development. William C. Smith (1977) finds archeological evidence of conflict or the threat of conflict in prehistoric times in the Columbia Basin. Perhaps pacifism is a recent development.

Note on the Spelling of Native Words

In writing words in the Indian languages I have used the orthography in general use among linguists working in this region. This system of spelling, with its unusual letters and diacritics, may look like the invention of elitist pedants designed to intimidate the uninitiated. But in fact we must have some such set of symbols to show the difference between one Native word and another. It doesn't really matter what they look like, of course, as long as we use them consistently. This system (sometimes called Americanist, since it is used for American Indian languages) builds on the Roman alphabet as used for most European languages, adding a few Greek letters, a device from Czech, and a few home-made inventions. The values of the symbols are best identified in groups according to the classes of sounds they represent.

The voiceless plosives are sounds made by cutting off the passage of air through the throat and mouth at some point along the way and then releasing it, either without audible friction (in which case the sound is a stop) or with audible friction (in which case it is an affricate). The symbols representing the voiceless plosives that occur in the languages of this region are:

p representing a stop sound like English p.

z an affricate made by pressing the tip of the tongue against the teeth and releasing it with a sound like th in English words like "thin" and "thorn." Giving z this value is my own usage; others have used t^θ. This sound is not common anywhere, though its glottal-ized (see below) counterpart occurs commonly in Halkomelem and the Saanich dialect of Straits.

t a stop, like English t.

c an affricate, like English ts, but treated as a single unit like the German z.

$\check{c}$ an affricate like English ch. The symbol is called "C wedge." (The wedge is the Czech device.)

λ unlike anything in English, an affricate made with the tongue in position for an l sound but released with lateral friction. The symbol is called "barred lambda." The sound is usually heard by English speakers as either a tl or a kl. This sound is not common in the Salishan languages, though its glottalized counterpart (see below) is.

k a stop like English k.

k^w a labialized or rounded stop, like English kw or qu in "quick" but treated as a single sound. The symbol can be called "K with raised W."

q a stop somewhat like a k, but whereas a k is made by raising the back of the tongue against the roof of the mouth, a q is made by pulling the root of the tongue back against the uvula. The difference can be hard to hear at first, and early in my work I often missed it, hearing q as k.

q^w a labialized q.

$ʔ$ the glottal stop, a common sound in English but generally noticed only in somebody else's accent, as in "bo'le" for "bottle"—unless that's the way you say it.

Voiced plosives do not occur in Halkomelem and Straits, the sources of most of the native words I have used, but some occur in Lushootseed and Twana. The symbols representing these sounds are:

b like English b.

d like English d.

$ʒ$ like English dz.

$\check{ʒ}$ like English j.

g^w like English gw.

Glottalized (or ejective) plosives have no counterparts in English or other

288

Western European languages. They are made by simultaneously stopping the passage of air with the lips (as for a p), the tongue against the ridge above the teeth (as for a t), etc. and closing the glottis (the vocal cords) so that the release can be made with a sharper, popping quality. All of the unvoiced plosives listed above have glottalized counterparts. Glottalization is indicated with a raised comma above the symbol for the unglottalized sound, thus $\dot{p}$ is a glottalized p, $\dot{t}$ a glottalized t, and so on.

Fricatives are made by partially stopping the passage of air so that there is audible friction. The symbols representing the fricatives that occur in the languages of the region are:

θ like English th in words like "thin" and "thorn."

s like English s. (Early in my work I recorded a sound as s, intending to represent an s-like sound made with the tongue farther forward. It turned out that this was better identified as a θ.)

$\dot{t}$ a lateral fricative, made with the tongue in the position for an l. This sound is unlike anything in English but it is what is written ll in Welsh. The symbol is called "barred L." It may be interpreted by English speakers as a combination of l and th or, like its affricate counterpart, as tl or kl.

$\check{s}$ is like English sh. The symbol is called "S wedge."

x a velar fricative, made with the tongue in position for a k or farther forward. In Mainland Halkomelem it sounds like the h in words like "human" and "huge" as I say them or perhaps like the German ch in "ich." Also written x^y.

x^w a labialized velar fricative. It sounds somewhat like the wh in words like "when" and "where" as I say them, but the friction is really farther back in the mouth rather than at the lips.

$\dot{x}$ a uvular fricative, like the ch in "Loch Lomond" or in "Bach," but with the tongue in position for q. The symbol can be called "back X."

$\dot{x}^w$ a labialized uvular fricative, like x but with the lips rounded.

h like English h in words like "hope," "hot," etc.

Resonants are nasals, liquids, and semivowels. The plain resonants present no major problems, being much as in English. They are:

m like English m.

n like English n.

η like English ng in "ring," "sing," etc.

l   like English l in "let," "lot," "loop," etc.

y   like English y in "yes," "you," "young," etc.

w   like English w in "wet," "wall," "wood," etc.

There are also glottalized resonants, made by constricting the glottis as the resonant is articulated. The symbols for them are *m̓* , *n̓*, etc., paralleling those for the glottalized plosives.

The vowel systems of the Native languages of the region differ from that of English in that they consist of fewer vowel phonemes (elements that make the difference between one word and another), but each phoneme can vary to a greater degree depending on its environment. Halkomelem and Northern Straits seem to have only five vowel phonemes, and so five symbols are quite enough to represent them. However, before I was convinced of this, I made distinctions that have turned out to be unnecessary. In a few articles I have not changed the vowel symbols I used earlier, and I have, of course, kept those appearing in words I have quoted from others. The vowel symbols have the following values:

i   as a phoneme represents a sound varying between the i of "machine" and the a of "gate." But a sound like a of "gate" may also be represented by *e*.

ε   as a phoneme represents a sound varying between the e of "bet" and the a of "bat." But the a of "bat" may also be represented as *ä*.

a   as a phoneme represents a sound varying between the a of "father" and the au of "caught" (as I say it, distinguishing it from "cot"). But the au of "caught" may also be represented as *ɔ*.

ə   as a phoneme represents a sound varying from the u of "butter" to the final a of "Canada" to the i of "bit" and the u of "put." But as a stressed vowel with the quality of the u of "butter" it has been written   ; as an unstressed vowel with the quality of the i of "bit" it has been written   ; and as an unstressed vowel with the quality of the u of "put" it has been written *ʊ*.

u   as a phoneme represents a sound varying between the oo of "boot" and the o of "rope."

Stressed vowels are marked *á*, *í*, etc., and long vowels are marked *a·*, *i·*, etc.

Bibliography

Abbott, Donald N.
1972 The Utility of the Concept of Phase in the Archaeology of the Southern Northwest Coast. Syesis 5:267-278.

Aberle, David F.
1959 The Prophet Dance and Reactions to White Contact. Southwestern Journal of Anthropology 15(1):74-83.

Adams, John W.
1973 The Gitksan Potlatch: Population Flux, Resource Ownership and Reciprocity. Toronto: Holt, Rinehart and Winston of Canada.
1981 Recent Ethnology of the Northwest Coast. Annual Review of Anthropology 10:361-392.

Adams, William Y., Dennis P. Van Gerven, and Richard S. Levy
1978 The Retreat from Migrationism. Annual Review of Anthropology 7:483-532.

Alvord, Benj., et al.
1857 Reports on Indian Affairs on the Pacific. Pp. 1-22 in 34th U.S. Congress, 3rd Session, House Executive Document No. 76.

Amoss, Pamela T.
1977 Strategies of Reorientation: The Contribution of Contemporary Winter Dancing to Coast Salish Identity and Solidarity. Pp. 77-83 in Blackman, ed. 1977.
1978 Coast Salish Spirit Dancing: The Survival of an Ancestral Religion. Seattle: University of Washington Press.

Anastasio, Angelo
1955 Intergroup Relations in the Southern Plateau. Ph.D. Dissertation in Anthropology, University of Chicago. [Published as Anastasio 1975.]
1975 The Southern Plateau: An Ecological Analysis of Intergroup Relations. Moscow: University of Idaho Laboratory of Anthropology.

Arctander, J. W.
1909 The Apostle of Alaska. The Story of William Duncan of Metlakahtla. New York: F. H. Revell.

Bagley, C. G., ed.
1915 Journal of Occurrences at Nisqually House, 1833. Washington Historical Quarterly 6:179-187.

Ballard, Arthur C.
1950 Calendric Terms of the Southern Puget Sound Salish. Southwestern Journal of Anthropology 6:79-99.

Bancroft, H. H.
1884 The Northwest Coast, vol 2, 1800-1846. History of the Pacific States Vol 23. San Francisco: The History Company, Publishers.
1886 Alaska, 1730-1885. History of the Pacific States, Vol 28. San Francisco: The History Company, Publishers.
1887 British Columbia, 1792-1887. History of the Pacific States, Vol 27. San Francisco: The History Company, Publishers.

Barbeau, Marius
[1950]Totem Poles. National Museum of Canada Bulletin 119.

Barber, B.
1941 Acculturation and Messianic Movements. American Sociological Review 6:663-669.

Barnett, Homer G.
1937 Culture Element Distributions: VII, Oregon Coast. University of California Anthropological Records 1(3):155-204.
1938a The Coast Salish of Canada. American Anthropologist 40:118-141.
1938b The Nature of the Potlatch. American Anthropologist 40:349-358.
1939 Culture Element Distributions: IX, Gulf of Georgia Salish. University of California Anthropological Records 1(5):221-295.
1942 The Southern Extent of Totem Pole Carving. Pacific Northwest Quarterly 33:379-389.
1955 The Coast Salish of British Columbia. University of Oregon Monographs, Studies in Anthropology No. 4. Eugene.
1957 Indian Shakers: A Messianic Cult of the Pacific Northwest. Carbondale: University of Southern Illinois.

Barry, J. Nelson
1929a Use of Soil Products by Indians. Oregon Historical Quarterly 30:43-52.
1929b Agriculture in the Oregon Country in 1795-1844. Oregon Historical Quarterly 30:161-168.

Bartholomew, George A., Jr., and Joseph B. Birdsell
1953 Ecology and the Protohominids. American Anthropologist 55:481-498.

Baumhoff, Martin A.
1963 Ecological Determinants of Aboriginal California Populations. University of California Publications in American Archaeology and Ethnology 49(2):155-236.

Beals, Ralph L., and Harry Hoijer
1959 An Introduction to Anthropology, 2nd ed. New York: Macmillan.

Belshaw, Cyril S.
1950 The Significance of Modern Cults in Melanesian Development. The Australian Outlook 4:116-125.

Benedict, Ruth
1932 Configurations of Culture in North America. American Anthropologist 34:1-27.

1934 Patterns of Culture. Boston: Houghton Mifflin.

Beattie, Owen B.

1985 A Note on Early Cranial Studies from the Gulf of Georgia Region: Long-heads, Broad-heads, and the Myth of Migration, in B.C. Studies 66:28-36.

Blackman, Margaret B.

1976 Northern Haida Ecology: A Preliminary Discussion. Paper presented at the Northwest Coast Studies Conference, Simon Fraser University.

Blackman, Margaret B., ed

1977 Continuity and Change in Northwest Coast Ceremonialism. Papers from a Symposium Presented at the 1974 Meetings of the American Anthropological Association in Mexico City. Arctic Anthropology 14(1):1-93.

Blanchet, F. N.

1910 Historical Sketches of the Catholic Church in Oregon and the Northwest. Ferndale, Washington.

Bloomfield, Leonard

1933 Language, New York: Holt.

Boas, Franz

1887 Zur Ethnologie Britisch-Kolumbiens. Petermanns Geographische Mitteilungen 5:129-133 and Tafel 7.

1891 The LkungEn. Pp. 563-592 in The Sixth Report on the Northwestern Tribes of Canada. Report of the 60th Meeting of the British Association for the Advancement of Science for 1890. London.

1891a The Nootka. Pp. 582-604 in The Sixth Report on the Northwestern Tribes of Canada. Report of the 60th Meeting of the British Association for the Advancement of Science. London.

1891b The Shuswap. Pp. 632-647 in The Sixth Report on the Northwestern Tribes of Canada. Report of the 60th Meeting of the British Association for the Advancement of Science. London.

1894 Indian Tribes of the Lower Fraser. Pp. 454-463 in The Ninth Report on the Northwestern Tribes of Canada. Report of the 64th Meeting of the British Association for the Advancement of Science. London.

1895 Indianische Sagen von der Nord-pacifischen Küste Amerikas. Berlin: A. Asher.

1897 The Social Organization and Secret Societies of the Kwakiutl Indians. United States National Museum, Annual Report for 1895. Pp. 311-738.

1898 Introduction to James Teit, Traditions of the Thompson Indians of British Columbia. American Folklore Society Memoir no. 6.

1899 Twelfth and Final Report on the North-Western Tribes of Canada. Pp. 628-688 in Report of the 68th Meeting of the British Association for the Advancement of Science. London.

1900 Conclusion, in The Thompson Indians of British Columbia, by James Teit. American Museum of Natural History, Memoirs 2:163-392.

1905 The Jesup North Pacific Expedition. International Congress of Americanists 13:91-100.

1909 The Kwakiutl of Vancouver Island. American Museum of Natural History Memoir 8:307-515.

1910 Die Resultäte der Jesup-Expedition. International Congress of Americanists 16:3-16. Vienna.

1911 Introduction. Handbook of American Indian Languages. Bureau of American Ethnology Bulletin 40:1:5-83.

1912   Changes in Bodily Form of Descendants of Immigrants. American Anthropologist 14:530-562. Reprinted as pp. 60-75 in Boas 1940.

1916   Tsimshian Mythology. Bureau of American Ethnology Annual Report 31:29-1037.

1921   Ethnology of the Kwakiutl, Based on Data Collected by George Hunt. Bureau of American Ethnology Annual Report 35, pts. 1-2.

1929   Classification of American Languages. Language 5:1-7. Reprinted as pp. 219-225 in Boas 1940.

1935   Kwakiutl Culture as Reflected in Mythology. American Folklore Society Memoir 28.

1938   Invention. Pp. 238-281 in General Anthropology. Franz Boas, ed. Boston: D. C. Heath.

1940   Race, Language, and Culture. New York: Macmillan.

Borden, Charles E.

1950   Preliminary Report on Archaeological Investigations in the Fraser Delta Region. Anthropology in British Columbia 1:13-27.

1951   Facts and Problems of Northwest Coast Prehistory. Anthropology in British Columbia 2:35-52.

1954   Some Aspects of Prehistoric Coastal-Interior Relations in the Pacific Northwest. Anthropology in British Columbia 4:26-32.

1969   Discussion of Papers Presented During the Symposium on Current Archaeological Research on the Northwest Coast. Northwest Anthropological Research Notes 3(3):255-261.

1970   Culture History of the Fraser-Delta Region: An Outline. B C Studies 6-7:95-122.

1975   Origins and Development of Early Northwest Coast Culture to about 3000 B.C. Canada. National Museum of Man Mercury Series. Archaeological Survey of Canada Paper 45.

1979   Peopling and Early Cultures of the Pacific Northwest. Science 203(4384):963-971.

Bouchard, Randy, and Dorothy I. D. Kennedy

1975   Utilization of Fish by the Colville Okanagan Indian People. British Columbia Indian Language Project, Victoria.

1979   Ethnogeography of the Franklin D. Roosevelt Lake Area. British Columbia Indian Language Project, Victoria.

Boyd, Robert T.

1985   The Introduction of Infectious Diseases among the Indians of the Pacific Northwest, 1774-1874. Ph.D. dissertation in anthropology, University of Washington.

Bruseth, Nels

[c.1950] Indian Stories and Legends of the Stillaguamish, Sauks and Allied Tribes, 2nd ed. Arlington, Washington: Arlington Times Press.

Butler, B. Robert

1957   Art of the Lower Columbia Valley. Archaeology 10:158-165.

Canada Department of Fisheries

1951-1958 British Columbia Catch Statistics.

Carlson, Roy L.

1979   The Early Period in Northwest Coast Prehistory. Paper presented at a Joint Session of the Canadian Archaeological Association and the Society for American Archaeology, Vancouver, 25 April 1979.

Carlson, Roy L., ed.

1970   Archaeology in British Columbia. Special Issue. B.C. Studies 6-7.

[1984] Indian Art Traditions of the Northwest Coast. Burnaby, B.C.: Archaeology Press, Simon Fraser University.

Chance, David H.
1973 Influences of the Hudson's Bay Company on the Native Cultures of the Colville District. Northwest Anthropological Research Notes, Memoir 2.

Clark, Ella
1955-1956 George Gibbs' Account of Indian Mythology in Oregon and Washington Territories. Oregon Historical Quarterly 56(4):293-325; 57(2):125-167.

Clemens, W. A., and G. V. Wilby
1946 Fishes of the Pacific Coast of Canada. Fisheries Research Board of Canada Bulletin 68. Ottawa.

Cline, Walter, et al.
1938 The Sinkaietk or Southern Okanagon of Washington. General Series in Anthropology 6.

Codere, Helen
1948 The Swai'xwe Myth of the Middle Fraser River: The Integration of Two Northwest Coast Cultural Ideas. Journal of American Folklore 61:1-18.
1957 Kwakiutl Society: Rank without Class. American Anthropologist 59:473-486.
1959 The Understanding of the Kwakiutl. Pp. 61-75 in The Anthropology of Franz Boas. Walter Goldschmidt, ed. American Anthropological Association Memoir 89.

Coffin, James, and Harold Driver
1974 Classification and Development of North American Indian Cultures. Paper Read at the 73rd Annual Meeting of the American Anthropological Association, Mexico City, 19-24 November 1974.

Cohen, Yehudi A., ed.
1968 Man in Adaptation: The Cultural Present. Chicago: Aldine.

Cohn, Werner
1962 Is Religion Universal? Problems of Definition. Journal for the Scientific Study of Religion 2:1.

Collins, Henry, et al.
1973 The Far North: 2,000 Years of American Eskimo and Indian Art. Washington: National Gallery of Art.

Collins, June McCormick
1950 Growth of Class Distinctions and Political Authority among the Skagit Indians during the Contact Period. American Anthropologist 52:331-342.
1974 Valley of the Spirits: The Upper Skagit Indians of Western Washington. American Ethnological Society Monograph 56. Seattle: University of Washington Press.

Colson, Elizabeth
1953 The Makah Indians. A Study of an Indian Tribe in Modern American Society. Minneapolis: University of Minnesota and Manchester University Press.

Cope, Leona
1919 Calendars of the Indians North of Mexico. University of California Publications in American Archaeology and Ethnology 16(4):119-176.

Cowan, Ian McTaggart
1940 Distribution and Variation in the Native Sheep of North America. American Midland Naturalist 24:505-580.
1945 The Ecological Relationships of the Food of the Columbian Black-tailed Deer, Odocoileus hemionus columbianus (Richardson), in the Coast Forest Region of Southern Vancouver Island, British Columbia. Ecological Monographs 15(2):109-139.

Cowan, Ian McTaggart, and Charles J. Guiguet
1956 The Mammals of British Columbia. British Columbia Provincial Museum Handbook No. 11. Victoria.
1965 The Mammals of British Columbia. British Columbia Provincial Museum Handbook No. 11, 3rd ed. rev. Victoria.
Cressman, Luther S.
1977 Prehistory of the Far West: Homes of Vanished Peoples. Salt Lake City: University of Utah.
Cressman, Luther S., et al.
1960 Cultural Sequences at The Dalles. American Philosophical Society Transactions n.s. 50(10).
Crosby, Thomas
1907 Among the An-ko-me-nums. Toronto: William Briggs.
1914 Up and Down the North Pacific Coast by Canoe and Mission Ship. Toronto: Missionary Society of the Methodist Church.
Curtis, Edward S.
1911-1916 The North American Indian, vols 7, 8, 9, 10, 11. Norwood, Mass.: Plimptom Press.
Cybulski, Jerome S.
1975 Skeletal Variability in British Columbia Populations. Archaeological Survey of Canada Paper 30. National Museum of Man, Mercury Series.
Dalquest, Walter W.
1948 Mammals of Washington. University of Kansas Publications, Museum of Natural History, 2:1-444.
Davenport, William
1959 Nonunilinear Descent and Descent Groups. American Anthropologist 61:557-572.
Dawson, George Mercer
1880 On the Haida Indians of the Queen Charlotte Islands. Pp. 10313-17513 in Report of Progress, Geological Survey of Canada, 1878-79. Ottawa.
Densmore, Frances
1943 Music of the Indians of British Columbia. Anthropological Papers no. 27. Bureau of American Ethnology Bulletin 136:1-199.
Dewhirst, John
1976 Coast Salish Summer Festivals: Rituals for Upgrading Social Identity. Anthropologica, n.s. 18:231-273.
Diebold, A. Richard, Jr.
1960 Determining the Centers of Dispersal of Language Groups. International Journal of American Linguistics 26:1-10.
Donald, Leland
1983 Was Nuu-chah-nulth-aht (Nootka) Society Based on Slave Labor? Pp. 108-119 in Tooker, ed. 1983.
Donald, Leland, and Donald Mitchell
1975 Some Correlates of Local Group Rank Among the Southern Kwakiutl. Ethnology 14:325-346.
Douglas, James
1840-1841 Journal, 1840-41. Typed copy in University of Washington Northwest Collection. Original in Bancroft Library, Berkeley, California.
1852 Letter to Wm. F. Tolmie, dated Fort Victoria, Dec. 6, 1852. Ms: typed copy in University of Washington Northwest Collection.

1854 Report of a Canoe Expedition along the East Coast of Vancouver Island. Journal of the Royal Geographical Society 24:245-249.

Driver, Harold E.

1939 Culture Element Distributions: X, Northwest California. University of California Anthropological Records 1(6):297-433.

1961 Indians of North America. Chicago: University of Chicago Press.

1969 Indians of North America, 2nd ed. Chicago: University of Chicago Press.

Driver, Harold E., and James L. Coffin

1975 Classification and Development of North American Indian Cultures: A Statistical Analysis of the Driver-Massey Sample. Transactions of the American Philosophical Society n. s. 65(3):1-120.

Drucker, Philip

1940 Kwakiutl Dancing Societies. University of California Anthropological Records 2(6):201-230.

1943 Archeological Survey on the Northern Northwest Coast. Bureau of American Ethnology Bulletin 133:17-142.

1950 Culture Element Distribution, 26: Northwest Coast. University of California Anthropological Records 9(3):157-294.

1951 The Northern and Central Nootkan Tribes. Bureau of American Ethnology Bulletin 144.

1955a Indians of the Northwest Coast. American Museum of Natural History Anthropological Handbook No. 10. Reprinted 1963: American Museum Science Books, Garden City: Natural History Press.

1955b Sources of Northwest Coast Culture. Pp. 59-81 in New Interpretations of Aboriginal American Culture History. Betty Meggers and Clifford Evans, eds. Washington: The Anthropological Society of Washington.

1965 Cultures of the North Pacific Coast. San Francisco: Chandler Publishing Co.

1983 Ecology and Political Organization on the Northwest Coast of America. Pp. 86-96 in Tooker, ed. 1984.

Drucker, Philip, and Robert F. Heizer

1967 To Make My Name Good: A Reexamination of the Southern Kwakiutl Potlatch. Berkeley: University of California Press.

DuBois, Cora

1936 The Wealth Concept as an Integrative Factor in Tolowa-Tututni Culture. Pp. 49-65 in Essays in Anthropology Presented to A. L. Kroeber. Robert H. Lowie, ed. Berkeley: University of California Press.

1938 The Feather Cult of the Middle Columbia. General Series in Anthropology No. 7.

Duff, Wilson

1952 The Upper Stalo Indians of the Fraser Valley, British Columbia. Anthropology in British Columbia Memoir 1. Victoria.

1956 Prehistoric Stone Sculpture of the Fraser River and Gulf of Georgia. Anthropology in British Columbia No. 5. Victoria.

1964 The Indian History of British Columbia. Vol. 1 The Impact of the White Man. Anthropology in British Columbia Memoir 5. Victoria.

Dumond, Don E.

1969 Toward a Prehistory of the Na-Dene, with a General Comment on Population Movements among Nomadic Hunters. American Anthropologist 71:857-863.

Dunn, John

n.d. Tsimshian Internal Relations Reconsidered: Southern Tsimshian. Ms.

Durkheim, Emile
1915 The Elementary Forms of the Religious Life, London: George Allen and Unwin.
Dyen, Isadore
1956 Language Distribution and Migration Theory. Language 32:611-626.
Elmendorf, William W.
1960 The Structure of Twana Culture. Washington State University Research Studies, Monograph Supplement 2:1-576.
1961 System Change in Salish Kinship Terminologies. Southwestern Journal of Anthropology 17:365-382.
1965a Some Problems in the Regrouping of Powell Units. Canadian Journal of Linguistics 10(2-3):93-107.
1965b Linguistic and Geographic Relations in the Northern Plateau Area. Southwestern Journal of Anthropology 21:63-78.
1971 Coast Salish Status Ranking and Intergroup Ties. Southwestern Journal of Anthropology 27:353-380.
Elmendorf, W. W., and Wayne Suttles
1960 Pattern and Change in Halkomelem Salish Dialects. Anthropological Linguistics 2:1-32.
Emmons, George T.
n.d. Notes, Photos, etc. on the Schwy-Why Legend. File in the British Columbia Provincial Archives.
Feder, Norman
1983 Incised Relief Carving of the Halkomelem and Straits Salish. American Indian Art Magazine 8(2): 46-55.
Fetzer, Paul
[1950-51] Nooksack ethnographic field notes. In possession of W. Suttles.
Fisher, H. D.
1952 The Status of the Harbour Seal in British Columbia, with Particular Reference to the Skeena River. Fisheries Research Board of Canada Bulletin 83.
Fitzhugh, E. C.
1858 Report No. 135, Bellingham Bay Agency, Washington Territory, June 8, 1857, of E. C. Fitzhugh, Special Indian Agent. Pp. 325-329 in Report of the Commissioner of Indian Affairs for 1857. Washington, D.C.
Fladmark, Knut R.
1975 A Paleoecological Model for Northwest Coast Prehistory. Canada. National Museum of Man, Mercury Series. Archaeological Survey of Canada Paper No. 43. Ottawa.
1978 The Feasibility of the Northwest Coast as a Migration Route for Early Man. Pp. 119-128 in Early Man in America from a Circum-Pacific Perspective. Alan L. Bryan, ed. Occasional Papers of the Department of Anthropology, University of Alberta, No. 1.
1979 Routes: Alternative Migration Corridors for Early Man in North America. American Antiquity 44:55-69.
Floyd, Patrick D.
1968 Aspects of the Economic Base and Population Distribution of the Haida, Southern Kwakiutl, and Georgia Strait Salish in Pre-Contact Times, and Some Implications of the Impact of Europeans. (Manuscript in possession of W. Suttles.)
Fort Langley Correspondence
1937 Fort Langley Correspondence. British Columbia Historical Quarterly 1:187-194.

Garfield, Viola E.

1945 A Research Problem in Northwest Indian Economics. American Anthropologist 47:626-630.

1951 The Tsimshian and their Neighbors. Pp. 5-70 in the Tsimshian: Their Arts and Music. Marian W. Smith, ed. American Ethnological Society Publication 18. New York: J. J. Augustin.

Garth, Thomas R.

1965 The Plateau Whipping Complex and Its Relationship to Plateau-Southwest Contacts. Ethnohistory 12:141-170.

Gibbs, George

1855 Report on the Indian Tribes of the Territory of Washington. Pp. 402-436 in Pacific Railroad Report, vol. 1. (Reprinted: Fairfield, Washington: Ye Galleon Press, 1972.)

1877 Tribes of Western Washington and Northwestern Oregon. Contributions to North American Ethnology 1:157-361.

Goldschmidt, Walter

1950 Social Class in America—a Critical View. American Anthropologist 52:483-498.

Golla, Victor

1976 The Origin of the Pacific Coast Athapaskan Languages. Paper presented at the Northwest Coast Studies Conference, Simon Fraser University, May 1976.

Gould, Richard A.

1966 The Wealth Quest among the Tolowa Indians of Northwestern California. Proceedings of the American Philosophical Society 110(1):67-89.

Grant, W. C.

1857 Description of Vancouver Island. Journal of the Royal Geographical Society 27:268-320.

Green, John

1968 On the Track of the Sasquatch, 2nd ed. Agassiz, British Columbia: Cheam Publishing.

Guédon, Marie-Françoise

1984 An Introduction to Tsimshian Worldview and Its Practitioners. Pp. 137-159 in The Tsimshian, Images of the Past: Views for the Present. Margaret Seguin, ed. Vancouver: University of British Columbia Press.

Guiart, J.

1951 Forerunners of Melanesian Nationalism. Oceania 22:81-90.

Gunther, Erna

1925 Klallam Folktales. University of Washington Publications in Anthropology 1(4):113-170.

1927 Klallam Ethnography. University of Washington Publications in Anthropology 1(5):171-314.

1928 A Further Analysis of the First Salmon Ceremony. University of Washington Publications in Anthropology 2(5):129-173.

1949 The Shaker Religion of the Northwest. Pp. 37-76 in Smith, ed. 1949.

Haas, Mary R.

1960 Some Genetic Affiliations of Algonkian. Pp. 977-992 in Culture in History. Essays in Honor of Paul Radin. Stanley Diamond, ed. New York: Columbia University Press.

1965 Is Kutenai Related to Algonkian? Canadian Journal of Linguistics 10:77-92.

Haeberlin, Hermann and Erna Gunther

1930 The Indians of Puget Sound. University of Washington Publications in Anthropology 4(1):1-84.

Halpin, Marjorie M.
1980 Investigating the Goblin Universe. Pp. 3-26 in Halpin and Ames 1980.
Halpin, Marjorie M., and Michael M. Ames, eds.
1980 Manlike Monsters on Trial. Vancouver: University of British Columbia Press.
Hansen, H.P.
1947 Postglacial Forest Succession, Climate, and Chronology in the Pacific Northwest. Transactions of the American Philosophical Society 37:1-130.
Harper, J. Russell, ed.
1971 Paul Kane's Frontier. Austin: University of Texas.
Hawthorn, Audrey
1967 Art of the Kwakiutl Indians and Other Northwest Coast Tribes. Seattle: University of Washington.
Hawthorn, H. B.
1968 Review of Philip Drucker and Robert F. Heizer, To Make My Name Good. Man n.s. 3:678-680.
Hawthorn, H. B., C. S. Belshaw, and S. M. Jamieson
1958 The Indians of British Columbia: A Study of Contemporary Social Adjustment. Berkeley: University of California Press and University of British Columbia.
Heizer, Robert F.
1943 Aconite Poison Whaling in Asia and America: An Aleutian Transfer to the New World. Anthropological Papers No. 24. Bureau of American Ethnology Bulletin 133.
Herskovits, M. J.
1938 Acculturation: The Study of Culture Contact. New York.
Hess, Thom
n.d. A Stem List of Northern Puget Salish. (Manuscript.)
1976 A Dictionary of Puget Salish. Seattle: University of Washington.
Hill-Tout, Charles
1902 Ethnological Studies of the Mainland Halkomelem Division of the Salish. Pp. 355-449 in Report of the 72nd Meeting of the British Association for the Advancement of Science. London.
1904a Report on the Ethnology of the Sicatl of British Columbia. Journal of the Royal Anthropological Institute 34:20-91.
1904b Ethnological Report of the StsEélis and Sk'aúlits Tribes of the Halkomelem Division of the Salish. Journal of the Royal Anthropological Institute 34:311-376.
Hockett, Charles F., and Robert Ascher.
1964 The Human Revolution. Current Anthropology 5(3):135-152.
Holm, Bill
1965 Northwest Coast Art. An Analysis of Form. Seattle: University of Washington Press.
1972 Crooked Beak of Heaven: Masks and Other Ceremonial Art of the Northwest Coast. Seattle: University of Washington.
Holm, Bill, and William Reid
1975 Form and Freedom: A Dialogue on Northwest Coast Indian Art. Houston: Rice University Press.
Holmes, Kenneth L.
1971 The Range of the California Condor (Gymnogyps Californianus) in the Nineteenth Century. Paper read at the Northwest Scientific Association Meeting, Moscow, Idaho, 16-17 April 1971.

Inglis, Richard, and George MacDonald
1975 5,000 Years of History on the West Coast. Canadian Geographical Journal 91(6):32-37.

Jackson, Roy I.
1953 Sockeye from the Fraser. The Beaver [March 1953] pp. 18-25.

Jacobs, Melville
1937 Historical Perspectives in Indian Languages of Oregon and Washington. Pacific Northwest Quarterly 28:55-74.
1959 The Content and Style of an Oral Literature: Clackamas Chinook Myths and Tales. Chicago: University of Chicago.
1964 Pattern in Cultural Anthropology. Homewood, Illinois: The Dorsey Press.

Jacobs, Melville, and Bernhard J. Stern
1947 Outline of Anthropology. New York: Barnes and Noble.

Jane, Cecil, trans.
1930 A Spanish Voyage to Vancouver and the North-West of America. Being the Narrative of the Voyage Made in the Year 1792 by the Schooners Sutil and Mexicana to Explore the Strait of Fuca. London: The Argonaut Press.

Jenness, Diamond
n.d. The Saanich Indians of Vancouver Island. Manuscript in the Archives of the Ethnology Division. Canada. National Museum of Man. Ottawa.
1943 The Carrier Indians of the Bulkley River. Bureau of American Ethnology Bulletin 133:469-586.
1955 The Faith of a Coast Salish Indian. Anthropology in British Columbia Memoir 3. Victoria.

Jennings, T. E., trans.
1937a Mission of the Columbia; Letter and Journal of Father J. B. Z. Bolduc [First published Quebec 1845] WPA projects 4185 and 5606, Seattle. Typed copy, University of Washington.
1937b Mission of the Columbia; Second Letter and Journal. (As above.)

Jessett, T. E.
1951 Anglicanism among the Indians of Washington Territory. Pacific Northwest Quarterly 42:224-241.

Jewett, S.G.
1953 Birds of Washington State. Seattle: University of Washington Press.

Jewitt, John R.
1815 A Narrative of the Adventures and Sufferings of John R. Jewitt. Middletown.

Jilek, Wolfgang
1974 Salish Indian Mental Health and Culture Change: Psychohygienic and Therapeutic Aspects of the Guardian Spirit Ceremonial. Toronto: Holt, Rinehart and Winston of Canada.
1982 Indian Healing. Shamanic Ceremonialism in the Pacific Northwest Today. Surrey, B. C. and Blaine, Washington: Hancock House.

Jorgensen, Joseph G.
1969 Salish Language and Culture, A Statistical Analysis of Internal Relationships, History, and Evolution. Indiana University Publications, Language Science Monographs 3. Bloomington.

Kendrew, W. G., and D. Kerr
1955 The Climate of British Columbia and the Yukon Territory. Ottawa: The Queen's Printer.

Kent, Susan
1980 Pacificism—A Myth of the Plateau. Northwest Anthropological Research Notes 14(2):125-134.

Kew, J. E. Michael
1970 Coast Salish Ceremonial Life: Status and Identity in a Modern Village. Unpublished Ph.D. dissertation in anthropology, University of Washington.
1980 Sculpture and Engraving of the Central Coast Salish. University of British Columbia Museum of Anthropology, Note No. 9.

Kinkade, M. Dale
1976 Areal Features. Paper presented at the Northwest Coast Studies Conference, Simon Fraser University, May 1976.

Kinkade, M. Dale, and J. V. Powell
1976 Language and the Prehistory of North America. World Archaeology 8:83-100.

Kirk, Ruth, with Richard D. Daugherty
1978 Exploring Washington Archaeology. Seattle: University of Washington Press.

Klokeid, Terry J.
1969 Notes on the Comparison of Wakashan and Salishan. Working Papers in Linguistics, Department of Linguistics, University of Hawaii, No. 7.

Knight, Rolf
1978 Indians at Work. An Informal History of Native Indian Labour in British Columbia, 1858-1930. Vancouver: New Star Books.

Kool, Richard
1982 Northwest Coast Indian Whaling: New Considerations. Canadian Journal of Anthropology 3:31-44.

Krauss, Michael E.
1973 Na-Dene. Current Trends in Linguistics 10:903-978.

Kroeber, A. L.
1909 Classificatory Systems of Relationships. Journal of the Royal Anthropological Institute 39:77-84.
1917 The Tribes of the Pacific Coast of North America. International Congress of Americanists 19:385-401. Washington.
1923 American Culture and the Northwest Coast. American Anthropologist 25:1-20.
1925 Handbook of the Indians of California. Bureau of American Ethnology Bulletin 78.
1939 Cultural and Natural Areas in Native North America. University of California Publications in American Archaeology and Ethnology 38.
1948 Anthropology. New York: Harcourt, Brace and Co.
1960 Comparative Notes on the Structure of Yurok Culture. Published with Elmendorf 1960.

Kroeber, A. L., and S. A. Barrett
1960 Fishing among the Indians of Northwestern California. University of California Anthropological Records 21(1).

Kuipers, Aert H.
1967 The Squamish Language. The Hague: Mouton.
1969 The Squamish Language: Grammar, Texts, Dictionary, Part II. The Hague: Mouton.
1970 Towards a Salish Etymological Dictionary. Lingua 26:46-72.

Lamb, W. Kaye, ed.
1960 The Letters and Journals of Simon Fraser, 1806-1808. Toronto: Macmillan Company of Canada.

Lane, Barbara Savadkin
1953 A Comparative and Analytic Study of Some Aspects of Northwest Coast Religion. Unpublished Ph.D. Dissertation in Anthropology, University of Washington.
Lantis, Margaret
1938 The Alaskan Whale Cult and Its Affinities. American Anthropologist 40:438-464.
Leach, E. R.
1950 Primitive Calendars. Oceania 20:245-262.
1954 Primitive Time-Reckoning. Pp. 110-127 in A History of Technology, vol. 1. Charles Singer, ed. New York: Oxford University Press.
Leacock, E. B.
1949 The Seabird Community. Pp. 185-194 in Smith ed. 1949.
Lee, Richard B., and Irven DeVore, eds.
1968 Man the Hunter. Chicago: Aldine.
Lemert, E. M.
1954 The Life and Death of an Indian State. Human Organization 13(3):23-27.
Levine, Robert D.
n.d. The Non-evidence for Haida as a Na-Dene Language. Ms.
Lévi-Strauss, Claude
1975 La Voie des Masques: Les Sentiers de la Creation. Geneva: Albert Skira.
1982 The Way of the Masks. Translated by Sylvia Modelski. Seattle: University of Washington.
Linton, Ralph
1943 Nativistic Movements. American Anthropologist 45:230-240.
Lowie, Robert H.
1956 Boas Once More. American Anthropologist 58:159-164.
McCurdy, David W., and James P. Spradley, eds.
1979 Issues in Cultural Anthropology: Selected Readings. Boston and Toronto: Little Brown.
MacDonald, George F.
1969 Preliminary Culture Sequences from the Coast Tsimshian area, British Columbia. Northwest Anthropological Research Notes 3:240-254.
McFeat, Tom, ed.
1966 Indians of the North Pacific Coast. Toronto: McClelland and Stewart. (Reprinted: Seattle: University of Washington Press, 1967.)
McIlwraith, T. F.
1948 The Bella Coola Indians. 2 vols. Toronto: University of Toronto Press.
McKelvie, B.A.
1947 Fort Langley, Outpost of Empire. Vancouver.
McKenny, T. J.
1868 Report of T. J. McKenny. Pp. 88-98 in Annual Report of the Commissioner of Indian Affairs for the Year 1868.
Martin, Paul S., George I. Quimby, and Donald Collier
1947 Indians Before Columbus. Chicago: University of Chicago.
Masson, L. F. R., ed.
1889-1890 Les Bourgeois de la Compagnie du Nord-Ouest. vol. 1. Quebec.
Matson, R. G.
1976 The Glenrose Cannery Site. Archaeological Survey of Canada Paper No. 52, National Museum of Man, Mercury Series.

Meany, Edmond S.
1942 Vancouver's Discovery of Puget Sound. Portland: Binfords and Mort.
Mitchell, Donald H.
1969 Site Survey in the Johnson [Johnstone] Strait Region. Northwest Anthropological Research Notes 3:193-216.
1971 Archaeology of the Gulf of Georgia Area, A Natural Region and Its Culture Types. Syesis 4, Suppl. 1.
Mooney, James
1896 The Ghost Dance Religion and the Sioux Outbreak of 1890. Bureau of American Ethnology Annual Report 17, pt. 2.
1928 The Aboriginal Population of America North of Mexico. Smithsonian Miscellaneous Collections 80(8):1-40.
Morice, A. G.
1910 History of the Catholic Church in Western Canada. 2 vols. Toronto: The Musson Book Company.
1923 Histoire de l'Eglise Catholique dans l'Ouest Canadien. 4 vol. Montreal.
Munro, J. A., and I. McT. Cowan
1947 A Review of the Bird Fauna of British Columbia. British Columbia Provincial Museum Special Publication No. 2. Victoria.
Murdock G. P.
1949 Social Structure. New York: Macmillan.
1960a Ethnographic Bibliography of North America, 3rd ed. New Haven, Conn.: Human Relations Area File Press.
1960b Cognatic Forms of Social Organization. Viking Fund Publications in Anthropology 29:1-14.
1967 The Ethnographic Atlas: A Summary. Ethnology 6(2).
Nash, Phileo
1937 The Place of Religious Revivalism in the Formation of the Intercultural Community on the Klamath Reservation. Pp. 375-422 in Social Anthropology of North American Tribes. Fred Eggan, ed. Chicago: University of Chicago.
Nelson, C. M.
1969 The Sunset Creek Site (45KT28) and Its Place in Plateau Prehistory. Washington State University. Laboratory of Anthropology, Report of Investigations, No. 47.
Nelson, Denys
1927 Fort Langley, 1827-1927: A Century of Settlement in the Valley of the Lower Fraser River. Fort Langley, B. C.
Newcomb, William W., Jr.
1974 North American Indians: An Anthropological Perspective. Pacific Palisades: Goodyear Publishing Co.
Newcombe, C. F., ed.
1923 Menzies' Journal of Vancouver's Voyages, April to October, 1792. Archives of British Columbia Memoir No. 5. Victoria.
Newcombe, C. F., W. H. Greenwood, and C. M. Fraser
1918 Preliminary Report of the Commission on the Sea-lion Question, 1915. Contributions to Canadian Biology, Sessional Paper No. 38a.
Niblack, Albert P.
1890 The Coast Indians of Southern Alaska and Northern British Columbia. Pp. 225-386 in United States National Museum, Annual Report for 1888.

Norton, Helen H.
1979 The Association Between Anthropogenic Prairies and Important Food Plants in Western Washington. Northwest Anthropological Field Notes 13: 175-200.

Olson, Ronald L.
1936 The Quinault Indians. University of Washington Publications in Anthropology 6(1):1-190.

Ott, George
1971 Thunder in Their Wings. Pp. 6-7 in Northwest Magazine, Sunday Oregonian 28 March.

Outram, D. N.
1956 Amount of Herring Spawn Deposited in British Columbia Coastal Waters in 1956. Fisheries Research Board of Canada, Pacific Biological Station, Nanaimo, B. C. Circular No. 42.
1957 Extent of Herring Spawning in British Columbia in 1957. As above, No. 46.
1958 The 1958 Herring Spawn Deposition in British Columbia Coastal Waters. As above, No. 50.

Pettigrew, Richard M.
1976 Lower Columbia Archaeology. Paper read at the Public Archaeology Conference, Oregon Museum of Science and Industry, 10 January 1976.
1977 A Prehistoric Culture Sequence in the Portland Basin of the Lower Columbia. Ph.D. Dissertation in Anthropology, University of Oregon.

Pickard, G. L., Director, Institute of Oceanography, University of British Columbia
1963 Personal communication. [Letter dated 13/ii/63 with table showing lowest tides during a 13-year period.]

Piddocke, Stuart
1965 The Potlatch System of the Southern Kwakiutl: a New Perspective. Southwestern Journal of Anthropology 21:244-264.

Pike, Gordon C.
1958 The Abundance and Distribution of the Northern Sea Lion (*Eumetopias jubata*) on the Coast of British Columbia. Journal of the Fisheries Research Board of Canada 15:5-17.

Powell, J. V.
1976 Chimakuan-Wakashan: Evidence of Genetic Relationship. Paper read at the Northwest Coast Studies Conference, Simon Fraser University, May 1976.

Powell, J. W.
1891 Linguistic Families of North America. Bureau of American Ethnology Annual Report 7:1-142.

Quebec, Diocese of
1839-74 Rapport sur les missions du Diocèse du Québec, qui sont secourues par l'Association de la Propagation de la Foi. Quebec.

Ray, Verne F.
1932 The Sanpoil and Nespelem: Salishan People of Northeastern Washington. University of Washington Publications in Anthropology 5.
1936 The Kolaskin Cult. American Anthropologist 38:67-75.
1938 Lower Chinook Ethnographic Notes. University of Washington Publications in Anthropology 7(2):29-165.
1939 Cultural Relations in the Plateau of Northwestern North America. Publications of the Frederick Webb Hodge Anniversary Publication Fund vol. 3. Los Angeles: Southwest Museum.

1942 Culture Element Distributions: XII, The Plateau. University of California Anthropological Records 8(2):99-262.

1955 Review of Franz Boas: The Science of Man in the Making, by Melville J. Herskovits, New York 1953. American Anthropologist 57:138-140.

1956 Rejoinder. American Anthropologist 58:164-170.

Richardson, Allan

1982 The Control of Productive Resources on the Northwest Coast of North America. Pp. 93-112 in Resource Managers: North American and Australian Hunter-Gatherers. Nancy M. Williams and Eugene S. Hunn, eds. Washington, D. C.: American Association for the Advancement of Science.

Riches, David

1979 Ecological Variation on the Northwest Coast: Models for the Generation of Cognatic and Matrilineal Descent. Pp. 145-166 in Social and Ecological Systems. P. Burnham and R. Ellen, eds. London and New York: Academic Press.

Rigsby, Bruce

n.d. Some Linguistic Insights into Recent Tsimshian Prehistory. (Manuscript.)

1969 The Waiilatpuan Problem: More on Cayuse-Molala Relatability. Northwest Anthropological Research Notes 3:68-146.

1971 Some Pacific Northwest Native Language Names for the Sasquatch Phenomena. Northwest Anthropological Research Notes 5(2):153-156.

Rivera, Trinita

1949 Diet of a Food-Gathering People, With Chemical Analysis of Salmon and Saskatoons. Pp. 19-36 in Smith ed. 1949.

Robinson, Ellen W.

1976 Harlan I. Smith, Boas, and The Salish: Unweaving Archaeological Hypotheses. Northwest Anthropological Research Notes 10:185-196.

Romanoff, Steven

1971 Fraser Lillooet Salmon Fishing. B.A. thesis in Anthropology, Reed College. Published 1985, Northwest Anthropological Research Notes 19:119-160.

Rostlund, Erhard

1952 Freshwater Fish and Fishing in Native North America. University of California Publications in Geography vol. 9.

Roth, L. R., ed.

1926 History of Whatcom County. Chicago and Seattle: Pioneer Historical Publishing Co.

Rounsefell, George A., and George B. Kelez

1938 The Salmon and Salmon Fisheries of Swiftsure Bank, Puget Sound, and the Fraser River. U. S. Department of Commerce, Bureau of Fisheries Bulletin no. 27.

Ruyle, Eugene E.

1973 Slavery, Surplus, and Stratification on the Northwest Coast: The Ethnoenergetics of an Incipient Stratification System. Current Anthropology 14:603-631.

Sanger, David

1968 The Chase Burial Site, EeQw: 1, British Columbia. National Museums of Canada Bulletin 244:86-185.

1970 The Archeology of the Lochnore-Nesikep Locality, British Columbia. Syesis 3, Supplement 1:1-146.

Sapir, Edward

1916 Time Perspective in Aboriginal North American Culture: A Study in Method. Canada, Department of Mines, Geological Survey, Memoir 90. (Reprinted as pp. 389-462 in Selected Writings, 1949).

1929 Central and North American Languages. Encyclopedia Britannica, 14th ed. 5:138-141. (Reprinted as pp. 169-178 in Selected Writings, 1949).

1931 Dialect. Encyclopedia of the Social Sciences 5:123-126. (Reprinted as pp. 83-88 in Selected Writings, 1949).

1949 Selected Writings of Edward Sapir. D. G. Mandelbaum, ed. Berkeley: University of California Press.

Sapir, Edward, and Morris Swadesh

1939 Nootka Texts. Philadelphia: University of Pennsylvania.

Schalk, Randall F.

1977 The Structure of an Anadromous Fish Resource. Pp. 207-249 in For Theory Building in Archaeology. L.R. Binford, ed. New York: Academic Press.

Scott, Leslie M.

1917 Soil Repair Lessons in Willamette Valley. Oregon Historical Quarterly 18:55-69.

Service, Elman R.

1960 Kinship Terminology and Evolution. American Anthropologist 62:747-763.

Sherzer, Joel

1973 Areal Linguistics in North America. Current Trends in Linguistics 10(2):749-795.

Silverstein, Michael

1974 Dialectal Development in Chinookan Tense-Aspect Systems: An Areal-Historical Analysis. International Journal of American Linguistics Memoir 29.

1976 Time Perspective in Northern and Western Penutian. Paper presented at the Northwest Coast Studies Conference, Simon Fraser University, May 1976.

n.d. Chinookans of the Lower Columbia. (Article written for vol. 7 of Handbook of North American Indians.)

Simmons, M. T.

1858 Report No. 81 of M. T. Simmons, Agent for the Indians of Puget's Sound District. Pp. 224-36 in Report of the Commissioner of Indian Affairs for 1858.

Simpson, Sir George

1847 Narrative of a Journey Round the World During the Years 1841 and 1842. 2 vols. London: Henry Colburn.

Smith, Marian W.

1940 The Puyallup-Nisqually. Columbia University Contributions to Anthropology 32.

1941 The Coast Salish of Puget Sound. American Anthropologist 43:197-211.

1947 House Types of the Middle Fraser River. American Antiquity 12:255-267.

Smith, Marian W., ed.

1949 Indians of the Urban Northwest. New York: Columbia University Press.

Smith, William C.

1977 Archaeological Explorations in the Columbia Basin, A Report on the Mesa Project, 1973-1975. Central Washington Archaeological Survey. Ellensburg, Washington: Department of Anthropology, Central Washington University.

Snyder, Sally

1954 Class Growth and Distinctions and Their Relation to Tribal Shifts in Northern Puget Sound. Paper read at the Northwest Anthropological Conference, Vancouver.

Snyder, Warren A.

1968 Southern Puget Sound Salish: Texts, Place Names and Dictionary. Sacramento Anthropological Society Paper 9.

Spain, David H., ed.

1975 The Human Experience, Readings in Sociocultural Anthropology. Homewood, Illinois: The Dorsey Press.

Spier, Leslie
1930 Klamath Ethnography. University of California Publications in American Archaeology and Ethnology 30:1-338.
1935 The Prophet Dance of the Northwest and its Derivatives. General Series in Anthropology no. 1.
1936 Tribal Distribution in Washington. General Series in Anthropology no. 3.
Spier, Leslie, Wayne Suttles, and Melville J. Herskovits
1959 Comment on Aberle's Thesis of Deprivation. Southwestern Journal of Anthropology 15(1):84-88.
Sprague, Roderick
1970 Editorial. Northwest Anthropological Research Notes 4(2):127-128.
Sprague, Roderick, and Grover S. Krantz, eds.
1977 The Scientist Looks at the Sasquatch. Anthropological Monographs of the University of Idaho, No. 3. Moscow: University Press of Idaho.
1979 The Scientists Looks at the Sasquatch (II). As above, No. 4.
Sproat, G. M.
1868 Scenes and Studies of Savage Life. London.
Stenzel, Franz
1975 James Madison Alden: Yankee Artist of the Pacific Coast, 1854-1860. Fort Worth: Amon Carter Museum.
Stern, Bernhard J.
1934 The Lummi Indians of Northwest Washington. New York: Columbia University Press.
Suttles, Wayne
1951a The Economic Life of the Coast Salish of Haro and Rosario Straits. Ph.D. Dissertation in Anthropology, University of Washington. Published as pp. 41-570 in American Indian Ethnohistory: Coast Salish Indians I (New York: Garland Publishing Inc., 1974 [with a misleading editorial introduction and without proper identification—W.S.]).
1951b The Early Diffusion of the Potato among the Coast Salish. Southwestern Journal of Anthropology 7:272-288. [No. 8 in this volume.]
1952 Notes on Coast Salish Sea-Mammal Hunting. Anthropology in British Columbia 3:10-20. [No. 12 in this volume.]
1954 Post-Contact Culture Change among the Lummi Indians. British Columbia Historical Quarterly 18:29-102.
1955 Katzie Ethnographic Notes. Anthropology in British Columbia Memoir 3.
1957a The "Middle Fraser" and "Foothill" Cultures: A Criticism. Southwestern Journal of Anthropology 13:156-183.
1957b The Plateau Prophet Dance Among the Coast Salish. Southwestern Journal of Anthropology 13:352-396. [No. 9 in this volume.]
1958 Private Knowledge, Morality, and Social Classes among the Coast Salish. American Anthropologist 60:497-507. [No. 1 in this volume.]
1959 Cultural Relativism, Cultural Evolution, and Popular Ideology. Western Humanities Review 13:311-319.
1960a Affinal Ties, Subsistence, and Prestige among the Coast Salish. American Anthropologist 62:296-305. [No. 2 in this volume.]
1960b Spirit Dancing and the Persistence of Native Culture Among the Coast Salish. Paper read at the Sixth International Congress of Anthropological and Ethnological

Sciences, Paris. Abstract published as pp. 495-496 in Actes du Ve Congrès Internationale des Sciences Anthropologiques et Ethnologiques, Paris 1960. Tome II, 2e vol. [No. 10 in this volume.]

1962 Variation in Habitat and Culture on the Northwest Coast. Pp. 522-537 in Akten des 34 internationalen Amerikanistenkongresses. Vienna: Verlag Ferdinand Berger. Reprinted as pp. 93-106 in Cohen 1968. [No. 3 in this volume.]

1963 The Persistence of Intervillage Ties among the Coast Salish. Ethnology 2:512-525. [No. 11 in this volume.]

1966 Review of Die Organisierung des indianischen Lachsfangs im westlichen Nordamerika, by Dietrich Treide. American Anthropologist 68:564-565.

1968a Coping with Abundance: Subsistence on the Northwest Coast. Pp. 55-68 in Man the Hunter. Richard B. Lee and Irven DeVore, eds. Chicago: Aldine. [No. 4 in this volume.]

1968b Review of To Make My Name Good: A Re-examination of the Southern Kwakiutl Potlatch, by Philip Drucker and Robert F. Heizer. American Anthropologist 70:1005-1006.

1972 On the Cultural Track of the Sasquatch. Northwest Anthropological Research Notes 6(1):65-90. [No. 6 in this volume.]

1977 Commentary. Pp. 84-88 in Blackman, ed. 1977.

1980 Sasquatch: The Testimony of Tradition. Pp. 245-254 in Halpin and Ames, eds. 1980.

1982 The Halkomelem Sxwayxwey. American Indian Art Magazine 8(1):56-65.

Suttles, Wayne, and William W. Elmendorf

1963 Linguistic Evidence for Salish Prehistory. Pp. 41-52 in Symposium on Language and Culture. Proceedings of the 1962 Annual Spring Meeting of the American Ethnological Society.

Swadesh, Morris

1950 Salish Internal Relationships. International Journal of American Linguistics 16:157-167.

1953a Mosan I: A Problem of Remote Common Origin. International Journal of American Linguistics 19:26-44.

1953b Mosan II: Comparative Vocabulary. International Journal of American Linguistics 19:223-236.

1956 Problems of Long-Range Comparison in Penutian. Language 32:17-41.

1962 Afinidades de las Lenguas Amerindias. Pp. 729-738 in Akten des 34 internationalen Amerikanistenkongresses. Vienna: Verlag Ferdinand Berger.

Swan, James G.

1857 The Northwest Coast; or, Three Years' Residence in Washington Territory. New York: Harper. Reprinted Seattle: University of Washington 1972.

1870 The Indians of Cape Flattery, at the Entrance to the Strait of Fuca, Washington Territory. Smithsonian Contributions to Knowledge vol. 6, article 8, no. 220.

Taylor, Herbert C.

1963 Aboriginal Populations of the Lower Northwest Coast. Pacific Northwest Quarterly 54:158-165.

Teit, James

1898 Traditions of the Thompson River Indians. American Folklore Society Memoir 6.

1900 The Thompson Indians. American Museum of Natural History Memoir 2(4):163-392.

1906a The Lillooet Indians. American Museum of Natural History Memoir 4(5):193-300.

1906b The Shuswap. American Museum of Natural History Memoir 4(7):447-758.

1912 Mythology of the Thompson Indians. American Museum of Natural History Memoir 12:199-416.

1928 The Middle Columbia Salish. University of Washington Publications in Anthropology 2(4):83-128.

1930 The Salishan Tribes of the Western Plateaus. Bureau of American Ethnology, Annual Report 45:25-396.

Thompson, Laurence C.

1973 The Northwest. Current Trends in Linguistics 10:979-1045.

Tooker, Elizabeth, ed.

1983 The Development of Political Organization in Native North America. 1979 Proceedings of the American Ethnological Society. Washington: American Ethnological Society.

Treide, Dietrich

1965 Die Organisierung des indianischen Lachsfangs im westlichen Nordamerika. Veröffentlichungen des Museums für Völkerkunde zu Leipzig 14. Berlin: Akademie-Verlag.

Turner, Nancy Chapman, Randy Bouchard, and Dorothy I.D. Kennedy

1980 Ethnobotany of the Okanagan-Colville Indians of British Columbia and Washington. B.C. Provincial Museum Occasional Paper No. 21. Victoria.

Underhill, Ruth

1944 Indians of the Pacific Northwest. Sherman Pamphlets on Indian Life and Customs, No. 5. Education Division, United States Office of Indian Affairs.

Vastokas, Joan M.

1966 Architecture of the Northwest Coast Indians of America. Unpublished Ph.D. Dissertation in Art History and Archaeology, Columbia University, New York.

Vayda, Andrew Peter

1961a A Re-examination of Northwest Coast Economic Systems. Transactions of the New York Academy of Sciences, Ser. 2, 32:618-624.

1961b Expansion and Warfare Among Swidden Agriculturists. American Anthropologist 63(2):346-358.

1966 Pomo Trade Feasts. Humanités, Cahiers de l'Institut de Science Économique Appliquée. (Reprinted pp. 494-500 in Tribal and Peasant Economies. Readings in Economic Anthropology. George Dalton, ed. Garden City, N.Y.: Natural History Press, 1969.)

Verhoeven, L. A., and E. B. Davidoff

MS Marine Tagging of Graser River Sockeye Salmon. International Pacific Salmon Fisheries Commission. New Westminster, B. C.

Voegelin, Charles F., and Ermine W. Voegelin

1966 Map of North American Indian Languages. American Ethnological Society Publication 20.

Vogel, Virgil J.

1972 The Indian in American History, 1968. Pp. 284-299 in This Country Was Ours, A Documentary History of the American Indian. Virgil V. Vogel, ed. New York: Harper and Row.

Voget, Fred W.

1956 The American Indian in Transition. American Anthropologist 58:249-263.

Wagner, Henry R.

1933 Spanish Exploration in the Strait of Juan de Fuca. Santa Ana, California: Fine Arts Press.

Wallace, Anthony F. C.
1956 Revitalization Movements. American Anthropologist 58:264-281.

Waterman, T. T.
1920 The Whaling Equipment of the Makah Indians. University of Washington Publications in Anthropology 1(1):1-67.

1922 The Shake Religion of Puget Sound. Smithsonian Institution, Annual Report for 1922. Pp. 499-507.

Weinberg, Daniela
1965 Models of Southern Kwakiutl Social Organization: General Systems. Yearbook of the Society for General Systems Research 10:169-181. (Reprinted pp. 227-253 in Cultural Ecology: Readings on the Canadian Indians and Eskimos. Bruce Cox, ed. Toronto: McClelland and Stewart, 1973.)

West, James
1945 Plainville, U.S.A. New York: Columbia University Press.

Weyer, E. M.
1932 The Eskimos, Their Environment and Folkways. New Haven.

White, Richard
1984 Native Americans and the Environment. Pp. 179-204 in Scholars and the Indian Experience. Critical Reviews of Recent Writing in the Social Sciences. Bloomington, Indiana: Indiana University Press.

Wickersham, James
1898 Nisqually Mythology. Overland Monthly 32:345-351.

Wike, Joyce
1941 Modern Spirit Dancing of Northern Puget Sound. Unpublished manuscript deposited in the University of Washington Library.

Wilkes, Charles
1845 Narrative of the United States Exploring Expedition during the Years 1838-1842. 5 vols. Philadelphia.

Wilson, Charles
1866 Report on the Indian Tribes Inhabiting the Country in the Vicinity of the 49th Parallel of North Latitude. Ethnological Society of London, Transactions 4:275-332.

1970 Mapping the Frontier. Edited by George F. G. Stanley. Toronto: Macmillan.

Wingert, Paul
1949a American Indian Sculpture, A Study of the Northwest Coast. New York: J. J. Augustin.

1949b Coast Salish Painting. Pp. 77-91 in Smith, ed. 1949.

1952 Prehistoric Stone Sculpture of the Pacific Northwest. Portland: Portland Art Museum.

Young, Mary M.
1970 Comments of "Sasquatchery". Western Canadian Journal of Anthropology 1(2):83-89.

Young R. B.
1954 British Columbia Pilot (Canadian Edition), vol. II: Northern Portion of the Coast of British Columbia, 3rd ed. Ottawa: Queen's Printer.

Index

314

316

320

KASKA
SEKANI
LIARD
Kechika River
Finlay River
NORTHERN
TUTCHONE
INLAND
TLINGIT
TAHLTAN
SOUTHERN
TUTCHONE
TSETSAUT
GITKSAN
Stikine River
Nass River
NASS
Alsek River
Skeena River
TLINGIT
EYAK
HAIDA
TSM

NORTH